P9-DVU-587

Disability Incarcerated

Disability Incarcerated

Imprisonment and Disability in the United States and Canada

Edited by

Liat Ben-Moshe, Chris Chapman, and Allison C. Carey

palgrave
macmillan

DISABILITY INCARCERATED
Copyright © Liat Ben-Moshe, Chris Chapman, and Allison C. Carey, 2014.

All rights reserved.

First published in 2014 by
PALGRAVE MACMILLAN®
in the United States—a division of St. Martin's Press LLC,
175 Fifth Avenue, New York, NY 10010.

Where this book is distributed in the UK, Europe and the rest of the world,
this is by Palgrave Macmillan, a division of Macmillan Publishers Limited,
registered in England, company number 785998, of Houndmills,
Basingstoke, Hampshire RG21 6XS.

Palgrave Macmillan is the global academic imprint of the above companies
and has companies and representatives throughout the world.

Palgrave® and Macmillan® are registered trademarks in the United States,
the United Kingdom, Europe and other countries.

ISBN: 978–1–137–39323–4 (hc)
ISBN: 978–1–137–40405–3 (pbk)

Library of Congress Cataloging-in-Publication Data

Disability incarcerated : imprisonment and disability in the United States and
Canada / edited by Liat Ben-Moshe, Chris Chapman and Allison C. Carey.
    pages cm
ISBN 978–1–137–39323–4 (hardcover : alk. paper) —
ISBN 978–1–137–40405–3 (pbk. : alk. paper)
    1. Sociology of disability. 2. Prisoners with disabilities—United States.
3. Prisoners with disabilities—Canada. 4. People with disabilities—Institutional
care--United States. 5. People with disabilities—Institutional care—Canada.
I. Ben-Moshe, Liat. II. Carey, Allison C.

HV1568.D5688 2014
365′.60870973—dc23   2013040052

A catalogue record of the book is available from the British Library.

Design by Newgen Knowledge Works (P) Ltd., Chennai, India.

First edition: May 2014

10 9 8 7 6 5 4 3 2 1

Contents

Foreword

Angela Y. Davis

Disability Incarcerated is an exciting development at the intersection of the fields of critical prison studies and disability studies. The anthology not only represents important scholarly work in these fields, but it also stages conversations across numerous borders, including the one separating the United States and Canada and those that strive to divorce scholarship and activism. When I was first introduced to the ideas explored in this collection, I remembered a scene from the era of my own incarceration. After being informed about a decision made by officials in the New York Women's House of Detention regarding the section of the jail where I would be housed, I was taken to the fourth floor into an area reserved, in the language of that period, for "emotionally and psychologically disturbed inmates." The only woman in that unit who was not entirely immobilized by the psychotropic drugs distributed to everyone there informed me that she was doing everything in her power to persuade the authorities to release her into the main population. She also sternly urged me to refuse to take the drugs.

When I tried to understand why a person arrested on political charges would be implicitly labeled "emotionally or psychologically disturbed," the most accessible frame of reference at the time was the well-publicized use of psychiatric institutions to punish political dissidents in other parts of the world. The fact that I was being similarly treated demonstrated, I thought, that the United States, despite its official protests vis-à-vis the then Soviet Union and China, also engaged in punishment practices that conflated political resistance with psychological disorders. I was especially struck by the fact that guards did indeed try to coax me to imbibe the medication indiscriminately distributed to the women there. After a legal injunction forced the authorities to transfer me to the main population, I learned from my fellow prisoners that the psychotropic medication I had been offered was probably either thorazine or chloral hydrate.

What surprised me even more than my assignment to the psych unit of the jail was the recognition that the prisoners I encountered in the main population were thoroughly familiar with the psychotropic medication regimes and treated them as an entirely routine phenomenon. I learned that many women in the main population were on the same drugs I had refused in the psych unit. Having been active in a number of campaigns in defense of political prisoners, I assumed I was somewhat knowledgeable about prison conditions, but since I had primarily encountered men's prisons, I was entirely unaware of the structural conflation of deviant and disabled women. At the time, although I lacked an analytical vocabulary to

understand this convergence, I suspected that that there was a far deeper significance to this experience than I was able to surmise. And indeed, over the last four
decades, my thoughts have periodically returned to that experience. But it was not
until I read *Disability Incarcerated* that I realized how important it is to pose such
probing questions about the complex intersections of imprisonment and disability.
This collection of essays asks the questions I wish I had known how to formulate
then and so many more that have only become possible in the aftermath of two
decades of intense research and passionate activism against the prison industrial
complex and after the emergence of fields of study and radical activism around the
category of disability.

The three largest contemporary psychiatric facilities, this volume dramatically
reveals, are jails: Cook County Jail in Chicago, L. A. County Jail, and Rikers
Island in New York. A direct consequence of the closure of psychiatric institutions
called for by progressive deinstitutionalization advocacy, this current crisis is also
an outcome of strategies proposed to trim national and state budgets. In general,
current policies of mass incarceration have led to a daily census count in US jails,
prisons, and other sites of imprisonment of almost two and a half million people. It
has been established by numerous researchers that the disproportionate number of
prisoners of color reveals how structural racism underpins what is often represented
as "due process." That aboriginal people in Canada are approximately ten times
more likely than nonindigenous people to be sent to jail reveals that Canada seems
to be following its southern neighbor's example by using imprisonment to deflect
attention from pressing social problems. In both the United States and Canada,
there are efforts currently underway to reduce the imprisoned population—ranging
from abolitionist strategies that are linked to broader demands for social justice to
calls for decarceration that will reduce the fiscal resources necessary to keep prisons functioning. If the radical core of prison abolitionism is not to be sacrificed on
the altar of fiscal responsibility, lessons from the deinstitutionalization movement
should be heeded.

The chapters in this collection do not simply seek to identify points of convergence of race, gender, class, sexuality, and disability within the framework of
historically developing modes of incarceration. Rather they also aim to transform
entrenched ways of conceptualizing imprisonment. They point out that carceral
practices are so deeply embedded in the history of disability that it is effectively
impossible to understand incarceration without attending to the confinement of
disabled people.

Preface: An Overview of *Disability Incarcerated*

Allison C. Carey, Liat Ben-Moshe, and Chris Chapman

"Is it surprising" asked Michel Foucault, "that prisons resemble factories, schools, barracks, hospitals, which all resemble prisons" (1995, 228)? Whether or not this is surprising, is it justifiable? A wide range of social service settings, including medical institutions, jails, detention centers, and even community services, such as group homes and day programs, share characteristics, philosophies, and goals that relate to rehabilitation through top-down evaluation and constrained freedom, routine, and physical space. In this book, we highlight connections among various sites of confinement and institutionalization with a particular attention to disability and its relevance to these diverse sites—both in terms of the heterogeneous "population" that gets abstractly collected together as "people with disabilities" and in terms of the processes of labeling, normalization, and marginalization upon which these settings rely and in which they participate. We suggest that disability has always been central to diverse practices of incarceration, alongside and interlocking with other forms of stratification. We do not claim that the diverse internments considered in this book are *all the same*; we believe, rather, that fruitful analysis emerges from considering both the similarities *and* the differences among diverse sites of confinement—in terms of the effects on those who are subjected to them, and in terms of the rationalizations that allow the rest of us to live with them. Of the latter, Foucault wrote,

> many factors determine power. Yet rationalization is also constantly working away at it. There are specific forms to such rationalization. The government of [people] by [people] – whether it is power exerted by men over women, or by adults over children, or by one class over another, or by a bureaucracy over a population – involves a certain type of rationality...Consequently, those who resist or rebel against a form of power cannot merely be content to denounce violence or criticize an institution...What has to be questioned is the form of rationality at stake. The criticism of power wielded over the mentally sick or mad cannot be restricted to psychiatric institutions; nor can those questioning the power to punish be content with denouncing prisons as total institutions. The question is: How are such relations of power rationalized? Asking this is the only way to avoid other institutions, with the same objectives and the same effects, from taking their stead. (1994, 324–325)

As we hope to demonstrate in the pages that follow, history has frequently replaced abolished institutions with "other institutions with the same objectives and the same effects" and so, following Foucault, the sphere of what he calls "political rationality" is one of the targets of our critique.

By bringing critical analyses of imprisonment centrally into conversation with critical analyses of institutionalization, and by bringing both into conversation with racism, colonialism, social welfare, and immigration policies, this book contributes to understandings of the shared and divergent political rationalities at work in making the confinement of diverse bodies seem acceptable and useful. This allows us to explore various ways that seemingly distinct and unrelated sites of mass incarceration are often interconnected in terms of their effects on individuals, populations, and society as a whole. For instance, when "Indian Residential Schools" closed, aboriginal children became shockingly overrepresented among those who were removed from their families by child welfare authorities; almost all of these children continued to be raised by non-Native people and many continued to be raised in institutional environments such as group homes (Churchill 2004; Fournier and Crey 1999; Smith 2005). In Canada, this became known as the "Sixties Scoop," although it continued beyond the 1960s. The effects of Residential Schools, the "Sixties Scoop," and the ongoing disproportionate apprehension of aboriginal children are related today to subsequent high rates of imprisonment among Aboriginal youth and adults (Thobani 2007, 124), as well as to the ongoing institutionalization of these survivors' children, sometimes now politically rationalized through the dividing practices of disability rather than race (Chapman 2012; LeFrançois 2013). Concurrent to these developments, when large state institutions for people with labels of psychiatric and intellectual disability closed in the United States, they reopened in many states as prisons and detention centers (Ben-Moshe 2011)—and the subsequent imprisonment of these populations in now penal settings coincided with an increase in imprisonment more generally. Disability, situated alongside other key lines of stratification such as race, class, nationality, and gender, is central to understanding the complex, varied, and interlocking ways in which incarceration occurs and is made out to be normal, natural, politically necessary, and beneficial. Sites of incarceration, such as medical institutions, nursing homes, and prisons, emerge and take shape in interaction with each other as various populations are sorted, identified, and treated according to rationalities and practices which, while different in many ways, all mark certain people as deviant and thus justify controlling what they can and cannot do.

This book has four primary goals. The first is to situate disability within the scholarship on prisons, criminal justice, and incarceration—and thereby to show that experiences of disabled people, and processes of disablement, are central to understanding the rationales, practices, and consequences of incarceration. The second is to expand notions of "incarceration" to encompass a wider variety of social settings and practices. The third is to explore and theorize various interlockings of incarceration and disability, being highly attentive to similarities and differences across constructed categories of identity, sites of incarceration, and geographical boundaries. Many antiprison activists have incorporated analyses of race, gender, and capitalism into their work but neglect disability, and many disability scholars and activists speak of disability-specific forms of institutionalization without fundamentally intersecting other sites of incarceration or other forms of oppression into their analyses. This call for connecting critical prison analyses with disability is also a call to pay attention to the lives of mostly poor people of color who are both disproportionately disabled (Puar 2012) and disproportionately incarcerated worldwide, and to bring this discrepancy to bear on what Chris Bell (2006) characterized as "White Disability Studies." Lastly, we aim to engage and invite further dialogue and collaboration among often unconnected scholars and activists to promote social change.

In this book, we sometimes focus on Canada,[1] sometimes on the United States, sometimes a little on each. While the border separating the two countries has real effects on people's lives, such as access to health care and access to state execution or "three strikes you're out" penal practices, it might also be important to keep in mind that, as Cherokee writer Thomas King writes, "the border doesn't mean that much to the majority of Native people in either country. It is, after all, a figment of someone else's imagination" (2003, 102). Drawing upon the materiality of the border where useful, and leaving it aside where it is not, also resonates with what Black Canadian Rinaldo Walcott (2003) writes of "diaspora sensibilities":

Diaspora sensibilities use the nation to make ethical claims and demands for social justice. Diaspora sensibilities speak to nations' limitations and demand nations be remade in a constant and restless ethical search for home. Home, in the diasporic framework, is an ethical place, not a narrative of containment. (23)

Throughout *Disability Incarcerated*, diverse authors and concerns come together in what we hope is a collaboration toward what Walcott calls an "ethical place," rather than a practice of containment or confinement. The lines between prison abolition and Disability Studies, or the lines between the United States and Canada, or any of the relevant lines between any us and any them, are lines that may sometimes be important, but they also need to be recognized for their limitations and need to "be remade in a constant and restless" search that is at once political and ethical. We imagine this book as one small contribution toward that restless search.

Entering into Conversation

The chapters are arranged in two sections to examine the interface of incarceration and disability both historically and today.

Part I, *Interlocking Histories of Confinement*, is framed by the opening chapter by *Chris Chapman, Allison Carey, and Liat Ben-Moshe* that provides a histori-cal overview of incarceration, developed with particular attention to interlockings across different incarceratory sites and practices as well as across populations and identity categories. Chapman, Carey, and Ben-Moshe discuss themes and theoreti-cal concepts relevant to incarceration, including a discussion of what constitutes incarceration, the impacts of colonialism, neo-colonialism, and globalization, and a call to reimagine the political inevitability of incarceration. This chapter provides our broad range of readers with the crucial historical and theoretical knowledge by which to problematize incarceration and contextualize the book's contributions.

The second chapter is *Chris Chapman*'s "Five Centuries' Material Reforms and Ethical Reformulations of Social Elimination." In this broad spanning history, Chapman argues that *how* and *where* people are incarcerated has transformed, but that *whether* or *who* is incarcerated has changed very little. Political rationalities shift over time, but each ethical reformulation serves to justify continued confinement of and violence against marginalized and oppressed populations. In contemporary times, this justification increasingly interlocks with liberal modes of political rationality that obscure domination by framing incarceration as both humane and essential to individual improvement, assimilation, and normalization. Despite the illusion of beneficence, sites of incarceration are fundamentally about containment and segregation.

In "Creating the Back Ward: The Triumph of Custodialism and the Uses of Therapeutic Failure in Nineteenth Century Idiot Asylums," *Phil Ferguson* explores the consequences experienced by those individuals deemed incurable within institutions justified through an ideology of cure. The back ward offered only a hellish existence of punishment and abandonment for its unfortunate residents. For administration, the back ward offered a disciplinary function—the threat of the back ward coerced many residents into following the rules. Moreover, categorization within the back ward identified one as hopeless and unable to progress, thereby blaming the individual for therapeutic failure. *Goeffrey Reaume* similarly problematizes the use of mental hospitals by showing the way in which the "treatment" of immigrants in a psychiatric asylum in the early twentieth century entailed their cultural rejection and expulsion from the nation. The asylum served as a rationale and a secure, temporary holding pen in the process of removing "undesirables" from the nation. Who was defined as undesirable and excluded was highly contextual and involved a range of identity categories. *Nirmala Erevelles* further explores this issue as she argues that disability came to serve a central role in the transformation of race oppression as the US moved from Jim Crow to supposed equality. Rather than producing equality, public educational systems now use disability to justify the punishment, isolation, and failure to teach "at-risk" children, many of whom are racialized and poor. Society has given up on these children, creating what has come to be called the school-to-prison pipeline.

Even as criticisms of institutionalization for people with disabilities grew, institutions proved challenging to reform or abolish. *Allison Carey* and *Lucy Gu* detail the tension experienced by parents of children with intellectual disabilities in the 1960s to the 1980s in deciding whether and how to reform or abolish the institution. While highly critical of institutional neglect and abuse, some parents still clung to the "services" provided by institutions, due to their concerns about the feasibility of community integration and their desire to preserve the institutional system as a legitimate "choice." Thus, parents paradoxically played a key role in advocating deinstitutionalization and in preserving the institutional system.

As we have moved toward deinstitutionalization, communities have attempted to erase reminders of institutional pasts. *Jihan Abbas* and *Jijian Voronka* study the ways in which, through architectural redevelopment, two Canadian communities are seeking to expunge the outward signs of incarceration based on disability, even while they continue to treat madness and intellectual disabilities as deficiencies to be fixed and erased. Like earlier institutional reforms, the buildings become more attractive, the rhetoric more palatable, but the push toward containment is still just as great. Connecting back with Chapman's argument regarding the shifting nature of incarceration, *Michael Rembis* argues that this history of institutionalization and deinstitutionalization is fundamental to understanding contemporary trends in mass incarceration. In "The New Asylums: Madness and Mass Incarceration in the NeoLiberal Era," Rembis outlines the growing connections between "deinstitutionalization" and the growth of mass incarceration from the 1960s to the present.

Part II—*Interlocking Oppression, Contemporary Lockdown and Contested Futures*—examines incarceration in modern society, a time often believed to be post-deinstitutionalization, and reveals the myriad ways people with disabilities remain contained, segregated, and excluded today. *Syrus Ware, Joan Ruzsa* and *Giselle Dias* begin these conversations with their chapter, "It Can't be Fixed Because It's Not Broken: Racism and Disability in the Prison Industrial Complex." This chapter posits that prisons are dangerous places, especially if you are racialized and disabled. Because of the ways that prisons are constructed, imagined, and maintained, rampant ableism and racism affect the daily lives of disabled, racialized prisoners. The authors explore how disability and experiences of racialization are constructed throughout the Prison Industrial Complex (PIC). While some people are confined by walls, modern medicine has transformed incarceratory options. *Erick Fabris* and *Katie Aubrecht* reveal the uses of psychiatric drugs as a form of physical and mental restraint. Such drugs are at times mandated with the promise of treatment, normalization, and progress, yet they often lead to addiction, impairments that result from the medication itself, and disempowerment.

Shaista Patel explores another way in which disability/madness and incarceration intertwine. Patel documents the narratives of madness that are used to explain Muslim terrorism and argues that these narratives not only inscribe the category of madness as inherently evil but also shore up biopolitical anxieties of a white nation by reinscribing madness as a racialized problem that needs to be contained for the protection of whites. Madness is used to mark "terrorists" as subhuman and not even worthy of rational consideration, requiring instead responses of violence and incarceration. Other "foreigners" are also marked and contained based on the interlockings of race, nationality, and disability. In "Refugee Camps, Asylum Detention, and the Geopolitics of Transnational Mobility, Disability and Its Intersections with Humanitarian Confinement," *Mansha Mirza* builds on our understanding of how humanitarian rhetoric is used to justify confinement, this time of refugees forcibly displaced from their homelands. According to Mirza, refugee camps and detention centers hold refugees in sites that are supposedly temporary, but are frequently long-term. They operate much like asylums and prisons, serving to classify, contain, and segregate. Mirza further examines how disability is contested, produced, and reproduced within the terrain of humanitarian confinement and transnational migration.

The future could hold more promise than just making incarceration "prettier" or more efficient. *Mark Friedman* and *Ruthie-Marie Beckwith* explore the work of self-advocates to overcome the stereotypes of persons with intellectual disabilities as incompetent, unable to benefit from education, and completely dependent on families and professional guidance, and instead position themselves as well-informed, tenacious leaders in the long-haul fight to emancipate their counterparts from large, state-run institutions. Their campaigns for freedom resulted in seismic shifts in how people with developmental disabilities were perceived and the manner in which they received services and supports. In the final chapter, *Liat Ben-Moshe* uses a broader lens to discuss "Alternatives to (Disability) Incarceration." She explores a range of strategies across populations to resist incarceration, reimagine social justice, and attain inclusivity. We hope people will bring these ideas into dialogue, and add to them, as we come to understand the devastating impact of institutionalization and mass incarceration, the fundamental role of disability in confinement, and possible alternative futures.

Note

1. Canadian readers may note that there is a disproportionate focus on Ontario and no mention of Quebec or Francophone Canada. We recognize this and hope this collection is the beginning of a much larger conversation. Of course, there are many other aspects of the interface of disability and incarceration that are also left unaddressed. Ultimately, we had to work within the confines of a single volume, recognizing that there is so much more to be said and done.

References

Bell, Chris. 2006. "Introducing White Disability Studies: A Modest Proposal." In *The Disability Studies Reader* (2nd ed), edited by Davis, L. J. (ed.). New York: Routledge.

Ben-Moshe, Liat. 2011. "Genealogies of Resistance to Incarceration: Abolition Politics within Deinstitutionalization and Anti-Prison Activism in the U.S 1950-Present." PhD diss., Syracuse University.

Chapman, C. 2012. "Colonialism, Disability, and Possible Lives: The Residential Treatment of Children Whose Parents Survived Indian Residential Schools." *Journal of Progressive Human Services* 24(2): 127–158.

Churchill, Ward. 2004. *Kill the Indian, Save the Man: The Genocidal Impact of American Indian Residential Schools.* San Francisco, CA: City Lights.

Foucault, Michel. 1995. *Discipline and Punish: The Birth of the Prison.* New York: Vintage.

———. 1994. "'Omnes et Singulatim': Toward a Critique of Political Reason." In *Power*, 298–325. New York: The New Press.

Fournier, Suzanne, and Ernie Crey. 1999. *Stolen from Our Embrace: The Abduction of First Nations Children and the Restoration of Aboriginal Communities.* Toronto, ON: Harper Collins.

King, Thomas. 2003. *The Truth about Stories: A Native Narrative.* Toronto, ON: House of Anansi Press Inc.

LeFrançois, Brenda A. 2013. "The Psychiatrization of Our Children, or, an Autoethnographic Narrative of Perpetuating First Nations Genocide through 'Benevolent' Institutions." *Decolonization* 2(1): 108–123.

Puar, Jasbir. 2012. "The Cost of Getting Better: Suicide, Sensation, Switchpoints." *GLQ* 18(1): 149–158.

Smith, Andrea. 2005. *Conquest: Sexual Violence and American Indian Genocide.* Cambridge: South End Press.

Thobani, Sunera. 2007. *Exalted Subjects: Studies in the Making of Race and Nation in Canada.* Toronto, ON: University of Toronto Press.

Walcott, Rinaldo. 2003. *Black Like Who? Writing Black Canada.* Toronto, ON: Insomniac Press.

Acknowledgments

This project stems out of numerous conversations at conferences, social gatherings, and workshops in which we started noticing the connections between doing disability studies and disability justice work, and doing antiprison, deinstitutionalization, antipsychiatry, and prison abolition work. We started meeting one another, some of whom became contributors to this book, discussing the lacuna in our respective fields that tended to either disability or incarceration but rarely both. Then, in 2009, Anthony J. Nocella II asked: "why don't we fill the gap ourselves?" Such a simple and profound question. We have taken up the challenge, we hope we did it justice, and we want to thank Anthony for the helpful suggestion and his initial help in conceptualizing this anthology.

The editors would like to thank all the phenomenal authors who contributed chapters to the book: Katie Aubrecht, Jihan Abbas, Ruthie-Marie Beckwith, Giselle Dias, Nirmala Erevelles, Erick Fabris, Phil Ferguson, Mark Friedman, Lucy Gu, Mansha Mirza, Shaista Patel, Geoffrey Reaume, Michael Rembis, Joan Ruzsa, Jijian Voronka, and Syrus Ware, as well as Robert McRuer for writing such a gracious and thoughtful epilogue to the anthology. We have learned so much from each other, and it has truly felt like a collaborative process at every step.

Special thanks goes to Angela Y. Davis, who has been a lightening rod in her commitment to critical interlocking analyses of incarceration (and a myriad of other issues), to which we hope to contribute in a small way through this anthology; and also for being extremely supportive of this project, from its initial conceptualization to writing the foreword and spreading the word.

We would also like to thank Palgrave Macmillan for taking on this project, and especially to Lani Oshima who has been a wonderful and supportive editor, helping us along and demystifying the publishing process. We also appreciate the often invisible labor done behind the scenes in the production of the book, from layout and design to sending the manuscript out for peer review. We appreciate the comments we received from Richard Scotch and Tanya Titchkosky on our prospectus and the feedback from our anonymous reviewers who encouraged us to "stay the course" while making the anthology stronger.

We would like to thank all the people who have been integral to the task of writing at the intersection of disability/madness and incarceration including, but not limited to, Susan Burch, Bernard Harcourt, Incite!, Jonathan Metzl, Leroy Moore, Robert Perske, Nicole Rafter, David Rothman, and the many people who have engaged in conversation and activism around these issues—especially those who are or have been institutionalized and incarcerated, in whatever capacity or incapacity. A special debt goes to Steven J. Taylor who has played a key role, along with so many others, in fighting against institutions for those labeled as disabled since the 1970s and whose work is not only pioneering, but unfortunately, more relevant than ever in these neoliberal times.

Liat would like to thank my partner in love and thought Deanna Adams, whose work has deeply shaped my knowledge of the workings on the school-to-prison pipeline, especially through the "pipe" known as special education.

Chris would like to thank Vic, Maayo, Kalye, and his many loved ones for support, inspiration, and challenge. He would also like to acknowledge the profound impact of the outrage and critique that he heard from people subjected to institutional sites in which he worked.

We want to end by thanking you, the reader, for taking the time and effort to read through this collection. It is meant to ignite a conversation, a dialogue, a movement. We hope you engage, contribute to the discussion, and carry it forward.

I

Interlocking Histories and Legacies of Confinement

Reconsidering Confinement: Interlocking Locations and Logics of Incarceration

Chris Chapman, Allison C. Carey, and Liat Ben-Moshe

Through this collection, we hope to engage in and inspire dialogue across people interested in imprisonment, institutionalization, and other sites of incarceration and segregation. Disability is of course a central component to our discussion as we consider how these sites uniquely and collectively shape the experiences of disabled people and how disability as a concept undergirds the development and workings of incarcerative systems. Because the work in this book crosses fields, examines multiple sites of incarceration, and attends to the interlocking of oppression, this chapter is designed to provide a broad historical and theoretical overview in order to showcase the intersections across sites and forms of inequality.

Undifferentiated Confinement and Its Early Critique

In disability scholarship, the rise and fall of the medical institution dominates the historical and theoretical landscape. One thing so compelling about histories of the medical institution is imagining that life was possible before it, which wears away its normative self-evidence. Indeed, just as there was a time before the medical institution, before eighteenth-century Europe and North America, there was a time when imprisonment had never been used anywhere as a primary form of punishment. It had been a temporary measure used under specific circumstances—often when the duration served a specific end, such as awaiting trial or being released upon paying a debt (Carrigan 1994; Foucault 1995; Guest 1997; Rothman 1971). Incarceration was not thought to have any benefit to inmates whatsoever, except perhaps deterrence. It was not any more "rehabilitative" than torture, banishment, or paying a fine.

Following traditions from England and France, the confinement of disabled people emerged early in colonial North America. Although social norms placed primary responsibility for dependents upon family, communities also developed formal mechanisms of care and control to handle instances when families would not or could not fulfill their obligations and when social problems such as vagrancy and theft emerged (Katz 1996). Criminalization and class oppression were thus central to the earliest forms of confining disabled (and nondisabled) people. One of the earliest institutions was the almshouse or poorhouse, which housed poor, disabled, widowed, orphaned, and sick people, in a relatively undifferentiated manner. In practice, early jails, poorhouses, and even "general hospitals," confined the same undifferentiated populations together. The only common theme was poverty because nobody with other options chose to live in any of these spaces. Wealthy people who were sick would never stay in a hospital, which was understood as a place of contagion rather than cure (Foucault 1994a); wealthy people were also less likely than today to be incarcerated for crimes, given that those jailed were most often sentenced for outstanding debts (Carrigan 1994; Guest 1997); and families with money were unlikely to institutionalize disabled loved ones until doing so became socially sanctioned.

People of color were rarely held in the earliest incarcerative sites, but for different reasons. It was not that racialized people had additional options from which they freely chose alternatives to confinement; rather, the ruling classes had other options for the control and elimination of racialized people. At this time, unrestrained violence was normatively and unapologetically used against enslaved and colonized peoples. Yet, except for this one significant exception, the earliest confinements housed the various populations that are still overrepresented among those incarcerated and institutionalized today (Chapman this volume).

These earliest imprisonments were contradictory in their orientation toward "care" and punishment, as are their descendants today. Supporters of the almshouse claimed that a formal system of institutional care would provide the worthy poor (those perceived as unfit for paid employment such as people with intellectual disabilities and the aged) with superior care, while deterring the unworthy poor (those who "could" work) from needless dependence and idleness. These two goals proved inherently contradictory (Ferguson 1994; Guest 1997). According to Ferguson (1994), in order to deter the unworthy poor, conditions in almshouses had to be sufficiently inhumane and abusive to motivate anyone who could work to do so, making compassionate care of the worthy poor impossible. Thus, abusive custodialism emerged as the accepted means of "caring" for disabled people. Furthermore, new laws against vagrancy and begging criminalized poverty, which increased the vulnerability of disabled people to penal imprisonment (Scheerenberger 1983). Disabled people incarcerated for begging were therefore inseparably confined for being "criminals," "paupers," and "disabled." The three stratifications came together in these new laws and earliest practices of segregating particular people away from "respectable society."

While it is well documented that the poorhouse was a catchall for all deemed dependent, unproductive or dangerous, it seems to be less often noted that this was equally true of early county jails and hospitals. Foucault (1988, 38) writes that French practices of mass incarceration began in 1657 with the creation of the "general hospital" and the "great confinement of the poor." Before long, one out of every hundred Parisians was incarcerated. Even after the differentiation of various confined groups had begun, due to efforts of reformers, the "treatment" of people in differentiated sites continued to be rationalized and practiced in ways understood as interrelated. This demands an interlocking analysis of them. For example, the National Conference on Charities and Corrections, founded in 1874 after confinement had become differentiated, was the leading authority on pauperism, insanity, delinquency, prisons, immigration, and feeblemindedness, because they were seen as so closely related (Trent 1994). In many ways, the only thing connecting the diverse populations who were first clustered together in the almshouse is that they have consistently been clustered together ever since, as the responsibility of sites of confinement, professional intervention in the community, or both.

Differentiated Confinement, Resonant Rationalities

The reformed differentiation of sites of confinement led to increased internment of diverse populations. Importantly, though, rather than being an imposition from government or business interests, this increase in confinement at first came largely out of the vigorous advocacy of progressive reformers and the advent of "moral treatment." In the eighteenth century, Pinel in France and Tuke in England described the then-normative approaches to psychiatric confinement as inhumane. They removed (some) patients' restraints and attempted to treat them in asylums. American psychiatric hospitals were also founded by progressive religious reformers, such as Dorothea Dix. Like Pinel and Tuke, Dix sought to liberate the "mad" from the oppressive conditions of chains and squalor, and to provide them with therapies—while still confined (Braddock and Parish 2003). Around this same time, the first institutions for blind people and "deaf mutes" also emerged. In 1818, the New York Institution for Deaf and Dumb was established (the American Asylum at Hartford was already operative), and the Perkins School for the Blind was established in Massachusetts in 1832. Dix herself founded a school for the blind, suggesting again that these diverse endeavors were intimately related. They were all oriented by the concern that confinement be specialized. Undifferentiated confinement was now an injustice, but specialized confinement could educate or rehabilitate.

In the United States, penitentiaries were created through the efforts of progressive religious reformers who sought more humane and efficacious forms of punishment than corporal punishments (Foucault 1995). Auburn prison opened in 1817 in Auburn, NY, and Quakers founded the Eastern State Penitentiary in Philadelphia in 1829. This was considered part of progressive social reform, and was followed in other parts of the United States and Canada in subsequent decades (Carrigan 1994). Early penitentiaries were not only imagined as the lesser of two evils, but they were also an experimental ground for other socially progressive innovations in architecture, hygiene, education, and moral reform (Rothman 1971; 1995).

Various incarcerative and institutional solutions grew in popularity throughout the 1800s (Ferguson 1994; Rothman 1971). By the mid-nineteenth century, systems of "care" were transforming into the more expansive, specialized, medical systems that would dominate the early twentieth century. In terms of political rationality (Chapman this volume; Foucault 1994b, 324–325), it was only in the 1800s that confinement was first conceptualized as doing anything useful for those confined. This was partly a result of developments in technologies of discipline within spaces of confinement (Foucault 1995; 2008), but it also relates to a growing secularization in Christian Europe. This disrupted the belief that people's lot in life was divinely predestined (Foucault 1994a). Now, for the first time in Christian Europe, it was believed that people could significantly alter the course of their lives. One could not only accrue wealth and status—as was evident in the new bourgeois class—but could also become educated, cultivated, sane, or "civilized" (Chapman this volume).

The idea of individual transformation intersected with the "treatment" of denigrated populations. Both the British New Poor Law and the Bill for the Total Abolition of Colonial Slavery (which abolished slavery in Canada and other British colonies) took effect in 1834, and both were premised on the idea that paupers and slaves could undergo tutelage to ready them for the responsibilities of "economic freedom" (O'Connell 2009). That paupers and Black people could ever handle such responsibilities was a new idea for ruling class Europeans. At this time, prisoners were first subjected to strict routines as a means of developing self-discipline. Faucher's strict timetable for prisoners, which would not have made sense to anyone a few decades earlier, was published only four years after the British New Poor Law and the Total Abolition of Colonial Slavery (Foucault 1995, 6–7). In the year previous to this timetable, the construction of New York's Utica State Lunatic Asylum began in 1837, and by the 1850s there were 30 such institutions in the United States (Braddock and Parish 2003). The then Province of Canada built its first "Lunatic Asylum" in Toronto in 1850 (Voronka 2008), which was just four years after the Government had resolved "to fully commit itself to Indian residential schools" in 1846 (Fournier and Crey 1999, 53). And only two years later, in the United States, Hervey Backus Wilbur undertook the first instruction of an intellectually disabled pupil in 1848 (Rafter 1997, 17), after which he became Superintendent of the first American "Asylum for Idiots" in Albany, NY, in 1851. Although there were widely divergent effects on the groups incarcerated in these various settings, which all emerged within a 17-year time span, they loosely share a structure of political rationality: under the right conditions imposed from above, degenerate, disabled, criminalistic, or uncivilized peoples can be brought "up" to normative standards. Theoretically, any person was now capable of achieving normalcy. This may sound like a welcome development, but it offered a very narrow conception of normalcy, and everyone was now measured against it, which was never previously the case (L. Davis 1995). Anything outside this narrow conception still required elimination, but such elimination could now be achieved by transforming individuals. As US Indian Commissioner William Jones put it, the goal of Indian Residential Schools was to "exterminate the Indian but develop a man" (in Churchill 2004, 14).

Furthermore, such previously impossible "development"—whether of slaves, First Nations, paupers, criminals, or intellectually, physically or psychiatrically disabled people—aimed toward integration into society as menial laborers. Residential Schools, penitentiaries, and the various specialized schools and institutions for disabled people never oriented their efforts toward graduates who would be leaders or professionals. The secular dream that people are masters of their own destiny only extended so far, and it intersected with the capitalist requirement for cheap labor.

Capitalism and Its Interlockings with Disablement and Confinement

Transformations within disability incarceration were propelled by the spread of capitalism, the reliance on institutions to manage social problems, the medicalization of intellectual disability, and the rise of eugenics (Rothman 1971; Trent 1994). Capitalism slowly and fundamentally transformed social norms regarding care, disability, and dependence. Growing capitalist markets required a vast pool of mobile and free workers, and traditional systems of charity were increasingly understood to undermine work ethic and encourage dependence. Reformers advanced distinct agendas for the able-bodied and disabled poor. The able-bodied were to be inculcated with work ethic and "motivated" to work—either by the denial of assistance or the provision of assistance in conditions wretched enough to make paid labor seem attractive. Those incapable of working were provided with custodial care and institutional segregation, but in inhumane conditions that underscored the horror of dependency (Ferguson 1994; Foucault 1988; Scull 1977).

When considering these histories, it should be remembered that some of those who were now "incapable of working" had previously been gainfully employed within more flexible and heterogeneous economic spheres in which requisite tasks and wages were more immediately and intimately negotiated, such as those within families and small communities (Edwards 1997; Snyder and Mitchell 2006). Some of the "non-productive" within industrial capitalism were easily identified, but differentiation based on psychiatric and intellectual disability proved more challenging. Medical, psychological, and educational professionals took on the task of sorting productive from unproductive (or unworthy from worthy) and managing appropriate "treatment." In reference to resultant practices of confinement, Foucault (1988) wrote: "Before having the medical meaning we give it, or that at least we like to suppose it has, confinement was required by something quite different from any concern with curing the sick. What made it necessary was an imperative of labor" (46). "Cure" was increasingly understood as "readiness for economic freedom," but this goal was made ever more challenging by a progressively competitive industrial labor market demanding fast-paced and standardized work. As optimism about specialized schools faded, superintendents began to emphasize the cost-effectiveness of institutions for lifelong custodial care (Noll and Trent 2004; Trent 1994).

From 1820–1850 there was also an increase in public concerns about crime as a hazard. Rothman (1995) asserts that this preoccupation with delinquency most likely had more to do with a society in flux than with actual rising rates of crime.[1] Reformers looked to prisons and the medical institution as a remedy for the resultant chaos (Reilly 1991; Rothman 1971). Within the walls of the institution or penitentiary, experts could create an environment that exemplified the principles of a well-ordered society and thereby (it was believed) cure inmates of insanity, deficiency, and deviancy. This occurred alongside the creation of the closed institutional spaces of Indian Residential Schools, which were politically rationalized as a means of "saving" the children from the "death of their race" (as a result of the social chaos resulting from colonialism, but narrated as social Darwinism)—which was considered inevitable by most White people at the time (Kelm 2005; King 2003; Neu and Therrien 2003).

Confinement's particularity was always contingent on interlocking power relations. The first institutions were marked by internal stratification, keeping the poor separate from privileged classes (Braddock and Parish 2003; Smith and Giggs 1988); while some wealthy families were able to pay for relatively comfortable institutional care for their loved ones, families with more moderate incomes had to accept institutional conditions which nobody would choose to inhabit. By 1860, 44 percent of the prisoners in New York State prisons were foreign-born, and these rates increased each decade thereafter (Rothman 1971). Aboriginal children in both Canada and the United States were often forcibly removed from their families by police and placed in Residential Schools, their parents occasionally imprisoned for resisting this (Churchill 2004, 17).

Medicalization, Eugenics, and the Return of Confinement as an End in Itself

Although early asylums were intended to provide temporary sanctuary and rehabilitation to those who were first time offenders, recently mad, temporarily impoverished, newly orphaned, and so on (Rothman 1971), they began housing those with long-term psychiatric disabilities, people serving life sentences, and children becoming adults in poorhouses and orphanages. Prisons and penitentiaries also held more "hardened criminals" than anticipated, and those convicted served very long sentences. Instead of being a means to an end, incarceration in the mid-nineteenth century became an end in itself. Today this is normatively unremarkable, but it would have been a travesty for the reformers who pushed for the rehabilitative prison (Foucault 1995).

Custodialism served the interests of the new helping professions. Institutions centralized treatment, research, and funding, and thus played an important role in the advancement of professionals concerned with the feebleminded (Rafter 1997). Medicine, social work, and other professions increasingly advocated eugenics, cementing a biological understanding of intellectual disability and the vital role of professional interventions (Carey 2003; Paul 1995). The rationality of eugenics was protecting society from social danger, and in many ways it was about criminalization, classism, sexism, racism, and homophobia as centrally as it was about disablism (Rafter 1997; Trent 1994). Eugenicists conflated the "strength" of one's intellect and morality, believing both were measurable through physiological, hereditary, and IQ testing.

Race, Gender, and Imprisonment in an Era of Slavery, Eugenics, and Emancipation

The history of eugenics, disability, and institutionalization cannot be radically separated from concurrent developments in the "scientific" study of race and sexuality. Discussing the second half of the nineteenth century, Somerville (2000) explores the relationship between physiological studies of African women and "female inverts" (lesbians), which took place concurrent to similar studies of paupers, convicted criminals, and diverse disabled people. These "concurrent" developments informed one another. For example, in 1866, Dr. Down isolated what came to be named Down Syndrome. However, drawing upon existing racist hierarchies, Down coined the term Mongolism. He wrote, "it is difficult to realize he is the child of Europeans, but so frequently are these characters presented, that there can be no doubt that these ethnic features are the result of degeneration" (cited in Clark and Marsh 2002, para. 12).

Eugenics was explicitly racist in its attempts to strengthen "population quality," defined in reference to Anglo-Saxon characteristics and moral codes (Black 2003; Larson 1995; McLaren 1990; Noll 1995; Thobani 2007). Although popular rhetoric frequently portrayed the faces of "feeblemindedness" and "insanity" as immigrants and women of color, institutionalization was initially reserved for Whites (Rafter 1988). Black people and immigrants were often denied any form of social assistance and left to fend for themselves (Carlton-LaNey 1999; Peebles-Wilkins and Francis 1990; Thobani 2007; Yee 1994), an exclusion that ironically protected them from the specific abuses of the disability system.

Snyder and Mitchell (2006, 88) note that it was not until the late 1940s that African Americans with disabilities were placed in medical institutions along with their White counterparts (see Erevelles this volume, for more on this). They also write that both English and German sources during the eugenics era portrayed the death of disabled people as beneficial to the nation, but Black people's lives were valued as exploitable labor. Folding disability back into the picture, they note that this "overlooks the mortality that always accompanies slave systems, particularly for human chattel who become disabled as a result of inhumane labor and living conditions or for those killed after being born with a disability on slave plantations" (122). Although people of color could be kept out of closed institutions through segregation, racially segregated spaces were never free from disability. The "inclusion" of African Americans in prisons only occurred following the abolition of the unapologetically violent practices of slavery (A. Davis 2003). Although, in practice, slavery continued in the convict leasing system, as a consequence of the thirteenth amendment's allowance for convicted "criminals'" enslavement (A. Davis 2000).

First Nations people were also normatively excluded from early penal and psychiatric incarceration. While sites of nearly exclusive White confinement based on disability were initially flourishing, both Canada and the United States attempted to incarcerate every single Aboriginal child in a residential/boarding school. These "schools" were incredibly violent, but were publicly rationalized through discourses of "pity" and "care"—rationales that in this respect had more in common with contemporaneous rationales of confining disabled people than Black people.

While Aboriginal and Black people were segregated from White settlers, Asians and other racialized groups were restricted from entering Canada and the United States (Thobani 2007). For those communities cautiously allowed to migrate (Jewish and Irish people, Eastern and Southern Europeans), immigration policy and institutionalization interlocked, rendering some confinements unnecessary; newcomers deemed degenerate were sent back to their home countries (Reaume this volume)[2].

Eugenics was also sharply gendered. Women could be institutionalized and sterilized for deviating from norms of sexuality and femininity (A. Davis 1983; Kline 2001; Rafter 1992; 1997). Imprisonment too was gendered. At the beginning of the nineteenth century, the majority of women convicted (of mostly petty crimes) endured, in some ways, worse conditions than men as prisoners, due to systematic abuse, exploitation, and a general lack of concern for them as a "constituency." When prisons and jails were erected, they did not take women into account.

Mill's (1869) On the Subjection of Women contrasts men's "privilege" with women's "disability." In this line of thinking, men were best rehabilitated through harshness, women through sympathy. In practice, any such distinction was precarious, but it marks two ends of a continuum that has constrained practices of confinement ever since—from "harshness" to "sympathy." Reform has consistently been constrained by these parameters, so that a given site of confinement might become more or less harsh but reform rarely transcended established practices of confinement.

Following emancipation, African American men and women were sent to prison for the most minor offenses of Jim Crow laws, and previously all-White prisons became filled with Black prisoners. After 1870, prison camps were established in the South, imprisoning emancipated slaves and exploiting their labor (Kurshan 1996). A two-tier system was created in which custodial and reformatory prisons were both established for women. The reformatories meant to rehabilitate female prisoners housed mostly White women, while custodial prisons were similar to men's prisons and housed mostly racialized women. Southern prisons had the worst conditions, were unsanitary, and lacked medical care (Kurshan 1996). Racism and sexism interlocked in such a way that racialized female prisoners appear to have been understood as "the kind of social threat" that—like male prisoners—required harshness rather than sympathy. Historical developments that are at once divergent, and inseparable, and intersecting, have worked together to create the diverse contemporary confinements that Foucault called "the carceral archipelago" (1995, 301). These developments established what Foucault called a "protective continuum," ranging from the medical to the penal. "These are the two poles of a continuous network of institutions…This continuum with its therapeutic and judicial poles, this institutional mixture, is actually a response to danger" (2003, 34), rather than precisely to illness or crime. Differentiated institutions were created, to classify, to control and treat danger, and to safeguard the rest of the population from the dangerous individual—as McLaren (1990) demonstrates of eugenics in Western Canada, Thobani of both colonization and immigration in Canada (2007), and Angela Davis (2003) of anti-Black racism in the rise of the US prison.

Out of discourses of the dangerous individual and the need to defend society, from the nineteenth century on, the medical and judicial become increasingly intertwined, with doctors "laying claim to judicial power, and judges laying claim to medical power" (2003, 39). According to Foucault, this emerged through discourses of abnormality and normalization, which are related to medical notions of illness and legal notions of recidivism, but in ways that always spill into one another. Psychiatry, for example, was not initially established in France as a specialization in medicine, but as a branch of public hygiene—of social safety. By codifying madness as both illness and danger, psychiatry gained legitimacy. And legal psychiatry was established at the very time that psychiatry was legitimizing itself as a scientific medical sub-specialization (Foucault 2003).

Resistance, Reform, and Reiteration

"Between 1950 and 1970, state authorities built, refurbished, and added to more public facilities than in any other period of American history" (Trent 1994, 250). Between 1946 and 1967 the number of residents in institutions for people with intellectual disabilities rose from 116,828 to 193,188—an increase of nearly twice the increase of the general population. In the face of deteriorating institutional conditions, accusations of abuse and neglect, and the scientific discrediting of eugenics, the medical institution and related programs still offered "sociological advantages" (Ladd-Taylor 2004) that led to their widespread use (Trent 1993). Institutions provided places of research and domains of power for institutional superintendents, served as a means to control and segregate a range of individuals perceived as socially deviant, and offered a cost-effective method to deal with lifelong dependency.

As the use of institutions continued to grow into the mid-twentieth century, criticisms mounted regarding institutions and programs such as compulsory sterilization. These criticisms emerged alongside, and intersected with, the many other radical political movements of the 1960s: Disability Rights and Prisoners' Rights movements gained new prominence; Indian Residential Schools began to give way to the "Sixties Scoop"; 32 different countries in Africa gained independence; and the Civil Rights and Black Power movements, American Indian Movement, Stonewall Riots, second wave feminism, and Vietnam War Protests raised many troubling social and political questions. Concurrent to these related developments, the dominance of the medical institutions began to decline for people with intellectual disabilities in the early 1970s (Trent 1994). The critique of institutions stated that: disability was manufactured and perpetuated by the systems that identified and labeled people as disabled; this often led to negative rather than positive consequences and primarily existed to exert social control; this was intrinsic to institutions and could only be ameliorated by ending institutional care; and institutions violated peoples' human and constitutional rights to life, liberty, and the pursuit of happiness. Kanner (1942), Sarason (1958), Scheff (1966), and Szasz (1961) were among the first scholars to apply labeling theories to disability. In *The Myth of Mental Illness*, Szasz argued that mental illness was only a label used to repress socially unacceptable behaviors and that psychiatrists were sanctioned by the state to enforce "normality." If psychiatrists were the police force for normality, then medical institutions were analogous to a prison for society's unwanted, unacceptable, and socially deviant. Goffman's (1961) *Asylums* compared mental institutions, prisons, boot camps, and religious cults, arguing that they share the features of "total institutions."[3] Human rights abuses were repeatedly documented in exposés (Blatt and Kaplan 1966; Deutsch 1948; Maisel 1946; Richardson 1946; Rivera 1972). World War II conscientious objectors who served in America's mental institutions led significant reform efforts, partly through such exposés (Taylor 2009). Nirje (1969) and Wolfensberger (1972) advocated that typical patterns of life, relationships, and roles be available to people with disabilities and that these qualities are essential to their development as people and citizens. But acclimatization to the local norms of an institution becomes a part of the problem for those incarcerated. Refuting that disabled people require protection from competition through segregation, Perske (1972) asserted that they deserve the "dignity of risk"; while Wald (1976) argued that disabled people have a right to privacy that is systematically violated in institutions and the broader service system. Parents and disabled people themselves organized to improve institutions and/or to replace institution-based services with community-based ones (Carey 2009, Carey and Gu this volume; Friedman and Beckwith this volume; Jones 2010). And Ferlerger argued in the groundbreaking Halderman v. Pennhurst (1977) that institutionalization violated the constitutional right to liberty. A later case, Olmstead v. L. C. (1999) found that unnecessary institutionalization was legally discrimination under the Americans with Disabilities Act. Such activism cumulatively transformed a system that at one time was as normatively unproblematized as today's prison, group home, or nursing home.

Thanks to efforts of survivors of institutions and other activists, many intellectually and psychiatrically disabled people today live outside large-scale institutions (Friedman and Beckwith this volume), which is a great accomplishment. Unfortunately, institutionalization has not ended. In 2009, 33,732 American people were still housed in large state institutions housing 16 people or more, and most states continue to channel a significant proportion of long-term care funding into institutions (Braddock et al. 2011). As with the reform of women's imprisonment a century earlier, resistance to institutionalization was constrained by the long-standing "curative" versus "custodial" and "sympathy" versus "harshness" parameters. The earliest prison reformers of the 1700s advocated for gentler and rehabilitative forms of punishment, and this same sentiment has motivated reform toward gentler institutionalization rather than abolition (Carey and Gu this volume). Just as institutions survived early criticisms of eugenics, so too did they survive mid-twentieth century legal and philosophical challenges. Their survival is not due to their success at providing treatment but is because they serve particular interests and rationalities, and because alternative models of service delivery are often blocked.

The large-scale institutionalization of disabled people, where it is rationalized as necessary specifically because of disability, has declined since the 1970s in the United States and Canada. And as institutions declined, community-based services emerged. But these have not offered the panacea that was desired. Like Ferguson noted regarding the similarities between the almshouse and the institution, so too are there similarities between community-based services and medical institutions. Community-based services are often run with a similar medical model and an asymmetry of power between staff and consumers (Drinkwater 2005; Rothman and Rothman 1984). They at times demand that people earn what should be basic rights to movement, privacy, and choice (Taylor 1988). They often create artificial homes and relationships without the true qualities (McKnight 1995).

Snyder and Mitchell (2006) suggest that current forms of surveillance, routine, and behavior modification in nursing homes, sheltered workshops, and so on, "remind us of a past that we had believed we had superseded and gesture toward a future we want to avoid" (135). They characterize these still existing institutions as continuities of a top-down model of power that is often assumed to have ended. Butler (2004) raises similar concerns discussing the indefinite detention of "terror suspects," as does Asad (2003) of contemporary police torture behind closed doors. Top-down and heavy-handed power relations continue, in spite of reforms narrated as movement toward kinder persuasions in which people subjected to them are more democratically involved in their negotiation. The two structures of power (top-down sovereign power and persuasive disciplinary power) coexist in even the most specific contexts and interactions. Narratives comparing today's programs favorably against "real institutionalization," might actually prevent the recognition of ongoing institutionalization today (Ahmed 2006; Drinkwater 2005; Heron 2007). Perhaps this is not a "post-institutionalization" era at all, but is rather one of different now-normative institutionalization.

Following Stiker's (2000) provocation that inclusion and exclusion are not mutually exclusive, community inclusion is continuous with longstanding practices and rationalizations of social control (Drinkwater 2005; Michalko 2002; Tremain 2005). People receive rights and inclusion only in exchange for conformity, normalization, self-support, silencing dissent, and erasing differences (Michalko 2002; Russell 1998; Snyder and Mitchell 2006; Stiker 2000; Titchkosky 2003). The tension between care and enforcing work in almshouses still informs disability policy, leading to "controlled integration" in which rights are offered or denied based on economic benefits to people without disabilities (Carey 2009). The "right" to be a part of the community is offered to those whose support is calculated as less costly, while institutionalization may be the only available option to those with more extensive care needs. The right to equal opportunity in the work place is provided for those considered viable workers, but income supports (which are always below the poverty line, following a similar logic of deterrence as early almshouses) are offered to others. "The disabled person is integrated only when disability is erased" (Stiker 2000, 152). And when such erasure is not achieved, integration is often not pursued at all.

The growth of the Prison-Industrial Complex, especially given its occurrence shortly following the massive closures of both medical institutions and Indian Residential Schools, further complicates the assumption that institutional forms of control are in any way behind us. The Prison-Industrial Complex could be defined as a complex web interweaving private business and government interests in the growing industry of incarceration and prison development (A. Davis 2003; Sudbury 2004). The public rationale behind the Prison-Industrial Complex is the fight against crime, but those drawing on this conceptualization note the implicit goals as profit making and social control of mostly men of color (Christie 2000; Gilmore 2006; Goldberg and Evans 1997). According to Parenti, the criminal (in) justice system and the privatization of prisons "manage and contain the new surplus populations created by neo-liberal economic policies" and the global flow of capital (1999). Goldberg and Evans (1997) connect the US practice of acting as policeman of the world to the exportation of specific penal regimes in what Sudbury (2005) has called "global lockdown." Canada's Prime Minister, shortly after apologizing for Indian Residential Schools (Harper 2008) and then denying Canada's history of colonialism (Canadian Business 2009), is now following the example of the United States in prison expansion (including building "Super Max" prisons). For the first time ever, in 2008, more than one in one hundred American adults was behind bars. In 2009, the adult incarcerated population in US prisons and jails was 2,284,900 (BJS 2010). The number of carceral edifices in the United States has also grown. From 2000 to 2005, the number of state and federal correctional facilities has increased by 9 percent, from 1,668 to 1,821 (BJS 2008). The United States incarcerates a greater share of its population, 737 per 100,000 residents, than any other country (Pew Center 2008). Race and disability play a significant role in incarceration rates. In 2006, Whites were imprisoned at a rate of 409 per 100,000 residents, Latinos at 1,038 per 100,000, and Blacks at 2,468 per 100,000. The number of prisoners with disabilities is not measured in the way that some races are, but in 2005 more than half of all prison and jail inmates were reported to have a mental health problem. Nearly a quarter of State prisoners and jail inmates with a mental health problem, compared to a fifth of those without, had served three or more prior incarcerations (Prison Policy Initiative 2008).

Framing imprisonment as the workings of the Prison-Industrial Complex aims to unhinge the normatively taken for granted one-to-one correspondence between crime and incarceration. As in other historical periods when incarceration rates have risen, the increase in the number of prisons and cells in recent decades is not correlated to any increase in crime. Prison abolitionists argue that it has rather been driven by capitalist greed and racist social control. The stated political rationalization behind imprisonment is the fight against crime, but the effects are profit making and the social control and removal of those same groups that were once enslaved, killed in colonial violence, or confined in poor houses and medical institutions. Furthermore, prisons are widely acknowledged to be unsuccessful in the deterrence or prevention of crime (A. Davis 2003; Goldberg and Evans 1997; Smith 2005), as was true even before they became the penalty for almost every crime (Foucault 1995).

Prison abolitionists suggest that the prison persists because it has become a core structure shaping social relations in our society—not just the relationships of those affected directly, but of everyone. Prison abolition is therefore not only about closing prisons, as that would not be enough. W. E. B. Du Bois, in *Black Reconstruction* (1956), discusses abolition as more than the negative process of tearing down. It is about creating social structures that assure equality. Du Bois insists that in order to truly abolish slavery, new democratic institutions are needed. Angela Davis (2003), following Du Bois, examines successful abolitions (of slavery, lynching, and Jim Crow segregation) and points to the gap between the change "that we fight for" and the change "that we actually achieve" (A. Davis 2007). The closure of even the most terrible institution, in isolation, does very little to contribute to more far-reaching societal outcomes of a radical participatory democracy in which all people have the opportunity to shape society.

Toward a Working Definition of Institutionalization, in Its Variety and Its Rough Coherence

Taking into account the wide range of sites that have evolved from the earliest undifferentiated confinements, today we need to ask: What is an institution? What is institutionalization? What is its relationship with imprisonment and other forms of physical confinement? Among what he called total institutions, Goffman (1961) included sites that featured no locked doors or bars on the windows. And yet his work may not adequately address the diverse mish-mash of institutional sites in our communities today. Centering these sites' relations to penal imprisonment, Foucault termed this mish-mash "the carceral archipelago" (1995). We are nuancing this slightly to call it an "institutional archipelago," made up of diverse services and spaces that all trace back to undifferentiated confinement and its ongoing reform—in which penalty is no more or less central than medical care or the right to education. However diverse, these sites also share something in common. It is not stated purpose, and it is not degrees of freedom of movement. These would have one separating the penal from the medical from the educational, or separating closed sites from community services, none of which honor the shared genealogy of the institutional archipelago or the resonances still felt across its diverse sites today.

What makes something an institution? Disability rights coalition Self Advocates Becoming Empowered (SABE) defines an institution as "any place, facility, or program where people don't have control over their lives" (2012). They thereby include many of today's "community-based services" under the umbrella of institutions. This is an important starting point. Many services that have emerged "post-deinstitutionalization" should be understood as institutions.

A difficulty with SABE's definition, however, is that there are countless noninstitutional contexts, such as many families, in which people have no control over their lives. Does the lack of control that many experience in families imply no distinction between a family and the broad range of sites and practices considered incarcerative and/or institutional in this volume? We do not think so. One difference may be that there is greater freedom on the part of those exercising authority in families, as compared to institutional sites in which even staff behavior is constrained by policies, norms, and surveillance. Staff members are not oppressed or affected the same way as those institutionalized; however, the institutionalization of staff/resident relations has a concrete effect on patients' ability to resist and gain some self-control, as well as on staff's agency to relate according to politics or values at odds with institutional norms and policies. Staff govern themselves in relation to many factors, but the added dimension of being disciplined as a "helping professional" or an employee of a particular institutional site also contributes to staff's parameters of freedom in responding to inmate, patient, resident, or consumer resistance (Chapman 2010; 2012).

Practices of power and domination, and of resistance and negotiation, in these sites have something in common that they do not share with noninstitutional sites.

To further consider this, we draw on the conceptualizations of everyday negotiations of power, domination, and resistance that Foucault (1982; 2006) and Bhabha (1994) articulate. Power relations shape encounters, and yet Foucault and Bhabha suggest that such encounters are nevertheless always unique. Their uniqueness is due to resistance and contestation on the part of those subjected to power, as well as to the varied responses to such resistance from those exercising power. Bhabha's colonial encounters, then, are both predictable systemic domination and radically unique negotiation. To analyze this complexity, Bhabha attends to the complex and contingent factors at play in a given interaction between two people, or two communities, which determine the parameters of freedom to negotiate relationships. He conceptualizes these complex determinants as the "Third Space" or "the space between" two people or communities in any given encounter (1994, 53–56). This "space" exceeds what can be concretely known, but conceptualizing it as "there" allows for certain interrogations of power.

There are aspects of "the space between" unique and widely variant staff/resident relations and negotiations that are roughly shared across diverse sites of confinement. For example, that prison personnel, like inmates, are under surveillance and scrutiny and are disciplined to interact with inmates in certain ways (Foucault 1995) is one aspect of Bhabha's Third Space that is equally applicable to asylums, group homes, sheltered workshops, day programs, and many other diverse sites of institutionalization. Policies and procedures manuals delimiting appropriate standardized responses to patient/inmate/consumer behavior is another component of this "space between." The rhetoric that obedience, following routines, and even the immersion in the physical space of the site are somehow beneficial and transformative is another. And the moral exaltation/denigration in which staff are disproportionately responsible for positive outcomes, while inmates/consumers are disproportionately responsible for negative outcomes is yet another.

Family and caregivers abuse many disabled people in their homes and, although this is related to disablism and would resonate in that sense with much institutional violence, such abuse would not share other aspects of the "space between" staff and residents that appears to feature somewhat consistently in confinement and community service settings. This line that we're suggesting can be useful is only "strategic," in the sense of Spivak's "strategic essentialism" (1993)—let's feel free to draw this line when it helps our analysis and activism, and let's highlight its imperfections, arbitrariness, and problems when that's most pressing.

Interlocking Analysis and Particularity

To propose a more thoroughly interlocking history is to suggest that the similarities and the distinctions across sites are important to consider, in terms of rationality, practice, and the effects on people who are incarcerated in diverse sites of confinement. For example, at least on paper the penal system offers certain protections to the accused and the prisoner, such as due process during the trial and sentencing procedures, a sentence of a specified duration, and protection against cruel and unusual punishment, while medical institutions allow the compulsory admittance of patients against their will based only on a medical diagnosis, an indefinite time of commitment, and "treatments" that can be painful and harmful, such as extended isolation, physical restraints, and electric shock "therapy" (Conrad and Schneider 1992; Goffman 1961; Snyder and Mitchell 2006; Szasz 2009).

Broadening the historical and institutional lens also enables innovative readings of historical changes. We do not wish to diminish the gains of the closure of many institutions. This has taken place, however, at roughly the same time as an unprecedented rate of American prison expansion beginning in the 1980s—and we want to encourage disability and prison activists alike to attend more closely to what this means and what can be done about it.

Moreover, one cannot comprehensively analyze and resist the massive prison machine today without a disability critique. Prisoners are not randomly selected and do not equally represent all sectors of society. A disproportionate number of persons incarcerated in US prisons and jails are disabled, poor, and/or racialized. Poverty is known to cause a variety of disabilities and disabling conditions (Puar 2012), as does the prison environment, due to: hard labor in toxic conditions; closed wards with poor air quality; emotional, physical, and sexual violence; the circulation of drugs and needles; and lack of medical equipment and medication (Russell and Stewart 2001). In 2007, 19-year-old Ashley Smith died in an isolation cell in Kitchener, Ontario. After an initial sentence of one month in a youth detention facility for throwing crabapples at a letter carrier, she was transferred among 11 institutions in five different provinces over four years. This enabled her to be held in isolation for much longer than legally allowed because she was never isolated in one institution beyond what is legal. She died under guards' direct observation, as they waited for her to go unconscious before intervening, as per their directives. The "treatment" she had received included extensions of her sentence, isolation, emotional abuse, physical restraint, pepper spray, and a restraint apparatus called "the wrap" (Gartner 2010). Her death was not only a result of disablism, and it was not only about the injustice of prisons; these systemic injustices worked together in particular ways.

There is also need for more critical engagement with the pervasive narrative of "the failure of deinstitutionalization." The hegemonic story is that deinstitutionalization led to "dumping people in the streets" who were unable to live non-institutionalized and so they ended up in prisons or homeless. There are crucial aspects left out of this story. This pervasive narrative steers our attention away from neoliberal policies that led simultaneously to the growth of the prison system, the reduction in affordable housing, and the lack of financial support for disabled people to live viably in the community. These discussions about homelessness individualize and psychiatrize what is properly a political, ethical, and socioeconomic issue. This shifts responsibility away from the state and its policies onto the human service sector who are charged with ameliorating the problem with individualistic mental health interventions and haphazardly available free meals or sleeping bags.

Colonialism and Neocolonialism

Incarceration is now normative worldwide, due to ongoing colonialism and neocolonialism[4]. Neocolonialism is the imposition of European/White settler/Global North ways of doing things, responding to social issues, and imagining human relations onto (for the most part) people of color in the Global South. Many have pointed out that neocolonialism is being mobilized to address problems stemming from colonialism. Ahmed (2004) writes,

> the West gives to others insofar as it is forgotten that the West has already taken in its very *capacity* to give in the first place...[P]ain and suffering,

which are in part effects of socio-economic relations of violence and poverty, are assumed to be alleviated by the very generosity that is enabled by such socio-economic relations. So the West takes, then gives, *and in the moment of giving repeats as well as conceals the taking* (22).

Julia Sudbury (2005) calls neocolonial impositions of imprisonment "global lockdown," saying they address social problems related to increasing disparity between rich and poor. The IMF and World Bank finance (and at times mandate the creation of) large custodial institutions in the Global South, despite critiques of such practices in both the North and the South. IMF Structural Adjustment Programs and international "free" trade agreements also lead to increased poverty, disability, and incarceration in the Global South. These neocolonial impositions, in some cases, have a positive effect on measures such as gross domestic product, but this does not "trickle down" in the way that some claim (Chaudry 2011). The effect of these interventions seems rather to be that the wealthy get wealthier, while the poor become even worse off. The result, then, on a societal level, is an increase in what some have called "relative poverty," which has been demonstrated to result in higher levels of the various social problems that prisons and other institutions are said to address (Wilkinson 2011).

This may appear to have little to do with disability and incarceration in North America, but this appearance is a result of the imaginary in which North America has no history of colonialism—as Canada's Prime Minister recently boasted to the G20, much to the outrage of First Nations groups (Canadian Business 2009). But, it is only through processes of colonial imposition that the sites and practices of confinement that we explore in this book have come to this land. Voronka (2008) writes that the sequestering of First Nations people onto Reserves and the construction of asylums for the sequestering of people with psychiatric disabilities were both central to Canadian "nation building," describing "sites of carceral containment as part of this colonizing project" (2008, 45). And contemporary First Nations' critiques of everyday details of life and social structures in the United States and Canada note that North America has never moved into a period that is "post"-colonial (Smith 2005; Turner 2006).

Conclusion: The Institution Yet to Come, and the Institutionalized Yet to Come

Closure of large institutions has not led to freedom for all disabled people—nor has it resulted in the radical acceptance of the fact of difference among us. Institutional life, whether in a prison, hospital, mental institution, nursing home, group home, or segregated "school," has been the reality, not the exception, for many disabled people, both throughout North American history since the poorhouse, and globally—again because of concrete impositions of colonialism and neocolonialism, here and the world over.

McRuer (2006) discusses what he calls "the disability yet to come," describing both the fear that nondisabled people have of becoming disabled and the notion that if anyone lives long enough, they will eventually become disabled in some way. For example, in describing the interlocking forces in her childhood that worked against her resistance and confidence (sexism and ageism in her family; racism that her family lived with), bell hooks names the ever-present threat of psychiatric incarceration if she does not follow the social mores of a Black girl.

> Questioning authority, raising issues that were not deemed appropriate subjects...that was crazy talk, crazy speech, the kind that would lead you to end up in a mental institution. "Little girl," I would be told, "if you don't stop all this crazy talk and crazy acting you are going to end up right out there at Western State."
>
> [M]adness...was the punishment for too much talk if you were female...[T]his fear of madness haunted me...I was sure [it] was the destiny of daring women born to intense speech. (1989, 7)

The ghost of forced confinement haunts everyone, but does so much more materially and immediately for marginalized populations, especially poor, racialized, and disabled people.

Derrida writes (1994, xix),

> no politics...seems possible and thinkable and *just* that does not recognize in its principal the respect for those others who are no longer or for those others who are not yet *there*, presently living, whether they are already dead or not yet born. No justice...seems possible or thinkable without the principle of some *responsibility*...before the ghosts of those who are not yet born or who are already dead.

How can there be accountability today to the childhood experience of bell hooks, a young Black girl threatened with institutionalization if she talked back to an adult? How can there be accountability to 19-year-old Ashley Smith, who died in her isolation cell in Kitchener just a few years ago? How can there be accountability to "Emily no. 049" who died in the Kuper Island Residential School and wasn't grieved by the White adults running the school because she was Indigenous, deaf, and "quasi-dumb" (Fournier and Crey 1999, 60)? How can there be accountability to "X.X." from Lennox Island whose toes had to be cut off due to severe frostbite in the Shubenacadie Indian Residential School, after having been exposed to severe cold as a punishment for running away (Chrisjohn and Young 2006, 54)? Or to the women forcibly sterilized or permanently incarcerated so that they wouldn't give birth to another generation of "feeblemindedness?" Or to emancipated slaves who found themselves working in similar conditions after being arrested for petty violations of Jim Crow laws? These are just some of the hauntings that need to inform politics, policies, activism, and scholarship today—real people who lived and died confined, or with the threat of confinement shaping the possibilities for their lives. And how can we live in a way that is also accountable, as Derrida says, to those "not yet born?" How can there be accountability to children who are born tomorrow or ten years from now—especially those who, because of disability, race, or class, are born disproportionately likely to live all or part of their lives in the terrible spaces of the carceral/institutional archipelago? This future "yet to come"—that of the Ashleys and the Emilys of tomorrow—is a looming presence that has to be lived with, that has to be contended with, today.

Notes

1. A similar phenomenon is at work today with widespread panic about mounting crime but no corresponding rise in crime rates (Gilmore 2006; Gottschalk 2006).
2. Patty Douglas (2011) documents how this in fact lives on in Canadian immigration policy and practice.
3. Chrisjohn and Young (2006) use Goffman's analysis and language in their discussion of Indian Residential Schools in Canada.
4. Aboriginal scholars tend to not place "neo" or "post" before "colonialism" in accounts of present-day North America and other White settler colonies. The argument is that colonization here has been continuous and that Canadian confederation and American independence brought about self-governance for settlers but not Aboriginal Nations. We therefore here distinguish "neocolonialism" in the Global South from ongoing colonialism in North America.

References

Ahmed, Sara. 2006. "The Nonperformativity of Antiracism." *Borderlands* 5(3).
———. 2004. *The Cultural Politics of Emotion*. New York: Routledge.
Asad, Talal. 2003. *Formations of the Secular: Christianity, Islam, Modernity*. Stanford: Stanford University Press.
Bhabha, Homi. 1994. *The Location of Culture*. New York: Routledge.
Bureau of Justice Statistics (BJS). 2010. *Correctional Populations in the United States 2009*. Washington, DC: U.S. Department of Justice.
———. 2008. *Census of State and Federal Correctional Facilities 2005*. Washington, DC: U.S. Department of Justice.
Black, Edwin R. 2003. *War against the Weak: Eugenics and America's Campaign to Create a Master Race*. New York: Four Walls Eight Windows.
Blatt, Burton, and Fred Kaplan. 1966. *Christmas in Purgatory: A Photographic Essay on Mental Retardation*. Boston, MA: Allyn and Bacon.
Braddock, David, and Susan Parish. 2003. "Social Policy Toward Persons with Intellectual Disabilities in the Nineteenth & Twentieth Centuries." In *Different But Equal: The Rights of People with Intellectual Disabilities*, edited by Stanley. S. Herr, Lawrence O. Gostin, and Harold H. Koh. New York: Oxford University Press.
Braddock, David, Richard Hemp, Mary C. Rizzolo, Laura Haffer, Emily S. Tanis, and Jiang Wu. 2011. *The State of the States in Developmental Disabilities: 2011*. Boulder: University of Colorado.
Butler, Judith. 2004. *Precarious Life: The Powers of Mourning and Violence*. New York: Verso.
Canadian Business, September 29, 2009. Accessed February 11, 2010. http://www.canadianbusiness.com/markets/cnw/article.jsp?content=20090929_172501_0_cnw_cnw.
Carey, Allison C. 2009. *On the Margins of Citizenship: Intellectual Disability and Civil Rights in Twentieth-Century America*. Philadelphia, PA: Temple University Press.
———. 2003. "Beyond the Medical Model: A Reconsideration of 'Feeblemindedness' Citizenship and Eugenic Restrictions." *Disability and Society* 18: 411–430.
Carlton-LaNey, Iris. 1999. "African American Social Work Pioneers' Response to Need." *Social Work* 44(4): 311–321.
Carrigan, D. Owen. 1994. *Crime and Punishment in Canada: A History*. Toronto, ON: McClelland and Stewart.

Chapman, Chris. 2012. "Colonialism, Disability, and Possible Lives: The Residential Treatment of Children Whose Parents Survived Indian Residential Schools." *Journal of Progressive Human Services* 24(2): 127–158.

———. 2010. "Becoming Perpetrator: How I Came to Accept Restraining and Confining Disabled Aboriginal Children." Presentation at PsychOut: A Conference for Organizing Resistance Against Psychiatry, Toronto.

Chaudry, Vandana. 2011. "Disability and the Neoliberal Indian State: The Perils of Community Participation." In *Research in Social Science and Disability*, vol 6, edited by Allison C. Carey, and Richard K. Scotch. Emerald Group Publishing Limited, 265–281.

Chrisjohn, Roland, and Sherri Young. 2006. *The Circle Game: Shadows and Substance in the Indian Residential School Experience in Canada*. Penticton, BC: Theytus.

Christie, Nils. 2000. *Crime Control as Industry: Towards Gulags, Western Style* (3rd ed.). New York: Routledge.

Churchill, Ward. 2004. *Kill the Indian, Save the Man: The Genocidal Impact of American Indian Residential Schools*. San Francisco: City Lights.

Clark, Laurence, and Stephen Marsh. 2002. "Patriarchy in the UK: The Language of Disability." Accessed June 11, 2012. http://www.disabilityarchive.leeds.ac.uk/authors _list.asp? AuthorID=217&author_name=Clark%2C+L.+and+Marsh%2C+S.

Conrad, Peter, and Joseph W. Schneider. 1992. *Deviance and Medicalization: From Badness To Sickness* (Expanded ed.). Philadelphia, PA: Temple University Press.

Davis, Angela Y. 2007. "How Does Change happen?" Accessed June 11, 2012. http:// www.youtube.com/watch?v=Pc6RHtEbiOA&feature=related.

———. 2003. *Are Prisons Obsolete?* New York: Seven Stories Press.

———. 2000. "From the Convict Lease System to the Super-Max Prison." In *States of Confinement: Policing, Detention, and Prisons*, edited by Joy James, 60–74. New York: St. Martin's Press.

———. 1983. *Women, Race, and Class*. New York: Vintage Books.

Davis, Lennard J. 1995. *Enforcing Normalcy*. London: Verso.

Derrida, Jacques. 1994. *Specters of Marx*. New York: Routledge.

Deutsch, Albert. 1948. *Shame of the States*. New York: Harcourt Brace.

Douglas, Patty. 2011. "Peripheral Belongings: Autism and Immigration Practice in Canada." Paper presented at the Society for Disability Studies Annual Conference, San Jose.

Drinkwater, Chris. 2005. "Supported Living and the Production of Individuals." In *Foucault and the Governmentality of Disability*, edited by Shelley Tremain, 229–244. Ann Arbor, MI: University of Michigan Press.

Du Bois, W. E. B. 1956. *Black Reconstruction in America 1860–1880*. New York: S. A. Russell.

Edwards, Marta. 1997. "Constructions of Physical Disability in the Ancient Greek World – the Community Concept." In *The Body and Physical Difference*, edited by David T. Mitchell and Sharon L. Snyder, 35–50. Ann Arbor, MI: University of Michigan Press.

Ferguson, Phillip M. 1994. *Abandoned to Their Fate: Social Policy and Practice Toward Severely Disabled People in America, 1820–1920*. Philadelphia, PA: Temple University Press.

Foucault, Michel. 2008. *Psychiatric Power: Lectures at the Collège de France, 1973–1974*. New York: Picador.

———. 2006. "The Ethics of the Concern for Self as a Practice of Freedom". In *Ethics: Subjectivity and Truth*, 281–301. New York: New Press.

———. 2003. *Abnormal: Lectures at the Collège de France, 1974–1975*. New York: Picador.

———. 1995. *Discipline and Punish: The Birth of the Prison*. New York: Vintage.

————. 1994a. *The Birth of the Clinic*. New York: Vintage.

————. 1994b. "'Omnes et Singulatim': Toward a Critique of Political Reason." In *Power*, 298–325. New York: The New Press.

————. 1988. *Madness and Civilization*. New York: Vintage.

————. 1982. "The Subject and Power." In *Michel Foucault: Beyond Structuralism and Hermeneutics*, edited by Hubert Dreyfus and Paul Rabinow, 208–226. Chicago, IL: University of Chicago Press.

————. 1978. "About the Concept of the 'Dangerous Individual' in Nineteenth-Century Legal Psychiatry." *International Journal of Law and Psychiatry* 1:1–18.

Fournier, Suzanne, and Ernie Crey. 1999. *Stolen from Our Embrace: The Abduction of First Nations Children and the Restoration of Aboriginal Communities*. Toronto, ON: Harper Collins.

Gartner, Hana. 2010. "Behind the Wall." *The Fifth Estate*. Canadian Broadcasting Corporation. Accessed February 7, 2013. http://www.cbc.ca/fifth/2010–2011/behindthewall/.

Gilmore, Ruth Wilson. 2006. *Golden Gulag: Prisons, Surplus, Crisis, and Opposition in Globalizing*. California: University of California Press.

Goffman, Erving. 1961. *Asylums*. New York: Anchor.

Goldberg, Eve, and Linda Evans. 1997. *The Prison Industrial Complex and the Global Economy*. Prison Activist Resource Center.

Gottschalk, Mark. 2006. *The Prison and the Gallows: The Politics of Mass Incarceration in America*. New York: Cambridge University Press.

Guest, Dennis. 1997. *The Emergence of Social Security in Canada*. Vancouver: UBC Press.

Halderman v. Pennhurst, 1977. 446 F. Supp. 1295.

Harper, Stephen. 2008. "Text of Prime Minister Harper's Apology." Accessed April 22, 2009. http://www.fns.bc.ca/pdf/TextofApology.pdf.

Heron, Barbara. 2007. *Desire for Development: Whiteness, Gender, and the Helping Imperative*. Waterloo: Wilfred Laurier University Press.

hooks, bell. 1989. *Talking Back: Thinking Feminist, Thinking Black*. Toronto, ON: Between the Lines.

Jones, Larry A. 2010. "Doing Disability Justice." Accessed February 8, 2013. www.lulu.com.

Kanner, Leo. 1942. "Exoneration of the Feebleminded." *American Journal of Psychiatry* 99(1): 17–22.

Katz, Michael B. 1996. *In the Shadow of the Poorhouse: A Social History of Welfare in America*. New York: Basic Books.

Kelm, Mary Ellen. 2005. "Diagnosing the Discursive Indian: Medicine, Gender, and the 'Dying Race.'" *Ethnohistory* 52(2): 371–406.

King, Thomas. 2003. *The Truth about Stories: A Native Narrative*. Toronto, ON: House of Anansi.

Kline, Wendy. 2001. *Building a Better Race: Gender Sexuality, and Eugenics from the Turn of the Century to the Baby Boom*. Berkeley: University of California Press.

Kurshan, Nancy. 1996. "Behind the Walls: The History and Current Reality of Women's Imprisonment." In *Criminal Injustice: Confronting the Prison Crisis*, edited by Rosenblatt, Elihu. Boston, MA: South End Press.

Ladd-Taylor, Molly. 2004. "The 'Sociological Advantages' of Sterilization: Fiscal Policies and Feebleminded Women in Interwar Minnesota." In *Mental Retardation in America*, edited by Steven Noll and James W. Trent Jr., 281–307. New York: New York University Press.

Larson, Edward J. 1995. *Sex, Race, and Science: Eugenics in the Deep South*. Baltimore: Johns Hopkins University Press.

Maisel, Alfred. 1946. "Bedlam, 1946." *Life Magazine*, May 6.

McKnight, John. 1995. "Regenerating Community." *Social Policy* 25(4): 54–58.

McLaren, Angus. 1990. "Creating a Haven for Human Thoroughbreds." In *Our Own Master Race: Eugenics in Canada, 1885–1945*, 89–106. Toronto, ON: McLelland & Stewart.

McRuer, Robert. 2006. *Crip Theory: Cultural Signs of Queerness and Disability*. New York: New York University Press.

Michalko, Rod. 2002. *The Difference That Disability Makes*. Philadelphia, PA: Temple University Press.

Mill, John Stuart. 1869. *The Subjection of Women*. London: Longmans, Green, Reader, and Dyer.

Neu, Dean, and Richard Therrien. 2003. *Accounting for Genocide: Canada's Bureaucratic Assault on Aboriginal People*. Halifax: Fernwood.

Nirje, Bengt. 1969. "The Normalization Principle and Its Human Management Implications." In *Changing Patterns in Residential Services for the Mentally Retarded*, edited by Robert B. Kugel, and Wolf Wolfensberger, 181–195. Washington, DC: President's Committee on Mental Retardation.

Noll, Steven. 1995. *Feeble-minded in Our Midst*. Chapel Hill, NC: University of North Carolina Press.

Noll, Steven, and James W. Trent Jr. 2004. *Mental Retardation in America: A Historical Reader*. New York: New York University Press.

O'Connell, Anne. 2009. "Building their Readiness for 'Economic Freedom': The New Poor Law and Emancipation." *Journal of Sociology and Social Welfare* XXXVI(2): 85–103.

Olmstead, Commissioner, Georgia Department of Human Resources et al., v. L. C. 1999. 527 U.S. 581.

Parenti, Christian. 1999. *Lockdown America: Police and Prisons in the Age of Crisis*. New York: Verso.

Paul, Diane. 1995. *Controlling Human Heredity*. Atlantic Highlands, NJ: Humanities Press.

Peebles-Wilkins, Wilma, and E. Aracelis Francis. 1990. "Two Outstanding Black Women in Social Welfare History: Mary Church Terrell and Ida B. Wells-Barnett." *Affilia* 5(4): 87–100.

Perske, Robert. 1972. "The Dignity of Risk." *Mental Retardation* 10(1): 24–27.

Pew Center on the States. 2008. *One in 100: Behind Bars in America 2008*. Washington, DC: The Pew Charitable Trusts.

Prison Policy Initiative (PPI). 2010. "Incarceration by Race and Mental Health Status." Accessed August 6, 2010. http://www.prisonpolicy.org/research.html.

Puar, Jasbir. 2012. "The Cost of Getting Better: Suicide, Sensation, Switchpoints." *GLQ* 18(1): 149–158.

Rafter, Nicole. 1997. *Creating Born Criminals*. Chicago: University of Illinois Press.

———. 1992. "Claims-Making and Socio-Cultural Context in the First Eugenics Campaign." *Social Problems* 39(1): 17–33.

———. 1988. *White Trash: The Eugenic Family Studies, 1877–1919*. Boston, MA: Northeastern University Press.

Reilly, Philip R. 1991. *The Surgical Solution: History of Involuntary Sterilization in the United States*. Baltimore, MD: Johns Hopkins University Press.

Richardson, Channing B. 1946. "A Hundred Thousand Defectives." *Christian Century* 63: 110–111.

Rivera, Geraldo. 1972. *Willowbrook: A Report on How It Is and Why It Doesn't Have to Be That Way*. New York: Random House.

Rothman, David J. 1995. "Perfecting the Prison." In *The Oxford History of the Prison: The Practice of Punishment in Western Society*, edited by Norval Morris and David J. Rothman. New York: Oxford University Press.

———. 1971. *The Discovery of the Asylum*. Boston, MA: Little, Brown.

Rothman, David, and Sheila M. Rothman. 1984. *The Willowbrook Wars*. New York: Harper and Row.

Russell, Marta. 1998. *Beyond Ramps: Disability at the End of the Social Contract*. Monroe, ME: Common Courage Press.

Russell, Marta, and Jean Stewart. 2001. *Disability, Prison and Historical Segregation*. Monthly Review, July–August issue.

Sarason, Seymour B. 1958. *Psychological Problems in Mental Deficiency*. New York: Harper and Brothers.

Scheerenberger, R. C. 1983. *A History of Mental Retardation*. Baltimore, MD: Brookes.

Scheff, Thomas J. 1966. *Being Mentally Ill: A Sociological Theory*. Chicago, IL: Aldine Publishing Co.

Scull, Andrew T. 1977. *Decarceration, Community Treatment and the Deviant: A Radical View*. Englewood Cliffs, NJ: Prentice-Hall.

Self Advocates Becoming Empowered. 2012. "Position Statement." Accessed February 21, 2013. http://www.sabeusa.org/user_storage/File/sabeusa/Position%20 Statements/ POSITION%20STATEMENT-Institutions.pdf.

Smith, Andrea. 2005. *Conquest: Sexual Violence and American Indian Genocide*. Cambridge: South End Press.

Smith, Christopher, and John Giggs. 1988. *Location and Stigma: Contemporary Perspectives on Mental Health and Mental Health Care*. Boston, MA : Unwin Hyman.

Snyder, Sharon L., and David T. Mitchell. 2006. *Cultural Locations of Disability*. Chicago, IL: University of Chicago Press.

Somerville, Siobhan B. 2000. *Queering the Color Line: Race and the Invention of Homosexuality in American Culture*. Durham: Duke University Press.

Spivak, Gayatri Chakravorty. 1993. *Outside in the Teaching Machine*. New York: Routledge.

Stiker, Henri-Jacques. 2000. *A History of Disability*. Ann Arbor, MI: University of Michigan Press.

Sudbury, Julia. 2005. *Global Lockdown: Race, Gender, and the Prison-Industrial Complex*. New York: Routledge.

———. 2004. "A World Without Prisons: Resisting Militarism, Globalized Punishment, and Empire." *Social Justice* 31(1/2): 9–30.

Szasz, Thomas S. 2009. *Coercion as Cure: A Critical History of Psychiatry*. New Brunswick, NJ: Transaction Publishers.

———. 1961. *The Myth of Mental Illness: Foundations of a Theory of Personal Conduct*. New York: Hoeber-Harper.

Taylor, Steven J. 2009. *Acts of Conscience: World War II, Mental Institutions, and Religious Objectors*. Syracuse, NY: Syracuse University Press.

———. 1988. "Caught in the Continuum: A Critical Analysis of the Principle of the Least Restrictive Environment." *Journal of the Association for the Severely Handicapped* 13(1): 41–53.

Thobani, Sunera. 2007. *Exalted Subjects: Studies in the Making of Race and Nation in Canada*. Toronto, ON: University of Toronto Press.

Titchkosky, Tanya. 2003. *Disability, Self, and Society*. Toronto, ON: University of Toronto Press.

Tremain, Shelley. 2005. "Foucault, Governmentally and Critical Disability Theory: An Introduction." In *Foucault and the Government of Disability*, edited by Shelley Tremain, 1–26. Ann Arbor, MI: University of Michigan Press.

Trent, James W., Jr. 1994. *Inventing the Feeble Mind: A History of Mental Retardation in the United States*. Berkeley: University of California Press.

———. 1993. "To Cut and Control: Institutional Preservation and the Sterilization of Mentally Retarded People in the United States, 1892–1947." *Journal of Historical Sociology* 6:56–73.

Turner, Dale. 2006. *This is Not a Peace Pipe: Towards a Critical Indigenous Philosophy*. Toronto, ON: University of Toronto Press.

Voronka, Jijian. 2008. "Re/moving Forward? Spacing Mad Degeneracy at the Queen Street Site." *Resources for Feminist Research* 33(1–2): 45–62.

Wald, Patricia M. 1976. "Principal Paper," in Chapter 1, "Basic Personal and Civil Rights." In *The Mentally Retarded Citizen and the Law*, edited by Michael Kindred, Julius Cohen, David Penrod, and Thomas Shaffer, 3–30. New York: Free Press.

Wilkinson, Richard. 2011. "The Age of Unequals." Accessed February 25, 2011. http://www.tvo.org/TVO/WebObjects/TVO.woa?videoid?774652544001.

Wolfensberger, Wolf. 1972. *Principles of Normalization in Human Services*. Toronto, ON: National Institute on Mental Retardation.

Yee, Shirley. 1994. "Gender Ideology and Black Women as Community-Builders in Ontario, 1850–1870." *Canadian Historical Review* 75(1): 53–73.

2

Five Centuries' Material Reforms and Ethical Reformulations of Social Elimination

Chris Chapman

Introduction

I once worked in an institution where almost all the children were Indigenous. Many were children of survivors of "Indian Residential Schools,"[1] and all had a disability diagnosis or suspected diagnosis recorded in their files (Chapman 2010; 2012). In wondering about historical developments through which places like this had emerged, I was surprised to find that North American timelines of the educationally oriented confinement of intellectually disabled people and of the Indian Residential School system mapped neatly onto one another. In the 1840s, both systems emerged, and their abolitions both began in the 1960s. What can be made of this? What historical developments paved the way for these new sites in the 1800s, and what legacies live beyond their specific abolitions, making contemporary incarcerations seem natural, politically neutral, and necessary (Ben-Moshe 2012; A. Davis 2003; Drinkwater 2005; Snyder and Mitchell 2006)? This chapter maps out tentative answers to these questions, exploring the "moral economies" (Ahmed 2010; Thobani 2007) circulating within five centuries' forms and reforms of social elimination, through reading "political rationalities" (Foucault 1994b, c) that narrate practices of power.

Although I follow Foucault, I draw connections he never spelled out between his various works, and I bring other histories of disability, racism, colonization, and incarceration into conversation with his writings. I first explore three developments that anteceded the various population-specific confinements of the 1800s, which I suggest paved the way for the new confinements of the 1840s and the contemporaneous discursive development of "the norm": first, the secularization of life, liberty, and the perpetration of atrocity, beginning in sixteenth-century Europe; second, the first mass confinement of poor Europeans in the seventeenth century; and third, the eighteenth century cross-referencing of political rationalities for eliminating or controlling various othered groups. I then explore reforms and narrative reformulations that occurred around the 1840s, and then around the 1960s, suggesting that legacies from each of these five reform periods live on.

Sixteenth Century: Secularizing Life, Liberty, and the Perpetration of Atrocity

Starting in the 1500s, Christian Europe gradually secularized what it meant to be both human and ethical. In the middle ages, self-contained Christian community was central to ruling-class moral economies of care and violence. Christian "charity" (*caritas* in Latin), in its original sense, meant indiscriminate love and compassion. This was the most important Christian virtue (I Corinthians 13:13) and was to be universally distributed. However, according to some medieval accounts, in order to be deserving of this "indiscriminate" and "universal" love, one had to be Christian. Various socially sanctioned medieval bouts of mass violence by Christians against Muslims, Jews, Roma, women deemed witches, and numerous peoples in the Global South, demonstrate that Christian charity or love was anything but indiscriminate. *Caritas* helps to understand the moral economies governing socially sanctioned violence at the time. That is, how were moral or ethical considerations abstracted from action, and how did the resulting abstractions accumulate or take away moral value for differently positioned groups? This can perhaps best be traced through attending to the ethical narratives or political rationalities surrounding a given material act. When medieval Christians tortured non-Christians, for example, it was often described as a means to bring about the victim's conversion, and so it could be imagined as folding someone into the flock of universal love. The Spanish Inquisition is the most famous systemic example of this. When Christians murdered non-Christians, it could be narrated as a means to personal salvation for the killer, who was acting as a conduit for divine justice and paving the road to God's kingdom on earth (Packett 2011; 2012; Pope Urban II 1095). It was even imagined to save the victim from the horror of living outside of Christ's love (Burke 1997). The crusades and witch burnings are two well-known illustrations of this. Violence transgressed Christian commandment (Matthew 5:39), and so it was only acceptable if narrated as following the will of God. Non-Christians could be narratively situated outside of the bounds of this "universal" fairly straightforwardly, but Christians could only commit violence against Christians if this violence was said to coincide with divine law in some exceptional way. And so it was: the torture of criminalized Christians was narrated as working toward their confession, and so therefore working toward God's forgiveness and the victim's eternal salvation. Death through such torture was deemed morally righteous because the victim might confess her sins with her dying breath, therefore achieving salvation. Violence against disabled people was also narrated within this moral economy: what we today call physical, intellectual, or psychiatric disability was accounted for by explanations such as a punishment for sin, the mark of Cain, demonic possession, or the work of the Devil (Barnes 1992; Stiker 1999; Wheatley 2010). At times, this exempted disabled people from *caritas* or framed violence against disabled people as divine justice.

A consequence of this moral economy was that when colonial Christianization efforts succeeded, new ethical dilemmas emerged about colonial violence. If colonized people converted, by what authority could Europeans kill, torture, or displace them? These were indeed "dilemmas," in that some Europeans critiqued colonial violence early on. Critical histories are sometimes criticized for reading the past through a contemporary lens, but just as our time features diverse accounts of right and wrong, so too did earlier periods. In 1542, for example, Bartolomé de las Casas wrote of Florida's colonization, "our Spaniards, with their cruel and abominable acts, have devastated the land and exterminated the rational people who fully inhabited it…The pretext was that these allocated Indians were to be instructed in the articles of the Christian Faith" (1542). De las Casas also spoke out against the slavery of Indigenous peoples of the Americas, which began with Columbus' first voyage (Churchill 1998). He suggested that African slaves could replace Indigenous ones (Tickell 2007a). From today's vantage point, it is difficult to reconcile his anticolonial critique with his anti-Black racism, but reading for his political rationality helps make sense of this. Las Casas dismisses the conquistadors' stated rationality—which he calls a "pretext"—and he counters their moral economy with an alternative one, which still allows for slavery and other forms of atrocity. According to his account above, one factor making the mass murder of Florida's Indigenous people abominable is that they are "rational people." Like many of his European contemporaries, Las Casas seems to have held that Africans were not "rational people." Clearly this is erroneous and racist, but that is not the only point we can take from reading his political rationality. This was centuries before diverse people were grouped together as "feebleminded," but in Las Casas we find an antecedent to later atrocities justified by designations of intellectual inferiority.

Another importance of Las Casas is that he drew from the available "discursive tradition" (Mahmood 2005) of his sixteenth-century Spanish Christianity in order to critique the brutality of what was being done using that same tradition as justification. This is significant to critical work on contemporary and historical oppression; Saba Mahmood (2005) illustrates how human agency is best accounted for by the various ways that we inhabit contingently available social norms, rather than imagining resistance to be outside of norms. Las Casas was a Dominican Friar who shared the discursive tradition that Spanish Inquisitors, Conquistadors, slave traders, and those who expelled Jewish people from Spain in 1492 drew upon in their political rationalities. However, he drew from this same tradition to critique (some of) his contemporaries' violences. Las Casas widely disseminated his critique and he achieved real change. However, as Angela Davis has said of more recent events (2007), there was a gap between the change Las Casas fought for and the change that came about. Early anticolonial critique had an impact, but sadly it largely impacted how continued violence was now to be politically rationalized. Religious rationalities no longer play the role they had previous to this development—not only in relation to colonial violence but also in penalty and disablement. Colonial "invaders branded the Mi'kmaq and other Native Americans as 'heathen savages'" (Paul 2006, 1), but this would not ethically suffice once First Nations began converting to Christianity. Either colonial violence would have to stop, or a European "conversion" of ethical narrative was needed. Thobani (2007) explains the resultant discursive shift:

> Colonized peoples were being converted to Christianity in large numbers across European empires, with the consequence that they acquired formal status as co-religionists of Europeans. This new religious status presented challenges to the legitimacy of their continued domination under divine law as heathens…Secular law enabled colonial hierarchies to be justified on the basis of scientific theories of race. (44–45)

According to Foucault (2003b), "Racism first develops with colonization…with colonizing genocide…[H]ow can you justify the need to kill people, to kill populations, and to kill civilizations? By using the themes of evolutionism, by appealing to a racism" (257). This new "scientific" justification for violence was subsequently generalized to justify dominance and violence within Europe. Initially formulated to justify "colonizing genocide," this "racism" was extended to justify the killing and abuse of those constituted as Europe's internal threats. In England at the time, poor people (including many disabled and criminalized people) were called "the pauper race," the aristocracy was referred to as "the Norman race," and so on. This use of "race" to articulate a diverse realm of otherness preceded the use of "feebleminded" to do so. It is therefore possible to read histories of oppression with a focus on this use of "race" and to argue that all oppression is an offshoot of racism. Similarly, it is possible to read histories of "feeblemindedness" and to argue that all oppression is an offshoot of disablism. But early uses of "race" differ from what is meant by race today, and historical "feeblemindedness" does not always refer to what is called intellectual disability today. I would suggest that our historical task is not to find the master trope of all oppression, but rather to trace how today's specific oppressions relate to particular histories that were at times parallel and discrete, at times intersecting, and at times mutually constitutive. For example, mobilizing the sixteenth-century conceptualization of race to describe both what we would call classism and colonial racism, in 1581 Blackwood justifies Norman rule in England by comparing it to European rule in America:

> The situation in England at the time of the Norman Conquest must in fact be understood in the same way that we now understand America...[W]e regard it as perfectly legitimate as we are doing the same thing...The Normans are in England by the same right that we are in America, that is, by the right of colonization. (cited in Foucault 2003b, 102–3)

In spite of Las Casas' critique of colonial violence 39 years earlier, Blackwell mobilizes the "right of colonization" in the Americas as so self-evident that it can justify British class oppression, which centrally affected British criminalized and disabled peoples. But what is Blackwell's "right?" Unlike earlier justifications for disablist and penal violence, monarchial rule, anti-Semitic pogroms, witch burnings, Crusades, the Inquisition, and early colonial slavery, torture, and mass murder, it makes no claim whatsoever to divine righteousness. It is a fully secular right of force, of domination, of having won.

Political power was increasingly narrated as a result of human agency, of overpowering other humans, and this cleared new ground for some Europeans on the bottom of what was previously considered a divinely ordained social order to articulate new narratives of resistance (Foucault 2003b). The later "dictatorship of the proletariat" succinctly sums up this new structure of imagining how to achieve alternative orders: becoming the stronger and more dominant faction is a dream only possible if significant agency is granted to humans rather than divine predestination or other forms of determinism. For the first time in Europe, social order was increasingly conceptualized as a result of cumulative historical human action and struggle—allowing for the emerging discourse of political struggle that we still generally take for granted: injustice is a historical accomplishment that resulted from "them" exercising power at "our" expense. This, in turn, requires "us" to exercise our power to bring about a future that is righted through force just as "we" were historically wronged through force (Foucault 2003b, 79).

While secularism enabled new interrogations of the social order, the exposure to alternative political systems also undermined the self-evidence of inequalities. Mi'kmaq activist and author Daniel Paul writes that "the social structures and democratic forms of government found in the Americas were deemed by European ruling classes as a serious threat to their own exercise of absolute power" (2006, 17). Revolutionaries from Marx and Engels (Engels 1884; Turner 2006, 34) to Benjamin Franklin (Johansen 1982; Paul 2006, 14) were directly inspired by the Iroquois Confederacy and other Indigenous governance systems. This included exposure to alternative systems of penalty (Smith 2005), as well as those of care, disability, and economic distribution. Of precolonial Mi'kmaq society, Paul (2006) writes:

> Because of the communal nature of the society and the abundance of food, poverty among the People was virtually unknown. Material things, other than clothing and household goods, were shared equally. Thus the old, sick, infirm and otherwise disadvantaged were protected from destitution. (18)

The new political struggles in Europe were initially met with explicit and unapologetic violence (Foucault 1995), and analogous extreme violence—on a larger scale in terms of numbers and effects—characterized the colonization of the Americas, so that "[f]our centuries after the European invasion began, all the civilizations of two continents lay in ruins and the remaining people were dispossessed and impoverished" (Paul 2006, 51). Although often not recognized as such, this is a history of present day disablement and criminalization. Indigenous people are now incarcerated at the highest per capita rate of any group in North America (Smith 2005) and "have rates of disability almost twice as high as the rest of the population of Canada" (Withers 2012, 8). Such statistics are best understood as the result of ongoing interlocking legacies of structural violence (Chrisjohn and Young 2006; Puar 2012).

Seventeenth Century: Confinement as an Available and Less Dangerous Means of Elimination

European ruling classes stopped relying primarily on explicit violence to quell political struggle—not owing to mercy, but to increasing inefficacy (Foucault 1995). If ruling-class violence had no divine sanction then it was clearly morally outrageous to those subjected to it. With the new secular dreams of human freedom, and with ritual violence increasingly backfiring as a strategy to maintain order, we can imagine a perceived need to do something, anything, otherwise. Perhaps "the great confinement of the poor" resulted from those in positions of influence looking to the already existing repertoire of strategies of control and elimination for anything that might be less dangerous to them. So while widespread explicit and unapologetic violence continued for two centuries against colonized and enslaved peoples, confinement was adopted for the elimination and control of undesirable white people in Europe and colonial North America. Confinement was already known to harm those confined and nobody had yet claimed it did anything beneficial (other than simple removal from society). Reformers protested against imprisonment as a generalized form of punishment (Foucault 1995, 114–120), and hospitals were not thought of as beneficial for curing illness until a century later (Foucault 1994a, 101–111). Mass confinement preceded the ends with which we associate it, and yet it was carried out on such a scale "that more than one out of every hundred inhabitants of the city of Paris found themselves confined...within several months" (Foucault 1988, 38). Confinement was not new, but this confinement was unprecedented in both scale and political rationality.

Fifty years previously (and just one year after the first permanent European settlement in what is now called Canada was established by French settlers), poor, disabled, and criminalized people had been dealt with very differently:

> a decree of the [French] Parlement dated 1606 ordered the beggars of Paris to be whipped in the public square, branded on the shoulder, shorn, and then driven from the city; to keep them from returning, an ordinance of 1607 established companies of archers at all the city gates to forbid entry to indigents. (Foucault 1988, 47)

The mass confinement of poor people in the 1600s was "a new solution. For the first time, purely negative measures of exclusion were replaced by the measure of confinement" (Foucault 1988, 48). When we read of beggars, paupers, or vagabonds, we are reading largely about diverse disabled people (from intellectually disabled, to blind, to missing a limb), who had not yet been cast under the generalized umbrella of disability but were rather lumped together by their poverty (Foucault 1988; Holmes 2001). And at this time their criminalization coexisted with "practices of community responsibility for poverty and disability" (Snyder and Mitchell 2006, 37). Disrupting the historical narrative of progressive social reform, these previously normative practices of community responsibility began to wane alongside the explicit violence that lived alongside them, as care and violence transformed together into practices of mass confinement. This initiated a move away from social control through explicit violence. It also initiated a move away from "outdoor relief" given to people in their homes toward "indoor relief," or the twinning of charity with confinement (Guest 1997, 12).

There is, however, a notable exception to this, and how we think it through is politically important. Slaves and colonized people were rarely incarcerated in the 1600s, which would remain so for some time. But this does not mean that histories of colonization, slavery, and racism are not histories of disablement or criminalization. Explicit and unapologetic torture and murder of slaves and colonized people remained wholly socially sanctioned, perhaps enabled by the biological and anthropological determinisms that now accompanied colonial violence, and which were not *yet* being used to narrate violence against disabled, criminalized, and poor Europeans.[2] And while such racist violence was widespread, it was not always exactly indiscriminate. It was more prevalent when inhumane legal or extralegal restrictions were said to have been transgressed, or when oppressive requirements of capitalist productivity were not met. Behaviors and conditions (including any number of disabilities) that might lead a poor eighteenth-century European to be placed in a poorhouse, general hospital, or county jail, would have often resulted in the torture or murder of an enslaved or colonized person. And, furthermore, from Las Casas' accounts of sixteenth-century Spaniards cutting off hundreds of Indigenous people's noses, lips, and chins in Florida, through to nineteenth-century Belgians cutting off Congolese forced laborers' right hands if they didn't harvest a set amount of rubber (1,308 right hands were amputated in one day in 1896, including those of children), colonization has often directly caused physical disability (Tickell 2007a,b)—as well as what is now considered psychiatric disability (Chrisjohn and Young 2006).

Eighteenth Century: A Genealogy of the Generalized Abstracted "Abnormal?"

Secularization enabled new ways of discerning who was eliminable and why, and the first mass confinement of diverse peoples set the stage for a new abstraction and generalization of "eliminables." Scientific accounts of human progress offered new narratives for justifying continuities of earlier targeted social elimination. As I illustrate below, Mi'kmaq people were not a Nation for Cornwallis; *Mi'kma'ki* and other colonized lands were narrated as inhabited by no one, as *terra nullius* in the new secular "international" law; French vagabonds held no more value for LeTrosne than wolves; and disabled and poor people were "nothing" for perpetrators of the great confinement. And as these narratives were emerging in the mid-eighteenth century, political rationalities for eliminating various distinct "others" cross-referenced and influenced one another.

In order to represent the end of public monarchial torture, Foucault graphically cites the 1757 public execution of attempted regicide Damiens to introduce *Discipline and Punish* (1995). Around the time of Damiens' execution, colonial relations in Canada were either characterized by unapologetic and brutal violence or were narrated as Nation-to-Nation relations (Turner 2006, 48). In early colonialism, as in poverty, charity, penalty, and what we call disability, there had been very clear lines drawn—however contingently and arbitrarily—between those who deserved love and those who deserved unbounded violence. In the 1700s, this line was no longer that of Christian versus heathen or heretic, and it was now more about apparent relevance than love. This division now coalesced around the idea of the perfectibility of "civilization." If you did not play some role in this perfectibility, including as slave labor, then you were not "against civilization," but you were irrelevant to it. You could therefore be left to your own devices, but only so long as you posed no threat to social order or social progress. A community or family could care for disabled people without the social pressure to confine that came with later eugenic discourse, and Europeans made treaties with largely self-governing Indigenous Nations. But if there was a threat to the social order, there were no bounds to the degree of violence considered acceptable.

Using Damiens' execution as a point of reference, the Royal Proclamation of 1763, in which all First Nations were recognized *as Nations* (King 2003, 130),[3] was only six years later. The practice of accepting difference and others' autonomy was therefore within the available repertoire of European ruling classes. However, as a counterpoint, only nine years before Damiens' execution, "Governor Cornwallis of Nova Scotia announced in 1749: "His Majesty's Council do promise a reward of ten Guineas for every Indian Micmac taken or killed" (cited in Paul 2009). Fourteen years before the Royal Proclamation, Cornwallis explicitly rejected Mi'kmaq nationhood, rather than simply ignoring it, which may not have been a viable option as happened in later colonial history (King 2003; Turner 2006). This rejection was key to his political rationalization: he said, "to declare war formally against the Micmac Indians would be a manner to own them a free and independent people, whereas they ought to be treated as so many Banditti Ruffians, or

Rebels" (Cornwallis, cited in Paul 2009). This call for mass murder was considered an acceptable "response" to Mi'kmaq raids, which of course were a response to the European takeover of what is now called Halifax (see Butler 2004 for a related analysis). This was *terra nullius* under European "international" law, so no action against the largely irrelevant Indigenous populations was deemed necessary, until they posed a threat. Once they posed such a threat, there were apparently no limits placed on what would constitute an acceptable level of violence "in response." According to Cornwallis, "it would be better to "root" the Micmac out of the peninsula decisively and forever" (cited in Paul 2009). In the new secular discourses of anthropological and biological determinism, Mi'kmaq people offered nothing to European notions of the perfectibility of civilization, whether or not they converted to Christianity. Once they posed a threat to European social progress, their intended genocide was narrated fully justifiable. And it was justified not by their religious status as it may have been in the past, but rather by comparing them to "so many Banditti Ruffians."

Fifteen years later, and seven after Damiens' execution, in 1764 LeTrosne inverted this analogy to make a resonant recommendation for French vagabonds, a criminalized population including diverse disabled people. He justified this by saying that vagabonds—like Mi'kmaq people in the European imagination of the day—were "in that state that one supposes existed before the establishment of civil society...A reward of ten pounds is given for anyone who kills a wolf. A vagabond is infinitely more dangerous to society" (cited in Foucault 1995, 88). It was widely stated that non-European societies "preceded civilization," and now this could be generalized to those who lived on the margins in Europe. Based on such newly articulated secular "similarities," analogous actions could be rationalized toward distinct groups. The effects of LeTrosne and Cornwallis were very different, but political rationalities brought them into a shared sphere of generalized, denigrated, otherness. Resonating with how Blackwell took for granted the "right of colonization" in the Americas to justify British class oppression, LeTrosne and Cornwallis each take for granted the other's right to kill and use it to justify their own.

The political rationality of the first mass confinement beginning in the 1600s, then, had little in common with that of later mass confinements of residential schools, asylums, schools for feebleminded or blind students, or the diverse incarcerative sites we have today. In rationality, the difference is that "the Hôpital Général had nothing to do with any medical concept" (Foucault 1988, 40). Those confined "were not given treatment; they were simply thrown into prison" (Foucault 1988, 9–10). The rationality of "the great confinement" was closer to that of killing than to later statements about education or rehabilitation. "Confinement merely manifested what madness, in its essence, was: a manifestation of non-being... [B]y confinement, madness is acknowledged to be *nothing*...[Confinement was] an operation to annihilate nothingness" (Foucault 1988, 115–16). When the social order of vast inequality had been widely accepted by Christians as divinely determined, no action against "nothingness" was required. But with increasing political instability, enabled by secular dreams of freedom and exposure to alternative social orders, worthless threats had to be eliminated. Given Foucault's description above of the great confinement as "an operation to annihilate nothingness," it is significant that Cornwallis offered equal payment for capture or killing. As long as the threat was "rooted" out, the means did not matter to him. And as "an operation to annihilate nothingness," the political rationality of the great confinement was very different from later confinements, which are usually accompanied by a promised rehabilitation and reintegration. But promises notwithstanding, to this day many of those confined have never been returned to any truly free community. The accepted (or ignored) death toll partly accounting for this fact suggests that, at least for "incorrigibles" (Foucault 2003a; Rafter 1997), people in closed sites are still worth nothing. Certainly the value of their lives is deemed less than the value of the moral imperative to rehabilitate.

Nineteenth Century: From Taking Life to Shaping Life and Letting Die

In 1620, a few decades before the "great confinement," "the first boarding school for aboriginal boys" was opened in what is now called Canada (Fournier and Crey 1999, 50). This one school, however, and scattered others over the next two centuries, was in some important ways distinct from what would later become the Residential School system. It would be more than two centuries before, in "1846, the government resolved at a meeting in Orillia, Ontario, to fully commit itself to Indian residential schools" (Fournier and Crey 1999, 53). The initial school surely cleared the ground for later developments, but it took a bureaucratic commitment on a massive scale so that "[f]rom the mid-1800s to the 1970s, up to a third of all aboriginal children were confined to the schools, many for the majority of their childhoods" (Fournier and Crey 1999, 53). Devastating as the first school very likely was for its students or inmates and their loved ones, it did not yet intimately affect the lives of all Indigenous people in Canada and the United States, as has been said of the subsequent system (Tinker 2004). And again, this timeline maps onto that in which both countries were attempting to incarcerate, sterilize, or both, all people deemed feebleminded.

My sense is therefore that the proliferation of schools for intellectually disabled or blind pupils, asylums, and Indian Residential Schools, beginning in the nineteenth century is best understood not only as a result of discrete developments relating to education, disability, or colonialism but also as a result of shared developments in white ruling-class political rationality. In the 1800s, the same generation of white ruling-class progressives and professionals transformed residential schools, penalty, charity, public education, and institutions for various disabled peoples. How did it come about that they felt responsible for change in all these distinct arenas?

As discussed earlier, the eighteenth century saw a cross-referencing in political rationality across geography and population, among European colonizers and ruling classes. This cleared the way for nineteenth-century intersections in social elimination practices, such as when racism and colonialism first mobilized confinement in Indian Residential Schools and postemancipation when African Americans were first among those massively deemed "in need" of incarceration and institutionalization (A. Davis 2003; Smith 2005; Snyder and Mitchell 2006, 88). Each occurred when public violence against Black and Indigenous people was no longer held as justifiable, reminiscent of the earlier shift that had transformed the public torture and killing of European convicts into their confinement. But in the 1700s, the ground had not yet been cleared for such racist confinements, due to the uneven transition from divine determinism to anthropological and biological determinism. That all vagabonds, Mi'kmaq, lawbreakers, or disabled people could be forcibly transformed into "productive members of society" was outside of ruling-class discourse in the 1700s. One could now narrate a shared lot of "less advanced" states, but mass efforts to remedy this, through rehabilitation and assimilation, on multiple fronts that were only then beginning to be narrated as "alike," would not yet have made sense.

Ever since the nineteenth century, we now usually confine people with a stated end in mind other than what Foucault called an "operation to annihilate nothingness." By housing so many people in closed spaces starting in the 1700s, unforeseen developments inadvertently emerged in the perceived utility of confinement. These closed-in spaces were originally imagined only negatively, in both penalty (Foucault 1995) and medicine (Foucault 1994a). In medicine contemporary to the great confinement, illness was to follow its natural course in the home or community. Hospitals, which were basically indistinguishable from jails or poorhouses, were believed to complicate disease through contamination with other illnesses. They were therefore only used by the very poor who were as likely to be housed in a poorhouse or county jail—depending on what was available, rather than on the purpose of the institution. Although this was changing, humans were still largely understood to have a natural place in the order of things and a predestined course for our lives (Foucault 1970, 370). The course of illness was also believed to be largely divinely determined. But as shifts began to occur in what was perceived and known, the previously taken for granted notion that doctors should interfere as little as possible (Foucault 1994a, 102) was displaced by an increasing secularized importance on human agency and on the scientific value of collecting the highest number of observations. Lennard Davis notes that the period of 1840–1860 marked "the coming into consciousness in English of an idea of "the norm'" (1995, 24)—the same period in which Foucault describes the shifts noted earlier in medical perception and when various specialized sites for the confinement of disabled people and the residential schools flourished. Like the advent of the "disciplines" that Foucault describes in his study of the prison, medical and statistical practices of tabulating the highest number of observations, comparing multiple people with the same illness in the same environment, and so on, were only possible because of a century of undifferentiated mass confinement. The application of "the norm" to populations, with its devastating effects on diverse peoples deemed "abnormal" or "deviant," would likely not have taken place without the material conditions of the great confinement and how the mish-mash of those confined began to be discursively conflated with racialized "others" in the seventeenth century.

The hospital, poorhouse, or jail was ideal for the emerging medical perception and practice. It was a closed site of restricted freedom in which many individuals could be organized, observed, and experimented upon so that their illnesses might be compared, contrasted, learned from and—now it was believed—more effectively known and cured. This transformed practices within, and narratives about, closed institutions. Snyder and Mitchell (2006) write that institutionalized disabled people have long been an easy source of research knowledge and bureaucratic management, which is "a primacy source of disabled people's oppression" (28–29). According to Anne Finger, "we must ask how public stripping of women with disabilities [in medical settings] comes to be described as nonviolent" (cited in Fellows and Razack 1994, 1055). Angela Davis (2007) asks resonant questions about imprisoned women. Starting in the 1800s, First Nations reservations too served as a contained space for experimenting with new medical and bureaucratic knowledges (Kelm 2005; Neu and Therrien 2003; Smith 2005). Colonial, disablist, and penal violence is normalized through these histories. Particular incidents of abuse that we tend to narrate as individually perpetrated need to be contextualized within the contingent parameters of such normalized everyday oppression.

In 1893, it was found that inmates of the Newark Custodial Asylum for Feeble-minded Women were being abused (Rafter 1997, 46–47). In 1916, Harley observed, "within two months of admission more than 10 percent of those institutionalized died" (cited in Snyder and Mitchell 2006, 91). In 1909, Bryce found that at "residential schools on the Prairies the death rate among students either while in the schools or immediately following discharge was 69 percent" (Kelm 2005, 375–376). Whatever the rationale for confinement, the high rates of trauma, injury, malnourishment, and illness in sites of confinement makes them disabling. And like Las Casas in the 1500s, the early 1900s found some ruling-class white settlers in North America critiquing the violence of the recently reformed and newly rationalized confinements. How did they continue to flourish when these unacceptable conditions were known? How do similar ones persist?

One factor seems to be what I'll call ethical narrations of selective intentionality, in which only certain outcomes are narrated as ethically significant or "on purpose" (see Knobe 2006, for a related discussion). In the political rationality surrounding diverse incarcerative settings since the mid-nineteenth century—and in the widely circulating liberal versions of their critique—the only ethically significant question appears to be whether the person confined is successfully transformed. Other outcomes, such as what happens to those who are not "successfully transformed," are thus rendered insignificant and unintentional. Foucault writes that the late 1700s marked "the emergence of a power that…consists in making live and letting die" (2003b, 247), so that "[p]ower no longer recognizes death. Power literally ignores death" (2003b, 248). Accordingly, progressive and professional rationalities were so selectively focused on making, shaping, and normalizing life that the resultant disablement and death was rendered a "side effect" rather than a significant outcome.

In terms of the narration of its perpetration, confinement from the 1840s to the 1960s was very different from that which began in 1657. Incarcerative sites no longer eliminated nothingness or worthlessness by intentionally eliminating people; people's elimination continued, but—if acknowledged—this was now an unfortunate side effect rather than an explicitly stated intention. There is a an important distinction, in political rationality, between Cornwallis' offer to pay equally for capture or killing, to root out Mi'kmaq people forever, and later statements that Residential Schools would "exterminate the Indian but develop a man" (William A. Jones, cited in Churchill 2004, 14).

The "killing" of indigeneity remained intentional at this time, but the ongoing taking of life was now narrated as nonintentional. In death toll, collective trauma, and social destabilization, the two periods would be hard to qualify as "better" or "worse." They were two different approaches to genocide. But in terms of how people who carried out genocide lived with themselves and made sense of what they were doing, something new had emerged. And the largely concurrent confinement of disabled and poor people to "annihilate nothingness," with no rationalization of treatment, and with nobody believing this would have any positive effects on confined people, is distinguishable from the optimistic "moral treatment" discourses that rationalized early schools for blind people, intellectually disabled people, and so on. The actual inefficacy and harm of the institutions that emerged in the mid-1800s is very important. But it may be just as important that the rationalities of previous confinements took inefficacy and harm for granted, and yet people were confined. From the mid-1800s on, this changed: disablist and colonial perpetrators still viewed some ways of being human worthless, but they now believed that worthless people could achieve worth by eliminating the part of them that was disabled, degenerate, uncivilized, or criminalistic. With the ongoing secular notion that we have no set place or path in life, with evolutionary, socialist, and bourgeois notions of perfectibility—even with the basic idea that time and events impact humans (Foucault 1970, 370)—came the practice, or perhaps just the dream, of eliminating "undesirable" traits not through death or permanent removal but through education, treatment, or discipline. This dream was a nightmare for many.

Rehabilitation seems clearly preferable to death or permanent incarceration, but it is not so simple. There was no shift in how diverse incarcerated people were valued in their difference—as Indigenous, deaf mute, political dissident, pauper, invert, and so on. Such divergent ways of being became ethically and politically conflated in the figure of the "abnormal" or "degenerate," formalizing the secularized generalization and abstraction of "otherness" that I suggest began earlier. And this formalization of abnormality did not lead to difference becoming more valued. The most significant shift was rather that generalized and denigrated "otherness" now held the potential for individual change, assimilation, education, and normalization. Humanity, society, *and individuals* could now be rid of feeblemindedness, savagery, madness, criminality, and so on. This is spoken about at this time distinctly in relation to diverse groups, but the essence is that individuals are alterable, changeable, and correctible. And only upon being altered, educated, assimilated, or rehabilitated does one become a worthwhile human: in 1882, Lord Milner described Britain's imperial task in Egypt as the making of "new men" (Asad 2003, 110, n12); in 1895, superintendent of "the prototype [U.S.] Indian Industrial School at Carlisle, Pennsylvania" Captain Richard Henry Pratt described the goal of Indian Residential Schools as to "kill the Indian, save the man" (Churchill 2004, 13–14). In this new political rationality, success or failure hinged only upon whether the "man" was "saved" by being made "new"; whether the person died or suffered was not the focus. The only ethically significant question was whether she was successfully civilized, assimilated, or cured. In 1913, Deputy Superintendent of Indian Affairs, Duncan Campbell Scott wrote that "fifty percent of the children who passed through these schools did not live to benefit from the education they received therein" without questioning the conditions creating this death toll (Churchill 2004, 34). Perhaps 164 years after Cornwallis' offer to pay equally for death or capture, Scott still imagined the death of "eliminables" as a mere move from one form of nothingness to another. In killing what is constituted as "defect," the potentially valuable human might be saved. And if the human dies as a direct result, there is no need to grieve because we had not yet "made" a valuable human from the defective one. Only defect dies.

Barely a generation passed before most disablist institutions built to shape life would reconceptualize their work as largely permanent removal, rationalized through eugenics. But the rehabilitative rhetoric of the 1840s reformulations survived the eugenics era and still lives on today. The various periods' political rationalities I discuss live alongside one another, which was also true historically. Thobani (2007) argues that Foucault's move from taking to shaping life is inadequate for understanding colonial violence in Canada because the disproportionate taking of Indigenous life by agents of the state continues. And Asad (2003) discusses how torture lives on within unofficial police custody practices. If we read Foucault for his attention to "political rationality" though, then the ending of the publicly socially sanctioned torture and murder of criminalized and First Nations persons is very significant, as is the ongoing torture and murder behind closed doors. It's also important that these material reforms and ethical reformulations happened unevenly and heterogeneously. At the height of eugenics, some intellectually disabled people were more likely to be subjected to rehabilitative institutionalization, others to purely custodial institutionalization, and others to public torture and murder—in part due to interlocking oppressions.

Many people inhabit several categories of denigrated otherness. But discursive and material oppression sometimes works to categorize people as only this or that, erasing other parts of a person, or at least momentarily eclipsing them. For example, James Allen (cited in Tickell 2007b) tells a terrible story about criminalization and disablement, although this is not how he frames it. It took place at the height of eugenic criminality, the year after *The Criminal Imbecile* was published (Rafter 1997, 143). Allen describes "a seventeen year old boy by the name of Jeff Washington in Waco, Texas in 1916. He was seriously mentally challenged. The wife of the farmer that he worked for was found dead. He was arrested, he was brought to trial" and he was found guilty. If Washington was white, he likely would have been labeled a "criminal imbecile" and confined in a eugenic institution for the rest of his life, as was the fate of many other intellectually disabled people convicted of crimes. But instead he was removed from the courtroom by a mob and, according to Allen, "16,000 people crowd[ed] the street to watch this boy be tortured...cheering the torturers on" (cited in Tickell 2007b). Washington was burned alive, repeatedly pulled out of the fire by a chain to prolong his suffering. While still alive, he was castrated and his fingers were cut off. This was the height of eugenic criminology. But that this was also the height of anti-Black lynching was what determined Washington's terrible fate.

Twentieth Century: An Ethics of Antidiscrimination; "the passion for similarity"[4]

Angela Davis (2003) invites us to learn not only from successful abolitions—of slavery, lynching, and Jim Crow segregation—but also from how these abolitions led to new institutions of control and violence, such as today's Prison Industrial Complex. In the 1960s, diverse confinements again transformed significantly, including how they were ethically narrated. It is now unacceptable to confine someone because of her or his membership in a "deviant population." But we still disproportionately confine the same "populations."

Today's political rationality says we do and must treat all populations equally. We now tend to rationalize today's perpetuation of historically continuous elimination through the new political rationality of antidiscrimination or equality-equals-sameness. This was selectively gleaned from liberal (as opposed to competing radical) discourses of the movements that abolished explicitly eugenic institutions, legal (or strict but extralegal) segregation of black people, Residential Schools, and explicitly racist immigration and voting restrictions. By insisting that treating different groups of people differently is only ever bad, we find peace with our own normative violence and extend the historical legacy of secular liberal individualism through which we have gradually begun to narrate what it is to be human for five centuries. The nineteenth-century narration of confinement as "curative" or "educational" lives on, now infused with a political rationality that emerged in the

1960s. We must treat everyone equally. We can't incarcerate someone for being poor, disabled, or Indigenous; we simply claim to treat Indigenous, poor, and disabled people the same as everyone else—in a historical and contextual vacuum. "Equality-equals-sameness" ethically justifies what we now perceive as inevitable, just, or helpful. Now, rather than assuming all disabled, poor, or Indigenous people require population-specific restrictions, services, or both, which would be "discriminatory," we only enforce these things when individuals are deemed "in need." Some are born more likely to be confined in one site, some in another, but some—as would have been true both 100 and 300 years ago—are unlikely to be incarcerated in any of them.

So what is equality-equals-sameness? In 1969, the Canadian Government attempted to assimilate all Indigenous people into the Canadian state (Turner 2006). This was nothing new, but its stated rationality was unprecedented. The proposed legislation was narrated as against discrimination or treating Indigenous people differently. Turner says it was rejected because Indigenous people want difference— namely, nationhood, land, and autonomy; not what all "Canadians" have.

Although distinct in many ways, something resonant is true of antidiscrimination and equality-equals-sameness in relation to disability justice. Not everybody needs a sign language interpreter or a quiet space to collect her thoughts. We aren't all the same. We may all benefit from inclusion and accessibility, but not "equally." The political dream of same and equal individuals bound together doesn't result in justice for all. Those needing anything whatsoever outside of constructed norms are imagined to be aberrations, which erases the continuities of structural violence that continue to determine how likely a given person is to be confined in this site or that.

Judge Barry Stuart says that nobody in the penal system wants "to increase the number of Indigenous people in jail, to increase the number of illiterate people in jail, to increase the number of people who are mentally challenged in jail—but that's what we're doing" (Rowlands and Stuart 2008). One hundred years ago, policy explicitly aimed to confine illiterate, Indigenous, and intellectually disabled people. And somehow we continue to do so.

Any needs specific to a particular othered group, however large, are rendered cumulative but discontinuous individual aberrations. Responses to construed aberrations such as disability, poverty, or indigeneity are conceptualized individualistically. We do not consider how life is made difficult for disabled people when material and nonmaterial social structures are created with nondisability in mind, or how we entrench colonialism by extending a unified (white/multicultural) state containing all political entities (Thobani 2007; Turner 2006). Instead we make a reform here, a consolation there, recognizing that equality-equals-sameness does not always prevent injustice, but unable to perceive how it feeds it. Whether rationalized as care or control, oppressive acts are rendered individually necessary and historically discontinuous. Predominant political rationalities have changed since earlier periods of confinement and elimination, but there has been little change in who gets forcibly removed from their homes and communities.

Discussion

The political rationalities of each of the periods discussed in this chapter live on today, unevenly and heterogeneously, alongside liberal discourses of equality-equals-sameness. The medieval European conflation of disability with sin and god's will is not entirely gone, as Michalko (2002) notes (165). That said, without the sixteenth century's initial secularization of what it is to be human, make history, and effect lives, nothing else described in this chapter would have made sense discursively. And thus none of it could have taken hold materially in the way that it did. The seventeenth-century political rationality that assigned "the same homeland to the poor, to the unemployed, to prisoners, and to the insane" (Foucault 1988, 39) appears to have been relatively short-lived, but only in a certain light. In the late 1700s, John Howard travelled across Europe,

> to all the chief centers of confinement—'hospitals, prisons, jails'—and his philanthropy was outraged by the fact that the same walls could contain those condemned by common law, young men who disturbed their families' peace or who squandered their goods, people without profession, and the insane...In a hundred and fifty years, confinement had become the abusive amalgam of heterogeneous elements. Yet, at its origin, there must have existed a unity which justified... [the holding together of] a group that to our eyes is strangely mixed and confused. (Foucault 1988, 44–45)

When Foucault describes those gathered together as "a group that to our eyes is strangely mixed and confused," was he being facetious? Reformers at the end of the eighteenth century were outraged by the proximity of these diverse groups of people. But isn't this strange grouping of people still those confined, just now separated from one another, in specialized settings dating back to Howard and other reformers? If one considers homeless shelters, group homes, supportive living centres, retirement homes, jails, half way houses, hospitals of various kinds, certain kinds of remedial schools, and so forth, are not the same diverse people still grouped together as fitting into the "them" that requires "indoor relief"? Normative political rationality no longer holds that they should all be assigned the same "homeland," but it remains self-evident that they should be segregated away from the rest of society. Every time a group home is built, every time someone can't imagine a world without prisons or psych wards, every time funding is available for a nursing home but not for care in one's own home, the fundamentals of the political rationalization of the "great confinement of the poor" lives on. Exactly where this "strangely mixed" group is held has to be understood as secondary to the fact that it had never before made sense to segregate such a "mixed" group, and that it has yet to stop making sense.

Furthermore, once someone is already deemed eliminable according to these centuries old divisions, higher death rates also continue to be somehow morally acceptable. This was true of the earliest sites of confinement through to the nineteenth-century acceptance of what was believed to be a 50 percent death rate in Indian Residential Schools. Thirty years later, the Nazis mass murdered disabled people as a part of "one of the most advanced and robust rehabilitation regimes" of the day (Snyder and Mitchell 2006, 123). If a disability could be "cured" (and the disabled person was not Jewish, Roma, queer, etc.), only then was she deemed worthy of living. It is now normatively agreed that this was immoral and assumed that this political rationality no longer exists. We "like to tell ourselves [stories] about injustices and atrocities and how most of them have happened in the past"

(King 2003, 127). But McGuire (2011) documents contemporary parents of autistic children speaking of killing their children in resonant terms:

> "I wanted a life without autism"...[said Dr. Karen] McCarron..."I tried very hard to get autism out of our lives", she said. She tried all the best therapies and interventions, she sent her [child] to all the right schools...
> (Defense lawyer) Wolfe: When you were suffocating your daughter, did you think you were killing her?
> [Dr. Karen] McCarron: No.
> Wolfe: Who did you think you were killing?
> McCarron: Autism. (316–18, 295)

In these very different contexts—Indian Residential Schools, the Nazi mass murder of disabled people, and parents taking their own autistic children's lives in the last decade—the importance of personal transformation outweighs the importance of lives, as it did in nineteenth-century acceptance of disproportionate death tolls in asylums and residential schools.

Political rationalities today selectively glean from the various options available from the last five centuries[5]—each period's ethical narration potentially available to justify our ongoing violences. For example, racism continues to significantly determine incarceration rates, early death rates, removal from one's home as a child, and the prevalence of various forms of disability (Puar 2012; Withers 2012). Although this is the case, racism is normatively narrated as bad and a thing of the past. As a result, in some instances it seems that the individualization accomplished through disablement discursively renders sites of blatant racism apparently nonracist or noncolonial. Shaista Patel's chapter in this volume suggests that this happens when the indefinite detention and torture of "terror suspects" are accompanied by claims that they are "mad." Elsewhere I (2012) suggest that the "residential treatment" of children of Indian Residential School survivors is discursively rendered noncolonial by the children's disability diagnoses. And Sherene Razack (2011) has found that Indigenous deaths in police custody are often discursively rendered noncolonial through medicalization (i.e., a death is said to have been caused by an individual's alcoholism rather than having to do with police racism).

Conclusion

This chapter describes historical political rationalities that still haunt us today. In the 1500s, Christian Europe began to move away from *caritas* and predestination toward secular accounts of what it is to be human and ethical. This enabled colonial violence to be "ethical" even after colonized peoples converted to Christianity. Secularization and the concurrent exposure to alternative social orders led to increased political instability within Europe. In response, the great confinement of the poor enclosed a wildly diverse group of people together for the first time. No one believed this did any good to those confined; it only removed their threat to ruling classes. Beginning with undifferentiated confinement in poorhouses and similar sites, and aided by new secular rationalities for social stratifications, perpetrators of the various forms of violence in Europe and its colonies began to draw comparisons with one another's actions and rationalities. Out of this, a new generalization of abstract denigrated "otherness" began to emerge, which was only later formalized in the figure of the "abnormal" or "deviant."

The grouping together of such diverse peoples in these spaces led to new narrations of the utility of confinement, resulting in both the disciplines and a new medical perception, concurrent to the development of statistics and the norm. This enabled new narratives about sites of confinement, so that they began to promise education, rehabilitation, and cure, but this had no effect on the valuing of people who remained outside of narrow concepts of the norm. When it began to be less normatively acceptable for Indigenous people and other racialized groups to be subjected to explicit violence, they too were folded into the "confinable," which was facilitated by earlier back-and-forth secular comparisons of European "undesirables" and racialized peoples. And finally, when explicitly eugenic and colonial institutions and legal racial segregation and restrictions on immigration were abolished in the mid-twentieth century, this was oriented by a liberal belief that everybody should be treated the same within a largely unchanged social order. However beautiful and well intentioned in theory, equality-equals-sameness lets us down as a pursuit of social justice. We claim to treat everyone the same, but the same populations that have been rendered "eliminable" for five centuries continue to be disproportionately impoverished, incarcerated, institutionalized, apprehended, medicalized, and killed.

Notes

1. Following Chrisjohn and Young (2006), I use this term to describe the system of schools that were called by various names across Canada and the United States.
2. This is Foucault's suggestion, noted above, that the new "racism" against internal (European) enemies was borne from discursive shifts in the context of colonizing genocide.
3. Likewise, concurrent with the US "Indian Wars," the first treaty between any First Nation and the US Government was the 1794 Treaty of Canandaigua with the Iroquois Confederacy. It followed the model the Iroquois had been using among Nations in the Confederacy for centuries, and the Confederacy had used it with Europeans for the first time two centuries previously with Dutch traders (Anderson 2001; Turner 2006).
4. Stiker (1999, 11).
5. If someone today mobilizes a normative moral economy from a previous era, however, they will be construed as aberrational—for example, if someone were to suggest that heathens or heretics should be incarcerated. Tellingly, their aberration would most likely be narrated using the secular dividing practices of psychiatry.

References

Ahmed, Sara. 2010. *The Promise of Happiness*. Durham: Duke University Press.
Anderson, Fred. 2001. "Wampum Belt: A History of America's First Treaty, with the Iroquois Confederacy." *The New York Times on the web*, January 7.
Asad, Talal. 2003. *Formations of the Secular*. Stanford, CA: Stanford University Press.
Ben-Moshe, Liat. 2012. "Genealogies of Resistance to Incarceration: Abolition Politics in Anti-Prison and De-Institutionalization Activism in the U.S. 1950-present." PhD diss., Syracuse University.
Barnes, Colin. 1992. *Disabling Imagery and the Media*. Halifax, England: The British Council of Organizations of Disabled People.

Burke, James. 1997. *An Invisible Object.* Connections 3, Episode 4. London: BBC.

Butler, Judith. 2004. *Precarious Life.* New York: Verso.

Chapman, Chris. 2012. "Colonialism, Disability, and Possible Lives: The Residential Treatment of Children Whose Parents Survived Indian Residential Schools." *Journal of Progressive Human Services* 24(2): 127–158.

———. 2010. "Becoming Perpetrator: How I Came to Accept Restraining and Confining Disabled Aboriginal Children." Paper presented at PsychOUT: A Conference for Organizing Resistance Against Psychiatry, individual.utoronto.ca/psychout/papers/Chapman_paper.pdf

Chrisjohn, Roland, and Sherri Young. 2006. *The Circle Game: Shadows and Substance in the Indian Residential School Experience in Canada.* Penticton, BC: Theytus.

Churchill, Ward. 2004. *Kill the Indian, Save the Man: The Genocidal Impact of American Indian Residential Schools.* San Francisco, CA: City Lights.

———. 1998. *A Little Matter of Genocide: Holocaust and Denial in the Americas, 1492 to the Present.* Winnipeg: Arbeiter Ring.

Davis, Angela. 2007. "How Does Change Happen?" [public lecture], http://www.youtube.com/watch?v=Pc6RHtEbiOA&feature=related.

———. 2003. *Are Prisons Obsolete?* New York: Seven Stories Press.

Davis, Lennard. 1995. *Enforcing Normalcy.* London: Verso.

De las Casas, Bartolome. 1542. *Brief Account of the Devastation of the Indies.* http://www.gutenberg.org/cache/epub/20321/pg20321.html

Drinkwater, Chris. 2005. "Supported Living and the Production of Individuals." In *Foucault and the Government of Disability,* edited by Shelley Tremain, 229–244. Ann Arbor, MI: University of Michigan Press.

Engels, Friedrich. 1884. *Origins of the Family, Private Property, and the State.* http://www.marxists.org/archive/marx/works/1884/origin-family/

Fellows, Mary Louise, and Sherene Razack. 1994. "Seeking Relations: Law and Feminism Roundtables." *Signs* 19(4):1048–83.

Foucault, Michel. 2003a. *Abnormal.* New York: Picador.

———. 2003b. *Society Must be Defended.* New York: Picador.

———. 1995. *Discipline and Punish: The Birth of the Prison.* New York: Vintage.

———. 1994a. *The Birth of the Clinic: An Archaeology of Medical Perception.* New York: Vintage.

———. 1994b. "'Omnes et Singulatim': Toward a Critique of Political Reason." In *Power,* edited by James Faubion, 298–325. New York: The New Press.

———. 1994c. "The Political Technology of Individuals." In *Power,* edited by James Faubion, 403–417. New York: The New Press.

———. 1988. *Madness and Civilization: A History of Insanity in the Age of Reason.* New York: Vintage Books.

———. 1970. *The Order of Things: An Archaeology of the Human Sciences.* New York: Vintage.

Fournier, Suzanne, and Ernie Crey. 1999. *Stolen from Our Embrace: The Abduction of First Nations Children and the Restoration of Aboriginal Communities.* Toronto, ON: Harper Collins Canada.

Guest, Dennis. 1997. *The Emergence of Social Security in Canada.* Vancouver: University of British Columbia Press.

Holmes, Martha Stoddard. 2001. "Working (with) the Rhetoric of Affliction: Autobiographical Narratives of Victorians with Physical Disabilities." In *Embodied Rhetorics: Disability in Language and Culture,* edited by James C. Wilson and Cynthia Lewiecki-Wilson, 27–44. Carbondale, IL: Southern Illinois University Press.

Johansen, Bruce E. 1982. *Forgotten Founders: Benjamin Franklin, the Iroquois, and the Rationale for the American Revolution.* Boston, MA: Harvard Common Press.

Kelm, Mary Ellen. 2005. "Diagnosing the Discursive Indian: Medicine, Gender, and the 'Dying Race.'" *Ethnohistory* 52(2): 371–406.

King, Thomas. 2003. *The Truth about Stories: A Native Narrative.* Toronto, ON: House of Anansi.

Knobe, Joshua. 2006. "The Concept of Intentional Action: A Case Study in the Uses of Folk Psychology." *Philosophical Studies* 130: 203–231.

Mahmood, Saba. 2005. *The Politics of Piety: The Islamic Revival and the Feminist Subject.* Princeton, NJ: Princeton University Press.

McGuire, Anne. 2011. "The War on Autism: On Normative Violence and the Cultural Production of Autism Advocacy." PhD diss., University of Toronto.

Michalko, Rod. 2002. *The Difference that Disability Makes.* Philadelphia, PA: Temple University Press.

Neu, Dean, and Richard Therrien. 2003. *Accounting for Genocide: Canada's Bureaucratic Assault on Aboriginal People.* Halifax: Fernwood.

Packett, Bob. 2012. "The Reasons for Going on a Crusade" [Podcast], http://www.summahistorica.com/podcast-archive.htm

———. 2011. "Crusader Privileges" [Podcast], http://www.summahistorica.com/podcast-archive.htm

Paul, Daniel. 2009. "Gov. Edward Cornwallis: British scalp proclamations: 1749 and 1750." http://www.danielnpaul.com/BritishScalpProclamation-1749.html

———. 2006. *We Were Not the Savages: Collision Between European and Native American Civilizations.* Halifax: Fernwood.

Pope Urban II. 1095. *The Speech at Council of Clermont,* According to Fulcher of Chartres. http://www.fordham.edu/halsall/source/urban2-fulcher.html

Puar, Jasbir. 2012. "The Cost of Getting Better: Suicide, Sensation, Switchpoints." *GLQ* 18(1): 149–158.

Rafter, Nicole Hahn. 1997. *Creating Born Criminals.* Chicago, IL: University of Illinois Press.

Razack, Sherene. 2011. "Timely Deaths: Medicalizing the Deaths of Aboriginal People in Police Custody." *Law, Culture and the Humanities.* http://lch.sagepub.com/content/early/2011/06/22/1743872111407022

Rowlands, Rose, and Barry Stuart. 2008. "Is Indigenization of the Justice System a Solution(?) and Restoring Social Control According to Culture and Tradition." Paper presented at Aboriginal Justice Forum, Vancouver, British Columbia.

Smith, Andrea. 2005. *Conquest: Sexual Violence and American Indian Genocide.* Cambridge: South End Press.

Snyder, Sharon L., and David T. Mitchell. 2006. *Cultural Locations of Disability.* Chicago, IL: The University of Chicago Press.

Stiker, Henri-Jacques. 1999. *A History of Disability.* Ann Arbor, MI: University of Michigan Press.

Thobani, Sunera. 2007. *Exalted Subjects: Studies in the Making of Race and Nation in Canada.* Toronto, ON: University of Toronto Press.

Tickell, Paul [Director]. 2007a. *The Colour of Money.* Racism: A History, Episode 1. London: British Broadcasting Corporation.

———. 2007b. *A Savage Legacy.* Racism: A History, Episode 3. London: British Broadcasting Corporation.

Tinker, George E. 2004. "Tracing a Contour of Colonialism: American Indians and the Trajectory of Educational Imperialism." In *Kill the Indian, Save the Man: The*

Genocidal Impact of American Indian Residential Schools, Ward Churchill, xiii–xlii. San Francisco, CA: City Lights Books.

Turner, Dale. 2006. *This is Not a Peace Pipe: Towards a Critical Indigenous Philosophy.* Toronto, ON: University of Toronto Press.

Wheatley, Edward. 2010. "Cripping the Middle Ages, Medievalizing Disability Theory." In *Stumbling Blocks Before the Blind: Medieval Constructions of a Disability.* Ann Arbor, MI: University of Michigan Press.

Withers, A. J. 2012. *Disability Politics and Theory.* Blackpoint, NS: Fernwood.

3

Creating the Back Ward: The Triumph of Custodialism and the Uses of Therapeutic Failure in Nineteenth-Century Idiot Asylums

Philip M. Ferguson

Introduction

In December 1965, Burton Blatt, along with photographer Fred Kaplan, made a series of visits to a variety of large public institutions for people with intellectual disabilities. They made special efforts at each facility to visit the "back wards" and document what they knew they would find. The photographic exposé (Blatt and Kaplan 1966/1974) of the abuse and neglect that had become standard "treatment" in these institutions helped stoke the fires of outrage and shame among both politicians and the public, leading to the large-scale movement of the people forced to live in these conditions back to the community. The population of these large, public institutions peaked in 1967 at about 230,000 individuals and has continued to decline to a current population just under 30,000 (Larson et al. 2013, 7).

Blatt and Kaplan undertook their efforts, in part, to document the conditions that had outraged then Senator Robert Kennedy when he had visited some of the institutions in New York a few months earlier. Blatt wanted to assure everyone that what the Senator had witnessed was the rule, not the exception, in the incarceration of people with intellectual disabilities in 1965. One did not have to know how the situation had devolved to such a state to recognize the horror of what had come to be.

> It is true that a short visit to the back wards of an institution for the mentally retarded will not provide, even for the most astute observer, any clear notion of the antecedents of the problems observed, the complexities of dealing with them, or ways to correct them. We can believe that the Senator did not fully comprehend the subtleties, the tenuous relationships, the grossness of budgetary inequities, the long history of political machinations, the extraordinary difficulty in providing care for severely mentally retarded patients, the unavailability of highly trained leaders, and the near-impossibility in recruiting dedicated attendants and ward personnel. But, we know, as well as do

thousands of others who have been associated with institutions for the mentally retarded, that what Senator Kennedy claimed to have seen he did see. In fact, we know personally of few institutions for the mentally retarded in the United States completely free of dirt and filth, odors, naked patients groveling in their own feces, children in locked cells, horribly crowded dormitories, and understaffed and wrongly staffed facilities. (Blatt 1974, *v*)

It has been almost a half-century since Blatt's observations of *Christmas in Purgatory*. Over the intervening years, we have become somewhat inured to the abuses of that earlier era. If conditions in the institutions that remain open are far from perfect, society seems to trust that the grossest of the conditions have been rectified. Yet people in North America remain familiar with the meaning of the term "back ward." The "back wards"[1] are where the worst abuses happened. Both in fact and in symbol, the back wards of institutions were those out-of-sight hellholes where the inmates with the most significant disabilities, the most challenging behaviors, the most hopeless of prognoses were abandoned. If back wards still exist then surely they are the exception rather than the rule. At least that is the hope. However, whether actual back wards still exist or not, metaphorical "back wards" still surely do.

My focus in this chapter is on the origin of the back ward rather than its demise. Where did the "back wards" that Blatt and Kennedy witnessed come from in the first place? What exactly were those "antecedents of the problems observed" that Blatt cited? This chapter reviews that history and argues that, in fact, there is a specific narrative to the evolution of the institutional "back ward" as an identifiable place where people with the most significant intellectual disabilities were to be incarcerated and largely forgotten.

As a physical location, institutional back wards in North America were created in the last half of the nineteenth century. This is not to say that there was no abuse or neglect before that time. Of course there was. Indeed, it was the documentation of existing abuses in county poor houses that was the ostensible justification for the creation of new, state institutions built along a new architectural and administrative model that included separate "wards" or "cottages" located at the back of the institutional grounds. However, actual wards or units located at the back of institutional settings were arrangements that American institutions borrowed from European institutions as an administrative solution to a problem of managing an increasingly custodial population. The so-called cottage plan for institutions allowed the creation of ever larger, congregate facilities where separate, individual units were built to house specific types and levels of inmates, with the most custodial classifications assigned to those units the furthest away from the administration building.

Especially in New York State, the debate over the "cottage plan" was both contentious and extended. Exploring that debate and how it evolved from roughly 1860 to 1915 allows a more detailed understanding of the power of the back ward as both symbol and artifact of institutional incarceration of people with the most significant intellectual disabilities. It leads to a series of additional questions that are specific to New York, but suggestive of larger institutional models throughout North America. Why were the details of institutional provisions for those individuals judged to be hopelessly idiotic or at least unimprovably demented or imbecilic so persistently contested in New York State and elsewhere? An adequate response to that question must quickly move beyond the specific issues and personalities to a larger question about the uses and abuses of the concept of "therapeutic failure" in the professionalization of care for people with intellectual disabilities in the nineteenth and early twentieth centuries.[2]

The creation of the back ward, then, becomes the story of the move from care to custody to incarceration. After reviewing the key points of this story, I argue that the details of developmental classification and institutional organization underlying the debate over custodial care reveal the beginnings of a model of service (a so-called continuum of care) for people with intellectual disabilities that still dominates today despite the diminishing role of the residential institution.

Locating Custody: The Debate over Separate or Congregate Care

In December 1906, some 60 years before Blatt's exposé, there were four state institutions in New York specifically charged with the care and treatment of feeble-minded[3] individuals. The names of the facilities were straightforward indications of their official purpose upon creation:

1. The Syracuse State School for Feeble-Minded Children (established 1852);
2. The State Custodial Asylum for Feeble-Minded Women (est. at Newark, 1878);
3. The Rome State Custodial Asylum (est. 1894);
4. The Craig Colony for Epileptics (est. at Sonyea, 1896)

The Syracuse facility—the second oldest public institution in the United States to focus specifically on the so-called feebleminded population—was the only one of the four to mention "school" and "children" in its name. This was suggestive of the facility's official emphasis on the remediation—and even cure—of youth with mild or moderate intellectual disabilities, with a projected return of many of its residents to life in the community as productive, if supervised, young adults. The Rome and Newark facilities, by contrast, are identified as "asylums" not "schools," and the official function of incarceration in these asylums was "custodial" in nature rather than curative or even ameliorative. The Craig Colony[4] facility clearly indicated its focus on individuals with epilepsy. For most institutional professionals of this era, epilepsy was, if anything, an even more dismal diagnosis than idiocy. Indeed, with some exceptions, epilepsy was often treated as a particularly hopeless category of feeblemindedness. According to one estimate, up to 98 percent of Craig's inmates were judged to be feebleminded (Hebberd 1912). In sum, two of the four "idiot asylums" in New York State at the dawn of the twentieth century were explicitly custodial in origin and purpose, and a third was implicitly custodial given the general view of incurability attributed to epilepsy.

It is, therefore, somewhat surprising to read in the Annual Report for the New York State Board of Charities how a special committee had set out in that same month of December 1906, to meet with the superintendents of the four asylums to discuss the very issue their institutions were designed to solve: what to do with the so-called custodial inmates that threatened to overwhelm the management of those custodial institutions? The summary of the meeting described the institution leaders as "greatly embarrassed" by the growing number of inmates "so demented as to be no longer capable of improvement, and to require, in the future, only custodial care" (New York State Board of Charities 1907, 24). The custodial asylums, in short, were seemingly ashamed that so many of their residents were, in fact, custodial. It had been at the behest of H. B. Wilbur, the first superintendent of the Syracuse State School, and others (especially Josephine Shaw Lowell[5]) that the Newark asylum had originally been established in 1878. Almost 20 years later, the creation of the institutions at Rome and Sonyea (Craig), New York, were likewise, in specific response to the complaint that the unimprovable inmates at Syracuse (and the county poorhouses) were crowding out the educational focus that was the prime mission of the facility.

If it was a familiar problem, the recommended solution coming out of the meeting also seemed strikingly repetitive, namely that the state should create another custodial asylum. However, the recommendation to create another asylum was not necessarily—or at least not primarily—to build the state's institutional capacity to handle larger and larger numbers of custodial inmates being admitted from the community. It was instead, to relieve the burden placed on the existing institutions by the custodial inmates already in residence.

> After consideration of the various phases of the problem, the superintendents and managers present adopted unanimously a resolution recommending the establishment of a new custodial asylum, to which may be sent all inmates of the four existing institutions intended for epileptics and the feeble-minded, who are no longer proper subjects for treatment and maintenance therein. (New York State Board of Charities 1907, 24)

The question arises as to why the administrators of asylums that had already been established as custodial in nature (as was true of three of the four New York facilities) were so adamant in their insistence that a new custodial asylum was needed? There were certainly social concerns about the dangers of the umimprovable classes to the safety of morals of the general public. However, in this situation the superintendents were discussing where, not whether, to incarcerate individuals. The people in question were already in custody. There were also certainly concerns of economics and efficiency. Getting rid of those inmates who were physically or cognitively unable to contribute to their own care could be a significant cost savings. However, economic concerns alone do not explain why the superintendents would be "greatly embarrassed" by discovering that their institutions had precisely the individuals for whom their facilities had been intended. Instead, their apprehension seems at least partly grounded in a concern with professional legitimacy and therapeutic skill. Regardless of the original purpose of the custodial facilities, once in charge of such a place, the superintendents were just as vulnerable to the professional need to demonstrate special expertise and discernment in the treatment of their residents. One of the by-products of this demonstration was the ability to make classificational distinctions where none had been made before. So, just as the almshouse managers had in earlier eras felt it necessary to sort the economic failures into separate subgroups of able-bodied poor and truly dependent; just as the insane asylum superintendents insisted on distinguishing the curable insane from the chronic; so did the idiot asylum leaders find it important to distinguish the truly custodial from those who could be somewhat useful and amenable to improvement.[6]

Regardless of its origins or merits, the recommendation of the State Board of Charities to create a new custodial asylum was not immediately acted upon by the state legislature. It was not until some five years later (1911) that Letchworth

Village was opened in downstate New York. More importantly, when opened, Letchworth was designated to receive individuals at all levels of functioning. It was to follow the pattern of congregate care adopted by virtually every other state and model itself as one of the all-purpose "villages of the simple" (Kerlin 1885, 174). Letchworth, in short, was both custodial and curative in official function. Despite the arguments of institution superintendents and State Board of Charities leaders, New York ended up following the rest of the country creating a network of idiot asylums across the state that were meant to "serve" all of those with *any* level of feeblemindedness. Asylums, in essence, were to create a continuum of care where separate cottages housed individuals with separate levels of support needs, while still connected organizationally under one administration. Instead of creating one or two institutions that were all "back wards," while others would supposedly have none, New York joined the other states in creating room for back wards at every institution.

The Move to Congregate Care

Interestingly, the last half of the nineteenth century was taken up with earlier versions of the same debate that the New York State Board of Charities was still considering in 1906. The earlier debates sometimes dealt with different sets of particular issues (e.g., economics, treatment regimens, prospects of cure or remediation, social welfare, ethical obligations). For a period of years, the arguments became bitter and personal. Yet they always revolved around a singular issue: what should be done with the growing number of individuals whose conditions remained impervious to professional help? Many of the details of this debate have already been ably recounted in histories of insane asylums (Dwyer 1987; Grob 1973; Schneider and Deutsch 1941; Tomes 1984), or as part of the story of the rise of idiot asylums in the last half of the nineteenth century (Ferguson 1992; Scheerenberger 1983; Trent 1994). However, it is useful to review the broad outlines of the debate as it initially took shape.

In the 1860s and 1870s, the questions being raised were mainly about what were increasingly referred to as the "chronically" or "incurably insane." At both a political and a professional level, this was a question of the centralization of state control and professional responsibility for chronic—and usually *poor* insane. The issue was the financial burden placed on the counties to care for these people, and also that they were being housed in terrible conditions in county poorhouses. In 1864, the New York State legislature authorized Dr. Sylvester Willard, in essence, to replicate a study done some 20 years earlier by Dorothea Dix and survey the conditions of the "insane poor" housed in the county poor houses across the state (Schneider and Deutsch 1941; Willard 1865). As did Dix, Willard found conditions that were largely appalling. Willard argued that the state should assume responsibility and take this growing segment of the almshouse population off the counties' hands.[7] Among most institution professionals, there was little opposition to the idea that the state needed to take over the care of this population.

However, if the first question of this era—"who" should be responsible for the custody of the incurably insane—was answered fairly quickly by the expanding role of the state, the next question of "where" that responsibility should be carried out evoked a longer debate. Both within New York—and then between New York officials and professionals in other states—the question was now where to house this new population. Should existing asylums simply be expanded with the full range of patients now accepted, going from those most amenable to "cure", or the so-called *acute* cases, to the most chronically disturbed patients destined to a lifetime of custody with little hope for cure (Dwyer 1987)? Or, should asylums be specialized to serve a specific subset of patients so that acute and chronically ill patients would be housed in separate asylums?

All of this played out from the late 1850s to the 1880s in reference to insane asylums. However, it quickly became clear that New York's path of creating totally separate asylums for those of insane and feebleminded populations found to be beyond help would be the exception rather than the rule. The other states, with a few variations, went quickly along the route of congregate asylums with acute and chronic cases served by the same institution and residing in separate cottages rather than creating entirely separate custodial institutions. The practical implications of the so-called cottage plan were important. The move to multilevel congregate care was greatly facilitated by a move away from the linear "Kirkbride model" of asylum architecture to the "cottage" system of separate buildings arranged on a single campus with each building—or cottage—housing 40–60 individuals of a specific type and functional level (Tomes 1984). Even in New York, where the specialized asylum persisted, institutions would come to follow this cottage design. It was cheaper, for one thing, to move away from the huge "bricks and columns" edifices favored by Kirkbride and the first generation of asylum superintendents, going instead to the simple, functional architecture of a basic two story box, dupli-cated multiple times around a central administration building. Equally important, however, the architectural move to separated buildings of simple design was inex-tricably bound in the policy decision to move to congregate care. In essence, the cottage system of separate buildings allowed the "best of both worlds": a congre-gate facility housing all levels of inmates but comprising an array of what could be characterized as separate mini-asylums in the form of cottages organized around various categories of therapeutic success and failure.

Early on in the debate, the economic utility of the cottage plan was not the pri-mary rationale used by backers of this approach. Perhaps the most vocal opponent of the move to create a separate insane asylum for the incurably insane was John Gray, who just happened to also be the superintendent of what was at the time the only state insane asylum in New York, based in the upstate city of Utica. Although his institution had from its beginning been focused on "acute" cases—returning those who were deemed incurable to the county poorhouses—Gray argued vocifer-ously that it would be much better to make the Utica asylum an all purpose insti-tution, rather than create a separate custodial facility as called for by the Willard Report. In the pages of the journal he edited, *The American Journal of Insanity*, Gray (as summarized by Grob 1994, 108) outlined his reasons for preferring the congregate care model to the separate asylum:

1. Places like Utica couldn't handle all of the acute cases;
2. Chronic cases still needed treatment;
3. Separate asylums for incurables would become unwieldy;
4. Absence of hope created an unhealthy atmosphere;
5. Chronic patients affixed with stigma of pauperism;
6. Families would resist putting their relatives in such places (i.e., asylums for incurables). (On Separate Asylums for Curables and Incurables 1865)

Even after the New York State legislature passed the law in 1865 authorizing the creation of the Willard Custodial Asylum, Gray could only imagine that it had been the result of distracted politicians. In an unsigned article that he almost certainly authored, the misguided action is explained:

> It should be borne in mind, however, that the measure was adopted by the State Government during a period of civil war, when the great question of the day absorbed every thought; and that the time and occasion were unfavorable to calm investigation and discussion of subjects of lesser moment. (On Separate Asylums 1865, 247)

Gray's position was opposed by several other institution professionals (H. B. Wilbur, George Cook, John Chapin) as well as members of the newly formed New York State Board of Charities. In the years immediately after the Willard Report was released, the response to Gray's opposition to a separate custodial insane asylum was presented in the pages of the very journal he edited. One of the main arguments was simply pointing to the failure of the Utica asylum to serve the chronic population that it now professed to want (Cook 1866).

> If one were to listen to what has been said in opposition to separate provision for the chronic insane in the State of New York, having no knowledge of their actual condition, he would suppose that they were now amply provided for in curative hospitals, and that some restless, dissatisfied theorists, not content to leave them in such good care, were, in violation of all professional and humane ideas, endeavoring to thrust them out and precipitate them into a hell, over the gateway to which shall be inscribed, "All hope abandon, you who enter here." (Cook 1866, 52)

Rather, Cook (1866) explained that the proposed custodial asylum would specialize in the distinct needs of the chronic insane, saving them from the degradation of the county poor houses where Gray and others apparently had been satisfied to let them remain. Facilities for the curable and incurable insane have "two distinct ends to be attained, requiring different construction, organization and management" (58). The "commingling" of the two groups would inevitably cause the institutional administration to "sacrifice the highest good of one class to the other. Need I add that the sacrifice falls mainly upon the chronic class?" (58).

Although the national debate had largely been settled by the end of the 1870s (Grob 1973) in favor of large congregate facilities, New York had taken a different path. The Willard State Asylum for the Chronic Insane was opened in 1869 (a similar facility was opened in Binghamton in 1879). By 1875 the institutional population of Willard had exceeded one thousand inmates (Grob 1973, 387). During this time, perhaps the most detailed defense of the separate custodial facility was provided by Hervey B. Wilbur. Wilbur, the superintendent at the Syracuse Idiot Asylum (later named the "Syracuse State School") was commissioned by the New York Board of Charities to do a report on insane asylums in Great Britain, which he presented to the Board in 1876. The report was generous in its praise of institutions in Scotland, England, and the community plan used in Gheel, Belgium. In essence, Wilbur's argument for separate custodial facilities had three points: First, creating separate, single purpose asylums would allow each individual facility to stay relatively small in size, thus allowing more personalized supervision; second, without the burden of aggressive medical intervention in pursuit of a cure, superintendents of custodial asylums could more easily embrace the British practice of nonrestraint as advocated by Connolly and others; and finally, a focus on custody rather than cure allowed institutions to use inmates in workshop and gardening occupations that were both financially helpful to the institution and behaviorally instructive to the inmates themselves.

Not only was Wilbur generous in his praise of the British asylums that he visited. His report was also generous and specific in its criticism of Gray and the Utica asylum (Wilbur 1876). After describing at some length, the economic and therapeutic benefits to be found in the small custodial insane asylums of Scotland, where inmates were given vocational responsibilities as part of their care, Wilbur turned to Gray's opposition to specialized custodial asylums in the United States:

> It may be said, and with truth, that it is a predominance of chronic cases that permits this large percentage of employment [of able-bodied inmates] in British asylums, but this same fact is true in American asylums generally. The theory is, not that our institutions have a greater proportion of recent [i.e. potentially curable] cases and, therefore, employment is impracticable, but it is a general want of faith in employment, as a means of treatment, in any form of insanity. (Wilbur 1876, 186)

Wilbur quotes Gray's dismissal of the Scottish model for use in America and then gives his unvarnished opinion of his fellow superintendent's argument: "This is the language of one who knows nothing, by observation, of the actual facts of the case" (187).

Despite Wilbur's report and the backing of the New York State Board of Charities and Corrections, even the custodial institutions in New York would gradually yield to the national trend for congregate care of the insane. By 1890, the New York legislature had passed the "State Care Act." While one major feature of the act was to clearly centralize the care of the insane poor as a state responsibility, the other feature was to undo the policy of separate custodial facilities begun in 1865. Indeed, the act mandated the "abolition of the legal distinction between cases of acute and chronic mental disease" (Schneider and Deutsch 1941, 97). What had been custodial facilities in Ovid (Willard) and Binghamton, New York, became congregate care insane asylums with regional responsibility for all of the insane poor within their geographic regions.

The debate over custodial versus congregate insane asylums overshadowed the agreement that both types of facilities would be built along the cottage plan of separate buildings. The back ward, in short, was a product of the need for a separate place to house the chronically insane. From the perspective of those with the most significant disabilities, the debate over the two models of institutions was a distinction without a difference. However, from the perspective of professional control and influence, the outcome was seen as critical. Perhaps for that reason the argument would continue in New York State for several more decades. The argument shifted from asylums for the insane to those for idiots, but the issues were virtually the same as were the outcomes.

Renewing the Debate: Wilbur, Kerlin, and the "Proper Care" of Custodial Idiots

As mentioned, Superintendent Gray and the backers of large, congregate asylums for the insane rather quickly carried the day in terms of institutional policy in most states. Even as Gray bemoaned the authorization of the Willard Asylum in 1865, he (anonymously but accurately) claimed that the larger debate over the arrangement of custodial care was already decided:

> There is, perhaps, no subject connected with provision for the insane, upon which the verdict of the profession has been more unanimous than their condemnation of asylums for incurables. If, as we have said, the chief source of chronic lunacy is the want of asylums for cure, it is obvious that we but palliate the evil by establishing institutions for the so-called incurable. (The Willard Asylum 1865, 207)

Wilbur did not agree with Gray's assessment and carried on the policy debate. Until his death in 1883, Wilbur pushed the notion of separate custodial asylums. However, much of his attention over those decades was focused on his primary area of professional expertise—the idiot asylum. It was against the backdrop of the debate about custodial insane asylums that the similar but delayed debate over custodial idiot asylums played out in New York and elsewhere.[8] Again, it was a debate that Wilbur was to lose, although—as we have seen—there were advocates in New York for separate custodial idiot asylums well into the twentieth century. Taking Gray's place in support of large congregate care facilities, housing all levels of idiots from the most educable imbecile to the most hopeless idiot, was one of Wilbur's few peers in terms of influence among idiot asylum superintendents, Isaac Kerlin of the Elwyn Asylum in Pennsylvania.

Both Wilbur and Kerlin were among the first generation of idiot asylum administrators. Unlike others of that generation(e.g., Samuel Gridley Howe and Edward Seguin), Wilbur and Kerlin were active participants in the move to establish the area of idiot asylum administration as its own medical and educational specialization, equal to but distinct from the better known field of insane asylum administration. Wilbur had actually preceded Howe and his "experimental school" for idiots—by a few months—in starting his private school in Barre, Massachusetts, in 1848 (Graney 1979). When New York started the country's second public idiot asylum in 1852, Wilbur became its first superintendent. He was to remain in that position until his death more than 30 years later. For his part, Kerlin gained notice and influence as the superintendent of the prominent institution opened outside of Philadelphia—the Pennsylvania (Elwyn) Training School—with both public and private inmates. Following Wilbur's pattern of longevity, Kerlin remained as superintendent of the facility for 30 years until his death in 1893. In 1876, both Kerlin and Wilbur were among the handful of superintendents who helped start the professional organization that would come to represent their field: the Association of Medical Officers of American Institutions for Idiots, Imbeciles and Feeble-Minded Persons.

Kerlin and the "Thoroughly Classified Institution"

In a report to his fellow superintendents in 1888, Kerlin laid out many of his reasons for preferring these larger asylums that housed all levels of idiots at one location, though separated into different cottages. In such facilities, Kerlin argued, there were economic benefits to the state, therapeutic benefits to the inmates, and what might today be called professional development opportunities for the staff.

1. Better medical care can be arranged for the "epileptic, paralytic, and scrofulous" children.
2. Under the expert eye of the superintendent, inmates may be easily moved back and forth from the "asylum branch" to the "education branch" as progress or deterioration occurs with specific individuals. Such movement would be much more difficult if the educational and custodial departments were not "in proximity."
3. Only in congregate institutions could the "custodials" benefit from the entertainment and cultural events provided by and for the higher functioning inmates (e.g., institution bands, theatrical productions, "stereopticon" showings).
4. The agricultural and industrial work of the physically able custodial inmates would have a "local market" in the institution itself. "[T]he gardening, laundering, and cobbling of our feeble-minded employés (sic) find here an exchange which will never be criticized by outside 'labor unions,' nor reached by 'labor legislation'" (80).
5. Just as inmates can be shifted around from one level of cottage to another, so may staff be moved from fairly unskilled work with custodial residents to more preferred (and better paid) work as matrons or teachers in the educational department.
6. Finally, and in an argument that most closely followed the concern expressed two decades earlier by John Gray, Kerlin maintained that the stigma and pessimism surrounding the hopeless care of custodial idiots would inevitably lead to what Gray referred to as an "unhealthy atmosphere" if isolated from other inmates more amenable to remediation. By contrast, when located within an "all-purpose" facility, the custodial department is maintained as a "medical philanthropy" so that it "can never sink to the hopeless, uninviting, and deplorable condition which attaches to the common thought of an utter and complete asylum for neglected idiocy" (Kerlin 1888, 80).

Kerlin summarized his defense of the congregate facility:

> In short, the experience at Elwyn attests to the economy, reasonableness, and humanity of embracing under the central administration of a general institution all the grades and classes of the idiotic and feeble-minded, living in segregate buildings, it is true, but allowed legitimate contact; each divisible from the other by a classification scientific but not rigid, yet no one group isolated from the Divine influences of hope and the human helps to improvement. (Kerlin 1888, 80–81)

At the same time that Kerlin made his case for his "all-comprehensive" institution, he made clear that the most severely disabled inmates—those who were assigned to the so-called asylum department—should be located at the back of such facilities, not the front. Cottages for these individuals were to be "more remote" and positioned "at some distance from the other departments—say from one-half to three-quarters of a mile" (Kerlin 1884, 260). For these facilities, big was better. Not only did size offer economies of scale, it offered a large enough population with which to demonstrate the diagnostic expertise of the asylum professionals. As mentioned earlier, taxonomic complexity—finding gradations and categories of idiocy where none had been found before—became for Kerlin and other leaders a key indication of specialized knowledge. All of that was possible only with facilities of a certain number and variety of inmate. As a result of this calculation, the very idea of small, custodial asylums was morally problematic for Kerlin:

> It is the small institution against which may be pronounced the objection of moral "hospitalism." The large, diffuse, and *thoroughly classified institution* is another affair, and can be to its wards and employés [*sic*] as cosmopolitan as a city. (Kerlin 1884, 262, emphasis added)

By the time of Kerlin's death in 1893, his plan for custodial cottages was fully implemented. The Elwyn facility had a four building "Hillside" complex matching Kerlin's policies for type of resident and distance from the other cottages. It was purely custodial in character. One building, for example, was designated for "helpless, idiotic and epileptic boys." Another (called "the chalet") was for "epileptic and paralytic girls" (cited in Hurd 1916, 507). Other states were gradually following the same model.

Wilbur and the Developmental Divide

For Wilbur and others in New York State, the argument for separate facilities for educable and uneducable feebleminded persons was at once more straightforward and less detailed. The custodial class of inmate was a diversion from the pedagogical purpose of the purely educational facility (such as the Syracuse Asylum). In language predictive of that used in 1906 by the special committee of the Board of Charities mentioned earlier, Wilbur stated clearly in his 1871 Annual Report that "The presence of these [unteachable ones] not only embarrasses the general management, but swells the average cost of taking care of the pupils generally" (Wilbur 1871, 11). Indeed, for a number of years after the opening of the Willard insane asylum in Ovid, Wilbur argued that one of the buildings at that facility should be dedicated to receive the custodial idiots gradually building up in number at Syracuse. The logic was obvious to Wilbur: "It would seem as if the mere presentation of the facts would suffice to ensure the necessary legislation" (12). By 1878, Wilbur reports to the other asylum superintendents that he and the Board of Trustees at Syracuse had always known that some alternative provision for custodial inmates would eventually have to be made. Keeping them at Syracuse was always thought, "not [to] be desirable" (Wilbur 1878, 96).

Wilbur's defense of separate facilities for custodial inmates can also be at least partly explained by his grudging insistence that his beloved institution at Syracuse was, at its heart, a school. Schools are for children. This was also a difference between idiocy and insanity, and therefore perhaps why Wilbur continued to fight for separate custodial idiot asylums even after the battle over separate insane asylums had been clearly lost. Insanity was seen largely as a disease of adults, while idiocy was almost always present from childhood. As a result, insane asylums had few children, while institutions for idiocy had many. Indeed, the earliest idiot asylums were often called "training schools" and barred admission of adults.[9]

The growing presence of adults represented a daily challenge to Wilbur's original conception of who he was and what he did. For him the developmental model of feeblemindedness was more about physical age than "mental age." If you were an adult, you did not belong in a school, even one exclusively designed for feeble-minded children. For Wilbur, there was a clear line of demarcation: if you had not moved far enough along the developmental scale to function independently or with only moderate supervision in the community, then you were custodial once you reached adulthood. This also helps explain why Wilbur argued for several years after the opening of the Willard asylum for the chronically insane, that custodial idiots could also be housed there. The point was that they were unimprovable adults; the source of their chronicity was not as important as its undeniable presence[10].

Wilbur's argument about the educational function of institutions for children with milder degrees of feeblemindedness highlights one of the important differences between asylums for idiots and those for the insane. When one reads the classification schemes that were emerging for the two separate populations, it is noticeable that the focus for classifying the insane was identification of different types of insanity. With idiocy, on the other hand, the emphasis tended to be on levels of impairment. Within idiot asylums of the late 1800s, in both Europe and North America, one sees the use of increasingly elaborate levels of developmental classification (Simpson 2007). In essence what we see in these schemes is a gradual adoption of a developmental model as the basic frame within which to understand feeblemindedness in all its forms. In this frame, the feebleminded person came to be portrayed very differently than the lunatic. Unlike insanity, feeblemindedness increasingly came to be understood as a premature interruption of the individual's gradual development or maturation from child to adult. Certainly this idea really gained dominance after the turn of the century with the rapid dissemination of the Binet intelligence test and its popularization of the concept of mental age.

As in the debate over separate, custodial insane asylums, Wilbur's position once again officially carried the day in New York State, while other states followed the advice of Kerlin and others building or enlarging large, congregate facilities with separate cottages for custodial inmates. As with the Willard Asylum, however, the official policy toward idiot asylums in New York steadily gave way to the congregate practice followed elsewhere. Kerlin even tried to rewrite Wilbur's endorsement of separate facilities as a misunderstanding that unjustly sullied his departed friend's reputation. Speaking specifically of the institution established at Newark, New York, Kerlin doubted Wilbur's support:

> I think that this whole matter of Dr. Wilbur's connection with the Newark institution should not be left in doubt. We do not want to embarrass the name of that good man with any possible mistake of today. All of us who have visited it and are studying the outcome of it, agree with Mrs. Kerlin that it is a palpable mistake. My own impression is that Dr. Wilbur had no intention of permanently separating the girls from the institution at Syracuse...The Newark institution will probably eventually become a general institution for the care and training of feeble-minded persons, irrespective of age and sex. (Kerlin 1891, 217)

Kerlin's prediction proved correct. Indeed, the defense of separate facilities was so discredited that it was thought that history should be revised so that Wilbur would not be associated with such a wrongheaded approach.[11]

Custodialism and the Creation of the Continuum of Care

What are we to make of this debate and its outcome? The immediate reasons for the triumph of the congregate care asylum are fairly easy to surmise. First, there were simple economies of scale to be had by building a smaller number of large facilities rather than a larger number of small ones. Indeed, the use of inmate labor to help run the asylums became a source of pride among superintendents. Walter Fernald of Massachusetts described the use of higher functioning female inmates to care for "the lowest grade idiots, paralytics [and] the helpless" as a way of showing the people of Massachusetts that "these trained girls can be of benefit to the state by caring for their more helpless associates" (Fernald 1891, 215). Kerlin himself bragged about maintenance costs at Elwyn decreasing from $250 to $100 per person because of the use of unpaid inmate labor. The male residents, for example, completely managed the institution bakery, "baking four to six barrels of flour daily at no expense for wages" (Kerlin 1891, 217).

A second reason was the administrative usefulness of having all of the clients at one setting, available to be moved and shuffled on relatively short notice. As Kerlin noted in listing his reasons for congregate care, the convenience of having the two populations—educational and custodial—in close proximity at one institution allowed such reassignments to happen more often. Of course, this also allowed the administrator a handy explanation for therapeutic failure: if a resident did not respond to intervention efforts, it was because of misclassification, not poor instruction. The failure to improve became a "success" of classification by simply moving the individual to the proper cottage following prolonged observation. Indeed, one senses that Kerlin's greatest sense of triumph came with the "thoroughly classified" institution that he was able to oversee at Elwyn. Elaborate classification of inmates became a powerful demonstration of professional legitimacy even if some of those classifications involved admission of therapeutic impotence.

Finally, it can be argued that the rapid adoption of the "cottage plan" itself was as much a cause as an effect of the move to large congregate care facilities. By moving to a model of institutional design that emphasized the use of small, separate, simple, cheaply constructed units (or cottages), the states could have their custodial cake and eat it too. Instead of building entirely separate custodial facilities, they were able to build the first back wards—institutions within institutions.

In the end, then, the only question that remains hard to answer is why Wilbur and his New York colleagues maintained their contrarian support for separate facilities for so long. A partial answer seems connected to Wilbur's own history. Wilbur saw himself as an educator first rather than an administrator (although he clearly acknowledged that role as well). In his closer ties to Seguin, he embodied a tradition of intervention and instruction that ran parallel to the other tradition of custody and control. His success, his claims to special expertise, were much more closely tied to educational outcomes than to administrative efficiencies. Both for Wilbur and his successors in New York, custodial inmates were more of an "embarrassment" than an opportunity.

So the issue of congregate versus separate can be seen not only as a debate over where inmates of various levels could best be served, but how professional claims to specialized knowledge could best be secured. A strategy of separate care would allow the superintendent to have the discretion of demonstrating the power of classification and assessment while focusing treatment on the salvageable minority. It gave the superintendent dominion over a smaller population but one with better prospects for valued treatment outcomes. The congregate care facility gave the superintendent control over the full range of individuals—the power to sort and serve as he saw fit on a continuing basis—where expertise is demonstrated by administrative efficiency as much as treatment efficacy (Ferguson 2002).

Conclusion

In today's formal support system for individuals with intellectual disabilities, a continuum of placement model has come to dominate the arrangement of services (Taylor 1988). In terms of schooling, students are placed somewhere along a continuum of more or less segregated settings running from the general education classroom on one end to entirely self-contained schools on the other (Ferguson in 2013). For vocational services, the continuum runs from supported employment in integrated work settings to sheltered work shops to segregated "day programs" where even the pretense of vocational activity is abandoned.

Finally, we have the residential continuum. Although small, community-based apartments and homes for adults with even significant intellectual disabilities have grown in number over the last few decades, the other options of the continuum have remained persistently in place. We still have large 10–20 bed group homes that often resemble nothing so much as the industrial and farm colonies started as offshoots of institutions more than a century ago. And finally, we still have the large, public congregate institution. As mentioned earlier, almost thirty thousand individuals continue to live in such facilities, with thousands more simply shifted to private versions of the public facilities. Yet, we know from years of practice and volumes of research that these remaining "back wards"—sanitized and improved as they may be—are not required to support individuals with disabilities. Eleven states have already demonstrated that by closing their large facilities (Larson et al. 2013, 7). In every state, there are individuals with the most significant disabilities being supported in family homes or in small community alternatives. Why does the continuum of placement continue to preserve its most segregated options?

Of course, there are multiple constituencies who continue to speak on behalf of these options (including some families and some disabled individuals themselves). Moreover, the intentions and preferences of individuals must be interpreted in the context of structural forces that nurture and shape those personal perspectives. Although financing segregated settings has become much more costly over the last three decades—as national and state standards of staffing and support have been established and enforced—the large, congregate care facility is still often seen as the best economic alternative among the many care options now available.

The historian's answer to such a policy conundrum might return to the debate from the nineteenth century. It is the continuing professional usefulness of therapeutic failure as both a diagnostic category and a location of service that makes today's back wards so resistant to change. The system within which professionals find themselves continues to reinforce the use of a physical location and conceptual justification for those whom professionals seem unable to help. Failure still needs a home, with or without a back ward attached.

Notes

1. The history of the term "back ward" and its usage as a reference to places where the individuals with the most "hopeless" conditions were kept would make an interesting study of its own. At least by the 1950s, the term was appearing in the titles of academic papers, with the obvious assumption that readers would understand the reference. One of the earliest such references (Martin 1950), described the meaning of the term as follows:

    Every mental hospital has one of these wards for the patients who are deteriorated but physically fit. The public thinks in terms of "The Snake Pit." The general practitioner thinks of these patients in such terms as "the hopeless and the damned." The hospital ward attendant usually feels that work with these patients lacks result, purpose, and prestige. The mental hospital doctor is usually preoccupied with his load of "new" patients, and these patients and their relatives make frequent demands upon his time and attention. (758)

2. By "therapeutic failure" I mean not just the failure of individuals to show improvement while under the care of professionals but also the "official" explanation of that failure as the result of the hopelessly unsalvageable nature of the individuals' disability (Ferguson 1992). Those individuals who "refused" to respond to the therapeutic regimen of the institution were now professionally ordained as chronic and beyond help. The problem was portrayed not as the inadequacy of the treatment but as the inadequacy of the person. For asylum administrators, the challenge presented by such individuals became the arrangement and location of their custody rather than continuing futile efforts at remediation.

3. The terminology used here will often include words or phrases that are no longer used or occur only as insults. However, during the times under discussion, the terms (e.g., feebleminded, idiotic, imbecilic, insane) were part of the clinical language of the emerging class of professionals in charge of their care in institutions.

4. The term "colony" in this institution's name was also meant to indicate a particular variant of the more familiar "cottage" model. The term ostensibly refers to the centuries old arrangement in Gheel, Belgium, where insane people were housed in the homes of towns people in Gheel. In the United States, a number of asylums in the nineteenth century started "farm colonies" as outposts of the main facility. These would typically be nearby the asylum, and have a resident family managing the farm and supervising 20–40 (male) inmates who were moved there. The products of their efforts were then used by the institution to defray costs. At Craig, the term "colony" was being used in a different sense, but still invoking at least an American perception of the Gheel arrangement. As the first Superintendent of the facility (William Shanahan) described the plan, the Colony was to differ from the cottage plan:

    This colony design includes not only the separation of the patients into detached buildings, but the arrangement of the cottages upon irregular lines and at different distances, in accordance with the situations of the various building sites, adapted to the self-support of the inmates through natural advantages for economy of administration, and for the successful prosecution of trades, industries and agricultural labors. (Shanahan 1912, 155)

    In practice, the facility came to resemble most of the other institutions built in this era along the cottage plan.

5. As Nicole Rafter has ably described in her book *Creating Born Criminals* (Rafter 1997), the "unlikely alliance" (p. 41) of Wilbur and Lowell in support of the Newark asylum was a case of dramatically different perspectives about people with disabilities coalescing around a shared outcome. To oversimplify the situation, Lowell wanted to protect society from the moral depravity of feebleminded women, while Wilbur needed a place for the unimproved residents of his facility at Syracuse to move as they became adults. For both, then, the Newark asylum was a common solution to two different problems.

6. At its core, the power of the concept of therapeutic failure is that it allows the professional to continue to claim success in the face of demonstrable ineffectiveness. Indeed, one way to demonstrate one's special expertise is to discover distinctions of classification where none had previously existed. So it was in this case as well: even among the custodial population, identification of the truly custodial creates a category of therapeutic failure where only generic ineffectiveness had been previously seen. The ability to diagnose permanent and inescapable failure in others was a demonstration of professional expertise.

7. Interestingly, Willard's report of 1865 did find some variation in the quality of care in the poor houses around the state. Many were, indeed, apparently terrible; however, others such as the facility in Westchester County were praised as models of humane and therapeutic care. Still, despite these mixed results, Willard's strong recommendation was to build a separate state asylum and mandate the placement of chronic poor insane.

8. This time lag between developments in "treating" the insane and similar developments in "treating" idiots is remarkably persistent throughout American history. The first public insane asylum (not counting the facility at Williamsburg) was opened in Worcester, Massachusetts in 1833. That was followed 15 years later with the opening of the first "experimental school" for idiots by Samuel Gridley Howe in 1848. The first officially custodial asylum, Willard, was authorized in 1865 (though not actually opened until 1869). The custodial idiot asylum at Newark, New York, was opened 13 years later in 1878. In the twentieth century, the population of insane asylums peaked in 1955, before a combination of new drugs, old economics, and civil rights concerns began the move to deinstitutionalize the mentally ill. The peak population for institutions for intellectually disabled individuals came some 12 years later in 1967. If one wants to make an educated guess at what official policy toward people with intellectual disabilities will be emphasizing in 10–15 years, there would be worse approaches than simply noticing what is happening to mental health policy today.

9. In his Annual Report for 1858, Wilbur extracted the relevant clause from the by-laws of the Syracuse Asylum specific as to who was—and was not—intended for admission:

> Children between the ages of seven and fourteen who are idiotic, or so deficient in intelligence as to be incapable of being educated at any ordinary school, and who are not epileptic, insane or greatly deformed, may be admitted by the superintendent, with the advice and counsel of the executive counsel. (Wilbur 1858, 28)

10. In his Annual Report for 1871, Wilbur mentions the plans for the chronic insane at Ovid (the Willard Asylum) and says a similar plan should be tried with the unteachable feebleminded. Indeed, he proposed that the law authorizing the Willard Asylum be changed to allow the admission of custodial idiots as well as the chronic insane. He had investigated the issue enough to discover that there was an empty building on the land for the asylum that he proposed to use for this population. "It would seem as if the mere presentation of the facts would suffice to ensure the necessary legislation" (Wilbur 1871, 12). His presentation of the facts,

however, did not suffice and he again reaffirmed his proposal in his Annual Report for the following year as well (Wilbur 1872). This time, the Board of Trustees endorsed his proposal for the Syracuse Asylum. It was all to no avail until Wilbur shifted his focus to support of the Newark Asylum as a separate custodial facility several years later.

11. Wilbur's worries about the Newark facility were primarily because of its restriction to women, not because of its custodial character.

References

Blatt, Burton. 1974. Introduction. In *Christmas in Purgatory: A Photographic Essay on Mental Retardation*, v–vi. Syracuse, NY: Syracuse University, Human Policy Press, Center on Human Policy.

Blatt, Burton, and Fred Kaplan. 1974. *Christmas in Purgatory: A Photographic Essay on Mental Retardation*. Originally published Boston, MD: Allyn & Bacon, 1966.

Cook, George. 1866. "Provision for the Insane Poor in the State of New York." *American Journal of Insanity* 23(1): 45–75.

Dwyer, Ellen. 1987. *Homes for the Mad: Life Inside Two Nineteenth-Century Asylums*. New Brunswick, NJ: Rutgers University Press.

Ferguson, Philip M. 2002. "Notes Toward a History of Hopelessness: Disability and the Places of Therapeutic Failure." *Disability, Culture and Education* 1(1): 27–40.

———. 1992. *Abandoned to their Fate: Social Policy and Practice Toward Severely Retarded People in America, 1820–1920*. Philadelphia: Temple University Press.

———. 2013. "The Present King of France is Feeble-Minded: The Logic and History of the Continuum of Placements for People with Intellectual Disabilities." In *Righting Educational Wrongs: Disability Studies in Law and Education*,(151–173), edited by Arlene S. Kanter and Beth. A. Ferri. Syracuse, NY: Syracuse University Press.

Fernald, Walter. 1891. Discussion. *Proceedings of the Association of Medical Officers of American Institutions for Idiotic and Feeble-Minded Persons* 15: 211–218 (Transcript of discussion by Fernald and others of paper by William B. Fish.)

Graney, Bernard J. 1979. "Hervey Backus Wilbur and the Evolution of Policies and Practices Toward Mentally Retarded People." PhD diss., Syracuse University.

Grob, Gerald N. 1994. *The Mad among Us: A History of the Care of America's Mentally Ill*. New York: Free Press.

———. 1973. *Mental Institutions in America: Social Policy to 1875*. New York: Free Press.

Hebberd, Robert W. 1912. "The Development of State Institutions for the Mentally Defective in this State for the Next Decade." *Proceedings of the New York State Conference of Charities and Correction* 13: 179–190.

Hurd, Henry. 1916. *The Institutional Care of the Insane in the United States and Canada*. Baltimore, MD: Johns Hopkins University Press.

Kerlin, Isaac N. 1891. "Discussion." *Proceedings of the Association of Medical Officers of American Institutions for Idiotic and Feeble-Minded Persons* 15: 211–218 (Transcript of discussion by Kerlin and others of paper by William B. Fish.)

———. 1888. "Status of the Work Before the People and Legislatures." *Proceedings of the Association of Medical Officers of American Institutions for Idiotic and Feeble-Minded Persons* 12: 64–83.

———. 1885. "Provision for Idiots: Report of the Standing Committee." *Proceedings of the National Conference of Charities and Correction* 12: 158–174.

———. 1884. "Provision for Idiotic and Feeble-Minded Children." *Proceedings of the National Conference of Charities and Correction* 11: 246–263.

Larson, Sheryl, Patricia Salmi, Drew Smith, Lynda Anderson, and Amy Hewitt. 2013. *Residential Services for Persons with Developmental Disabilities: Status and Trends Through 2011*. Minneapolis: University of Minnesota, Research and Training Center on Community Living, Institute on Community Integration.

Martin, M. G. 1950. "A Practical Treatment Program for a Mental Hospital "Back" Ward." *American Journal of Psychiatry* 106: 758–760.

New York State Board of Charities. 1907. "Report of the Committee on Idiots and Feeble-Minded." *Annual Report* 40: 171–178.

"On Separate Asylums for Curables and Incurables." 1865. *American Journal of Insanity* 22: 246–252.

Rafter, Nicole H. 1997. *Creating Born Criminals*. Chicago, IL: University of Illinois Press.

Scheerenberger, Richard C. 1983. *A History of Mental Retardation*. Baltimore, MD: Paul Brookes Publishing.

Schneider, David M., and Albert Deutsch. 1941. *The History of Public Welfare in New York State, 1867–1940*. Chicago, IL: University of Chicago Press.

Shanahan, William T. 1912. "History of the Establishment and Development of the Craig Colony for Epileptics Located at Sonyea, N. Y." *Epilepsia* A3(2): 153–161.

Simpson, Murray. 2007. "Developmental Concept of Idiocy." *Intellectual and Developmental Disability* 45(1): 23–32.

Taylor, Steven J. 1988. "Caught in the Continuum: A Critical Analysis of the Principle of the Least Restrictive Environment." *Journal of the Association for Persons with Severe Handicaps* 13(1): 45–53.

Tomes, Nancy. 1984. *A Generous Confidence: Thomas Story Kirkbride and the Art of Asylum-Keeping, 1840–1883*. New York: Cambridge University Press.

Trent, James W. Jr. 1994. *Inventing the Feeble Mind: A History of Mental Retardation in the United States*. Berkeley, CA: University of California Press.

Wilbur, Hervey B. 1878. "The Status of the Work." *Proceedings of the Association of Medical Officers of American Institutions for Idiotic and Feeble-Minded Persons* 3:96–97.

———. 1876. "Management of the Insane in Great Britain." In *Annual Report*, New York State Board of Charities 9: 175–207.

———. 1872. *19th Annual Report*. New York State Idiot Asylum. Syracuse, NY.

———. 1871. *18th Annual Report*. New York State Idiot Asylum. Syracuse, NY.

———. 1858. *6th Annual Report*. New York Idiot Asylum.

"The Willard Asylum and Provision for the Insane." 1865. *American Journal of Insanity* 22(2): 192–212.

Willard, Sylvester D. 1865. "Report on the Condition of the Insane Person in the County Poorhouse of New York." *Assembly Documents*, New York: New York State Assembly.

4

Eugenics Incarceration and Expulsion: Daniel G. and Andrew T.'s Deportation from 1928 Toronto, Canada

Geoffrey Reaume

Introduction

Daniel G. was admitted to 999 Queen Street West Asylum in Toronto on the same day as Andrew T: January 3, 1928. Both would be deported back to their countries of origin that same year after being incarcerated on their way to expulsion as "mentally defective" immigrants. This chapter seeks to understand what happened to them at a time when disabled people subject to deportation had no real say in their own fate. To provide context to their stories and the legalistic snare in which they were entrapped, the social and legal background to their status in Canadian society, or more accurately, their "spoiled" status in Canadian society, are analyzed (Goffman 1963; 1986).

The incarceration of people classified as having some sort of a mental disability was suffused with race, gender, class, sexual, and disability characteristics in Canada as elsewhere (Appignanesi 2007; Menzies 2002; Menzies and Palys 2006; Metzl 2009; Mitchinson 1991; Taylor 2009; Ussher 1991). Incarceration of native born Canadians could end up becoming a life sentence in institutions for people labeled "mentally deficient," as John Radford and Deborah Carter Park show (Radford and Park 1993, 387). Similarly, during the early decades of the twentieth century, people confined in institutions for people labeled mentally ill in Ontario could and did spend decades behind prisonlike walls. In these sites, treatment was little more than a mixture of exploitative patient labor, long periods in a regulated bath called hydrotherapy to supposedly calm "excited" individuals, various sedatives and, toward the middle of the century, invasive and barbaric physical interventions such as lobotomy (Reaume 2000; 2008). For the purposes of this chapter, however, the focus is not on experiences of long-term incarceration in a Canadian context but rather on how incarceration in psychiatric hospitals, in 1920s Toronto in particular, was an intermediate station in the process of expulsion back to one's country of origin as a rejected resident of Canada. While race and class are shown as of central importance in the experiences of the two men whose lives and expulsions are recounted here, it is also evident that, for one of these men, advantageous racial and ethnic categorization did not help in the long run, as his status as a mad immigrant trumped whatever social advantages he had as a member of the dominant linguistic and cultural group. It is also essential to point out the bureaucratic mechanisms Canada shared as part of the British empire, in which it was possible to "dispose" of unwanted people deemed disabled from one part of the empire to the other. British imperialism made such expulsions easier for officials on both sides of the Atlantic by having in place a common communication network which made expulsion all that more efficient when set in motion between Canada and Britain, than was the case outside the empire, as occurred between Canada and Poland. Ultimately confinement leading to expulsion as a disabled person is shown as the motivating factor above all in how these two immigrants were viewed by those who determined their fate, which ultimately was to be expelled with the intention of long-term confinement—though not in Canada where "foreign" disabled people were not welcome.

Legal and Eugenic Context

As Robert Menzies (1998) and Ena Chadha (2008) show in their respective articles, Canadian immigration laws in the early twentieth century became increasingly punitive by expanding the time period a person could be deported after arriving in the country. It was not a coincidence that this was a time when large-scale immigration, followed by the political and social turmoil in the aftermath of World War I, led to prejudices toward certain "types" of immigrants. This included people who were other than English, particularly white or northern European, persons with real or perceived disabilities, as well as individuals considered as politically suspect in the first "Red scare" following the 1917 Bolshevik seizure of power in Russia (Francis 2010). All of these factors influenced the expansion of who came under the federal Canadian Immigration Act when amendments were made between 1906 and 1919. The Immigration Act was revised during this period so that a person who was deemed mentally disabled after arriving and taking up residence in the country could be deported. In 1906 the law allowed deportation within two years of arrival, in 1910 the law was amended to allow deportation within three years of arrival, and finally in 1919 a person could be expelled for up to five years after arrival if judged as coming under the law's provisions (Chadha 2008, 7–8, 12; Menzies 1998, 154–158). These revisions were facilitated by the involvement of reputed "experts" on immigrants deemed "mentally defective" such as Toronto Psychiatrist C. K. Clarke. He helped to influence policy makers in Ottawa to expand the criteria for exclusion both in terms of the years allowed to ensnare someone and by his claim that upwards of half of asylum inmates were immigrants, which he claimed was nearly three times the overall number of Ontario's residents who were born outside Canada (Chadha 2008, 11–12).

By 1927, when another Immigration Act revision was promulgated, the main group of people targeted were those deemed as spies, political radicals, and people with varying categories of mental disabilities (Chadha 2008, 16). Thus, the year before Daniel and Andrew (the immigrants who are the focus of this chapter) were deported, Canadian immigration officials were provided with ever stricter and more expansive laws in which people regarded as having a mental disability of some kind were subjects for incarceration and deportation, which clearly indicates the eugenic character of this legislation. That the weight of these immigration laws fell upon people from a working-class background, as was the case with both immigrants upon whom this chapter focuses, is reflected as well in the impact of such eugenically motivated measures elsewhere (Grekul, Krahn, and Odynak 2004;Gould 1981; 1996; McLaren 1990; Park and Radford 1998). Racist notions of who was superior and inferior suffused the eugenic agenda and influenced all manner of policies, including that which pertained to immigrants, as Stephen Jay Gould (1981; 1996) has shown in regard to the United States and Angus McLaren (1990) to Canada.

The anti-Semitic racist beliefs of eugenics proponents were present in Canada as elsewhere, though there were also prominent Jews in this country and abroad who supported eugenics in the early twentieth century. Eugenics appealed to them, as it did to so many others, owing to its anti-disability message that sought to rid the world of people labeled "mentally defective" (McLaren 1990, 76–77; Uzarczyk 2007). Nevertheless, among poor immigrants who endured the full brunt of these laws and who were not part of the public discussion about these ideas swirling around elites in 1920s Toronto, there can be no doubt that these eugenic laws were experienced as encompassing class, religious, and race prejudice. Carolyn Strange notes that powerful Toronto Police Magistrate George Denison, who held the post for over 40 years until 1921, "openly subscribed to a racial schema in which Jews were 'neurotic,' southern Europeans 'hot-blooded,' Chinese 'degenerate,' and Native peoples and blacks 'savage' and 'primitive.' In contrast, Protestant Anglo-Celtic Canadians sat at the top of the racial hierarchy..." (Knowles 2000; Strange 1995, 16;) With views like this among the top law enforcement officials in the city, it is no wonder that immigrants from marginalized communities were easy prey to state intervention and deportation when the opportunity arose.

Yet, while English speaking immigrants from the British Isles undoubtedly had a degree of privilege bestowed on them by being part of the dominant linguistic and cultural group in places like Toronto, they also had to endure eugenic based prejudices from the local elite related to class and disability. For as Angus McLaren observes, while British eugenicists thought native born people who left the United Kingdom for Canada were among the best "stock," "Canadian eugenicists tended to assume the opposite, that the failed and ineffectual dregs of Britain were being dumped on the Dominion" (McLaren 1990, 57). These attitudes were transformed from words to deeds in which direct intervention occurred in the lives of people in their own neighborhoods, in hospital wards, and ultimately, by forcing them onto a ship out of the country to a fate that is usually impossible to trace.

Daniel G.

Daniel G. was a 21-year-old man when he was admitted to Toronto Psychiatric Hospital in October 1927, less than a year and a half after he arrived in Toronto in May 1926 (Daniel G. patient file).[1] A poor laboring man, Daniel was originally from rural Poland and spoke little English, with few possessions other than the clothes on his back (Daniel G, Ward Admission Record, January 4, 1928).[2] After arriving in Halifax from Danzig, Daniel traveled to Toronto where he lived with his brother and worked in tailor shops in the Jewish quarter of town until he quit because of "not feeling well" (Daniel G, Clinical Chart, January 4, 1928). Daniel stated he had worked for ten months in Toronto until July 1927, where he toiled for four months dying fur for 14–15 hours a day starting at eight in the morning, earning 12 dollars a week, as well as operating a machine in an embroidery factory.

Originally told by a doctor to rest in bed after first complaining of illness, Daniel then had visions that summer of death stalking him. He seemed to feel better when on October 8, 1927, three days after the start of Yom Kippur, Daniel "became quite excited and began to preach in the synagogue saying he was the creator" (Daniel G, Clinical Record, October 15, 1927).[3] He was taken home and, four days later, admitted to the Toronto Psychiatric Hospital where he stayed until the beginning of January 1928 when he was transferred to the Toronto provincial psychiatric hospital at 999 Queen Street West. Throughout his time in hospital, it was clear that there were language barriers most Canadian-born patients of European background did not have to face, as well as insecurity about whether or not he would be allowed to stay in the country.

After responding to the admitting Queen Street doctor that Warsaw was the capital of Poland, the physician noted "This was about the only question he could answer" (Daniel G., Clinical Record, January 4, 1928). Yet, elsewhere in the same file it is plain that communication between Daniel and his doctors was impeded by language barriers on both sides. Daniel is frequently recorded as singing and talking to himself "in his native tongue"— presumably Hebrew or Yiddish as he is also recorded as speaking in the "Jewish language" several times (Daniel G., Clinical Record, October 17, 24, 1927; Clinical Chart, January 11, 14, 16, 1928).[4] In spite of this observation, during the admission interview at the provincial hospital on Queen Street, his clinical file does not indicate that this would have impeded his ability to answer questions in a language with which he was not conversant. While Daniel was not viewed as a threat to himself or anyone else, his views of himself as the messiah and ideas that his brother was plotting to poison him led to his being locked up. Yet, while the precipitating cause that led to his confinement was hearing voices, Daniel also told doctors at Queen Street upon admission in January 1928 that "this was all a bluff" and refrained from telling them the content of his "hallucinations." Almost immediately after this statement, Daniel is recorded as stating his messianic beliefs that "he is the Jewish God and has been since the Jewish New Year, about five months ago" [sic—the Jewish New Year would have been three months earlier]. These views were first recorded shortly after his admission to the Toronto Psychiatric Hospital in the fall of 1927 when the doctor declared that "he says that he is the god of the world and that all people are Jews, that he is the father of all people" while bluntly telling another doctor a few weeks later, "I am the Jewish God, I own all the world. You don't think so. Go to hell then" (Daniel G., Clinical Record, October 24, 1927; Physician's Statement of Patient's History, November 15, 1927). Daniel also accused his brother Saul of trying to poison him owing to Daniel being a "Jewish god," and was recorded as saying that the people who said they were his relatives "are not his true relatives at all." He also mentioned that electricity was sent into his body by external agents. Although he described himself as "a trifle nervous," Daniel claimed that there was nothing wrong with him (Daniel G., Clinical Record, January 4, 1928).

While at the Toronto Psychiatric Hospital, Daniel's diagnosis was first given as Dementia Praecox, or schizophrenia as it was later more commonly known.[5] This diagnosis was considered the most hopeless label a psychiatric patient could receive from a physician, something which occurred to both individuals with whom this chapter is concerned. Two days later Daniel was recorded as showing "a naturalness of expression and a playfulness in his replies suggestive of manic reaction." His personality comes through in his file, as when he is recorded stating that he wants "all the people to go to hell," and that "I want to sleep, eat and have a good time, and the world belongs to me" (Daniel G., Clinical Record, October 24, 1927). These comments indicate that whatever language barriers existed he was able to communicate effectively in some ways. When he was transferred from the Toronto Psychiatric Hospital to the provincial asylum on Queen Street, Daniel was diagnosed as having "manic excitement" but less than three weeks later this was changed to Catatonic Dementia Praecox, even though nothing in his file hints at him being in a state of catatonia as he was physically and verbally quite active at this time (Daniel G., Clinical Record, January 5 192[8]; January 23, 1928). Indeed, during his first month at the Queen Street asylum, Daniel is recorded during hydrotherapy treatment when he was immersed for hours on end in supposedly calming bath water, as "somewhat euphoric," "pleasant and affable," and engaging in "a lot of loud talking and singing while in the bath" though he was quieter a few days later (Daniel G., Clinical Record, January 9, 11, 21, 1928). By mid-March when daily records of his time in the Queen Street asylum end, though he would remain there for over five more months, he was recorded as "somewhat depressed." Evidently he no longer rejected his brother's existence who was recorded as having spoken with Daniel, and he no longer blamed Saul for trying to poison him and instead claimed this noxious substance was because of electric shocks from an unknown source for which he needed "some good medicine to relieve this condition" (Daniel G, Clinical Record, March 13, 1928).

While Daniel's Jewish faith is not explicitly stigmatized with anti-Semitic remarks in the file, his religion and heritage are repeatedly emphasized, both in the characterization of his speaking "the Jewish language" and in his foreignness as a Polish immigrant. That he was an observant Jew appears most certain given his feelings that he was a god, which he preached at the synagogue a few days before being confined. Moreover, he is frequently recorded as singing or talking in his native tongue, which may have been him praying at times, as when a nurse recorded at the Queen Street hospital that Daniel in January 1928 was "standing along side of bed talking in Jewish language out the window," and another time as "Talking loudly in the bath to himself in his own language" (Daniel G., Clinical Chart, January 5, 6, 11, 16, 1928, March 10, 1928).[6] The one entry on his hair in his entire file notes that it was "long and black" which is consistent with the style worn by Orthodox Jewish men, unlike most other men in Toronto during this period when long hair was not common for males (Daniel G., Clinical Chart, January 3, 1928). He was therefore in every respect looked upon and recorded as foreign in appearance, language, and manner. Whatever "othering" Daniel was subjected to, he clearly made numerous attempts to be friendly by talking in an amicable way with both the nurses and other patients as is indicated in his clinical chart (Daniel G., Clinical Chart, January 5, 8, 10, 12, 14, 1928; March 15, 1928).[7] Thus, this sense of "otherness" to those who recorded his time in this hospital did not prevent him from reaching out to those around him in a way that was more welcoming than were the state and medical officials who so wished him to be gone from Canada.

The state did not wait long after his admission in October 1927 to begin the deportation process. Within six weeks of his first admission to Toronto Psychiatric Hospital, notice was sent by James Mitchell from the Canadian Department of Immigration and Colonization that Daniel had "appealed against my decision when I ordered his deportation; I am in receipt of advice from the Department that the appeal has been dismissed and his deportation will be carried out as soon as the necessary passport can be secured from the Polish authorities for his return"

(Daniel G., Mitchell to Farrar, December 1, 1927). His fate was thus sealed very early after being incarcerated; all that remained was getting the proper papers in order. A provincial health department official, however, noted that such papers were not received as quickly as they wanted. When writing to the Queen Street hospital superintendent in late December about the pending transferal of Daniel, H. M. Robbins wrote: "This patient is a case for deportation...but as you probably know from previous experience, the Government of Poland have not been prompt in assisting us with their cases of deportation"(Daniel G., Robbins to Superintendent, December 28, 1927). A month later, James Mitchell from the Department of Immigration requested, on behalf of the Consul General of Poland, that doctors send him a brief medical history of Daniel, including his diagnosis and whether or not he would require someone to travel with him and if he would need further hospitalization upon reaching his home country. The required letter was sent in which Daniel was noted as needing "careful oversight," though he was also known as nonthreatening, including toward himself; confinement in Poland was also recommended. Extraordinarily, Daniel is characterized in this letter for the Polish authorities as "unable to carry on any intelligent conversation," without any reference to the language barriers he encountered with people who did not speak Polish, Hebrew, or Yiddish. Nor is there reference to his limited ability to speak English, or to the fact that his medical file clearly records his engaging in comprehensible conversations with both fellow patients and staff (Daniel G., Mitchell to Fletcher, January 24, 1928; Superintendent "To Whom It May Concern," January 25, 1928). Nothing further is recorded on the deportation process until mid-June when the federal Immigration agent noted that the Polish government had Daniel's passport and was preparing to find a place in an asylum in Poland for him upon his enforced return (Daniel G., Mitchell to McKay, June 15, 1928).

In the meantime, as the deportation process continued to make its way through bureaucratic and diplomatic channels, efforts were made to get Daniel's daily fee paid by Jewish organizations. Daniel's brother Saul told hospital officials in late 1927 that he did not have money to pay this cost and thus Daniel was made a public ward (Daniel G., Robbins to Superintendent, December 28, 1927). However, by the following summer the Jewish Immigrant Aid Society of Canada had agreed to pay for the one dollar a day cost of Daniel's room and board for the entire time of his confinement at the provincial asylum on Queen Street since his admission on January 3, 1928. The account was honored in full with Executive Secretary, A. J. Paull writing to the Queen Street hospital bursar that the Toronto office of the Jewish Immigrant Aid Society stated that they "are glad to inform you that they will take care of the maintenance" of Daniel G. (Daniel G., Mitchell to Robbins, July 7, 1928; Paull to Bursar, July 24, 1928). This amount was paid for every day of the eight months he was confined in 999 Queen Street. His deportation, therefore, could not have been hastened by a financial motive to release a "pressing burden" on the state as Daniel was thus otherwise financially supported (Daniel G., Paull to Steward, March 14, 1929; Boag to Jewish Immigrant Aid Society, July 3, 1929).[8] In spite of this support, Daniel was discharged from the provincial hospital in Toronto on Queen Street on August 31, 1928 as the first part of his deportation from Canada back to Poland (Daniel G., Discharge papers, September 1, 1928). The letter from the hospital's Assistant Superintendent, which was to accompany him back to his native country, gave his diagnosis as Dementia Praecox and noted that Daniel "has shown neither suicidal or homicidal tendencies while here and at the present time is considerably improved" (Daniel G., Assistant Superintendent

"To Whom It May Concern," August 28, 1928). Almost half a year earlier the hospital's medical superintendent had written to a local representative of the Jewish Immigrant Aid Society that Daniel's "chances of recovery are poor" (Daniel G., Superintendent to Miss Cohen, March 14, 1928). The contradiction between these two reports indicates the nebulous character of his diagnosis that served as a convenient basis upon which to confine and expel an unwanted mad immigrant who was originally from a foreign, non-English speaking land and who, moreover, belonged to a religious minority that had long been subjected to discrimination in both his native and adopted lands.

In addition to the evidence in his file which notes that he appealed (and lost) the deportation order, we can be certain of Daniel's opposition to his deportation by several other brief comments he made, which are recorded in his clinical chart by nurses at the Queen Street hospital. Referring to his having left Poland when he "wasn't a year old" a nurse recorded in January 1928 that "He likes Canada, thinks it is a fine country + never intends to go back [to Poland]" (Daniel G., Clinical Chart, January 8, 1928). A few days later, undoubtedly in recognition that Canadian authorities did not want him to remain in the country, he was recorded as saying "that his home is in U.S.A. + he wants to go back there" (Daniel G., Clinical Chart, January 11, 1928). His final recorded statement makes it clear what his views were on being incarcerated in the provincial hospital when he informed a nurse that "he dont [sic] want to stay here. Says I want my own people[.] I want out of here" (Daniel G., Clinical Chart, March 10, 1928). Ending his incarceration and stopping his related expulsion from the country was out of Daniel's control. All he could do was to voice some form of protest, which is what the records show he did do to no avail. Another man from another country, though one perceived as less "foreign" among Canadian officials, had some local avenues of support to prevent his forced departure, though, as seen, his expulsion was not only assured, it was even swifter than Daniel's deportation.

Andrew T.

Andrew T. was a 42-year-old married laborer with two children when he was confined in Toronto's Queen Street asylum on the same day as Daniel G., January 3, 1928, after being transferred from the Toronto Psychiatric Hospital. Unlike Daniel, who had no other disability recorded, Andrew was recorded as being both deaf and of "defective" appearance; though judging from the records in his file, he did have some hearing ability as he is recorded as having heard conversations at various times. Andrew accused his wife, whose first name is not recorded anywhere in the file, of having affairs with local men who arranged romantic trysts with her, while also believing that coworkers engaged in plots against him both on and off the job; he was diagnosed by one of the admitting physicians as having Paranoid Dementia Praecox, or paranoid schizophrenia (Andrew T., patient file; Admission papers, December 20, 1927; Mental Examination statements, December 21, 1927).[9] Like Daniel, Andrew too was a first time admission to a psychiatric hospital in Toronto (or anywhere else as far as their records indicate) and, like Daniel, he too expressed opposition to his incarceration. Andrew demanded to know the reason for his confinement and when admitted to the hospital "knelt down and prayed that he and his wife would be spared..." (Andrew T., Clinical Record, January 4, 1928). By 1928 Andrew had lived in Canada with his wife, who was also from Britain, for a total of almost nine years since 1911. Their first period of Canadian residence was for four years during which he toiled in a foundry until 1914. They returned to England in 1915 when Andrew served a year in the British Army during World War I. They remained together in their home country for eight years. He returned to Toronto in August, 1923, a date which would turn out to be crucial for his eventual deportation. During this latter period he worked at several jobs, including the public transit company, gas company, and a button factory among other places, until being employed at a local electrical company. He quit the latter position because of on-the-job conflicts and illness two weeks prior to being arrested and incarcerated in the hospital. His idea that his wife was "leading an immoral life" led him to locking her up several times, along with their daughter, in their house believing she was in league with men who were trying to poison him (Andrew T., Clinical Record, December 17, 1927, January 4, 1928). His wife said he quit work after he complained for several weeks of plots to get him fired, which she investigated and reported to be unfounded (Andrew T., Clinical Record, December 17, 1927, January 4, 1928).

According to his wife, after he quit work he became "uncontrollable" at home. This included Andrew believing in conspiracies, going around to neighbors asking them to sign a petition against his wife's behavior, locking his wife and daughter indoors, and finally being arrested after his wife called the police, one of whom was her own brother on an occasion when Andrew asked her for a razor for unknown purposes (Andrew T., Clinical Record, December 19, 1927). Though he denied that he had gone around with a petition about his wife, Andrew confirmed the rest of what she reported. He did not fault her for mentioning that he spoke about being poisoned since he thought it came from gas that he continued to report smelling on the hospital ward. Andrew also felt it was "somebody other than his wife" engaging in these plots; he did not mind his wife's visits, but he wished his brother-in-law did not visit because of his apparent role in physically restraining and incarcerating him (Andrew T., Clinical Record, December 29, 1927). Since his madness was of sudden onset, according to his wife only a matter of two months from when Andrew started believing in plots against him at work leading to turmoil at home, the diagnosis was uncertain in that it was believed he might later improve. Nevertheless, he was given the most hopeless diagnosis possible, as far as recovery prospects were concerned among physicians at both the Toronto Psychiatric Hospital and Queen Street provincial asylum: "Paranoid Dementia Praecox" (Andrew T., Clinical Record, January 5, 1928 [TPH]; January 23, 1928 [999]).[10] Unlike Daniel, whose plight was unknown beyond people immediately involved, the situation of Andrew and his family was publicized in a local newspaper when political pressure was exerted to try to prevent the deportation of himself and, eventually, his wife and their two children.

In early March 1928, an article in a Toronto newspaper appeared which noted that Andrew was about to be deported because he had not yet lived as a citizen for five consecutive years in the country. By this time, Andrew had lived in Toronto for a total of almost nine years, from 1911–1915 and since August 1923; although neither time was for five consecutive years, it was nearly so for his second period of residence. It needs also to be mentioned that, as discussed earlier, the five year provision was only in effect since 1919. When he had left Canada in 1915 he had been in the country for over the existing three year maximum limit imposed by law in 1910, after which expulsion was no longer possible. Thus, if the earlier time period had been taken into consideration on its own narrow legal limits, he should not have been subjected later to expulsion since he had surpassed the residency requirement then. Evidently, this no longer counted, and his file does not indicate consideration of his earlier length of residence by the authorities in their drive to expel him. No doubt, the soon approaching fifth year anniversary of his second arrival also helped to speed up his deportation proceedings. As well, the fact that immigrants to Canada from Britain did not need to get their papers in order from a foreign government, as was the case with Daniel, since they were all subjects of the same crown authority emanating in Britain. This allowed the bureaucratic machinery to act even more speedily in Andrew's case since no third party government officials needed to be involved, as was necessary for people born in Poland.

The collaboration of medical, legal, and state bureaucracies within the British empire, which helped to quickly "process" Andrew's deportation, did so owing to the connections developed between authorities in both countries as part of the empire. The context of eugenics deportations from Canada was based on a moral panic engineered internationally by pro-eugenics physicians and public officials on both sides of the Atlantic. In Canada, where three million immigrants arrived between 1896 and 1914, including Andrew T. and his wife during their initial residency, pro-imperialist psychiatrists such as C. K. Clarke had long advocated expelling people deemed "unfit" because of either their race or medical diagnoses (Dowbiggin 1995, 607). Links between Canadian and British officials were part of well-established contacts between members of the empire, as well as with wider international medical circles elsewhere. In 1912, Canadians were among more than seven hundred people from around the world who went to London as part of an international eugenics conference (McLaren 1990, 23). By the time Andrew T.'s expulsion was in process in 1928, pro-eugenics ideas were firmly entrenched among state and medical bureaucracies in both Canada and Britain. While his being a citizen of the colonial "mother country' undoubtedly helped him to gain entry to Canada, this same colonial link helped to more efficiently sever his relationship with the country he wanted to call home, through expedited bureaucratic methods that both countries shared.

According to the local newspaper article, which mentioned that Andrew, his wife, and their two children were all subject to deportation, their life together had not been regarded as traumatic until just before this episode: "The family has looked upon the land of their adoption as a veritable Utopia until the severity of last winter and the resulting lack of remunerative employment everything went awry and the father, incapacitated through worry now finds himself an inmate of the Queen street mental hospital pending the execution of the deportation order" (Andrew T., newspaper article in file). The deportation would have already proceeded but for the intervention of local municipal politicians and a Senator in Ottawa who was also the council's lawyer and who had the order delayed. Noting that the family house was "well kept," a reporter also recorded that Mr. T. "had spent every cent on returning to this country in order to provide for a cosy nook for his loved ones" (Andrew T., newspaper article in file). The article explained that less than a year after he had returned to Canada in 1923, Mrs. T. and their two children joined him in May 1924. At first, all proceeded well with work and a small home. A period of unemployment caused Andrew distress, and though he secured other work, afterwards he began to act more suspicious of his wife and other people he knew which led to his confinement. On February 23, 1928 Mrs. T. received a letter that stated that in five days her husband would be deported and she should bring his belongings to the hospital. In the meantime, she and her two children would be allowed another six months leeway before a decision on their status in the country would be made (Andrew T., newspaper article in file).[11]

Mrs. T. said, "What can we do if we are deported to England?...We have no friends living there and all our money is invested in getting the home together. If they only give us a chance when dad becomes well his job is open for him and besides while I can work, we are not likely to become public charges..." (Andrew T., newspaper article in file). Upon Andrew's confinement, the mother's allowance board sent five dollars per week to the family. When this ended the local municipality approved four dollars a week in support, with Deputy Reeve I. E. Woolner stating "the council were doing everything in their power to have the [deportation] order canceled" (Andrew T., newspaper article in file). These efforts were motivated by the clearly felt sense of injustice that a man and his family were under threat of deportation even though the individual concerned had been in the country for well past the five years required to prevent such an occurrence, though not continuously as a result of volunteering for war service. Said Deputy Reeve Woolner, "a man going home to enlist should not have lost his Canadian status. The family have no friends in England and why send a family to England with an insane father. It's up to the province to look after this man" (Andrew T., newspaper article in file). The day after this article was published, 999 Medical Superintendent McKay wrote to Deputy Provincial Secretary Robbins that, while quiet on the ward and not violent or a danger to himself, Andrew's "outlook for recovery" was "the reverse of hopeful" as, in addition to persecutory ideas mentioned already, he had threatened to kill his wife which "must be treated seriously" (Andrew T., Superintendent to Robbins, March 6, 1928). His deportation therefore proceeded forthwith with a recommendation that Andrew be institutionalized "on arrival" (Andrew T., Superintendent "To Whom It May Concern," February 24, 1928).

While awaiting expulsion, in addition to expressing opposition to his deportation, Andrew was also busily engaged in patient labor, such as polishing the floors and general cleaning duties that are repeatedly mentioned in the records of his brief three month confinement at the Queen Street hospital (Andrew T., Clinical Record, January 9, 17, 1928; Clinical Chart, January 7, 11, 12, 14, 15, 1928, March 13, 14, 1928). On April 3, 1928, Andrew was reported in his file as discharged from the psychiatric institution in the process of being deported from the country in the company of an Immigration Officer. His Clinical Record notes "On leaving the hospital his condition showed some slight improvement. He is still quite paranoidal toward his wife and while waiting to leave the Hospital told me she was downstairs bothering him" (Andrew T., Clinical Record, April 3, 1928; deportation papers, April 4, 1928). An idea of the financial despair he was in can be gleaned from his medical file which records that three months before he was deported Andrew could not pay any of the expenses for his deportation, nor could anyone else in his personal life and that there were no known relatives back in England, just as his wife had stated in the newspaper article.[12]

An undated letter from Andrew after he arrived in Birmingham gives a local address, though it is not clear whether it is a hospital or a private residence. In this letter he wrote that he asked the ship's doctor: "what charge I was deported on + he could not answer me + he only asked me about money and I told I had not got any, as I travelled [sic] all the way through without a cent + I told the Dr that my wife was on the boat + the children...she was using Telepathy all the way to Liverpool + I have neither seen her or the children since I left the Hospital......"(Andrew T., Letter "To Dr Hay and Supertendent [sic]" from Andrew T., undated, Birmingham,

England). This is the last definite word of Andrew's existence in his file. His reference to his wife and children on board may have related to his ideas when in the asylum that his wife, in particular, was nearby and thus he thought the same on the ship back to Britain. Given the evidence in his file that Mrs. T and her two children were given a six-month reprieve after Andrew T's expulsion before deciding whether to deport them, there is no reason to believe that they left when he did. What happened to all of them in the long run is not known.

Conclusion

The preemptory way in which people like Daniel and Andrew were deported reflects the administratively strict manner in which their lives were so quickly dispatched from Canadian shores. Barbara Roberts (1988) writes how, once the process was in place, there was next to nothing someone subjected to a deportation order could do to stop it:

> Deportation was an administrative, not a judicial matter; therefore, prospective deports did not have the rights that they would have had in a judicial process. The administrative proceeding was based on a hearing in front of a panel of officers of the Department who were appointed by the Minister...The single operative right, as far as most cases were concerned, was the right to appeal the decision of the Board of Inquiry to the Minister of Immigration. If the hearing had been carried out according to the regulations, following the procedures outlined in the Act, the proper forms filled out, the proper phrasing used, and the evidence adduced in standardized ways according to directives issued by the Department, then there would seldom be a basis for overturning the decision...The Immigration Act gave officials of the Department the power to determine and administer deportation with virtually no interferences from the courts or Parliament." (Roberts 1988, 36)

This helps to explain both the quick dismissal of Daniel's appeal of his deportation and the failure of political pressure from local politicians and a Senator to stop Andrew's expulsion. Yet nothing can explain their incarceration and expulsion more than their status as immigrants deemed mad. In this sense, their relatively short-term Canadian incarceration needs to be understood as being intended as long-term confinement through expulsion to a mental institution in their home country, as was recommended in deportation documents for both Daniel and Andrew. This was a potentially grim future for both men, given that they were both labeled with the most "hopeless" diagnoses at that time for mad people—Dementia Praecox. What happened to them is unknown other than that that they were both sent back unwillingly to their native lands.

In Daniel's case, there can be little doubt as to the fate that awaited him in the long run. As he would have been 22 years old upon deportation in 1928 and in good physical health, it is more than likely that he was still alive when Nazi Germany invaded and conquered Poland in 1939, 11 years later almost to the day from when he was deported. As a Jew and, if he was still alive and in a psychiatric hospital, a psychiatric patient, his life was of no value to his country's conquerors and he would almost certainly have been murdered along with millions of fellow

Jews and thousands of psychiatric patients.[13] While no one in 1928 could foresee what would happen in Europe over a decade later, there is no doubt that the international connections made by pro-eugenics physicians and policy makers on both sides of the Atlantic created a climate of intolerance, which led to the expulsions of people deemed disabled. The incarceration, deportation and, ultimately, perhaps the murder of Daniel G. had he still been alive in 1939, was prepared for in an increasingly intensified process of exclusion and persecution under the aegis of eugenics legislation in Canada and internationally.

In his study of the connections between American and German eugenics advocates before and during the Nazi period, Stefan Kuhl (1994) has shown the significance of international collaboration in the international eugenics movement in fostering a climate that made the lives of people like Daniel G. all the more precarious. As Kuhl notes, the publication in German of a well known 1913 book about eugenics policies in the United States helped to forge these links, "since it allowed European eugenicists insight into events on the other side of the Atlantic" (Kuhl 1994; 2002, 17). This collaboration included the participation in international eugenics conferences by Canadian academics and doctors in 1912, 1921, and 1932 (McLaren 1990, 25, 128). All of this meant that to be incarcerated and deported as a foreign-born mad person became a matter of routine policy, no matter what the impact on the individual concerned. One does not find a shred of concern expressed by state or medical officials in the documents regarding either Daniel G. or Andrew T. about the impact that deportation would have on them.

Daniel G., being a Jew, would have been targeted for murder in the Nazi killings, whether or not he had been a psychiatric patient. Yet, his status as a psychiatric patient in 1928 and his subsequent designation as being unwanted under eugenic immigration policies promoted in Canada, as part of the wider international eugenics movement, is what led to his being deported back to Poland over a decade before it became a site of mass extermination for Jews. His incarceration and expulsion offer a horrific reminder of the devastating consequences of the international movement to implement eugenic immigration policies on people deemed disabled, like this young man. In his case it literally meant the difference, over time, between life and death. For Daniel G., it would have almost certainly been the latter.

Andrew, in contrast, is not as sympathetic a person as is Daniel. As his case file shows, he abused his wife and locked both her and his daughter in the house and threatened her physically, all in contrast to Daniel who was never at any time recorded as threatening anyone. Andrew also toiled long hours and, while apparently somewhat better off than Daniel in that he had saved enough to buy a small house for his family, both men were poor working-class laborers whose class background militated against their being regarded with anything but contempt by officials who adhered to eugenic immigration policies that sought to rid Canada of foreign born, economically marginalized mad people who ended up in asylums.

There is no doubt that both men were experiencing some form of madness given their recorded statements, which undoubtedly was used to disparage and diminish their worth as human beings, particularly as immigrants. The social stressors that influenced these views are difficult to trace in regard to Daniel's madness, which was expressed in the belief that he was the messiah in addition to his denial of the existence of members of his family at times. Andrew's madness can be seen in his recorded statements and handwritten letters in his file, in which he wrote that his wife was plotting against him along with others, which, at least insofar as his wife is concerned, was not the case. Uncertain employment conditions also contributed to his distraught mental state. Evidence also shows that Mrs. T. was actually trying to prevent her husband's deportation, that she supported him with visits while he was in hospital and, even if allowing for the fact that she too might eventually be deported if he was expelled, the newspaper article makes it clear that she wanted him to stay in Canada and she also had feelings of care and concern for him. Thus Andrew had local supports, even local political support from politicians, which was unusual for an immigrant classified as an unwanted disabled person. So too did Daniel have support, even if not quite so well connected as Andrew's family, which would have enabled him to continue to stay in the country had officials been more amenable to his remaining. His brother Saul also visited him in hospital, and the financial aid of the Jewish Immigrant Aid Society indicates there was wider community support from fellow Jews, at least in regard to his hospital costs. That Daniel received such monetary support, and that Andrew had a long history of employment until shortly before he was confined as well as a supportive family and house to return to, disproves the idea of their being a "burden" on society, one of the standard claims of the eugenics movement (Lombardo 2008, 7–11; McLaren 1990, 52–55).

That both men were still subjected to deportation in spite of such supports, and given the ethnic and racial privileges that Andrew had by dint of his country of origin and his many years of prior residence in Canada—though interrupted by war service that did not seem to make any difference to Canadian officials—underlines the clear motives that influenced their expulsion by the state. No matter what their background or country of origin, their status as mentally disabled immigrants trumped everything else about them, and thus they were incarcerated on the road to expulsion to what was intended to be longer term confinement back in their home countries. It is clear that it was their categorization as mentally disabled above all else that led to their incarceration and then expulsion as unwanted people whose mental state and foreign birth, no matter how much others were supporting them locally, superseded all else. Like so many before and after them, Daniel G. and Andrew T. were deported as a result of their "spoiled" status as mad immigrants, devoid of worth to elite policy makers and medical officials in their adopted land.

Notes

1. Daniel G., Patient File # 12001 Archives of Ontario, RG 10, Series 20-B-2, Queen Street Mental Health Centre Casefiles, Admissions and Readmissions. All documents referring to Daniel G. cited below are contained in this patient file. Owing to Ontario's confidentiality laws governing access to provincial psychiatric patient records that are less than one hundred years old the actual name and patient file number for Daniel G. are anonymous using pseudonyms, though his actual initials are "D.G." and his patient file can be found in Box Q120. Daniel's clinical records give two dates for his arrival in Canada from Poland: May 3, 1926 recorded in the October 24, 1927 Toronto Psychiatric Hospital Clinical Record and November 29, 1926 recorded in the January 4, 1928 999 Queen Street Clinical Record. Because it is recorded he quit work in July 1927 after feeling ill, and had worked by then for ten months in Toronto, it will be assumed that the earlier arrival date is the correct date because he could not have worked this length of time had he arrived in November 1926 and stopped working the following July.

2. Ward Admission Record, January 4, 1928. No clothes or possessions of any kind are noted on this form as belonging to Daniel when he was admitted to 999 Queen Street West, though less than three months earlier, his ward admission papers from the Toronto Psychiatric Hospital, dated October 12, 1927, list ten clothing items with their being of "fine quality and condition." Polish Jews in early twentieth century Toronto "were the least prosperous of the local Jews in this period…" Stephen A. Speisman, *The Jews of Toronto: A History to 1937* (Toronto: McClelland and Stewart, 1987), 173.

3. Clinical Record, October 15, 1927. His brother was the only relative noted as living in Toronto as Daniel's parents were recorded as living in Poland where his father worked in the clothing industry, while two sisters are mentioned, whose existence Daniel denied, but their place of residence is not stated (October 24, 1927 Clinical Record). His brother said Daniel's madness was of sudden onset. A calendar for October 1927 records that Yom Kippur started on Wednesday, October 5, 1927, three days before Daniel preached in the synagogue, can be found at: http://www .rocketcalendar.com/calendar/1927–10 (Downloaded on March 23, 2011).

4. In his clinical record from the Toronto Psychiatric Hospital which was sent over to Queen Street asylum with Daniel at the time of his January 1928 admission, an entry from October 17, 1927 states he is a "somewhat undernourished foreigner who speaks and understands very little English" though another entry from two days earlier notes that he "can read and write in English and Hebrew." On October 24, 1927 an entry notes "He has been singing in his native tongue…" and on the same date it is recorded that "it is impossible to follow up questions because of his inability to speak English." References to Daniel speaking in the "Jewish language" can be found in his Clinical Chart, distinct from the Clinical Record, the former being handwritten by nurses the latter being typed by doctors. See Clinical Chart January 14, 1928 entry: "talking to a nurse, asks is she is a princess + if she can talk jewish [sic]," indicated he could speak some English to make himself understood. Daniel is also recorded as "crying to himself" and "talking to a visitor in jewish [sic] language" in this same entry. Similar references can be found in Clinical Chart entries for January 11 and 16, 1928.

5. Diagnostic criteria for "dementia praecox" were developed by German Doctor Emil Kraepelin in the 1890s, while the refinement of these concepts into "schizophrenia" was promoted by Swiss physician Eugen Bleuler in 1911. This latter term was not commonly used until at least the 1930s. The diagnosis, "schizophrenia," begins to appear in Ontario provincial psychiatric hospital reports in 1933. J. Hoenig, "Schizophrenia: Clinical Section", in *A History of Clinical Psychiatry: The Origin and History of Psychiatric Disorders*, edited by German Berrios and Roy Porter (London: Athlone, 1995), 342–344; Trevor Turner, "Schizophrenia: Social Section", in *A History of Clinical Psychiatry: The Origin and History of Psychiatric Disorders*, edited by German Berrios and Roy Porter (London: Athlone, 1995), 349–350. Geoffrey Reaume, *Remembrance of Patients Past: Patient Life at the Toronto Hospital for the Insane, 1870–1940* (Toronto, ON: Oxford University Press Canada, 2000), 16–17; 264 n58.

6. Clinical Chart, January 11, 1928. Both entries were made on the same day, five hours apart. Daniel is also recorded as "Singing tunes/songs in foreign language" by another nurse a few days before: Clinical Chart, January 5 and 6, 1928. While visitors are mentioned a few times in his file, the only person specifically identified as a visitor in Daniel's file was his brother, Saul, while other times no name was recorded other than a friend who visited, for example: "Sitting up in bed reading a letter [with] his friend." Clinical Chart, March 10, 1928. Whether Daniel was able to observe the Jewish Sabbath and dietary laws in a way that accorded with his faith

is not mentioned in the records. Daniel was also recorded in his January 16, 1928 Clinical Chart as "lying in bed + head covered" which may also relate to Orthodox Jewish religious practices for men.

7. References to his friendliness with nurses and talking with other patients can be found in: Clinical Chart, January 5, 8, 10, 12, 14, 1928; March 15, 1928. All of this indicates he must have been able to speak some English or communicate in some way to have been understood because there was no reference to other patients or nurses conversing with Daniel in his native tongue.

8. The final two months of Daniel's confinement was paid by the Jewish Immigrant Aid Society in early 1929 when they sent in a $62.00 check for July and August, 1928. A. J. Paull, Executive Secretary, Jewish Immigrant Aid Society of Canada, Montreal, to Steward, Ontario Hospital, Toronto, March 14, 1929; J. A. Boag, Steward, Ontario Hospital, Toronto, to Jewish Immigrant Aid Society, Toronto, July 3, 1929 (enclosing final receipt for payment). This check completed payment for the entire eight months Daniel spent in 999 Queen Street West. Irving Abella and Harold Troper write that the Jewish Immigrant Aid Society was originally founded by the Canadian Jewish Congress in 1919, however it fell apart owing to internal disputes so that: "It lay moribund, little more than a name on stationary letterhead, until the rise of Hitler in Germany and the growth of Fascist organizations in Canada." Irving Abella and Harold Troper, *None Is Too Many: Canada and the Jews of Europe, 1933–1948* (Toronto, ON: Lester & Orpen Dennys Limited, 1983), 10. Such judgment seems too harsh. The evidence in the patient file of Daniel G. provides clear proof that the Jewish Immigrant Aid Society, four and five years before Hitler came to power, provided material support to an impoverished Jewish immigrant and thus was, in his life at least, "more than a name on stationary letterhead."

9. Andrew T., Patient File # 12002 Archives of Ontario, RG 10, Series 20-B-2, Queen Street Mental Health Centre Casefiles, Admissions and Readmissions. Admission papers, Patient history form signed by T. H. Brunton, December 20, 1927; Mental Examination statements signed by W. T. Parry, C. M. Crawford, December 21, 1927, Toronto. All documents referring to Andrew T. cited below are contained in this patient file. Owing to Ontario's confidentiality laws governing access to provincial psychiatric patient records that are less than one hundred years old the actual name and patient file number for Andrew T. are anonymous using pseudonyms, though his actual initials are "A.T.," and his patient file can be found in Box Q120.

10. Andrew T., Clinical Record, Toronto Psychiatric Hospital, January 5, 1928. This entry was the last made on Andrew at the Toronto Psychiatric Hospital after he was transferred. The diagnosis made at 999 Queen Street is in Clinical Record, January 23, 1928.

11. Article from March 1928 newspaper pasted into Andrew's Clinical Record after January 17, 1928 entry. Owing to Ontario's confidentiality laws, the exact date and name of this newspaper cannot be provided because it was found in a patient file and access to it will reveal the patient's and family's identity. In addition to the comments in the newspaper article about the expulsion order, see the letter in Andrew's file from James Mitchell, Department of Immigration and Colonization, Toronto, to Mrs. A. T., February 23, 1928.

12. Information contained on a form addressed to The Superintendent of Immigration, signed by Medical Superintendent F. S. Vrooman, January 5, 1928. Andrew also had no financial support for his hospitalization and thus he was placed on a public ward. See the form in his file entitled: "Office of the Public Trustee" dated January 5, 1928 signed by 999 Queen Street Hospital Superintendent F. S. Vrooman, which

notes that Andrew was placed on the free ward and that this was his first admission. There is an odd postscript to this story: more than three months after his deportation, the local secretary of the Canadian Legion wrote to the 999 Medical Superintendent stating that a man identified only as having the same last name as Andrew T. was causing his wife, Mrs. T., serious problems and was previously under deportation order, which the correspondent wanted enforced. The superintendent wrote back to say an immigration official was looking into this matter, though nothing further is recorded in the file. No first names or initials beyond Mr. and Mrs. T. are identified and as the address supplied by the Legion officer for this particular married couple is different from the home address of the man who was deported in April it seems unlikely this was the same person. Furthermore, their poor family circumstances and the question of how he could have afforded to travel back to the country so soon when he left with nothing and how he could have regained entrance given his very recent history of deportation suggest that this latter identified person was not the same man deported to Britain in April, a destination that a letter makes clear Andrew T. arrived at for certain. See letters in Andrew's file: Charles Nash, Canadian Legion, Toronto, to Superintendent, 999, July 13, 1928; 999 Superintendent to British Empire Service League, Toronto, July 17, 1928.

13. Psychiatric patients in Poland, along with Jews, were early victims of Nazi barbarism in that country. Gotz Aly notes that "two SS commandos murdered more than 10,000 mentally ill people from October 1939 to spring 1940...The murdered were German patients from Pomerania, Germans and Poles from West Prussia and Polish, Jewish and German patients from the Warthegau [area of Poland annexed by Nazi Germany] – a total of at least 10,000 people." Gotz Aly, *Final Solution: Nazi Population Policy and the Murder of European Jews* (London: Arnold, 1999), 70.

References

Abella, Irving, and Harold Troper. 1983. *None Is Too Many: Canada and the Jews of Europe, 1933–1948*. Toronto, ON: Lester & Orpen Dennys Limited.

Aly, Gotz. 1999. *Final Solution: Nazi Population Policy and the Murder of European Jews*. London: Arnold.

Andrew T., Patient File, Box Q120, 1928, Archives of Ontario, RG 10, Series 20-B-2, Queen Street Mental Health Centre Casefiles, Admissions and Readmissions.

Appignanesi, Lisa. 2007. *Sad, Bad and Mad: Women and the Mind-Doctors from 1800*. Toronto, ON: McArthur & Company.

Chadha, Ena. 2008. "'Mentally Defectives' Not Welcome: Mental Disability in Canadian Immigration Law, 1859–1927." *Disability Studies Quarterly* 28(1). http://www.dsq-sds.org/article/view/67/67

Daniel G., Patient File, Box Q120, 1928, Archives of Ontario, RG 10, Series 20-B-2, Queen Street Mental Health Centre Casefiles, Admissions and Readmissions.

Dowbiggin, Ian. 1995. "'Keeping this Young Country Sane': C.K. Clarke, Immigration Restriction, and Canadian Psychiatry, 1890–1925." *The Canadian Historical Review* 76(4): 598–627.

Francis, Daniel. 2010. *Seeing Reds: The Red Scare of 1918–1919, Canada's First War on Terror*. Vancouver: Arsenal Pulp Press.

Goffman, Erving. 1963/1986. *Stigma: Notes on the Management of Spoiled Identity*. New York: Simon & Schuster.

Gould, Stephen Jay. 1981/1996. *The Mismeasure of Man*. New York: W. W. Norton.

Grekul, Jana, Harvey Krahn, and Dave Odynak. 2004. "Sterilizing the 'Feeble-minded': Eugenics in Alberta, Canada, 1929–1972." *Journal of Historical Sociology* 17(4): 358–384.

Hoenig, J. 1995. "Schizophrenia: Clinical Section." In *A History of Clinical Psychiatry: The Origin and History of Psychiatric Disorders*, edited by German Berrios and Roy Porter, 336–348. London: Athlone.

Knowles, Norman. 2000. "Denison, George Taylor." *Dictionary of Canadian Biography Online. (1921–1930) Volume XV.* http://www.biographi.ca/009004 -119.01-e.php?&id_nbr=8101

Kuhl, Stefan. [1994] 2002. *The Nazi Connection: Eugenics, American Racism, and German National Socialism*. New York: Oxford University Press.

Lombardo, Paul A. 2008. *Three Generations, No Imbeciles: Eugenics, the Supreme Court and Buck v. Bell*. Baltimore, MD: Johns Hopkins University Press.

McLaren, Angus. 1990. *Our Own Master Race: Eugenics in Canada, 1885–1945*. Toronto, ON: McLelland & Stewart.

Menzies, Robert. 2002. "Race, Reason, and Regulation: British Columbia's Mass Exile of Chinese 'Lunatics' aboard the *Empress of Russia*, 9 February 1935." In *Regulating Lives: Historical Essays on the State, Society, The Individual, and the Law*, edited by John McLaren, Robert Menzies, and Dorothy Chunn, 196–230. Vancouver: University of British Columbia Press.

———. 1998. "Governing Mentalities: The Deportation of 'Insane' and 'Feebleminded' Immigrants Out of British Columbia from Confederation to World War II." *Canadian Journal of Law and Society* 13(2): 135–178.

Menzies, Robert, and Ted Palys. 2006. "Turbulent Spirits: Aboriginal Patients in the British Columbia Psychiatric System, 1879–1950." In *Mental Health and Canadian Society: Historical Perspectives*, edited by James Moran and David Wright, 149–175. Montreal and Kingston: McGill-Queen's University Press.

Metzl, Jonathan M. 2009. *The Protest Psychosis: How Schizophrenia Became a Black Disease*. Boston, MA: Beacon Press.

Mitchinson, Wendy. 1991. *The Nature of Their Bodies: Women and Their Doctors in Victorian Canada*. Toronto, ON: University of Toronto Press.

Park, Deborah C., and John P. Radford. 1998. "From the Case Files: Reconstructing a History of Involuntary Sterilisation." *Disability & Society* 13(3): 317–342.

Radford, John R., and Deborah Carter Park. 1993. "'A Convenient Means of Riddance': Institutionalization of People Diagnosed as 'Mentally Deficient' in Ontario, 1876–1934." *Health and Canadian Society* 1(2): 369–392.

Reaume, Geoffrey. 2008. "A History of Lobotomy in Ontario." In *Essays in Honour of Michael Bliss: Figuring the Social*, edited by Elsbeth Heaman, Alison Li, and Shelley McKellar, 378–399. Toronto: University of Toronto Press.

———. 2000. *Remembrance of Patients Past: Patient Life at the Toronto Hospital for the Insane, 1870–1940*. Toronto, ON: Oxford University Press Canada.

Roberts, Barbara. 1988. *Whence They Came: Deportation from Canada, 1900–1935*. Ottawa, ON: University of Ottawa Press.

Speisman, Stephen A. 1987. *The Jews of Toronto: A History to 1937*. Toronto, ON: McClelland and Stewart.

Strange, Carolyn. 1995. *Toronto's Girl Problem: The Perils and Pleasures of the City, 1880–1930*. Toronto, ON: University of Toronto Press.

Taylor, Steven J. 2009. *Acts of Conscience: World War II, Mental Institutions and Religious Objectors*. Syracuse, NY: Syracuse University Press.

Turner, Trevor. 1995. "Schizophrenia: Social Section." In *A History of Clinical Psychiatry: The Origin and History of Psychiatric Disorders*, edited by German Berrios and Roy Porter, 349–359. London: Athlone.

Ussher, Jane. 1991. *Women's Madness: Misogyny or Mental Illness?* Amherst: University of Massachusetts Press.

Uzarczyk, Kamila. 2007. "'Moses as Eugeniker'? The Reception of Eugenic Ideas in Jewish Medical Circles in Interwar Poland." In *Blood and Homeland: Eugenics and Racial Nationalism in Central and Southeast Europe, 1900–1940*, edited by Marius Turda and Paul J. Weindling, 283–297. Budapest: Central European University Press.

5

Crippin' Jim Crow: Disability, Dis-Location, and the School-to-Prison Pipeline

Nirmala Erevelles

Introduction

This chapter describes the removal of marked bodies from public generative spaces, such as schools, to restrictive spaces of isolation, violence, and shame, such as prisons. I argue that it is urgent to deploy a more complex analysis of these removals that have brutal consequences not only for those "removed" but also for the possibility of imagining a more inclusive radical transformational politics. The title of this chapter "Crippin' Jim Crow" references the historical practice of legalized removal via separation that was extended to an entire society based on the social category of race as theorized in contemporary analyses in Critical Race Theory and that I now bring to bear on a more recent analytic, "crippin'" from the relatively younger field of Critical Disability Studies. "Crippin'" according to disability studies' scholar Robert McRuer (2006) refers, in part, to critical analytic practices that explore how "cultures of ability/disability are conceived, materialized, spatialized, and populated...[within] geographies of uneven development [and] are mapped onto bodies marked by differences of race, class, gender and ability" (72). In referencing the term "crippin'," McRuer also marks its coincidental association with the Los Angeles-based street gang Crips, whose members often become disabled as a result of gang violence and who are often also confined in incarcerated spaces like prisons. As such, the title of this chapter, "Crippin' Jim Crow" marks the transhistorical confluence of the legacy of plantation slavery and Jim Crow with the more contemporary violence of mass incarceration to foreground a complex intersectional politics of race, class, and disability where incarcerated bodies become profitable commodities in the neoliberal prison-industrial-complex of late capitalism.

In this chapter, I am not just bringing race and disability together in an analytical marriage of convenience, nor am I arguing that racial oppression is like disability oppression and vice versa. Rather, I argue that "becoming disabled" (Erevelles 2011) or "coming out crip" (McRuer 2006) is an historical event with different implications for different bodies that foreground almost simultaneously the painful antagonisms and promising alliances that emerge out of these historical continuities/discontinuities of removal/segregation/incarceration. More specifically, in the latter section of this chapter, I discuss public schooling—that much celebrated space where children are presumably nurtured into productive and accomplished young adults ripe with the promise of our collective futures. But this chapter, once it crosses the threshold of the schoolhouse door, rather than tripping lightly toward a rosy optimism, takes a dismal turn to follow a more brutal trajectory—the school-to-prison pipeline—that emphasizes what La Paperson (2010) has called the "dirty work of schooling" (8).

The school-to-prison pipeline is a "multidimensional process that funnels large numbers of minority students from the classroom into the adult prison system" (Aul IV 2012, 180). This trajectory maps out the problematic continuities between mass schooling and mass incarceration, where one subset of students located at the complex intersection of race, class, and disability find themselves as social outlaws for almost the entire span of their lives in school and thereafter. Here, I invoke the school-to-prison pipeline not merely to refer to the education and criminal justice systems but also to a complex network of laws, rules, and policies supported by the exploitative political economy of late capitalism that Michelle Alexander (2010) has called the New Jim Crow.

Throughout this chapter, I mark the significant ways in which the social category of disability animates this analysis of mass incarceration in its casual insistence on "compulsory able-bodiedness" (McRuer 2006, 2). Compulsory able-bodiedness, just like compulsory heterosexuality, insists that what is both moral and desirable in the neoliberal social contexts of late capitalism is necessarily heteronormative and nondisabled. In these contexts, disability is required to be simultaneously hypervisible and yet invisible in the medicolegal measurement of social and moral worth, serving as the yardstick that resurrects social difference only to hasten its instantaneous disappearance. Therefore, I map out the oppressive consequences of disability's disappearing act on "outlaw" bodies by invoking the transgressive analytic of "coming out crip" or "crippin'" as described earlier.

In the first section, I make the case for "coming out crip" in the confining contexts of mass incarceration. I then follow with a description of how race and disability as historical constructs "become" pathologized via the violent practices of plantation slavery and the subsequent enactment of Jim Crow laws within the exploitative political economy of a burgeoning capitalism. Next, making an analytical leap into more contemporary times, I draw on Alexander's (2010) book, *The New Jim Crow* to mark the historical continuities between the Jim Crow laws of yesteryears and the more contemporary "postcolonial ghetto" (La Paperson 2010) as spaces that continue to outlaw bodies located at the intersections of multiple difference. Arguing that mass-incarcerations are not limited to large institutional settings such as asylums and prisons, the last section describes how disability becomes the animating logic of dis-location that hustles racialized youth along the dreadful trajectory of the school-to-prison pipeline via the everyday normative practices of schooling. Finally, I briefly discuss the implications of this analysis for transformative praxis.

"Coming out Crip" in Incarcerated Spaces

Disability has been rarely mentioned in the context of mass-incarcerations, except for very few exceptions. One such exception is Liat Ben-Moshe's (2011; 2013) scholarship where she points out that discussions relating to mass incarceration seldom include institutions for people with intellectual disabilities or psychiatric hospitals.

Ben-Moshe, however, is careful not to conflate the prison and the asylum together, and in doing so points to their contrary differences. The prison, though punitive in nature, nevertheless has protections in place like due process and sentencing limits, however imperfect they may be (see Chapman, Ben-Moshe, and Carey, this volume). On the other hand, the asylum, although purportedly for rehabilitative care, is involved in the involuntary confinement of its inmates justified by a medical diagnosis that includes an indefinite time of confinement often accompanied by painful treatments such as extended periods of isolation, physical restraints, and electric shock "therapy"—none of this with the inmate's consent. Moreover, even after the spate of deinstitutionalizations that began in the mid 1950s and that closed down mammoth-sized institutions/hospitals, the smaller community living arrangements that have replaced the large institution continue to warehouse their disabled clients in isolated communities. Ironically, many former institutions have now been reopened as prisons, inadvertently reaffirming the painful relationship between institutionalized rehabilitative care and mass incarceration (Ben-Moshe 2011).

One reason disability is seldom mentioned in the context of mass incarceration is the implicit assumption that such confinements are medically necessary for people with intellectual and psychiatric disabilities. In fact, two recent mass killings in the United States in 2012—the shooting deaths of 12 people in an Aurora, Colorado movie theater by the 24-year-old James Holmes and the shooting deaths of 20 children and 8 adults that included the shooter, 21-year-old Adam Lanza at Sandy Hook Elementary School in Newtown, Connecticut—has resurrected a heated public discussion on dangerous stereotypical representations of people diagnosed with mental illnesses/disabilities. Margaret Price (2011) in her book, *Mad at School* describes similar representations of the undergraduate student Seung-Hui Cho who killed 30 people at Virginia Tech University in 2007 and Steve Kazmierczak who killed 6 people at Northern Illinois University in 2008. Although the media downplayed the fact that at least three of these shooters were young white men with easy access to assault rifles, much was made of the allegation that all four men were presumably diagnosed with a mental illness/disability. Price insightfully points out that in each of the public discourses surrounding these mass killings, mental illness/disability appears as the dividing line—the fearsome Other—that sign "of deviance that will separate the killers from 'us'" (151).

Even within radical social theory, disability continues to be perceived as the natural site of abnormality and fearsome difference—the "abject." Drawing on psychoanalytic theory, Julia Kristeva (1982) argues that the abject threatens our illusory notions of the autonomous, normative Self because it represents those terrifying aspects of the Other (disability) that "disturbs identity, system, order" (4), so that we actively repress all memory of its existence from our consciousness. Similarly, Tobin Siebers (2010) describes normative associations of disability with "an aesthetics of human disqualification" (23) where disabled people "are disqualified...found lacking, inept, incompetent, inferior, in need, incapable, degenerate, uneducated, weak, ugly, underdeveloped, diseased, immature, unskilled, frail, uncivilized, defective, and so on" (23). Fiona Kumari Campbell (2009) explains that this negative ontology is propagated via the structural practice of ableism because the "presence of disability upsets the modernist craving for ontological security" (13). Thus, it is no surprise that even radical social theorists of difference distance themselves from any thoughtful discussion of disability because disability remains the acceptable line of separation between "us" and "them." One could also argue that a similar negative ontology is used against criminalized people where the very real walls of the prison serve to separate the "moral us" from the "depraved them."

That disability is implicated in the uneasy alliance between race, class, and criminalization may be apparent in the narrative I will now share with you. As the Parent Teacher Association (PTA) president in my daughter's elementary school—a Title I school (where at least 60% of its students are from underprivileged families and are eligible for either free or reduced lunches provided by the state)—I organized a monthly activity where parents relieve teachers from lunch duty and supervise students in the cafeteria. To most precocious students, the sight of a substitute promises limitless possibilities for fun, and so, to put it simply, we parents had our work cut out for us. And so one afternoon, in the process of trying to gently encourage a little decorum at the table, I called on one of the more boisterous fourth graders (who happened to be African American) and asked his name, which he proceeded to give me to the immense amusement of his classmates. The words were barely out of his mouth when one of the support staff—a "nice" white woman challenged the boy, "That's not your name. Jeremiah is your real name. That's a lie (and then turning to me continued in the same loud voice)...He's lying! That's not his name. They learn to lie about their names from their parents. They see their parents lie about their names at home to get away from creditors and from the police and then their kids do it in school too. It's like what they do in their community. It's something they are used to doing."

I was too shell-shocked to find words of rebuttal. In less than a minute, the "nice" staff member had transformed a popular student antic into proof of the pathology of the individual student, his parents, and even his entire community. I call it "pathology" rather than "labeling" because she was doing much more than just remarking on his misbehavior. Rather, she was—as the act of pathologizing demands—marking the origins, causes, developments, consequences, and manifestations of deviation from some imagined norm. This is what Foucault (1980) called "bio-power"—"an explosion of numerous and diverse techniques for achieving the subjugations of bodies and the control of populations" (140). Here, unlike sovereign power that is based on the threat of death, biopower is exercised in an attempt to preserve (normative) life by deploying "the power to qualify, measure, appraise, and hierarchize" (144) via the social institutions of law, medicine, and education, among others.

Disabled people know full well the horrors of this enactment of biopower that has historically associated disability with a dangerous pathology. For example, the deployment of the medical model of disability has justified the continued segregation/removal/incarceration of disabled people to special education classrooms, alternative schools, asylums, and segregated residential institutions. Similarly, people of color are also painfully aware of these horrors through their own experiences of segregation/removal/incarceration via the Middle Passage, slavery, lynchings, Jim Crow, reservations, barrios, urban ghettos, segregated schools, boarding schools, alternative schools, and ultimately the prison-industrial-complex. But even at this moment of shared experience, I want to mark the very real painful antagonisms that keep disrupting any easy possibility of alliance as we carefully sort through the problematic relationships unearthed in our analyses of criminality, danger, disability, class, and race.

This relationship between disability, criminality, class, and race is fraught. Most radical scholars have traditionally conceived of disability as a biological category, as an immutable and pathological abnormality rooted in the "the medical language of symptoms and diagnostic categories" (Linton 1998, 8). Disability studies scholars, on the other hand, have described disability as a socially constructed category that derives meaning and social (in)significance from the historical, cultural, political, and economic structures that frame social life (Erevelles 2011; McRuer 2006; Oliver 1990). In fact, disability exposes the "implicit assumptions inherent in creating the social hierarchy that invest the list [of social categories] with meaning, [in the first place]" (Kudlick 2005, 60) and as a result, disability can be theorized as constitutive of most social differences, including race (Baynton 2005; Erevelles 2011; James and Wu 2003).

It is in this context that I invoke the analytic practice of "coming out crip." McRuer (2006) argues that "coming out crip" entails "coming out as what you already are (but not repeating the dominant culture's understanding of that faithfully)…[as well as] coming out as what you are apparently not" (70–71). I argue that this analytic practice is critical to a radical analysis of mass incarceration, because it chronicles the disruptive emergence of disability not in its expected role as abject deviance, but rather as the animating force at the intersections of multiple differences. Here, mass incarceration represents for a terrified public the reassuring barrier between the mainstream population and its outcasts in its fervid project of policing "compulsory able-bodiedness." This was witnessed in the aftermath of the shootings in Connecticut (that I referred to earlier) that highlighted an unusual agreement between many quarters of the political left and conservative right regarding the active policing and possible institutionalization of those saddled with the questionable diagnosis of mental illness/disability.

"Coming out crip" in discourses of mass incarceration is not, however, a resurrection of disability as merely the by-product of brutal oppression. If "coming out crip" celebrates the transformative potential of disability and queerness to unsettle and radically rewrite abject identities (McRuer 2006), I argue that to even reimagine these discursive possibilities necessitates an engagement with the social conditions that constitute disability in relation to other categories of difference. I, therefore, situate disability not as the condition of "being" but of "becoming," and this "becoming" is an historical event, and further, it is its material context that is critical in the theorizing of bodies at the intersections of multiple difference (Erevelles 2011). Specifically, my analysis focuses on the historical contexts in which the body "becomes" a commodity of exchange in the neoliberal prison-industrial-complex of late capitalism, and on how this "becoming" proliferates a multiplicity of discourses of disability, race, class, gender, and sexuality. It is to this analysis that I now turn.

Crippin' Jim Crow

In her thought-provoking book, *The New Jim Crow*, Michelle Alexander (2010) describes how the relentless focus on the War on Drugs by the US criminal justice system disproportionately targets underprivileged, poorly educated African Americans who are basically warehoused in prison and who are then released to face lifelong job discrimination, elimination from juries and voter rolls, and even disqualification from food stamps, public housing and student loans. The nearly one million African Americans behind bars (NAACP 2014), with even more experiencing legalized discrimination and permanent social exclusion as a result of a criminal record, has produced what Alexander calls a new racial under-caste, relegated to the margins of mainstream society. Alexander argues that this new racial under-caste now occupies a political and social space not unlike Jim Crow—the legalized racial caste system that emerged in the Southern US states, post Reconstruction. This "New Jim Crow" (56), she argues, has "functioned relatively automatically, and the prevailing system of racial meanings, identities, and ideologies [are naturalized and]...explained in race neutral terms" (56–57). As a result, Alexander argues that much like their grandparents before them, many poor African American communities continue to be legally subject to an explicit system of control and social and political exclusion, even among incredulous assertions that the United States is now a postracial society.

Although Alexander claims that this group is defined largely by race, I argue that this group is defined at the crucial intersection of race, class, and disability. Interestingly, Alexander almost intuitively gestures toward such an analysis. In marking the historical continuities between Jim Crow laws and mass incarceration, she writes that, "the degraded status of Africans was justified on the grounds that Negroes, like the Indians, were an uncivilized lesser race, perhaps even more lacking in intelligence and laudable human qualities than the red-skinned natives" (25). Here, Alexander seems unaware that disability as deviant pathology is utilized to assign African slaves a degraded self-worth. This unawareness results in her nonrecognition of the constitutive relationship of race and disability where racialized bodies became disabled and disabled bodies became racialized within the specific historical conditions of a burgeoning capitalism (Erevelles 2011).

In her essay "Mama's Baby, Papa's Maybe: Notes on an American Grammar," Hortense Spillers (1987) locates the "origins" of African American subjectivity in the (trans)Atlantic slave trade that starts with the unimaginable violence during the Middle Passage, continues through the dehumanization of slavery, and finally concludes by exposing dominant conceptualizations of the contemporary "Black Family" as a tangle of pathology. However, just like Alexander's book, Spillers' essay, detailing the historical practices that enabled the black body to be pathologized, is as much about disability as it is about race, even though the word "disability" is not mentioned once in her essay. I find this startling because the "scene[s] of *actual* mutilation, dismemberment, and exile" (67) that Spillers' describes in her essay produce disabled bodies—black disabled bodies without gender, without genitalia, without subjectivity—who in an ironic turn are transformed into commodities that are exchanged in the market for profit. I call it ironic because it is in this "becoming" disabled that the black body is at the height of its profitability for the slave masters and it is the historical, social, and economic context of this "becoming" that I foreground.

But profitability in colonialist/protocapitalist contexts has its even darker side. If profits could not be realized from the enslaved body, then of what value is the body? In the introduction, Chapman, Ben-Moshe, and Carey draw on Sharon Snyder and David Mitchell's work to argue that "both English and German sources during the eugenics era portrayed...the death of disabled people as a benefit to the nation" just as enslaved black bodies were deemed a benefit to the nation so long as they represented a valuable labor force. Thus, in a curious complication, although on the one hand "becoming disabled" as described in Spillers' text rendered black bodies as profitable to slave masters, this profitability was only temporary because it "overlooks the mortality that always accompanies slave systems, particularly for human chattel who become disabled as a result of inhumane labor and living

conditions or for those killed after being born with a disability on slave plantations" (Snyder and Mitchell 2006, 122).

To the ship crew of mostly European men undertaking the Middle Passage,
those bodies, "black as Ethiops, and so ugly, both in features and in body, as
almost to appear (to those who saw them) the images of a lower hemisphere" (De
Azurara as qtd. in Spillers 1987, 70) were nothing more than cargo to be trans-
ported to the New World by sea and to be traded for unimaginable profit because
of their obvious "physical" impairments. Here, the conceptualization of black
subjectivity as impaired subjectivity is neither accidental nor metaphorical. Rather
it is precisely at that moment when one class of human beings was transformed
into cargo that black bodies become disabled and disabled bodies become black.
Further, it is also important to note that blackness itself does not stand in for skin
color. *Black* and *disabled* are not just linguistic tropes used to delineate difference,
but are, instead, materialist constructs produced for the appropriation of profit
in an historical context where black disabled bodies were subjected to the most
brutal violence. Spillers describes the brutal violation of black flesh with "eyes
beaten out, arms, backs, skulls branded, a left jaw, a right ankle, punctured; teeth
missing, as the calculated work of iron, whips, chains, knives, the canine patrol,
the bullet" (67).

Although Spillers (1987) describes these markings on the flesh as "the concentration of ethnicity" in a culture "whose state apparatus, including judges, attorneys, 'owners,' 'soul drivers,' 'overseers,' and 'men of God,' apparently colludes
with a protocol of 'search and destroy'" (67), I argue that these same markings
on the flesh, quite simply, also produce impairment. Here, impairment is not just
biological/natural, it is also produced in a historical, social, and economic context
where the very embodiment of blackness and disability "bears in person the marks
of a cultural text whose inside has been turned outside" (p. 67). Here, the historical conditions of a nascent colonialist transnational expansion of capitalism are
responsible for the violent reconfiguration of the flesh such that it becomes almost
impossible to even imagine the sovereign subject, now mutually constituted via
race, disability, and gender as a dehumanized commodity. Thus, rather than posing
a simple causal effect (viz. that slavery produces disability), I argue, on the other
hand, that both disability/impairment and race are neither merely biological nor
wholly discursive, but rather are historical materialist constructs imbricated within
the exploitative conditions of transnational capitalism.

A similar imbrication of race and disability can be observed in the historical
context of Jim Crow. Interestingly enough, one story of the origin of the term
"Jim Crow" describes how in 1830, a white, minstrel show performer, Thomas
"Daddy" Rice, blackened his face with charcoal paste or burnt cork in imitation of
a crippled, elderly black man dancing and singing the lyrics to the song, "Jump Jim
Crow." Here, yet again, is an often unremarked intimate association of race and
disability that materialized into legal statutes that "enforce[d] and reinforce[d] the
compulsory crippling and enfeeblement of entire 'colored populations'" (Schweik
2009, 186). Here, yet again, black bodies and disabled bodies are inextricably
intertwined in the punitive patrol of bodily boundaries.

Alexander (2010) locates the origins of Jim Crow in the backlash against the
gains earned by the former slaves during the Reconstruction Period enacted by the
southern elite plantation class. Following the civil war, the dearth of social laws
and customs to maintain white control gave rise to white elite fears of a possible
insurrection by an angry mass of black men. It was in this context that vagrancy

laws and other laws accusing African Americans of "mischief" and "insulting gestures" were utilized to incarcerate large numbers of African American men who then became part of the convict labor force and who thus reentered into yet another system of extreme repression and control. Moreover, the severe agrarian depression of the late 1880s and 1890s enabled an unlikely alliance between poor /working class whites and African Americans in the south. Thus, it was around this time that the white elite fearful of a possible challenge to its social and economic power proposed a slew of segregation laws intended to drive a wedge between poor whites and African Americans—laws that later came to be known as Jim Crow. Thus, by the turn of the century, every state in the South supported laws that sanctioned racial ostracism in virtually every aspect of social life that extended to schools, churches, hospitals, prisons, cemeteries, asylums, etc. (Alexander 2010). Jim Crow, therefore, enabled even lower class whites to maintain some sort of psychological superiority over African Americans.

In many ways the vagrancy laws just described above appear to be the precursor to the "ugly laws"—public ordinances that were proposed in the late 1800s that barred any "person who is diseased, maimed, mutilated, or...deformed, so as to be an unsightly or disgusting object" (293) to remain in public view or else be to fined or imprisoned (Schweik 2009). Schweik argues that these unsightly beggar ordinances were used to define a certain form of despised whiteness—disabled white trash—and therefore functioned as an "allegory of identity" (185), fleetingly exposing the very real class antagonisms and ableist assumptions in an already racially stratified society. Recognizing "ugly laws" as part of the same project as Jim Crow, Schweik observes that such ordinances reveal an oppressive "investment in, the disciplining of, the anxious management of skin...loaded with social as well as medical significance" (187).

Alexander (2010), in marking parallels between Jim Crow and mass incarceration, echoes Schweik's observation when she argues that

> what it means to be a criminal in our collective consciousness has become conflated with what it means to be black (193)...For black youth, the experience of being "made black" often begins with the first police stop, interrogation, search, or arrest. The experience carries social meaning – *this is what it means to be black* (194)...For the [racial caste] system to succeed...black...[youth] must be labeled criminals before they are formally subject to control...This process of being made a criminal is, to a large extent, the process of "becoming" black. (195)

Here, Alexander describes "becoming" black as a "'body-based' disqualification" (Snyder and Mitchell 2006, 400) that presumes an in-built inferiority/ deviance that being biologically encoded would therefore be almost impossible to transcend. What Alexander misses in her analysis is that disability serving as the "master trope of human disqualification" (Mitchell and Snyder 2001, 3) is deployed to give oppressive credence to this flawed equation: criminal = black youth. Here, remapping the historical continuities with earlier times, the simultaneous process of "becoming black" AND "becoming disabled" described uncritically as "natural" deviance foregrounds a complex intersectional politics of race, class, and disability that is used to justify the incarceration of "outlaw" bodies that eventually become profitable commodities in the neoliberal prison-industrial-complex of late capitalism. Furthermore, the historical continuities between Jim Crow, the ugly laws, and the contemporary context of mass incarceration mirror in many ways eugenic ideologies that imagined a "uniquely modern utopian fantasy of a future world uncontaminated by defective bodies — either disabled, racialised, or both at the same time" (Mitchell and Snyder 2003, 861).

Compulsory Able-Bodiedness in the Postcolonial Ghetto

McRuer (2006) has argued that the recognition of compulsory able-bodiedness as an organizing practice in social life enables us to "question the order of things, considering how and why it is constructed and naturalized; how it is embedded in complex economic, social, and cultural relations; and how it might be changed" (2). Compulsory able-bodiedness is brought to bear on the body via the *normate* (Garland-Thomson 1996, 8), the cultural Self whose boundaries are marked by its opposing twin—the disabled other—the very embodiment of corporeal differ-ence. The material effects of these ableist practices result in the removal or erasure of disability or both, even in social practices that purport to be inclusive. In fact, conditions for the inclusion of disabled people in mainstream society require their assimilation (via special education, rehabilitation, and assistive technology), their removal (via segregation, institutionalization, incarceration) or their complete anni-hilation (euthanasia, abortion of disabled fetuses) (Campbell 2009; Siebers 2008; Snyder and Mitchell 2006). Disability, therefore, becomes "the boundary condition that resides just on the other side of hope...the condition one must escape rather than improve" (Ferguson 1987, 63).

Shifting the locus of analysis from the individual to the social, compulsory able-bodiedness becomes the ideological and material means to separate mainstream society from its dangerous outcastes. Here, pathological discourses of disability are used to justify the oppressive binary cultural constructions of normal/pathological, autonomous/dependent, competent citizen/ward of the state, and the social divi-sions of labor (Erevelles 2011). In the context of Jim Crow, Alexander (2010) points out that the continued need to "prevent the 'amalgamation' with a group of people considered intrinsically inferior and vile" (27) perpetuated the current stereotypes of black men as "aggressive, unruly predators" required to be forcibly separated from the general population. Thus, while the US South was patrolled by Jim Crow laws, the more liberal US North East was safe guarded-via the ghetto—"a third vehicle [the first being slavery and the second Jim Crow] to extract black labor, while keeping black bodies at a safe distance, to the material and symbolic benefit of white society" (Wacquant 2009, 202).

Wacquant (2009) likens the ghetto to an "ethnoracial prison" and the prison to a "judicial ghetto" (205). He theorizes both these spaces as "socio-spatial device[s] that enable a dominant status group...to simultaneously *ostracize and exploit* a subordinate group endowed with *negative symbolic capital*" (204). Although the ghetto serves as an "urban condom" (Richard Sennett qtd. in Wacquant 2009, 205) protecting urban residents from the polluting intercourse of its outcasts, the prison cleanses the urban space from the pollution of natural and dangerous deprav-ity. Moreover, the concurrent loss of jobs in the inner city and the gradual retrench-ment of social welfare in response to the neoliberal policies of less government intervention and their corresponding association with social stigma have created a breakdown of the social order in the inner city. Here, the ghetto and the prison combine into a single carceral continuum that has entrapped "a redundant population of younger black men (and increasingly women)...in a self-fulfilling cycle of social and legal marginality" (207). Here the trajectory from the ghetto to the prison is one of circularity (akin to a hamster's wheel) and as a result functions "as an ancillary institution for caste preservation and labor control" (Wacquant 2009, 207) in US society.

La Paperson (2010), on the other hand, theorizes the ghetto not as "a fixed sociological space...[but rather as] a dislocating procedure" (10)—that draws on the "apparatus of empire" (21) to exclude, contain, and control the proliferation of excessive bodies. According to La Paperson, the ghetto is constituted by three critical elements: "(i) *walls* that serve to contain bodies; (ii) legal and civil *divestment* that ensures educational, social, and economic deprivation of those contained, and (iii) *racial marking* where minority status is assigned to those bodies that are contained" (10). To these three elements I would add a fourth—the signifying practice of compulsory able-bodiedness that is the wellspring of these dis-locations.

Compulsory able-bodiedness as a practice of dis-location is the cornerstone of the ghetto, both hypervisible and yet invisible in its workings. For example, La Paperson argues that the ghetto is not where black people live but rather where blackness is contained. Here compulsory able-bodiedness patrols the boundaries of the ghetto to maintain this racial isolation such that the ghetto "becomes" the excess of white/pure space—"that which is left over, the matter out of place" (13). Here, liberal discourses point to the racial and economic isolation in the ghetto as nurturing a culture of poverty (a "natural" state of hopelessness). This is contrasted with the place of "universal rights" that exists outside the ghetto where rational and "normal" enlightened subjects apparently exist. The ghetto is also imagined as a "zone of violence" even though violence occurs not because of what "happens" in the ghetto, but rather because of what "is done" to the ghetto and its inhabitants (La Paperson 2010). Moreover, because of its feared pathology, there is also always the move to destroy the ghetto, to always shift its inhabitants someplace else—such that it becomes a space that is always open for continuous dispersal; of going "nowhere for good" (21). Thus the "ghetto" is not just a space but "a portable status that can be cast onto bodies—some are temporarily and selectively branded, others inescapably so (19)...[such that if mapped]...it would be a palimpsest, a map of absences — of what used to be there — or perhaps a map of the condemned" (21). See Abbass and Voronka (in this book) for a description of how institutions for those labeled feebleminded also represent a palimpset—a trace of past dis-locations.

In La Paperson's (2010) vivid conceptualization of the ghetto, disability is both hyper visible, yet invisible; its (re)appearances/disappearances dependent on the capricious practices of compulsory-able-bodiedness. At one moment, it shows its hand in the social construction of dangerous and depraved pathology (disability) assigned to underprivileged bodies of color (race and class) located within the exploitative political economy of late capitalism; at another moment it disappears into obfuscating discourses that represent this pathology (disability) ascribed to these raced and classed bodies as innate/natural. In either case the dis-locating context of the postcolonial ghetto ultimately results in foregrounding "a map of the condemned" inhabited by bodies (at the intersection of race, class, and disability) branded (temporarily or permanently) as so dangerously criminal as to require expulsion or incarceration. In this way, compulsory able-bodiedness as dis-locating practice rules the (postcolonial) ghetto.

Reading the School-to-Prison Pipeline via Crip Politics

In this section, the locus of analysis shifts to public education where I draw parallels between the dis-locating practices of public education, the postcolonial ghetto and the segregational statutes of the New Jim Crow. I argue that the "New Jim Crow" naturalizes racial inferiority in educational contexts such that students located at the critical intersections of race, class, and disability are conceived of as "public enemies" (Winn and Behizadeh 2011, 156) subject to the unforgiving authority of zero-tolerance policies. Zero-tolerance policies were instituted when Congress passed the Gun-Free Schools Act in 1994 requiring any state receiving federal funds to suspend or expel, for at least one calendar year, any student who brought a firearm to school. More recently, zero-tolerance policies have evolved into a "nondiscretionary approach that mandates a set of often severe, predetermined consequences to student misbehavior that is to be applied without regard to seriousness of behavior, mitigating circumstances, or situational context" (Aul IV 2012, 182).

One problematic outcome of zero-tolerance policies is that everyday student infractions have now become criminal offenses that cause referrals to the juvenile justice system. Zero-tolerance policies also infringe on students' rights to due process because student explanations are not heard before an impartial official, and these "hearings" are often held without parents being present. More troubling, when transferred to the alternative school system, students cannot challenge these transfers on the grounds that they are being deprived of public education. Further, the Supreme Court has not come to any conclusion about how the right to not incriminate oneself (also known as Miranda rights in the United States) is to be applied when school officials question students (Aul IV 2012). Thus, zero tolerance policies are a fast track to being committed involuntarily to the school-to-prison pipeline.

Alexander (2010) describes the school-to-prison pipeline "as numerous interinstitutional actions that collectively undereducate and overincarcerate students of color at disparate rates" (104). For example, Smith (2009) reports that although blacks and Latinos each accounted for 17 percent of US K-12 enrollment, they respectively comprised 30 percent and 20 percent of all twelfth-grade suspensions and expulsions. Before twelfth grade, black students were two to five times more likely than whites to be suspended at a younger age leading some researchers to name this the "cradle-to-prison track" (Heitzeg 2009, 2). The repercussions for moving along this track are immense. According to Smith (2009), 69 percent of all incarcerated adults never finish high school, 75 percent of juveniles in adult prisons fail to complete tenth grade, and 33 percent of all incarcerated juveniles do not have a fourth-grade reading level proficiency. Most critically, high school dropouts are three-and-a-half times more likely to become incarcerated than high school graduates.

The overrepresentation of black and Latino students in the school-to-prison pipeline is justified by invoking Jim Crow ideologies of black men as innately dangerous and depraved. For example, even though school security and zero-tolerance was beefed up in the wake of the mass shootings in April 1999, perpetrated by four suburban white male students at a high school in Columbine, Colorado, the excessive policing and punishment as a result of these policies has been directed mostly at inner city African-American and Latino youth. This is because echoing Jim Crow laws of an earlier time, African American and Latino youth continue to be represented as dangerously depraved and mentally imbalanced as a result of their "aberrant biology."

Michelle Jarman (2012) has drawn conceptual yet contrary connections between the violent practices of white-on-black lynchings and eugenic castration during Jim Crow. Although both lynchings and castrations enacted similar barbaric mutilations that operated outside the law, white-on-black lynching was the murderous public spectacle consumed as a communal cultural event, whereas eugenic castration was administered by white medical doctors to white "feebleminded" inmates behind institutional walls. Jarman, argues that notwithstanding their differences, both modes of sexualized violence had the collective effect of normalizing and legitimizing each other because "each responded to...a culturally produced fear...of a threat animalistic and sexual, to the sanctity of normative white heterosexuality" (100). Thus, the logic of disability (feebleminded) as dangerous pathology also implicated in the construction of black men as dangerous (sexual) predators justified the most violent practices of Jim Crow and eugenic criminology. Similarly, Ferri (2010) explores the "the entangled histories of racism and ableism embedded in the construction of mental deficiency" (134) that continued to place African American students in segregated special education classrooms because they were perceived as threats to the "normal" practices of schooling (Erevelles, Kanga, and Middleton 2006).

A similar logic operates with the New Jim Crow. One example in contemporary contexts is represented in this quote from *The Weekly Standard*:

On the horizon, therefore, are tens of thousands of severely morally impoverished juvenile super-predators. They are perfectly capable of committing the most heinous acts of physical violence for the most trivial [reasons]...They fear neither the stigma of arrest nor the pain of imprisonment. They live by the meanest code of the meanest streets, a code that reinforces rather than restrains their violent, hand-trigger mentality. In prison or out, the things that superpredators get by their criminal behavior – sex, drugs, money – are their own immediate rewards. Nothing else matters to them. (DiIulio qtd in Farmer 2010, 371)

Here, the intersecting discourses of race and disability as pathological deviance are deployed to create "moral panic...the means of orchestrating consent by actively intervening in the space of public opinion and social consciousness through the use of highly rhetorical and emotive language, which has the effect of requiring that 'something be done about it'" (Farmer 2010, 372). Margaret Price (2010) describes a similar "moral panic" around people diagnosed with mental illness in the aftermath of recent mass shootings. So pervasive is this pathological rhetoric that in November 2003, in the racially diverse Stratford High School in Goose Creek, South Carolina, officers in SWAT team uniforms and bulletproof vests raided the school and forced students as young as 14 years old to the ground in handcuffs at gunpoint while their bags were searched with gun sniffing dogs.

No drugs or guns were found and the most noteworthy fact regarding this raid was that the children who were searched were all black.

I was surprised how easily discourses of moral panic drawing on the rhetoric of black pathology and the practices of compulsory able-bodiedness were the part of everyday conversations of liberal middle class parents at my daughter's elementary school with students from diverse race and class backgrounds. In a recent conversation with some of these parents, moral panic ruled the day in the obvious terror the parents felt about sending their children (especially their young daughters) to the same middle school with low-income pre-teens of color—the very same students their daughters were friends with in elementary school. When I asked the parents how it was that we could promptly transform these inquisitive, gentle, fun-loving children into potential criminals within the brief moments of a conversation without any proof of their potential for violent notoriety, they assured me that this was inevitable because of the presumed pathological deviance in their families and their communities. Furthermore, many parents assured me that the effectiveness of the tracking systems (ability grouping) in public education would prove to be the first line of defense in separating "us" from "them." Perhaps, especially telling is that the parents showed no reticence in this conversation with me (a woman of color)—a situation that painfully demonstrates that these parents assumed that our class alliances (us) would trump any and all racial alliances (them) that I might have claimed with the racialized other. Thus, in this way, discourses of racism and ableism intersect within the broader social logic of class antagonisms to segregate even within a presumably free, equitable, and democratic public education.

Additionally, La Paperson's (2010) conceptualization of the postcolonial ghetto is especially critical to describe how outlaw bodies are excluded, contained, and controlled in special education, alternative schooling, and the school-to-prison pipeline. Unlike the overseas colony that served as "imperialism's outpost," the postcolonial ghetto serves "as imperialism's outcast: the alley and the underground of imperial outlaw" (21). In these "ghettoized zones in schools...the rights of students are suspended, and state agents are allowed free reign to implement any set of neocolonial educational and disciplinary tactics...violence that would never be permitted in their privileged counterparts" (18). Here the shift to the ghetto is not an "accident of discrimination" (8), but rather a deliberate act of dis-location by the school system.

It is easy to see how self-contained special education classrooms and alternative schools in US public education serve as postcolonial ghettoes. Here, definitions of disability as intransigent pathology are used to justify segregation along the axes of race and class under the questionable guise of "special" education and rehabilitation. Claiming or passing as normal while maintaining a distance from the "real" aberrancy of disability is amply rewarded in educational contexts. Put simply, "we" MUST try really hard not to be like "them." To all those who cannot pass for normal, there is always quarantine—the condition of temporary enforced isolation. To quarantine requires space, preferably secluded, but also one that can easily be patrolled to protect the outside from those on the inside.

In the moral geography of schooling, one such quarantined space is the alternative school where students who are deemed at risk for school failure are forced to attend (Lehr, Tan, and Ysseldyke 2009). It is a little terrifying to note that according to 2001–2002 data, the numbers of students isolated in these quarantined spaces exceeded more than 613,000. Students are banished from regular classrooms because they are perceived to be at a higher risk of substance abuse, suicide, sexual activity and teen pregnancy. Nearly twelve percent of the students who attend alternative school are identified with emotional and behavioral disabilities and have IEPs (Individualized Educational Plans). Yet, many of these alternative schools privilege the punitive over the pedagogical or the therapeutic, becoming the dumping ground of at-risk students whom teachers are too terrified to teach. In this way, disability serves as an "outlaw ontology" used to justify the exclusion of individuals in the postcolonial ghettoes of public schooling.

Additionally, I argue that "becoming" black and "becoming" disabled are not merely discursive events but are material constructs shaped by the political economy of educational opportunity and social segregation that frame the lives of those students on the fast track to the school-to-prison pipeline. The harsh reality is that most of these low-income students of color are caught in what Fine and Ruglis (2009) have referred to as "circuits of dispossession" fueled by economic practices that systematically funnel public education funding to private enterprises; swell the profits of testing companies, private vendors, and textbook publisher professionals; increase the police-in-school and military recruitment budgets. As a result, low-income youth of color slowly disappear from educational spaces that could offer them an alternative to the numbing promise of lifelong incarceration. This sorting process is further exacerbated by housing policies that ghettoize those perceived as deviant, rampant racial and class segregation in public education fueled by regressive economic policies of school funding through property taxes, and through the pedagogical practices of tracking that disproportionately place minority students in underachieving schools and classrooms (Smith 2009). Most significantly, these low-income schools are also organized via a prisonlike atmosphere with little motivation to build and sustain relationships among students and their peers or between students and teachers or school staff—all of which are becoming secondary to budget line items assigned for the management of Black and Brown bodies (Smith 2009; Winn and Behizadeh 2011).

I argued earlier that "becoming disabled" is an historical event mediated via the political economy of the social. This is also true in schools. Steele and Aronson (1995) have argued that low-income students of color wrestle with the historically derogatory threats of being viewed as innately deviant and constantly live in the fear of doing something that would inadvertently confirm that stereotype. They call it stereotype threat. In the specific context of zero-tolerance policies and its associative practices, the very act of surveillance serves as a physical representation of a threat whether or not students are actively conscious of it (Farmer 2010). And contrary to popular belief, the threat of constant surveillance does very little to reform the soul or normalize conduct; rather it has led to increased raids, confiscation of student property, interrogations, zero-tolerance suspensions, and ultimately juvenile detention centers and prison.

Additionally, many incarcerated juveniles are often diagnosed with questionable labels such as disruptive behavior disorders (e.g., conduct disorder, oppositional defiant disorder), substance abuse disorders, schizophrenia, psychosis, and self-injurious behavior. Conservative estimates claim that about ten percent of juvenile detainees have recently thought about suicide, with ten percent having attempted suicide over their lifetimes (Abram et al. 2008). Moreover, as many as many as 79 percent of juveniles labeled as mentally ill are thought to meet the criteria for multiple disorders, with 60 percent believed to be displaying symptoms of three or more disorders. Most of these children receive little or no interventions with the likelihood of treatment increasing if the juvenile is a non-Hispanic white, younger detainee, processed as a juvenile rather than an adult, and with a past history of treatment. In a case study of the New Orleans schools, it was reported that both pre- and post-Katrina, students of color with disabilities lacked resources for intervention programs that should have been illegal under IDEA—The Individual with Disabilities' Education Act (Tuzzolo and Hewitt 2006/2007).

I note here that members of the psychiatric survivor movement have protested the excessive control medical practitioners have on the lives of people diagnosed "mentally ill" and have argued that many of the treatments used have deprived them of their autonomy, respect, and human rights (Mollow 2006). This perspective, however, is challenged when brought to bear on those living at the intersections of race, class, and disability. For example, Anna Mollow's (2006) insightful analysis of Meri Nana-Ama Danquah's memoir, *Willow Weep for Me: A Black Woman's Journey through Depression* foregrounds how this memoir complicates disabled people's critiques of the psychiatric model of mental illness because, for African American women with depression, the problem does not lie in the involuntary administration of questionable treatments, but the lack of access to any form of treatment at all.

In school contexts, McWilliams and Fancher (2010) point out that the failure to evaluate for disabilities while in school, contributes to a demonstrated racial "suspension gap" that negatively impacts communities of color—the black community in particular. They describe what they call a manifestation review where a team of school officials are required to decide (1) whether the conduct in question was caused by or had a direct and substantial relationship to the child's disability; or (2) that the conduct in question was the direct result of the school's failure to implement the IEP (Individualized Education Plan). McWilliam and Fancher report that in affluent school districts black students, often poor, are denied the support that an individual behavior plan can provide because the predominantly white administration assumes these students are *choosing* to act out. The matter is further complicated by the tendency of teachers and school officials to define disruptive white youth as in need of medical intervention rather than suspension under zero tolerance policies. This occurs in a context where social class, insurance coverage, and race are key indicators of who receives treatment and who is disciplined. In this way, it is the reality of political and economic factors that deny low-income students of color with disabilities not only corrective and educational supports but also enable schools to refuse to reinstate students expelled due to zero tolerance policies. Thus, when youth get in trouble and the school refers them to alternative schools or the juvenile criminal system, they experience a kind of "civic death" (Wacquant 2005), where they are made unable to fully participate in school processes (Farmer 2010, 376) and also in civic life later on.

Low-income students of color when labeled with a disability are, therefore, caught in an oppressive yet contradictory logic. Put simply, as per the illogic of the manifestation review, for African American students being labeled a potential superpredator foregrounds a biological determinism that is absurdly couched in a language of choice. In other words, he is a natural born killer and so he "choses" to kill. On the other hand, assigning white students with a disability label also implies a "natural" deficiency, but one outside the realm of "choice" and therefore worthy of pedagogical or other intervention. Clearly, as per this logic, "coming out crip" in public education has different outcomes for different bodies located at the intersections of race, class, and disability.

Conclusion: The Political Economy of Crip Politics

Michel Foucault's (1977) *Discipline and Punish* has drawn analogies between the birth of the prison and the social organization of schooling in the eighteenth century. According to Foucault, institutions such as schools regarded the student body as both an object and target of power and utilized various technologies of discipline so as to make the body completely docile. Those whose bodies challenged the rigidity of this discipline and proved to be "unruly bodies" (Erevelles 2000), came to be known as "social outcasts of education" (Noguera 1995, 194), and student populations who are designated as social outcasts of education are not just disabled students, but also include nondisabled students of color who are labeled "at-risk": pregnant teens of color from low income neighborhoods; students who exhibit low English proficiency who are also seen to skew performance scores and are often excluded from these evaluations; and some gay, lesbian, bisexual, and transsexual students who are deemed emotionally unstable and socially isolated.

There is rarely a "biological" basis for these labels (disability, at-risk). It is also generally understood that the assignment of these labels are arbitrary—I would say historical—rooted in the very American Grammar book that Spillers (1987) discusses in her essay. The material consequences of these assignments are horribly damaging—students move from segregated classrooms to alternative schools to becoming school dropouts to becoming completely alienated from the labor market and the wider social world and eventually many find themselves in prison—a humiliating passage along the school to prison pipeline. This phenomenon reproduces what I call the (post) modern version of the Middle Passage/Jim Crow that continues the historical tradition of transforming children of color into "diseased, damaged, and disabled Negroes deemed incurable and otherwise worthless" (Goodell as quoted in Spillers, 68), commodities used to feed the prison industrial complex and served up again for consumption via the media (through TV shows like COPS, Oz, and the news) in another brutal conflation of pleasure and profit. We now have the production of another social pathology blamed on the violent historical construction of the special education student living in the postcolonial ghetto still bearing the wounds of broken flesh marked by the violent lashes of history.

Although this pathologization is most definitely unwarranted in that it presumes that deviance is endemic to black bodies, there is another complication to this argument. Many authors in both education and legal studies have noted that the material conditions of poverty/inferior educational resources and structural racism actually create conditions for both diagnosed and undiagnosed learning disabilities/emotional challenges and mental illness. Failure to be identified with these disabilities prevents these students from gaining access to services/resources/supports that would enable them to tentatively traverse the very treacherous terrain of schooling. It should be noted also that these learning disabilities/emotional challenges and mental illnesses are not the sole purview of low income youth of color. And while almost all students with disabilities have experienced navigating the special education systems in public education as a nightmare, those from upper middle class families have avoided the one-way road to lifelong incarceration—as a result of ardent advocacy/access to outside resources and sometimes just simple class and race privilege.

Going back to the incident in the cafeteria, this should have been a simple reprimand (laughingly given to the mischievous child)—one that I have often seen happens to students from more privileged race/class backgrounds. "They're feisty! Boys will be boys! He's a special one!" But what little Jeremiah received was no simple reprimand but a public pathologization of an entire population. Terrifyingly, this is not an isolated incident but a general strategy of power enacted against low income students of color, as documented in the considerable literature both in education and legal studies that have sought to explain the removal of African American males, in particular, from regular classrooms via in-school suspensions/alternative school enrollment/expulsion and finally prison.

I want to end on a more positive note. The possibility of a radical coalitional politics for transformative praxis can only happen if we are open to complex understandings of the embodied experiences of disability, in a continuum from the most desirable way of being in the world—a radical crip politics—to the more sobering reality of how it can be experienced in very painful and terrible ways. The difference lies not in discursive meanings of disability per se but in the historical contexts in which it is manifested—and it is our relentless focus on those conditions that may enable us to move toward more transformative praxis.

References

Abram, Karen, Jeanne Y. Cho, Jason J. Washburn, Linda A. Teplin, Devon C. King, and Mina K. Dulcan. 2008. "Suicidal Ideation and Behaviors among Youths in Juvenile Detention." *Journal of the American Academy of Child and Adolescent Psychiatry* 47(3): 291–300.

Alexander, Michelle. 2010. *The New Jim Crow: Mass Incarceration in the Age of Colorblindness*. New York: The New Press.

Aul IV, Elbert. 2012. "Zero Tolerance, Frivolous Juvenile Court Referrals, and the School-to-Prison Pipeline: Using Arbitration as a Screening-Out Method to Help Plug the Pipeline." *Ohio State Journal of Dispute Resolution* 27: 180–206.

Baynton, Douglas. 2005. "Slaves, immigrants, and suffragists: The uses of disability in citizenship debates." *PMLA: The Publication of the Modern Language Association* 120(2):562–566.

Ben-Moshe, Liat. 2013. "'The institution yet to come:' Analysing Incarceration Through a Disability Lens." In *The Disability Studies Reader, 4th edition*, edited by Lennard J. Davis. New York: Routledge.

———. 2011. *Genealogies of Resistance to Incarceration: Abolition Politics within Deinstitutionalization And Anti-Prison Activism in the U.S. 1950-Present.* PhD diss., Syracuse University.

Campbell, Fiona Kumari. 2009. *Contours of Ableism: The Production of Disability and Abledness*. New York: Palgrave MacMillan.

Erevelles, Nirmala. 2011. *Disability and Difference in Global Context: Towards a Transformative Body Politic*. New York: Palgrave Macmillan.

———. 2000. "Educating Unruly Bodies: Critical Pedagogy, Disability Studies, and the Politics of Schooling." *Educational Theory* 50(1): 25–57.

Erevelles, Nirmala, Anne Kanga, and Renee Middleton. 2006. "How Does It Feel to Be a Problem? Race, Disability, and Exclusion in Educational Policy." In *Who Benefits from Special Education? Remediating [Fixing] Other People's Children*, edited by Ellen Brantlinger, 77–99. Mahwah, NJ: Lawrence Erlbaum.

Farmer, Sarah. 2010. "Criminality of Black Youth in Inner-City Schools: 'Moral panic,' Moral Imagination, and Moral Formation." *Race, Ethnicity, and Education* 13(3): 367–381.

Ferguson, Philip. 1987. "The Social Construction of Mental Retardation." *Social Policy* 18(1): 51–56.

Ferri, Beth. 2010. "A Dialogue We've Yet to Have: Critical Race Studies & Disability Studies." In *Troubling the Foundations of Special Education: Examining the Myth of the Normal Curve*, edited by Curt Dudling-Marling, 139–150. New York: Peter Lang.

Fine, Michelle, and Jessica Ruglis. 2009. "Circuits and Consequences of Dispossession: The Racialized Realignment of the Public Sphere for U.S. youth." *Transforming Anthropology* 17(1): 20–33.

Foucault, Michel. 1980. *The History of Sexuality Volume 1: An Introduction*. New York: Vintage.

———. 1977. *Discipline and Punish: The Birth of a Prison*. New York: Random House.

Garland Thomson, Rosemary. 1996. *Extraordinary Bodies*. New York: Columbia University Press.

Heitzeg, Nancy. 2009. "Education or Incarceration: Zero Tolerance Policies and the School to Prison Pipeline." *Forum on Public Policy* 1–21.

James, Jennifer C., and Cynthia Wu. 2006. "Editors' Introduction: Race, Ethnicity, Disability, and Literature: Intersections and Interventions." *MELUS :Multi-Ethnic Literature of the U.S.* 31(13): 3–11.

Jarman, Michelle. 2012. "Dismembering the Lynch Mob: Intersecting Narratives of Disability, Race, and Sexual Menace." In *Sex and Disability*, edited by Robert McRuer and Anna Mollow, 89–107. Durham, NC: Duke University Press.

Kristeva, Julia. 1982. *Powers of Horror: An Essay on Abjection*. New York: Columbia University Press.

Kudlick, Catherine J. 2005. "Disability History, Power, and Rethinking the Idea of "the other."" *PMLA-Publications of the Modern Language Association of America* 120(2): 557–561.

Lehr, Camilla A., Chee Soon Tan, and James A. Ysseldyke. 2009. "Alternative schools: A synthesis of state-level policy and research." *Remedial & Special Education* 30:19–32.

Linton, Simi. 1998. *Claiming Disability: Knowledge and Identity*. New York: New York University Press.

McRuer, Robert. 2006. *Crip Theory: Cultural Signs of Queerness and Disability*. New York : New York University Press.

McWilliams, Mark, and Mark P. Fancher. 2010. "Undiagnosed Students with Disabilities Trapped in the School-to-Prison Pipeline." *Michigan Bar Journal* 28–33.

Mitchell, David, and Sharon Snyder. 2003. "Race, Disability, and the Making of an International Eugenic Science, 1800–1945." *Disability & Society* 18(7): 843–864.

———. 2001. *Narrative Prosthesis: Disability and the Dependencies of Discourse*. Ann Arbor, MI: University of Michigan Press.

Mollow, Anna. 2006. "'When Black Women start going on Prozac:' Race, Gender, and Mental Illness" in Meri Nana-Ama Danquah's "Willow Weep for Me." *MELUS -Multi-Ethnic Literature of the U.S.* 31(3): 67–99.

National Association for the Advancement of Colored People (NAACP). 2014. Criminal Justice Fact Sheet. Accessed Feb 1, 2014. http://www.naacp.org/pages/criminal-justice-fact-sheet

Noguera, Pedro. 1995. "Preventing and Producing Violence: A Critical Analyses of Responses to School Violence." *Harvard Educational Review* 65: 189–212.

Oliver, Michael. 1990. *The Politics of Disablement: A Sociological Approach*. New York: Palgrave MacMillan.

Paperson, La. 2010. "The Postcolonial Ghetto: Seeing Her Shape and His Hand." *Berkeley Review of Education* 1(1): 5–34.

Price, Margaret. 2011. *Mad at School: Rhetorics of Mental Disability and Academic Life*. Ann Arbor, MI: University of Michigan Press.

Schweik, Susan C. 2009. *The Ugly Laws: Disability in Public.* New York : New York University Press.

Siebers, Tobin. 2010. *Disability Aesthetics.* Ann Arbor, MI: University of Michigan Press.

————. 2008. *Disability Theory.* Ann Arbor, MI: University of Michigan Press.

Smith, Chauncee D. 2009. "Deconstructing the Pipeline: Examing School-to-Prison Pipeline Equal Protection Cases through a Structural Racism Framework." *Fordham Urban Law Journal* 36:1009–1049.

Snyder, Sharon, and David Mitchell. 2006. "Eugenics and the Racial Genome: Politics at the Molecular Level." *Patterns of Prejudice* 40(4–5): 399–412.

Spillers, Hortense. 1987. "Mama's Baby, Papa's Maybe: An American Grammar Book." *Diacritics: A Review of Contemporary Criticism* 17(2): 65–81.

Steele, Claude M., and Joshua Aronson. 1995. Stereotype Threat and the Intellectual Test Performance of African Americans. *Journal of Personality and Social Psychology* 69(5): 797–811.

Tuzzolo, Ellen, and Damon T. Hewitt. 2006/2007. "Re-building Inequity: The Re-emergence of the School-to-Prion Pipeline in New Orleans." *The High School Journal* 90(2): 59–68.

Wacquant, Loic. 2009. *Punishing the Poor: The Neoliberal Government of Social Insecurity.* Durham, NC: Duke University Press.

Winn, Maisha T., and Nadia Behizadeh. 2011. "The Right to be Literate: Literacy, Education, and the School to Prison Pipeline." *Review of Research in Education* 35: 147–171.

6

Walking the Line between the Past and the Future: Parents' Resistance and Commitment to Institutionalization

*Allison C. Carey and Lucy Gu**

Introduction

There is a growing body of research on the role of parents in disability rights activism. Some of this scholarship positions parents as early advocates who still today fight selflessly for the rights and needs of their children (Blum 2007; L. Jones 2010). Other work, however, criticizes the role of parents in the disability rights movement and positions them as a barrier to social change, especially insofar as they espouse models of disability rooted in tragedy, medical narratives, and paternalism (K. Jones 1998; Kittay 2009; Landsman 2009).

Increasingly, scholarship has attempted to resist the dichotomous portrayal of parents as martyrs or oppressors and to instead reveal the complexity of parents' roles in pursuing and hindering the movement toward disability rights. Parents may accept medicalization to pursue normalization, but they may also use medicalization as a means to claim disability rights and accommodations through diagnosis (Landsman 2005; Ong-Dean 2005; Prussing et al. 2005). Their activism may promote inclusion or the perpetuation of institutional and segregated care (Carey 2009; L. Jones 2010; Panitch 2008). Parents are not and have not been a unified group with a unified philosophy.

In this historical case study, we examine the ways in which a leading state-level parents organization, The Arc of Pennsylvania (PARC),[1] both supported and confronted the institutional system in Pennsylvania. Our focus is primarily Pennsylvania from 1950 to 1980, a time period when the state was receiving national attention for both its institutional scandals and its efforts at reform. We draw on the archives of the Governors' papers relevant to parent activism and institutionalization throughout the 1950s to the 1970s and PARC's newsletter, the *Pennsylvania Message*. This analysis reveals the ways in which parents understood and confronted the institutional system. PARC's strategy noticeably evolved throughout this time period. In the 1950s and early 1960s, they focused on institutional expansion and reform as they also encouraged the growth of community services as an alternative to institutional care. At this time, institutions and community services were seen as complimentary service systems offering parents a range of options, a position referred to as the "continuum of care." In the late 1960s, PARC moved to a position of "No New Institutional Construction." This position encouraged deinstitutionalization to end overcrowding, but allowed institutional placement for those who desired or "needed" it. In the 1970s, PARC sought to close Pennhurst; however, they did not seek to close all Pennsylvania's institutions. Indeed, only in 2011 did PARC participate in a lawsuit to deinstitutionalize all of Pennsylvania's institutions, now called "state centers" for people with developmental disabilities.

The changes in their political stance in part resulted from a growing recognition that the state could not or would not reform institutions. But an examination of these changes also highlights the pragmatics of the positions taken by PARC. Rather than pursue the ideological position of full closure of the institutions in the 1970s, PARC accepted a smaller victory by closing Pennhurst. They then spent approximately 15 years struggling to ensure that individuals who moved out of Pennhurst had adequate housing, services, and supports within the community. Meanwhile, other Pennsylvania institutions remained open. This history is also used to examine the impact of parental division, the tension between parent agendas and disability rights, and PARC's responses to these issues.

Pennsylvania's Institutions Pre-1968: The Continuum of Care

Samuel Gridley Howe justified the establishment of the first publicly funded school for "idiots" in 1847 by advocating for their right to an education and extolling the benefits to society of training individuals otherwise left dependent (Trent 1994). Soon thereafter, the creation of specialized institutions to care for and train people with intellectual disabilities became the dominant political response to intellectual disability; however, because of overcrowding and underfunding, institutional administrators quickly disregarded their mission to educate and train and instead ran large-scale custodial warehouses (Ferguson 1994; Noll and Trent 2004; Rothman 1971; Trent 1994). Pennsylvania's history closely paralleled these national trends. In 1852, Dr. Alfred L. Elwyn founded Pennsylvania's first privately run residential school for individuals diagnosed as "feeble-minded," the Pennsylvania Training School for Feebleminded Children (later named Elwyn). In 1893, the Pennsylvania state legislature authorized the construction of Pennsylvania's first public institution for people diagnosed as feebleminded: the State Institution for the Feeble-Minded of Western Pennsylvania, which would later become known as Polk State School. In 1903, the legislature authorized the construction of a second institution, the Eastern Pennsylvania State Institution for the Feeble-Minded and Epileptics, later known as Pennhurst State School. Polk and Pennhurst were both expected to house at least 800 patients, but each grew to house more than three thousand patients at their peak populations. They also shared a similar initial charge to serve two types of patients: "trainables" who were expected to receive an education and return to the community and "custodial cases" who were defined as unable to care for themselves and were expected to reside throughout their lives at the institution. Both Polk and Pennhurst, however, soon became primarily custodial institutions with little in the way of treatment or educational programming. The Commonwealth of Pennsylvania would eventually run six institutions for people with intellectual disabilities, five of which continued to operate in 2012 as "state centers" and serve more than one hundred "consumers" at each site.

Owing to the philosophy, lack of funding, devaluation of institutional patients/ inmates, minimal qualifications of underpaid staff, and social isolation of the institution, America's institutions deteriorated into sites of abuse and neglect. This trend also occurred in Pennsylvania. Indeed, by the 1930s, criticism of the deplorable conditions in Pennsylvania's institutions was both public and common. In 1937 Pennsylvania Governor George H. Earle said of his investigation into Pennsylvania's institutions that he "found conditions that were so lacking in humaneness as to be almost unbelievable in a great civilized Commonwealth" (Earle 1937, 1). Despite Earle's purported commitment to improving the institutions, Albert Deutsch's 1946 photographic exposé documented horrendous conditions at the Philadelphia State Hospital. In 1947 in response to the public outcry after Deutsch's exposé, Governor James H. Duff promised to support a "curative approach" and transform the institutions into places of treatment (Duff 1947). Despite this promise, by the 1950s Polk State School was operating at 33 percent more than its capacity with one physician per six hundred patients. Pennhurst State School and Hospital was operating 18 percent above its capacity with a documented need for an additional three hundred attendants and medical social workers (Department of Public Welfare 1955–1958). A 1960 official report of the Pennsylvania Department of Public Welfare stated, "We need to face the fact, however, that we daily skirt the brink of tragedy. Despite the millions we have spent and are spending on construction and maintenance, too many of our patients still live under overcrowded, hazardous, and unsanitary conditions. Too many of our buildings present a picture of dilapidation..." (Department of Public Welfare 1960, 54).

Criticism of institutions steadily grew and came from varied sources such as journalists and the Mental Health Foundation and the National Committee for Mental Hygiene (Taylor 2009). Adding to these voices were parents of children diagnosed as "mentally retarded."[2] PARC was the largest of these parent organizations in Pennsylvania, and, in their activism, they advocated for services, both institutional and community-based, and criticized the current service system.

Before the 1950s, Pennsylvania parents were not well organized, they hesitated to criticize the system because of fear of negative repercussions targeted at their families, and when they did complain they typically expressed individual-level concerns. In 1949, parents founded the Pennsylvania Association for Retarded and Handicapped Children, and parents soon became increasingly vocal in their criticism. They did not however immediately urge the closure of institutions. Rather, in the 1950s and early 1960s, PARC blamed institutional problems on the lack of funding and overcrowding and saw institutional expansion, reform, and community services as linked solutions. By this logic, the problems of the institutions could be rectified through providing a "continuum of care," a range of services, both in the community and through the institutional system, to meet the varied needs of people with mental retardation (Taylor 1988). This conceptual framework allowed PARC to appease parents who supported the perpetuation of the institutional system and parents who demanded services in the community. In line with their position thus far, the continuum of care positioned institutional and community-based services as complimentary, not competing, models of care, which were both valuable in meeting the varied needs of a diverse population. Indeed, through the early 1960s, PARC's newsletter, *The Pennsylvania Message*, never mentioned abolishing the institutional system.

Institutional Expansion

To offer some examples of the push for institutional expansion, in the early 1950s parents launched a letter writing campaign to urge Governor Fine to address overcrowding at Polk through institutional expansion and funding for community services. One of the most eloquent of the letters was written by a member of the Greater Pittsburgh Association of Parents and Friends of Mentally Retarded Children who urged Governor Fine to expand access to institutional care:

> Dear Governor Fine: When your children were born, you were blessed with normal children – not blind, not deaf, nor mentally retarded. If you had not been so blessed, your blind child would have a good school to attend. The deaf child would be given every opportunity to overcome his handicap in a good school. However, your mentally retarded child would probably still be on a waiting list – a long, long waiting list – awaiting admittance to a State School for Mentally Retarded Children...
>
> A little over a year ago, twelve desperate parents organized the Greater Pittsburgh Association of Parents and Friends of Mentally Retarded Children...These parents, 20,000 of them, in Allegheny County, pay school taxes, but most of their children are not able to attend public schools and because of the lack of space and facilities in State Institutions, are made to stay at home, friendless, innocent children who should have the same opportunities every other child born should have...Our children are all future patients for Pennsylvania State Schools, but there is no room for them now or for years to come. They have been barred from Special Classes in public schools so they are kept at home alone and friendless...
>
> It is within your power, as Governor of this State, to change this unhealthy situation. A mentally retarded child is not a temporary problem- it is a lifetime problem. He must be given the opportunity to live in his own world, with friends of his own kind – not made to bear the abuse of normal children who never realize how cruel they can be – and also from society in general who never heard of the problem of mentally retarded children because nobody ever made any effort to help these children publicly as they have polio or cerebral palsy victims...We have been visitors at Polk State School and have found it to be a beautiful haven for these innocent children who cannot live in normal society. They are happy and clean and busy children. Even their parents look happy and at peace with the world. Their children are happy and safe for the rest of their lives. These parents can die knowing their child will still be happy and taken care of. We, who must wait and wait for years do not have that peace- ours is a 24 hour a day worry. (Ruth H. 1952)

In 1952, PARC President Martin Papish urged Governor Fine to build a third institution for mentally retarded children (Papish 1952). In 1957, when a tour of the state institutions revealed chronic overcrowding, Pennsylvania's House passed House Bill one thousand seven hundred postponing admissions. Rather than support this decision, PARC President Mrs. Philip Elkin wrote to Governor George Leader urging institutional expansion and the guarantee of institutional placements for those on the waitlist, stating, "The Commonwealth has the obligation of caring for the mentally retarded who require institutionalization...Surely the only possible solution to the program of admissions is to reopen them! (Elkin 1957, 1).

Because parents were still committed to the institutional system, they relied heavily on collaborative strategies for reform rather than confrontational ones. Confrontation, especially the use of public exposés, was seen as placing the whole institutional system at risk because the state might entertain the notion of abolishing it. Parents instead used strategies such as building alliances with politicians, letter-writing, phone-calling, and demanding state investigations to expose conditions to politicians. (Segal 1970). As discussed by Brockley (2004, 132), parents saw institutions as "both a resource and a restriction." For parents who could not care for their child or who desired but could not afford professional treatment or education for their children, the state institution was often perceived as their only option. Parents therefore played a key role in pushing for institutional expansion (L. Jones 2010). Other parents, though, resisted the domination of the institution and pressured politicians and professionals to provide quality care in the community (Brockley 2004; L. Jones 2010). In these struggles, complex narratives of rights emerged, as some parents fought for their children to have a right to lifelong security and support through institutional care, while others began framing a right to live in the community with services provided there (Carey 2009). PARC tried to bridge these positions by advocating both institutional improvement and expansion as well as the development of services in the community.[3]

Institutional Reform

Though a fundamental shift in position did not occur until the late 1960s, parents in the early 1960s began pressing more stridently for institutional reform and for the provision of services located in the community. The growing ambiguity regarding institutions is vividly revealed in PARC's newsletter, the *Pennsylvania Message*. The newsletter frequently ran positive articles showcasing the merits of state institutions. In fact, some articles read like advertising copy. A 1965 (p. 2) article, "Recreation at Laurelton State School and Hospital," offered the following description: "On this beautiful campus, housed in buildings of native stone, live about 900 mentally retarded girls and women...The philosophy of Laurelton State School and Hospital is to recognize the dignity and worth of each individual entrusted to our care." The full page article described the many opportunities for residents, including "seasonal parties and dances" with live music, an active recreational program run by trained staff, hiking, bowling and many opportunities for play. Indeed, the article presented the primary challenge for residents as the difficulty they faced in learning how to have fun and enjoy the opportunities at Laurelton "when their experiences before Laurelton have deprived them of so much" (p. 2). Laurelton was presented as an ideal environment, preferable to the cruel world from which they had come.

The promotion of institutions, however, was by no means the only discourse. Indeed, articles detailing the merits of institutions were increasingly placed in the broader context of criticism and suggestions for reform. Coverage of Polk State School and Hospital offers a fitting example. The *Pennsylvania Message* reported in 1965 that Polk was operated under conditions of severe overcrowding ("Lawrence County" 1965). In contrast, a 1966 article praised its progress in educational training. The article concluded on an uplifting note: "Future developments affecting treatments, training, and education look promising and interesting for the retarded in residential schools" ("Polk develops..." 1966, 9).

Coverage of other institutions reveals the same inconsistencies in message. In February 1968, the *Pennsylvania Message* ran a positive article on the development of psycho-social habilitation at Pennhurst, which was presented as a step toward the provision of opportunities to every resident and the eradication of the poor conditions. The program's philosophy was described as recognizing "that the retardate, whatever his mental state or physical condition, is a human being deserving the fullest assistance possible..." (Schaffer and Looker 1968, 3). The very next volume (April 1968) offered strident criticism of the political system that had underfunded its "medieval institutions," described as "antiquated" with "corridors of despair" ("Focus on Guilt" 1968, 1). However, the next volume (September 1968) contained another positive article, this time about Hamburg State School and Hospital. The article stated, "A peaceful world of trees, grass, love, and care is available to the patients at Hamburg State School and Hospital..." (Edelson 1968, 5).

These examples illustrate the ways in which PARC encouraged hope for the institutional system while simultaneously criticizing it. When discussing institutional reform, PARC considered many possible types of reform and actively attempted to serve many interests. One type of reform was to position the institution as the hub of an expansive system of care, similar to the hopes of the institutional founders in the early 1900s. The institution, according to this model of reform, would be the center for training professionals, identifying and diagnosing people with mental retardation, providing services in-house and to those who lived in the community, and coordinating community-based services. Discussions of the Elwyn School best represent this model. Elwyn was a private, well-funded institution with a reputation that remained relatively unsullied in the institutional scandals that rocked Pennsylvania. Renamed the "Elwyn Institute," Elwyn directors emphasized the wide range of services offered including education, treatment, diagnosis, vocational rehabilitation, and recreation (in contrast with the typical custodial institution). In such a model of reform, the institution remained a vital and indeed the central component of the continuum of care.

Such lofty dreams were rarely imagined for public institutions. Rather, two hopes seemed to dominate the discourse in PARC newsletters: to modernize and humanize the institution and/or to reduce and specialize it. Modernizing and humanizing the institutions involved several possible facets: architecture, programming, staffing, and organizational philosophy. The creation of a humane institution necessitated buildings that embraced new models of construction and spatial geography. At times this ambitious goal was reduced to specific architectural details like removing cement block interior walls and chicken wire fencing, which were now said to symbolize the "institutional mentality" and instead using oak veneer and "an attractively designed lattice screen" to partition large rooms into intimate living spaces ("Architectural Conference" 1968, 1). Reformers also pushed to ban the "cages" used to contain infants and "crib cases."

More substantive architectural changes involved the creation of smaller facilities on the institutional "campus." For example, the Laurel House School created cottage units "for 18 persons in each group, arranged as to avoid crowding and to provide more privacy and homelike living arrangements than are frequently permitted the retarded individual living in a residential facility" ("New Residential Facility for Southeastern Area" 1968, 1). For massive institutions like Pennhurst, reformers considered creating a series of smaller institutions on the grounds of Pennhurst, each to house five hundred residents ("New Residential Facility for Southeastern Area" 1968). Ironically, although framed here as "reform," "colony models" had been among the earliest institutional designs. As Ferguson (this volume) shows, the colony model did little to humanize or individualize the institution, but rather served professional interests in supporting a thoroughly classified population in which all activities were determined by one's diagnosis. Institutional professionals and administrators hoped to loosely replicate increasingly popular models of group homes and community-based housing under the institutional umbrella, while ignoring that institutional rules, hierarchy, structure, and the isolated environment completely altered the experience of living in a "small" residence. PARC, though, encouraged these architectural reforms, as they were seen as more humane than mass congregate bedrooms. PARC also continued to demand the state reduce the number of patients at Pennhurst and Polk down to a population size below one thousand people, close to their original charge, which is not a radical stance by today's standards but would have been a considerable reduction in size, given that each institution housed more than three thousand patients.

Although administrators and state officials tended to focus on the physical aspects of the institution such as size and construction, parents also demanded changes in staffing, training, and programming. Federal funding streams supported construction rather than staffing and programming (Trent 1994), and therefore the state's answer to the institutional problem always seemed to be more buildings (albeit differently designed) and more beds. But what would become of the people in the buildings? Parents pushed for more staff and programming, with limited success. Scandals at Pennhurst, for example, led to the creation of new staff positions, especially in direct care and a reduction of staff-patient ratio. Polk developed a "stimulating" new educational program ("Simulating Community..." 1968), which served 615 residents (of 3,000+) for several hours one day per week.

The call to individualize treatment and services became a common mantra, to be accomplished by increasing the number of staff members and training them in best practices of care. Toward that goal, in 1968 PARC reprinted a brochure created by the Minnesota Department of Public Welfare to train staff regarding dehumanizing and humanizing practices using a series of comic strip images ("From Dehumanization to Dignity" 1968, 4–5). The comic strip vividly yet simply displays the point that both prisons and institutions shared common dehumanizing practices, such as referring to people as labels and numbers, scheduling routine care like showers only on certain days and times, having mail opened and inspected, and being locked behind closed doors. High quality care instead required an approach that supported the dignity of the individual. Patients treated with dignity had privacy in the bathrooms and showers, received encouragement and praise, were recognized and treated as individuals, owned and had access to personal items, and had a say in whether and how they participated in treatment and activities.

The notion of the continuum of care and the growing prevalence of community services led to questions not only about quality of institutional care but also for whom institutional care was appropriate. Some individuals wanted institutions to continue to serve all those in need of care, whether the need be owing to severity or type of disability, absence of family supports, or absence of community services. Others saw institutions playing an increasingly specialized role, serving only those with severe and multiple disabilities, those who needed 24 hour care, and/or individuals with significant medical needs ("Scranton's Allied Services..." 1967). The best strategy to conquer institutional overcrowding and the long wait lists, according to PARC leaders, was to provide an array of services in the community, leaving large-scale, centralized institutions available to those with the greatest needs.

While situating institutions as part of the continuum of care, PARC began to more clearly articulate that most people could and should be served in the community. For most individuals community services were more cost-effective, produced better outcomes, and were more humane than institutional services. This stance, however, legitimated institutional care as appropriate for some individuals.

Through the 1960s, PARC tried to both critique the institutional system and advocate for a varied set of reforms, but they failed to develop a consistent narrative for when, why, and for whom institutions should be available and how they would interact with community services. Parents became increasingly divided. Parents with institutionalized children primarily sought investments in the institutional system while other parents sought the development of community-based services. PARC tried to represent all of these parents in advocating access to a range of high-quality options at affordable prices with state support. They also sought to simultaneously collaborate with and criticize state officials. By the late 1960s and early 1970s, however, it became increasingly clear that the talk of reform was not leading to significant improvements in the public institutional system.

Although PARC had waited for reform for two decades, by the late 1960s PARC was increasingly disillusioned with the institutional system and the political system that seemed unable to reform it. They had been pushing for reform since their formation in 1949, and the institutions were no better. National concern regarding institutional care was growing. Research on labeling, social control, and "normalization" argued that treating people as deviants only led to and reinforced deviant behavior. Burton Blatt's 1966 exposé, *Christmas in Purgatory*, shocked the nation through the graphic depiction of the isolation and neglect in institutions. PARC decided that the time was ripe to capitalize on the national shift in sentiment toward institutions in order to demand reform. In 1968, PARC lent its support for a public exposé of Pennhurst State School and Hospital. *Suffer the Little Children* aired in 1968 as a 5 part series on NBC10, a local Philadelphia based station. After the series aired, the *Pennsylvania Message*'s headline read "Focus on Guilt." PARC publicly demanded that the state reduce the overcrowded conditions, end the abuse of patients, create more staff positions, raise staff pay, and dismiss Pennhurst's superintendent.

Their decision to use vocal and public criticism of the institutions not only energized many individuals to action but also quickly alienated some parents and professionals. Former PARC president Paul R. Reed (1968, 1) wrote to Governor Shafer criticizing PARC's tactics rather than the state's woeful administration of institutions, stating "I disagree completely with the tactics recently displayed by the Pennsylvania Association for Retarded Children in publicizing certain alleged conditions at Pennhurst. Whether true or not, charges brought forth in such a manner hurt, rather than help the retarded. It sickens one to ponder the anguish and anxiety which have been needlessly imposed upon those who have children in Pennhurst and other state schools." In contrast with the traditional PARC strategy of cooperation with state officials, Reed said "I view with apprehension the Association's change in mode of operation." Finally, he added, "Dr. Potkonski has been an excellent administrator, and I hope you will not accede to PARC's demands for his dismissal." The Pennhurst Parents and Staff Association also made a public statement in support of the Pennhurst superintendent and in opposition to PARC's initiatives. As PARC grew increasingly critical of institutions, it faced increasing divisions among its previous allies and supporters.

Cracks in the Continuum: No New Construction

PARC had hoped that public embarrassment would force the state to respond. The state did respond, but PARC was deeply frustrated with its proposal. PARC wanted a significant infusion of money into the institutions to reduce their populations and increase the quality of care, as well as funding to support the growth of community services. The administration, however, focused only on channeling more money into institutional construction. The Pennsylvania Department of Public Welfare (DPW) proposed to build a new four-story building on the Pennhurst grounds, announced with no promises regarding staffing, programming, or funding for community services.

PARC opposed the project. It had never before directly opposed state expenditures to expand the institutional system. PARC president Harold Nathan (1968, 1) wrote to Governor Shafer, "The Pennsylvania Association for Retarded Children has come to a crossroads however. When considering the length of the waiting list, the waiting time for admission to State schools and hospitals and the heartache which this causes the individual families, it is still better to say we would rather have no building than to go ahead with the construction of this outmoded, outdated, four-story construction."

Despite PARC's concerns, DPW went ahead and requested more than twenty-three million dollars to renovate and build at Pennhurst. Twenty-three million dollars would be channeled into the same site by the same administration, with no promises of reductions in size, funding for staffing or programming, or investment in community services. PARC again opposed this request. In a letter to Pennsylvania legislators, PARC President James R. Wilson argued that the proposal "not only violates modern architectural and program concepts for the retarded, it also negates the community-based mandate of the MH/MR Act of 1966... We appeal to you to determine who really stands to gain from this perpetuation of an oversized institution predestined to suffer from escalating operational costs and a population twice the size, according to OMHMR's own statement, of that required for effective programming..." (Wilson 1970a, 1, italics in original). In testimony to the House Appropriations Committee, Wilson (1970b, 1) stated, "It is not our intent to deny the critical need for adequate Capital Budget appropriations to protect and program properly for mentally retarded persons who require residential services. It is our intent however to cause the department either to justify the way it proposed to use this $23,757,000 or to find other more acceptable ways to meet the residential service needs of retarded persons." Wilson went on to argue that institutional care cost more, violated modern standards, misdirected money away from the community, and was inconsistent with modern best practices. PARC took a similar stance regarding other institutional construction. PARC opposed construction costing half a million dollars that proceeded at the Southeastern Hospital at Byberry and a ten million dollar construction project at Western State Hospital ("Construction Changes at Byberry" 1971; "State Scraps Building Plan" 1970–1971).

Through these actions, PARC moved from supporting a range of services to a position of "No New Construction" with regard to new large buildings or major expansion on institutional property ("PARC Convention Reaffirms..." 1972, 1). According to PARC, all major funding for new construction should be directed toward community services. Moreover, encouraged by Gunnar Dybwad (former executive director of the National Association for Retarded Children), PARC increasingly came to see institutional preservation and community care as competing rather than complimentary paths toward meeting the needs of people with intellectual disabilities ("Death Knell May Sound on M.R. Institutions" 1971). In an article entitled, "What Prompts PARC's Action Toward Institutions," the author explained, "This pouring of public dollars into an archaic and deteriorating residential system in turn perpetuates the shortage of community services which, in turn, accentuates the urgency for the creation of additional residential services which are storing up an ever larger number of individuals since those ready to return to the community cannot be released because of the inadequacy of supportive community services. A vicious circle indeed" (1973, 4).

The continued political deadlock between the Pennsylvania administration and PARC led PARC to reverse their long support of the institutional system, and their goals became more clearly articulated: to reduce institutional populations, prevent "unnecessary" institutionalization, and provide community alternatives. By the early 1970s, discourse in the *Pennsylvania Message* was almost solely negative when reporting on institutions, except when reporting on efforts by institutions to involve institutional residents in the community or move them to the community. Headlines included "Violations Charged at Cresson School" (1973), "Hearing Over the Closing of Pinehill" (1973), "Special Commission Investigates Human Medical Experimentation in State Institutions" (1973), "Peonage Ends in Court Order" (1974), and "Deinstitutionalization: Convention's Key Issue" (1974). PARC's work toward institutional reform became more rights-focused as they worked on halting human experimentation, banning "cages" used as beds, advocating pay for inmate labor, and enforcing a uniform set of institutional standards.

Two things are important to consider regarding the position of "No New Construction." First, although PARC was by this time less ideologically supportive of institutions, their shift seems to be in large part *a response* to a series of inadequate proposals for reform by the state. Had the state promised to channel money into more training and staffing in institutions, as well as more community services, as PARC had requested, it seems likely PARC would have continued to support the continuum of care. A second and related point, the position of no new construction was not the same as advocating for the closure of institutions. Despite PARC's goals of deinstitutionalization and avoiding unnecessary institutional placement, they still believed in the need for large-scale, centralized institutions. Alongside the "No New Construction" position, they articulated a "commitment recognition," in which they recognized that large institutions would continue to exist and should receive appropriate funding for maintenance and programming. More shocking perhaps, they still claimed a "right" to institutional placement. In their 1973 "Bill of Rights for Pennsylvania's Retarded Citizens" (p. 1), the first right articulated specified:

(1) **State Schools and Hospitals should be regarded as part of residential services which are part of community services.** Every retarded person, if at all possible, should be kept within his family and community circle; and the family should receive sustained professional reinforcement. If the child cannot be cared for and properly trained at home, then he should live in a foster home or in a community-based residence. If care in an institution becomes necessary, it should be in surroundings and under circumstances as close to normal living as possible. (Bold included in original)

Thus, despite their shifting philosophy and sharp and sustained criticism of institutions, PARC still supported a need for and even a right to institutionalization.

The "commitment recognition," combined with "no new construction," was in part a practical stance in recognition of the reality that it might be decades before community services had grown sufficiently to serve all persons identified with mental retardation; in the meantime, individuals in institutions deserved proper care. It was also likely a strategy to appease the parents and community members who had not yet come to understand or appreciate PARC's shifting priorities. Many community members and parents still assumed that the best way to improve care for people with intellectual disabilities was to invest in state institutions. For example, after *Suffer the Little Children* aired in 1968, the governor's office received more than one hundred letters, as well as petitions with more than three hundred signatures, expressing concern regarding Pennsylvania's institutions. Almost none of the letters suggested closing Pennhurst, and few even mentioned developing community services. Instead, they focused on improving Pennhurst, expressed general concern, and/or asked for unspecified changes/improvements (for examples see Mrs. Marie W. 1968, Mrs. Ellen S. 1968, and Mrs. Elizabeth S. 1968). Particularly problematic was resistance to PARC's goals by parents with institutionalized children, because these parents held the same claim to represent the interests of their children. If these parents organized separately, PARC would lose its claim to speak for the parents of people with intellectual disabilities.

Given the intransigence of the state, PARC turned to attorney Tom Gilhool to examine the feasibility of a lawsuit claiming the right to treatment as a strategy to force the state to reform the institutions. Gilhool suggested a lawsuit related to the right to education instead. Unlike the right to treatment, the right to education for all children was established in Pennsylvania legislation, and recognition of this right for children with disabilities would simultaneously enhance services in the community and improve treatment and education in the institutions. The fight for education helped to energize, mobilize, and unify parents. In 1971, PARC won a historically path-breaking court case, PARC v. Commonwealth of Pennsylvania, which guaranteed children with disabilities the right to "a program of education and training appropriate to his learning capacities" (PARC v. Commonwealth 1971, 1266). In the wake of this victory, PARC shifted its attention to capitalize on its success, creating initiatives to identify children outside of the educational system, parent training programs related to securing the right to an education, and mechanisms to assess the quality of educational program.

While PARC focused on educational initiatives, institutional reform shifted to the back-burner for a few years. The *Pennsylvania Message* provided fewer articles related to institutions, and work toward institutional reform decelerated. However, PARC leaders argued that the provision of public education had a "profound effect" ("Right to Education' Becomes Reality" 1973, 2) on children with disabilities, including those in institutions. They claimed that three thousand six hundred residents were now being educated with the oversight of the Department of Education, and many institutionalized children were now experiencing some level of community integration and educational programming ("'Right to Education' at Ebensburg" 1973). PARC also worked to develop community services beyond education, creating the service infrastructure to support deinstitutionalization.

Deinstitutionalization and Partial Closure

Within a few years, PARC again ramped up their efforts toward deinstitutionalization with another court case. Twenty-one year old Terri Halderman, a resident of the Pennhurst State School and Hospital who had suffered numerous injuries while living there, and her mother, Winifred Halderman, stepped forward to become the lead plaintiffs, joined by 7 other residents and the Parents and Family Association of Pennhurst. They charged Pennhurst with violating patients' rights and sought the improvement of conditions and services at Pennhurst. After the case began, Congress passed the 1975 Developmental Disabilities Assistance and Bill of Rights Act (referred to as the DD Act) that affirmed that individuals with developmental disabilities had the right to receive individualized treatment in the least restrictive environment. At this point, the United States Department of Justice and PARC joined the lawsuit, transforming the case into a class action suit representing all patients at Pennhurst.

After testimony regarding the abuse and neglect at Pennhurst, Judge Broderick came to the dramatic conclusion that "minimally adequate habilitation cannot be provided in an atmosphere such as Pennhurst. As the Court has heretofore found, Pennhurst does not provide an atmosphere conducive to normalization which is so vital to the retarded if they are to be given the opportunity to acquire, maintain, and improve their life skills. Pennhurst provides confinement and isolation, the antithesis of habilitation" (Halderman v. Pennhurst State School 1977, 1319). Judge Broderick became the first judge to mandate that all residents be moved into community placements, in effect ordering the closure of Pennhurst.

Broderick's historic decision was not applauded by everyone, and forces began to line up to prevent the closing of Pennhurst, including labor unions, superintendents and some parents (Carey 2009). The parents who filed the case had sought to improve conditions at Pennhurst, and some were dismayed when Judge Broderick ordered its closure. Pennhurst parent leader Rev. L. David Schlosser told a local newspaper, "One of the options ought to be an institution, not necessarily Pennhurst. We ought to have a range of options or alternatives" (Rebenkoff 1979). For these parents, large scale institutions were a desirable option to maintain. Ultimately the case came before the United States Supreme Court (Halderman v. Pennhurst 1981). The Court did not find that federal law, specifically the DD Act, conferred the right to treatment. Sent back to the state, the state appellate court upheld Broderick's decision. In 1984, after ten years of litigation, the parties involved signed the final settlement agreement and proceeded with plans to close Pennhurst State School and Hospital and thereby replace large, inflexible institutions with hundreds of small programs in the community.

This was a monumental victory, yet a strangely limited one. Although Pennhurst was closing, other large institutions in Pennsylvania remained in place. Broderick had declared that habilitation could not take place at Pennhurst, but he did not declare that all state institutions had to close. In fact, resources for the establishment of community services were diverted so dramatically to eastern Pennsylvania as deinstitutionalization proceeded that the growth of community services in other parts of the state slowed. In 1979 the legislature passed the Community Services Act that stressed the right to "effective, integrated services under conditions least restrictive to personal liberty." (New Community Service Legislation Developed 1979); however, this still was not the death knoll for institutions. More interestingly perhaps, PARC did not immediately use the Pennhurst legal precedent nor this new law to sue to close other Pennsylvania institutions. Instead it relied on the former strategies of exposés and negotiations to improve institutional conditions, rather than close them. For example, frustrated with the lack of improvement at

Polk State Center, in 1979 PARC released a statement to the news detailing the numerous problems at Polk including a drowning determined to be because of staff negligence. At the time, Polk still had more than one thousand residents. In 1976 PARC members visited Hamburg, a six hundred person facility. Despite over-crowding and insufficient programming, the article in the *Pennsylvania Message* stated, "the investigators cited recent improvements and reported that conditions are comparable to or better than, those at the state's 10 other similar institutions." In fact, the article noted that PARC investigators were "pleased with" the posi-tive attitudes of staff (Residential Services Team Visits Hamburg 1976). Again in 1980, PARC participated in a review of the Hamburg Center, and they found again insufficient programming and services. Rather than demand closure, the review committee recommended that Hamburg move from a medical model to a rehabili-tative model "where the emphasis is placed on programming" (Hamburg Center Reviewed 1980, 5).

Thus, the Pennhurst case by no means meant the end of large-scale institu-tionalization in Pennsylvania. It led to the closure of one institution while others remained open, and parents still engaged in the same struggles over reform using the same tactics. Again, this seems to be for rather practical purposes. After declar-ing institutionalization unconstitutional, it seemed unrealistic to deinstitutionalize throughout all of Pennsylvania, given the paucity of community services. PARC focused its energies on ensuring that deinstitutionalization of Pennhurst residents preceded in a safe, humane manner. In particular, they worked to ensure that each resident had a transition plan including housing and supports so that deinstitution-alization would not lead to mass homelessness. Deinstitutionalization of Pennhurst took at least 15 years, and in the meantime, other institutions remained open.

Discussion

The 1950s, 1960s, and 1970s were years of transition with regard to PARC's posi-tion on institutions as they moved from promoting expansion, to opposing con-struction, to deinstitutionalization and limited closure. Similar political trends have continued to allow state centers to persist today. In 1999 the United States Supreme Court affirmed the right to live in the community in Olmstead v. L.C. (1999), yet the Commonwealth of Pennsylvania continued to operate five "state centers": Ebensburg, Hamburg, Polk, Selinsgrove, and White Haven. In 2011, 1,159 people lived in these 5 centers (Institute on Disabilities 2011).[4] State officials argued that these state centers are not in fact institutions. Rather, they say state centers are run on the same philosophies and practices as other community service sites: a respect for rights, individualized treatment, and the provision of "everyday lives" to people with disabilities ("State Centers" 2011).

Advocates yet again had to turn to the courts. In Benjamin v. the Department of Welfare (2011), the Disability Rights Network with the support of PARC and other organizations filed a suit on behalf of residents of state centers charging the state with violations of the Americans with Disabilities Act and Section 504 of the Rehabilitation Act for imposing unnecessary segregation. The Court found in favor of the Disability Rights Network and a settlement has been negotiated in which the state must develop a plan of transition for all state center residents who are qualified to receive community services, desire them, and have no guardian in opposition.

Both the present day continuation of and resistance against large-scale congregate housing and services were paved in Pennsylvania's history of reform. Deinstitutionalization and the prevention of "unnecessary" institutionalization were prioritized, rather than closing the institutions. Deinstitutionalization is not necessarily the same as closing the institutions. Deinstitutionalization may mean moving people out as community services are available, moving those deemed "able to benefit from community services," or reducing institutional populations as residents die. Indeed, as noted in Benjamin v. DPW, "individuals institutionalized in [Pennsylvania's] state centers are significantly more likely to leave those centers through death than through community placement" (Benjamin v. Department of Public Welfare Brief of the US as Amicus Curiae 2009). PARC historically sought to abolish appalling conditions, reduce the numbers of people in institutions, and expand community services, not close down all institutions. This is not to say that PARC has not asserted the need to close state centers; in 2009 PARC published a position statement "Close State Centers" that affirmed the right to live and receive services in the community. Yet even after the success of the Benjamin v. PDW case, Robert Meek of the Disability Rights Network told reporters that, "No one's kicking out people who want to stay there...We would like the state to be more responsive to people who are ready to go" (Moore 2011). He continued on to explain that they are "not looking to close state facilities, but rather provide community-based services to residents who want them." Thus, even after Pennhurst, Olmstead, and Benjamin, the goal is presented as access to the community rather than closure of the institutions.

This difference is a significant one and relates to the framing of rights. Indeed, the rhetoric of choice and rights has been just as important in maintaining institutions as in closing them. The Olmstead decision affirmed a person's right to receive community-integrated services. This right is based on choice, not mandate, offering people the right to choose among services in the continuum of care, and thereby maintaining the legitimacy of institutions as a choice. Taking a stand to close institutions represents a different view of rights, one that argues that the state cannot restrict the liberty of individuals based on disability, even if some parents and individuals with disabilities might choose this option (Community Imperative 1979). Historically, PARC has typically positioned itself within the framework of choice. In this rhetoric of choice, we see a conflict over who actually controls the choice. Even in the Benjamin decision, those who want to leave and have family in support of this decision are prioritized for deinstitutionalization. Those who have guardians who oppose the move are not to be moved. The state therefore still supports that parents and guardians have the right to maintain the institutional residence of their wards against their wishes.

To consider the issue of parent activism, it may seem easy to position parents for or against institutionalization, and more broadly for or against disability rights, but the history is much less clear. Parents like Eleanor Elkin fought strenuously for the right to education and for institutional reform, yet also for institutional expansion. Parents fought primarily for services perceived to support the well-being of their children and families, and they used a rights-rhetoric to do so; therefore it was not unusual for parents to fight for the right to education, to community services, to medical care, *and* to institutional "services." Parents did not split over the issue of segregation or institutionalization simply or even primarily due to ideology at first; their division was driven by the state's refusal to adequately fund and advance institutional reform and community services, thereby pitting parents who still wanted to support institutional expansion against other parents who felt that the continuum of care was infeasible.

The question of rights and parents' role in these questions though clearly became a dilemma for PARC and the parents' movement. The divisions around institutionalization and the growing Disability Rights Movement made clear that parents and their disabled offspring may have different and conflicting interests. Therefore, organizations like PARC had to decide whether they were primarily a parents' organization or a disability rights organization. Early in its history PARC was largely an organization of parents and allies, and it sought to represent the needs and demands of a wide range of parents, including fighting for improvement in the institutions at the same time they fought to expand services in the community. Parent activists believed they could come together to fight for the best interests of their children, and that parents' interests were the same as their children's interests. However, the conflicts over institutions divided parents and pushed PARC to consider who it was serving: parents or people with disabilities. As PARC moved toward demanding institutional closure, parents—PARC's main organizational base—also became a significant potential hindrance. Thus, PARC began to reposition itself as an advocacy organization supporting people with disabilities and their family members, rather than an organization of parents and their allies. Yet, PARC's tie to family members has always been strong, and they continue to serve as a resource for parents and family members while they simultaneously advocate for disability rights.

We also see a lack of conceptualization regarding the definition of an institution and its impact. PARC demanded smaller buildings without chicken wire and cages. Once Hamburg had "typical" furniture and 120 people, is this small enough, nice enough? PARC demanded dignity, respect and individualized services. Does an individualized support plan "prove" these criteria are met? Recent definitions have focused more heavily on choice and the relational patterns within a setting. If someone chooses to be in an institution, is it no longer an institution? There are also significant debates over who gets to choose, especially when a disability is significant.

Self-Advocates Becoming Empowered (SABE) argues that any setting that denies choice and segregates people based on disability is an institution, and they demand the closure of all segregated, congregate services including group homes, day centers, and sheltered workshops. However, ARC chapters run many services that are segregated and deny people with disabilities particular choices in their daily life. As PARC had invested in the institutional system, it has invested heavily in the modern system of segregated "community" services. Reform will mean again confronting parents who are heavily invested in systems they helped create and who believe that they have a right to choose particular services for their sons and daughters, as well as confronting the larger state and professional systems. However, PARC clearly weighs ideology and pragmatics. If they end segregated or "special" services, will communities step up to promote inclusion? Will employers employ people with significant disabilities? How is inclusion funded and supported? As with institutional reform, PARC has advocated inclusion at the same time that it supports a wide range of segregated congregate services. Just as the goals in the 1960s and 1970s seemed unclear and contradictory, so too today PARC experiences tensions in the degree to which they should support, reform or end models of segregated community services, and parents continue to play different and complex roles in the debates around integration and supporting a largely differentiated, segregated system of services.

Notes

* Author's Note: We would like to thank Richard Scotch and Jennifer Bridges for their assistance in this project, and the editors for their feedback.

1. Founded as the Pennsylvania Association for Retarded and Handicapped Children, the organization then became the Pennsylvania Association for Retarded Children, then the Pennsylvania Association for Retarded Citizens, and most recently The Arc of Pennsylvania. For simplicity sake, we will use the abbreviation PARC throughout this time period regardless of the full name.
2. Mental retardation was the dominant terminology from the 1950s through to the 1990s used to describe someone identified as having an IQ of 70 or below and significant deficits in adaptation. The current terminology is intellectual disability; however, we will rely on the terminology of the time period.
3. Despite the growing resistance, institutions still garnered tremendous support from parents, the medical community, and politicians. Between 1946 and 1967 the number of residents in institutions for those labeled as "mentally retarded" rose from 116,828 to 193,188—an increase of 65 percent, nearly twice the increase of the general population (Trent 1994).
4. As of the June 20, 2011 census, 275 residents lived in Ebensburg, 120 in Hamburg, 293 in Polk, 310 in Selinsgrove, and 161 in White Haven.

References

"Architectural Conference." 1968. *Pennsylvania Message* 4(1): 1.
Benjamin v. The Department of Public Welfare of the Commonwealth of Pennsylvania, U.S. Court of Appeals, Third Circuit, Opinion April 15, 2011.
Benjamin v. Department of Public Welfare, Brief of the US as Amicus Curiae in Support of Plantiffs' Motion for Summary Judgment. 2009. Accessed June 2012. http://www.ada.gov/olmstead/documents/benjamin_brief.pdf
"Bill of Rights for Pennsylvania's Retarded Citizens." 1973. *Pennsylvania Message* 9 (2): 4.
Blum, Linda. 2007. "Mother-blame in the Prozac Nation: Raising Kids with Invisible Disabilities." *Gender and Society* 21(2): 202–226.
Brockley, Janice. 2004. "Raising the Child Who Never Grew." In *Mental Retardation in America*, edited by Steven Noll and James W. Trent Jr., 130–164. New York: New York University Press.
Brune, Jeffrey A. In press. *Disability Stigma and the Modern American State*. Cambridge, UK: Cambridge University Press.
Carey, Allison. 2009. *On the Margins of Citizenship: Intellectual Disability and Civil Rights in Twentieth Century America*. Philadelphia, PA: Temple University Press.
"The Community Imperative." 1979. Center on Human Policy at Syracuse University. Accessed June 2012. http://thechp.syr.edu/community_imperative.htm
"Construction Changes Sought at Byberry." 1971. *Pennsylvania Message* 7(2): 4.
"Death Knell May Sound on M.R. Institutions." 1971. *Pennsylvania Message* 7(2): 1–2.
"Deinstitutionalization: Convention's Key Issue." 1974. *Pennsylvania Message* 9(4): 1.

Duff, James H. 1947. "News Release, Office of the Governor." Papers of Governor James H. Duff, Pennsylvania State Archives, Manuscript Group 190, Official Papers, Mental Health, GM1445, Box 25, News Releases, 8–9–1947.

Earle, George Howard III. 1937. "Remarks of George H. Earle, Governor of PA, at ground-breaking ceremonies, Laurelton State Village, Inaugurating the first construction of the State Authority Institutional Building Program, Thursday, September 23, 1937, at 11am est." Papers of Governor George Howard Earle III. Earle, Pennsylvania State Archives, Manuscript Group 342, Official Papers, Speeches 1937–1938, Box 15, 3 Page Document.

Edelson, Maxine A. 1968. "College "Student Aids" Lend Hand at Hamburg." *Pennsylvania Message* 4(4): 8.

Elkin, Eleanor (Mrs. Phillip). August 2, 1957. Letter from Mrs. Phillip Elkin to Honorable George M. Leader. Papers of Governor George Leader, Pennsylvania State Archives, Manuscript Group 207, subject index – Pennsylvania Association for Retarded Children, 1955–1959, 9–0260 Carton 59, Folder 1.

Ferguson, Philip M. 1994. *Abandoned to Their Fate: Social Policy and Practice toward Severely Disabled People in America, 1820–1920.* Philadelphia, PA: Temple University Press.

"Focus on Guilt and Commonwealth of Excellence?" 1968. *Pennsylvania Message* 4(3): 1.

"Governor Readies Major Statement on Retarded – Wide Implication Expected in Response to PARC Concerns." 1970. *Pennsylvania Message* 6(1): 1.

H., Ruth. 1952 (September 25). Letter from Ruth H. to Governor John S. Fine. Papers of Governor John S. Fine. Pennsylvania State Archives. Manuscript Group 206, Mental Health 1951–1954, General Correspondence, 9–0031, Box 29, Folder 20.

Halderman v. Pennhurst State School. 1977. 446 F. Supp. 1295.

"Hamburg Center Reviewed." 1980. *Pennsylvania Message* 25(3): 5.

"Hearing Over the Closing of Pinehill." 1973. *Pennsylvania Message* 9(3): 2.

Institute on Disabilities. 2011. "Writing IM$Q Considerations for State Center ICF/MRs." Accessed June 2012. http://www.slideserve.com/humphrey/writing-im4q-considerations-for-state-center-icf

Jones, Kathleen. 1998. "'Mother Made Me Do It': Mother-Blaming and the Women of Child Guidance." In *Bad Mothers*, edited by Molly Ladd-Taylor and Laura Umanksy, 99–126. New York City: New York University Press.

Jones, Larry. 2010. *Doing Disability Justice.* Raleigh, NC: lulu.com Publishers.

Kittay, Eva. 2009. "Forever Small: The Strange Case of Ashley X." *Hypatia* 26(3): 610–631.

Landsman, Gail. 2009. *Reconstructing Motherhood and Disability in an Age of "Perfect Babies."* New York: Routledge.

"Lawrence County." 1965. *Pennsylvania Message* 1(2): 4.

Moore, Marcia. 2011. "Ruling a Threat to State Centers." *The Daily Item*, Sunbury Pa., January 28. Accessed June 2012. http://dailyitem.com/0100_news/x135631006/Ruling-a-threat-to-state-center/print

Nathan, Harold. October 30, 1968. Letter from Harold Nathan, President of PARC, to Governor Raymond Shafer. Papers of Governor Raymond P. Shafer. Pennsylvania State Archives. Manuscript Group 209. Shafer Papers, MG 209, General File Pennhurst and PA state schools and hospitals, 9–1109, Box 75, Folder 6

"New Community Service Legislation Developed." 1979. *Pennsylvania Message* 24(2): 12.

"New Residential Facility for Southeastern Area to Feature Small Groups, Community Relationships." 1968. Pennsylvania Message 4(3): 1.

Noll, Steven, and James W. Trent Jr. 2004. *Mental Retardation in America: A Historical Reader.* Chapel Hill, NC: University of North Carolina Press.

Olmstead, Commissioner, Georgia Department of Human Resources et. Al. v. L. C. 1999. 527 U.S. 581.

Ong-Dean, Colin. 2005. "Reconsidering the Social Location of the Medical Model: An Examination of Disability in Parenting Literature." *Journal of Medical Humanities* 26(2/3): 141–158.

Panitch, Melanie. 2008. *Disability, Mothers, and Organization: Accidental Activists.* New York: Routledge.

Papish, Martin F. November 3, 1952. Letter from Martin F. Papish to Governor John S. Fine. Papers of John S. Fine. Pennsylvania State Archives. Manuscript Group 206. Mental Health 1951–1954, General Correspondence, 9–0031, Box 29, Folder 20.

"PARC Convention Reaffirms Position on 'Construction' and 'Transfer.'" 1972. *Pennsylvania Message* 8(3): 1.

Pennsylvania Department of Public Welfare, n.d. Release from Department of Public Welfare, "Unofficial Fact Sheet of Background Data on Polk State School." Papers of Governor George Leader, Pennsylvania State Archives, MG 207, General File, 1955–1958, Series of institutional inspections, 9–0284, Carton 81, Folder 12.

———. 2011. "State Centers." Accessed June 2012. http://www.dpw.state.pa.us /foradults/statecenters/index.htm.

———. 1960. "Public Welfare Report, June 1, 1958 – May 31, 1960." Harrisburg: Commonwealth of Pennsylvania. Papers of Governor David Lawrence. Pennsylvania State Archives. Manuscript Group 191. Lawrence General Files, Public Welfare 1959–1960, 9–0470, Box 79, Folder 5.

"Peonage Ends in Court Order." 1974. *Pennsylvania Message* 9(2): 1.

"Polk Develops Behavioral-Social Approach to Treatment, Training, and Education of Residential Retardates." 1966. *Pennsylvania Message* 2(2): 9.

Prussing, Erica, Elisa J. Sobo, Elizabeth Walker, and Paul S. Kurtin. 2005. "Between 'desperation' and Disability Rights: A Narrative Analysis of Complimentary/ Alternative Medicine Use by Parents for Children with Down Syndrome" *Social Science and Medicine* 60(3): 587–598.

Rebenkoff, Marie. 1979. "Pennhurst Parent Group Organizes to Delay Move." *Suburban and Wayne Times* Wayne, Pa.), June 28.

"Recreation at Laurelton State School and Hospital." 1965. *Pennsylvania Message* 1(3): 2.

Reed, Paul R. 1968. Letter from Paul R. Reed to Governor Raymond Shafer. Papers of Governor Raymond P. Shafer. Pennsylvania State Archives. Manuscript Group 209, General File – Pennhurst and Pennsylvania State Schools and Hospitals, 9–1109, Box 75, Folder 8.

"Residential Services Team Visits Hamburg." 1976. *Pennsylvania Message* 11(3): 10.

"'Right to Education' Becomes Reality." 1973. *Pennsylvania Message* 9(4): 2.

"'Right to Education' at Ebensburg." 1973. *Pennsylvania Message* 9(4): 6.

Rothman, David J. 1971. *The Discovery of the Asylum.* Boston: Little, Brown.

S., Elizabeth. July 24, 1968. Letter from Mrs. Elizabeth S. to Governor Raymond Shafer. Papers of Governor Raymond P. Shafer. Pennsylvania State Archives. Manuscript Group 209, General File Pennhurst and PA State Schools and Hospitals, 9–1109, Box 75, Folder 8.

S., Ellen. July 12, 1968. Letter from Mrs. Ellen S. to Governor Raymond Shafer. Papers of Governor Raymond P. Shafer. Pennsylvania State Archives. Manuscript Group 209, General File Pennhurst and PA State Schools and Hospitals, 9–1109, Box 75, Folder 8.

Schaffer, M. Harris, and Brian B. Looker. 1968. Psycho-Social Habilitation – Pennhurst State School and Hospital." 1968. *Pennsylvania Message* 4(1): 3.

"Scranton's Allied Services Dedicates Residential Facility." 1967. *Pennsylvania Message* 3(3): 4.

Segal, Robert M. 1970. *Mental Retardation and Social Action*. Springfield, IL: Charles C. Thomas.

"Simulating Community at Polk Stimulates Resident Development." 1969. *Pennsylvania Message* 5(3): 5.

"Special Commission Investigates Human Medical Experimentation in State Institutions." 1973. *Pennsylvania Message* 9(3): 5.

"State Scraps Building Plan." 1970–1971. *Pennsylvania Message* 7(1): 7.

Taylor, Steven. 2009. *Acts of Conscience: World War II, Mental Institutions and Religious Objectors*. Syracuse, NY: Syracuse University Press.

———. 1988. "Caught in the Continuum: A Critical Analysis of the Principle of the Least Restrictive Environment." *Journal of the Association for the Severely Handicapped* 13(1): 41–53.

Trent, James W. Jr. 1994. *Inventing the Feeble Mind: A History of Mental Retardation in the United States*. Berkeley, CA: University of California Press.

W., Marie Walton. n.d. Received August 2, 1968. Letter from Mrs. Marie W. to Governor Raymond Shafer. Papers of Governor Raymond P. Shafer. Pennsylvania State Archives. Manuscript Group 209, General File Pennhurst and PA State Schools and Hospitals, 9–1109, Box 75, Folder 8.

"What Prompts PARC's Action Toward Institutions." 1973. *Pennsylvania Message* 9(2): 1.

Wilson, James R. March 10, 1970a. Letter from James R. Wilson to Honorable Hugh E. Flaherty, Sec for Legislation and Public Affairs. Papers of Governor Raymond P. Shafer. Manuscript Group 209. General File – Pennhurst and PA State Schools and Hospitals, 9–1109, Box 75, Folder 6.

———. March 6, 1970b. Testimony presented to House Appropriations Subcommittee to Study Department of Public Welfare Institutional Capital Appropriations. Papers of Governor Raymond P. Shafer. Manuscript Group 209. General File – Pennhurst and PA State Schools and Hospitals, 9–1109, Box 75, Folder 6.

"Violations Charged at Cresson School." 1973. *Pennsylvania Message* 9(1): 5.

7

Remembering Institutional Erasures: The Meaning of Histories of Disability Incarceration in Ontario

Jihan Abbas and Jijian Voronka

Introduction

Disability policy and the institutionalization and deinstitutionalization process provide the opportunity to critically reflect on social policy and praxis, with a specific emphasis on the construction of disability through projects of social and spatial exclusion. March 2009 saw the closure of the last of Ontario's remaining institutions for persons with intellectual disabilities,[1] and the move from spatially confining mad people[2] toward self-governance through community care are the current moments in Ontario's history of spatial incarceration. Whatever the province's commitment to policies of "inclusion," the process of deinstitutionalization itself, and the ways in which these former sites of containment are being redeveloped, help illuminate a continuing legacy of exclusion. It is critical then to understand that "deinstitutionalization" does not equal inclusion, as inclusion must be conceptualized as more than simply the physical relocation of certain bodies. We argue here that the redevelopment of sites of disability incarceration works to, on the one hand, erase the history of Ontario's legacy of segregating disability from the larger community through confinement, control, and surveillance, and at the same time works to further the policy rhetoric that disabled people are currently well integrated within community contexts.

The Total Institution and the Construction of Disability

As Park and Radford (1999) note, policies related to disabled people have historically tended to favor spatial exclusion. In fact, they argue the last half-century of disability policy has been "preoccupied with questions of social and spatial positioning" (Park and Radford 1999, 71). Of specific interest to this work is what has been referred to as the "asylum era," a roughly 120 year period starting in the 1850s in Ontario that includes the building of institutions for mad people and persons with intellectual disabilities. What these policies, and the structures and sites built to support them illustrate, is that questions about disabled people's place in society have almost always been answered with social and spatial exclusion, "characterized by discourses of 'defect', 'deviance' and 'threat'" (Park and Radford 1999, 72). These sites then reflect the powerful ways that disability has been socially constructed through policy discourse and action. What is important then is the way that the institution as a space shaped how disability came to be understood, and more importantly, how policies of social and spatial exclusion were influenced by these early policy discourses.

Of note in any analysis of the construction of intellectual disability is that as a category, "intellectual disability" poses very real interpretive challenges as we have no way of knowing if individuals would still be categorized as such across different times and different spaces (McDonagh 2009). As a category then, McDonagh (2009) argues that intellectual disability must be viewed like other "broad cultural notions of intelligence... [as] packed with ideas and preconceptions about gender, class, ethnicity, religion, and other socio-cultural markers" (5). As Park and Radford (1999) note with respect to their analysis of institutionalization:

> Clearly we are not necessarily dealing with intellectual disability *per se* but with individuals who were targeted by legal and medical agents and institutionalized on the pretext of being idiotic, moronic, feebleminded, mentally, deficient, mentally retarded and...on the assumption of being socially and economically marginalized. (77)

As Oliver (1990) argues, the development of the total institution reflects a form of social control to address these bodies through the proliferation of "prisons, asylums, workhouses, hospitals, industrial schools, and colonies" (32). As characterized by Goffman (1961), the total institution can be understood

> As a place of residence or work where a large number of like-situated individuals, cut off from wider society for an appreciable period of time, together lead an enclosed, formally administered round of life. (XIII)

What emerges then is the role of the institution in a wider project of social control and exclusion. As Park and Radford (1999) note "once institutionalized, few people escaped the 'total institution'" (94). Locking up the mad has a long history, one that varies across spatial sites. While some nations have earlier histories of building asylum spaces specifically to contain lunatics (such as London's St. Mary of Bethlam, founded in 1247 and catering to those deemed mad by the fourteenth century), the shift to mad asylum spaces in modern form, operating in conjunction with emerging scientific understandings of explaining madness (such as through phrenology) really took anchor in the early nineteenth century. It was within these confined settings, where mad people were monitored, typified, and categorized, that "mental illness" and "the mentally ill" were able to emerge through examination. The more modern-day disciplines of psychiatry and psychology were able to build cartographies of characteristics, disorders, and diagnostics based on bodies contained within asylum spaces.. Thus it was partially through confinement that madness was able to be known and rationalized by emerging experts in the field (Porter 2002).

This chapter seeks to explore the powerful cultural, symbolic, and material meaning that disability incarcerative settings have, and how they contribute to building and sustaining our understanding of disability as "states of exception" (Agamben 2005). Further, we investigate how the rehabilitation and rewriting of these sites' histories work to interact with Ontario's meta-narrative understanding of itself as caring, benevolent, and progressive in its relation to "the disabled." We seek to explore how, through two case studies of the ways these sites of containment are being reconstructed, we can disrupt this story through marking a counter-narrative, one that refuses to forget the recent past, nor uncritically accept the progressive promise of a better future.

Rideau Regional Centre

The Institution as a Built Environment

The developments of Canada's "Regional Centres" (institutions for persons with intellectual disabilities) have their roots in the "mid-Victorian 'idiot asylum'" (Radford and Park 1999, 71). As Radford and Park (1999) further note, "the succession of uses for the asylum [were] accompanied by a constantly changing vocabulary of classification, diagnosis, and recommended treatments" (71). While the rhetoric surrounding the purposes of such sites and supposed attributes of those confined within them are important, an examination of the built environment as a spatial project of exclusion is important to consider as it shapes our collective understanding of the "place" of intellectual disability.

Built-in an area of high unemployment, the first wing of the then "Eastern Hospital for Defectives" in Smiths Falls, Ontario, opened in January 1951 (Simmons 1982). The province's institutions for persons with intellectual disabilities (later to be called Regional Centres) were generally constructed outside urban centres (Radford and Park 1999). Historian Harvey Simmons (1982) argues that the result of this project in Smiths Falls "was a massive custodial institution whose design recalls the madhouses of the eighteenth and nineteenth centuries" (160). Simmons (1982) describes Rideau Regional Centre (RRC) as:

> A main corridor running the length of the institution was over one-third of a mile long, while on either side in a series of 'H's' aligned side by side were the various [wards]. The cross corridors were one-fifth of a mile long. (160)

Rideau Regional was thus "the very model of a custodial institution" (Simmons 1982, 162). The physical construction of this site speaks to notions of threats posed by those it was built to confine, as even the smallest details in the architecture spoke to assumptions about the dangerous nature of those to be confined behind its walls. RRC is well hidden from the passing roadway by a long tree-lined driveway. Indeed, because of its placement off the main road and behind a tree line, the true scope of RRC can only be seen from an aerial view. In this sense, RRC (and other institutions for persons with intellectual disabilities) reflect Goffman's (1961) original description of the total institution: "total character is symbolized by the barrier to social intercourse with the outside and to departure that is often built right into the physical plant, such as locked doors, high walls, barbed wire, cliffs, water, forests, or moors" (4). The institution then lies at the heart of policies of social exclusion, and the success of these sites hinges on both repressive and ideological functions:

> It is repressive in that those who either cannot or will not conform to the norms and discipline of capitalist society can be removed from it. It is

ideological in that it stands as a visible monument for all those who currently conform but may not continue to do so – if you do not behave, the institution awaits you. (Oliver 1999, 165)

This description by Oliver speaks to why the function of the institution was, and continues to be, of such importance to disabled individuals and advocates. Although many may have escaped its clutches early in their life, the threat of institutional responses remains a very real possibility as the place of disabled persons remains unequal and tenuous.

The spatial geography of these sites also serves to reinforce an important piece of disability history that speaks to experiences of exclusion, oppression, and incarceration. These experiences cannot, and should not, be easily forgotten. Both the atmosphere and design of these facilities reflect an expectation that those confined within them act "in a subhuman fashion" (Wolfensberger 1975, 8). These notions influence the physical geography itself as the environment is built to reflect an "abuse-restraint" mentality (Wolfensberger 1975:8). These environments includes the following characteristics:

Indestructible material used for walls and floors; partitions constructed from unbreakable, wire-enmeshed, and shatterproof glass; sturdy furniture with minimized moving parts; high ceilings and recessed and shielded lights; soundproofing; and things like television sets being placed above reach and often behind a protective housing. (Wolfensberger 1975, 8)

The areas occupied by residents include the following features that speak to expectations and limitations on those who reside on these kinds of facilities:

Locked wards; doors that lock from the outside and open only outward; inaccessible and locked areas for residents within living units; barred and reinforced windows; enclosed outdoor areas; inaccessible light switches that can only be accessed by staff; water and air temperatures controlled by staff; screened radiators; restrictions for residents to carry matches and lighters; a lack of privacy reflected in a lack of partitions, curtains or doors; a lack of individual property and possessions; and the segregation of men and women residents as well as staff and residents. (Wolfensburger 1975, 9–10)

These features ensure residents enjoy minimal choice and control within their living environment (Wolfsenberger 1969). While some features may have been modified over time, many of these architectural features remain and stand in stark contrast to the shifting discourse around intellectual disability that promoted dignity, choice, inclusion, and greater independence.

The Redevelopment of Rideau Regional Centre

While the purpose and history of this site are evident in every single physical characteristic of its design, the redevelopment process has systematically attempted to strip these realities away. In her own research around the reworking of the St Lawrence Hospital in Bodmin, United Kingdom (a former asylum), Claire Cornish (1997) explores deinstitutionalization and its impact on the human and physical geography of this site. What she uncovers is a "stigmatized" space that is not easily forgotten and poses challenges with respect to reconceptualization outside its function for undesirable individuals (Cornish 1997). While a space may be reworked to suit changing purposes, the "built infrastructure remains firm" (Cornish 1997, 105). This firmness is in part what makes reconceptualizing RRC, with all its architectural nods to confinement and control, a difficult task.

Those cosmetic changes that did occur to RRC over time serve as an important reminder of an ongoing development process that is linked to contested and shifting discourses. Indeed, as Cornish (1997) notes, the renaming process itself speaks to these shifting identities. With respect to RRC, while its physical geography may have remained largely intact, the social construction of this site and its purpose shifted over time with changing policy discourses that were reflected in various name changes. Originally referred to as the "Eastern Hospital for Defectives" (Simmons 1982), it would eventually be named the "Ontario Hospital School, Smiths Falls" upon its opening in 1951. Later, in 1967, it was renamed the "Rideau Regional Hospital School"; and finally in 1974 became "Rideau Regional Centre" (Ontario Ministry of community and Social Services 2011). These name changes speak to an ongoing process of rebranding that enabled the space to, at least on the surface, reflect shifts within developmental policy discourses and the place of intellectual disability. Yet, while these name changes signified an evolution to the outside world and policy makers, the spatial elements intrinsic to this site persisted and continued to restrict and influence the daily lives of residents. Divorced then from shifting policy rhetoric, RRC remained a site of control and confinement for those who were deemed unable to conform within a community setting. Indeed, I (JA) had the opportunity to visit the site on several occasions over the last decade and until its closure in 2009, many residents' daily routines still reflected the rhythm of isolated wards, and although there were some minor architectural enhancements (i.e., separated sleeping areas), many residents still appeared to exercise very little control over their daily lives (i.e., when to get up, when and what to eat etc.).

While it is important to acknowledge the ongoing process of repurposing these sites through policy discourse and rhetoric, the deinstitutionalization process presents an important opportunity to critique the redevelopment and remaking of these sites and to examine the impact these processes have on disability histories. RRC serves as a good case study for both the making, and later, attempted remaking of a degenerate space, as the built environment itself was constructed to respond to very specific notions about how persons with intellectual disabilities should be segregated, managed, and treated. The process of deinstitutionalization, the province's administration of these now-empty spaces, and the subsequent sale reveal much about official efforts to make the histories of these sites and individuals confined within them invisible.

This history and the kinds of discourses that have shaped RRC are contrasted to their representation in official documents from the Ontario Realty Corporation (ORC) about this site and its potential for redevelopment. These documents include site specifics and an expression of interest among other "redevelopment" material and the Ministries own reflection around this site. What is most telling in this redevelopment process and related real estate literature, is that the very narratives that once served to justify these sites, their architecture, the spatial exclusion, and their history of incarceration are completely absent in these promotional materials (along with the histories of those once confined within these sites). In describing RRC now, the ORC reframes this site in a way in which it is no longer an out-of-the-way space to hide and confine undesirable individuals, but rather a convenient space in "close proximity" to Ottawa, Toronto, Montreal, and the USA (ORC, Expression of Interest 2007a). The site, built to confine people with intellectual disabilities, and designed and constructed to cope with the dangers these individuals were thought to present, is no longer an indestructible and inescapable custodial institution but rather an "expansive property" that includes a "complex" boasting impressive corporate amenities. These include an 800-seat auditorium, gymnasium, indoor swimming pool, cafeteria, and laundry and conference facilities (ORC, "Rideau Regional Centre Eastern Ontario" 2007b). There is no mention here of the living wards that account for a good portion of the main building's layout and purpose. According to the ORC, the property is appropriate for many uses including schools, university and college campuses, conferences and training facilities, hotels and resorts, research or health industry facilities, and residential and food preparation facilities (ORC, "Rideau Regional Centre Eastern Ontario" 2007b). Completely absent in this material is what the site was built for and who was housed in it for more than 50 years, although there is a passing reference to the Ministry of Social and Community Services "using" the site (ORC, "Rideau Regional Centre Eastern Ontario" 2007b). In another ORC sales brochure, there is brief reference to the site as the "former" "Rideau Regional Hospital School," and "most recently" the former "Rideau Regional Facility" administered by the Ministry of Community and Social Services (ORC, Sales Brochure 2010). Yet these materials never mention the site's earliest identities like the "Eastern Hospital for Defectives" or the "Ontario Hospital School, Smiths Falls." However, because the ministry itself neglects to mention the "Eastern Hospital for Defectives" on their own history of developmental services website, it is clear this early reference to the site has already been erased from the new and sanitized retelling of this space.

Reading through the ORC's official material related to the redevelopment, the history of confinement at this site and its role in exclusionary policies are completely erased through a strategic and deliberate reconfiguring/contextualizing of this space. Once a site purposefully placed outside of large urban centres, and hidden from public view behind long-winding and tree-lined drives, this spatial project of exclusion is erased and rebuilt through a new public discourse that ignores the history of this site and instead reframes this space as a desirable and convenient asset.

The Sale of Rideau Regional Centre

In the spring of 2011, the ORC confirmed they were close to a sale and had identified a "preferred prospect" (EMC News Smiths Falls, "RRC sale is nearing completion" May 26, 2011). Later the ORC confirmed RRC had been conditionally sold (Lake 88.1, "No comment from province on regional centre sales negotiations" June 2011), yet in late July reports surfaced that indicated an ongoing heritage assessment of RRC was creating delays in finalizing the sale process (EMC News Smiths Falls, "Plans to designate RRC heritage delays land sale" June 30, 2011). While at the time of writing I do not have any specific results around this heritage assessment, at the time of its sale (in July 2011) the new developer did note that the results of this assessment do indicate specific heritage significance that require some restrictions to the development process (Nease 2011). The issue of heritage significance for the *architecture* of this site does pose an interesting question with respect to the history of the physical site itself versus the lived histories of those once confined behind its walls. Indeed, while it seems there are histories worth preserving within the very bricks and mortar of this space, one is left to wonder what, if anything, will become of the individual histories of those who lived behind these walls?

In July 2011, the ORC confirmed that 345 acres with 50 interconnected buildings that comprise the former RRC had been sold for $100,000 (Ottawa Citizen, "Province sells former home for disabled for $100,000" July 13, 2011), to a local residential housing developer (CBC News, "Rideau Regional Centre site sold in Smiths Falls" July 11, 2011). The new owner confirmed plans to develop a residential seniors' complex that targets "active" seniors (40% of the proposed development of the site) as well as light commercial use of the remaining areas (Nease 2011). These new developments for the former RRC are interesting as its proposed reincarnation as a seniors' complex keep the purpose of the site as a "residential" facility intact—although repurposed through individual living units (Nease 2011). One also wonders, given very real concerns within the disability community that many young disabled adults continue to find themselves in care facilities fashioned for an aging population, if RRC's newest reincarnation will again lead to another generation of adults with intellectual disabilities behind these very walls. Again, just like in its earliest development, the former RRC site is being celebrated publically as it has the potential to give the struggling local economy a boost (CBC News, "Rideau Regional Centre site sold in Smiths Falls" July 11, 2011).

Redeveloping the Queen Street Site

From Lunatic Asylum to "Toronto's most Life Changing Address"

The Provincial Lunatic Asylum was Upper Canada's first asylum space, opening its doors in January 1850, a century before the opening of RRC. It was built at a time when white settlers were preoccupied with spatially containing various degeneracies, which included the criminal, the racialized, Aboriginals, and others (Dowbiggin 1997; Gilman 1985). At the time, madness was approached as a degenerative illness, hereditary in nature, which lurked, sometimes dormant in the body, passed down through tainted genes, but that could be exacerbated by social stressors. Thus, madness as a degenerative illness was something that was "incubated by the parents and visited upon the children, it had no precise borders, but it involved a progressively intensifying tyranny of the body over the spirit or soul" (Pick 1989, 51). Further, as I have noted in earlier work, madness was understood as a degeneracy that was triggered by urbanity, and must be kept from the social in order to protect its purity and progress. In addition,

> This mad degeneracy that lurked in the body with the potential to threaten the community became a philanthropic project – one which sought to contain madness in order to protect the new Canadian citizenry. Thus, mad degenerates were met with middle-class intervention that called for discipline, regulation, and temperance in the name of nation-building. When those interventions failed, they were often sent to built sites of carceral containment." (Voronka 2008: 48)

This threat of "urban crisis" allowed for the justified expense and efforts involved in building Upper Canada's first asylum space, referred to as the Howard building (named after its architect). Before this, the mad had been contained in jails, and the asylum was understood as a curative improvement on other institutional settings of the times. The building was modeled after Cambridge University, a U-shaped neo-classical design, planned at 584 feet, "designed to contain each "class" of patient within his or her own environment" (Hudson 2000, 210). The Howard building was never fully finished as planned because of over-budget; however, funds were found to build a ten foot wall, which would eventually fully enclose the grounds (Crawford in Hudson 2000, 61). The workers who built these walls were often unpaid patient laborers who were contained within the asylum (Reaume 2000). By the end of the nineteenth century, Ontario had opened seven public asylums, with the Queen Street site working "as the flagship of the provincial system. At the turn of the twentieth century no state institution loomed larger on the Canadian social landscape than the asylum" (Dowbiggin 2011, 44).

Since its erection, the Queen Street site has always been understood as a "prob-lemed" site in need of interventions—be they structural, medical, or philosophical (for a full history of the Queen Street site, please see Hudson 2000; Reaume 2000). During its 160-year tenure, the site has undergone a number of structural changes, be they nineteenth and mid-twentieth century additions, or the large-scale early 1970s redevelopment of the site, which saw a number of early structures (including the original Howard building) demolished to make way for more modern build-ings. Removal of old incarceration sites (while the practice continues) works to eradicate the histories of a site's antiquated carceral interventions, and allows for the emergence of a new meta-narrative, one that puts the "care" back into mental health. For instance, to the modern eye, the Howard building's sinister presence was understood as "a highly visible reminder of a previous era of treatment of the mentally ill from which, thankfully, we have emerged" (Museum of Mental Health Services 1993, 21). The demolishment and continual rehabilitation through redevelopment of the site work to continually regenerate the image of medical men-tal health practices, as they continue to change. For instance, it was within the Howard building that a century of violent practices were performed, including arsenic, insulin and metrazol "therapies," electroconvulsive shock, and loboto-mies. The Howard building thus personified in material form "reminders that the building contained therapies that were useless, [and] of the often futile nature of their efforts to help the insane" (Hudson 2000, 214).

Further, the site's continual philosophical restructuring can be traced through its persistent renaming. Because language is power, and there is power in language, official language producers with the will to choose how to name a site use such posi-tioning to reframe the material meaning of a space through language that reflects the philosophical conceptions of madness at a given moment. Similar to the RCC's multiple renaming, the Queen Street site has been known as: the Provincial Lunatic Asylum (1850–1871); Asylum for the Insane, Toronto (1871–1907); Hospital for the Insane, Toronto (1907–1919); Ontario Hospital, Toronto (1919–1966); 999 Queen Street West (1966–1976); Queen Street Mental Health Centre (1976–1998); and in its current formation, when the Queen Street Mental Health Centre amal-gamated with three other Toronto mental health and addiction sites in 1998, to form the Centre for Addiction and Mental Health (CAMH) (Everett 2000, 38; Reaume 2000, 6). Each renaming signifies a philosophical and cultural shift in approach to madness, and renaming of the site works to mark the space as modern-ized, cutting edge, and most currently—recovery oriented. As Dr. Catherine Zahn, current president of CAMH notes, "The language of the day is inclusivity. It is the idea of inclusion, to reduce prejudice and reduce opportunities for discrimination of people who have issues in their lives" (Boyle 2010). How we name and speak of things work to change the meaning behind actions. But should the language of inclusivity be used when many people within the site are still being held and undergoing treatments against their will?

Respectability through Redevelopment

Soon after the Queen Street site's amalgamation into CAMH in 1998, yet another redevelopment to the 27-acre site was proposed. Plans put into action involve eventually closing the three other amalgamated sites (Addiction Research Foundation, the Clarke Institute of Psychiatry, the Donwood Institute) and condensing them all onto the Queen Street site at 1001 Queen Street West. According to the master plan, the new design will work to break up the site as one solely used for incarceration and intervention, and to move it progressively forward into a mixed-use urban village hub that blends with the surrounding (recently gentrified) Parkdale community. Envisioned is a "casual mixing between staff, clients/patients and visitors of CAMH with the surrounding community, [which] will occur naturally on public sidewalks, parks, shared community facilities and cafes, restaurants and shops that will occupy the street level of buildings. CAMH uses will be integrated with other uses to *create a safe, comfortable and welcoming place where the stigma of the institution can disappear into the rhythm of normal daily activities associated with city living*" (Urban Strategies August 2002, 5, italics mine). Early planning on the redevelopment emphasized normalizing the Queen Street site's practice (including continued involuntary incarceration) and changing attitudes toward the site by "breaking down barriers to eliminate stigma" (CAMH, Redeveloping the Queen Street Site, 2011b).The need to improve on the public image of the Queen Street site has been ongoing work. How is incarceration made palpable? Oftentimes framed under the rhetoric of ending the stigma associated with being a patient at the site, what is often left unmentioned is how redevelopment of this site, and thus an erasure of its history, works to further CAMH's working maxim as Canada's largest mental health and addictions teaching hospital, and a leading innovator in research.

Improving the public relations of the site works to solidify it as a professional hospital like any other: reifying madness as a biomedical illness, psychiatrists and other psy professionals as legitimate professionals, and improving the overall reputation of a site with a dark history. Indeed, when the site underwent prior redevelopment in the 1970s, hope was expressed that the new developments would improve the image of psychiatric care in the public imaginary. In regards to the old Howard building:

> The dark, fortress-like 1850 building was the focus of many local horror stories and for years children were threatened with incarceration at Queen Street that the new environment combined with the new programs it helped stimulate, would create a better public image for the hospital: "when we pull the old building down, we will pull down the old mythology with it." (Kelner, quoted in Pos 1975, 2)

Thus, making a site of incarceration into a hub of respectability is one of the processes through which the current redevelopment should be understood.

The current redevelopment project is entitled "Transforming Lives Here." The project, as promoted through CAMH's website, is to undertake the building of "a new kind of hospital for the twenty-first century—advancing treatment, revitalizing our community, and changing attitudes toward those with mental illness and addictions." This "new" hospital built on the same grounds that 160 years ago gave birth to a new asylum space built on the philosophy of moral therapy, will now "provide a healthy environment that promotes recovery" (CAMH, Redeveloping the Queen Street Site, 2011b). This new "recovery" approach to the old problem of curing madness will be promoted through built environment (for recent critical reflections on the recovery model as it has been integrated into mental health service systems, please see Mental Health "recovery" Study Working Group 2009; Poole 2011). In the past, spatial treatment of mad people has ranged from enclosed asylum spaces outside city centers, cottage-style rural retreats, and units within medical hospitals. Our current professed method of spatial regulation, following the large-scale deinstitutionalization that began in the 1950s, operates under the language of "community integration." However, while most receiving mental health and addictions services live outside of institutional settings, they can still be tied to compulsory treatment conditions.

For instance, Ontario's Mental Health Act "provides psychiatrists with powers to detain, restrain, and impose (for therapeutic purposes)" treatments on individuals involuntarily if they are deemed a threat to themselves, others, or unable to care for themselves (Fabris 2011, 107, 109). Furthermore, Community Treatment Orders can be enacted on individuals who fit the legal criteria. These Orders mean that people can be released conditionally from institutions, so long as they comply with the treatment plan that has been prepared in advance of their release into community. These Orders often require individuals to receive "psychiatric care and supervision while living in the community and be able to 'comply' with the treatment plan...The 'community treatment plan' may include any conceivable treatment or appointment, and may assign monitoring and information-sharing tasks to the person's family, community members, and helpers or agencies beyond the facility" (Fabris 2011, 111). While many mad people now negotiate service provision on an out-patient basis, mental health "centers" still continue to have in-patient (and involuntary incarceration) provisions, offering mixed-use of the site to people and dividing them along the lines of who can come and go, and those that are forced to stay.

The redevelopment of CAMH, however, emphasizes the former, those that use this "mental health hub" as if it were a visit to the doctor. And, importantly, as if it were a visit to any other hospital—further linking "mental illness and addictions" to that of physical illness, as if it were one and the same (like, diabetes: not curable but containable through proper treatment management)—and thus constructing discourses that maintain that madness should be conceptualized, treated, and funded in the same manner. Indeed, the redevelopment is intent on changing the site's community legacy, from one of shackles to that of wings. Crucial to remember is that the intent of the redevelopment is not solely to create a "normalized living environment that will provide an important component of client recovery and healing" (CAMH, New Neighbours in the Urban Village, 2011a), as the rhetoric professes. It will also work to change the community legacy of the degenerate site, and there are substantial institutional investments in doing so.

One of the goals of the redevelopment is "bring[ing] together the best research, clinical, education, health promotion, and policy experts in one place to change the future of mental health and addictions" (CAMH, Redeveloping the Queen Street Site, 2011b). In improving the façade of this site of incarceration, to one that better meets the image of scientificity, progress, and modernity, those that work there in professional capacities are more likely to understand themselves, and be understood by others, as, for example, neuroscientists rather than carceral gatekeepers. This works to justify and solidify often forceful mental health service tactics that continue to happen on-site (such as involuntary incarceration, forensic units, much debated electroconvulsive treatments) and to spatially solidify the psy professions, ones that are under renewed query and critique for their methods and research (see Miller and Rose 2008; Whitaker 2010).

Integrating Normalcy into Incarcerational Settings

Most marked about the reconstruction is that after more than a century and a half of the land being solely used as a site to contain madness, the grounds are being redeveloped for mixed use, whereby CAMH "will convert our 27-acre site on Queen Street West into a welcoming, integrated community, weaving together new cutting-edge CAMH facilities with shops, residences, businesses, parks, and through-streets to create an inclusive, healing neighbourhood. Nothing quite like this has ever been done before" (CAMH, Redeveloping the Queen Street Site, 2011b). Hitherto, the buildings on this 27-acre public hospital were all used for institutional means. But times have changed (as we are repeatedly told), and the site post-mixed-use redevelopment "will contain a balance of uses that will draw people into the site, promote street-level activity, help reduce the lingering stigma of "999 Queen," and add to the energetic and dynamic neighbourhood of Queen Street West."(CAMH, New Neighbours in the Urban Village, 2011a). What this means on the ground is that through redevelopment, about half of the development blocks will be for CAMH use, and the other half will be used for non-CAMH uses. In effect, the site in its current redevelopment is being broken up into institutional and noninstitutional settings, and the legacy of the land as a mad site is being fractured under the name of community integration and—ultimately—commercial gain.

The site is currently in the midst of Phase 1b of the redevelopment, which is expected to be completed in summer 2012 at an estimated cost of $341 million (Boyle 2010). The Queen Street site saw its 1954 Administration building demolished in winter of 2010, and in its place, the first (and so far only confirmed) non-CAMH development will take root, on a prominent piece of property located at the southwest corner of the Queen Street and Ossington avenue intersection. A heavily trafficked piece of land that is now suddenly commercially in demand because of the gentrification of the surrounding neighbourhood, this block of land will be developed into "street-level retail shops...[and] above the shops there will be seven floors of much-needed affordable rental housing. The 179 new units will range from bachelors to three-bedroom apartments" (CAMH, New Neighbours in the Urban Village, 2011a). The valuable land is being leased to Forum Equity Partners and developed by Verdiroc Development Corporation. Whether the stores and apartment buildings will cater to the mad population, who often rely on limited financial resources from Ontario's Disability and Workfare programs, or rather cater to the catchment of people who are looking to move into the trendy neighborhood, remains to be seen.

Breaking up the site into mixed-use provides a normalized appearance to a space that still practices as an institution. But normalization, as Disability Studies scholars have insisted, should never be the goal (McRuer 2006; Michalko 2009; Snyder and Mitchell 2006). As both the site and the subjects it serves are professed to be stigmatized, the question remains is the response to stigmatization normalization? As Titchkosky (2000) notes, those "who possess the potential to stigmatize people are referred to as the "normals." Normals are those who have many different attributes but who do not, in the interactional situation in question, have an attribute of difference...Normalcy is the unmarked site from which people view the stigma of disability" (204). Further, subject-making is dependent on the organization of difference in order to solidify notions of particular persons as exemplar citizens. As Thobani (2007) notes, it is through what she calls the exaltation process, where particular human characteristics, as rendered through hegemonic powers, are drawn upon and exalted to delineate and distinguish these subjects as representative of a nation's ideal and governing citizenry, and those others, differentiated through this process, as not. It is taken for granted by exalted subjects that the quest to normalize stigmatized mad attributes, "conditions," and characteristics is the best way to "fix" the problem of madness as it is presented. But disability and mad scholars are pushing back against this quest to normalize, insisting that there can be value, benefit, and knowledge derived from maintaining difference (Ingram 2007; White 2009; Fabris 2011).

One also has to consider—in whose interest does normalizing practices within mad sites benefit? Should a site that still continues to enact forced incarceration, forced medical treatment, seclusion and restraints, and conditional releases be considered a normal site within our everyday community? Rather, these practices are allowed to take place because these spaces work as sites of exception where mad people are legally understood as extraordinary citizens who can be made governed when it is assessed that they are unable to govern themselves. This governance can take the form of regulation through forced incarceration within mad sites, a form of "spatial segregation that is legally produced and authorized" (Razack 2010, 92). Evicted from some laws, and taken up through others, mad subjects are made known not only through the law but also through what spaces they can and cannot occupy. Further complicating matters of spatial regulation, Community Treatment Orders (CTO's), and chemical restraints now extend beyond mad sites of exception and well into the community, and the once clear spatial organization and delineation between how mad sites and mad people are organized within spatial configurations has blurred. As Fabris (2011) notes, enforced drug compliance can work as chemical restraints, as "imposed drug treatment acts on the brain to limit the body, as any restraint does, and over time as any prison does" (115). This spatial dispersal of mad people into communities while still under forced compliance through treatment plans produces a public anxiety that now extends beyond the realm of mad sites (Cross 2010).Thus the simplistic quest to normalize a site and its actions does not address the public panic of the mad being among us. And attempts to normalize actions such as physical, environmental, and chemical restraints, that are in actuality exceptional ones often enacted through force, should be questioned.

Connected to this question of normalizing sites of exceptions is that of how the urban village design works to mask the incarceration that will still be taking place within the future mixed-use site. The design will pair shopping, leisure, and rental suites next door to buildings such as the innocuously named "Intergenerational Wellness Centre" (which is quoted within a newspaper as having "the feel like a hotel"), a planned in-patient building, where some will be staying involuntarily (Boyle 2010). Normalizing institutional settings as part of the urban landscape, and having them blend in with everyday surroundings, shouldn't be the goal of deinstitutionalization. The design works to mask what is taking place within the site. Consider the above-discussed street level shops along Queen Street and the rental units that will sit atop the building. Queen Street is the most heavily trafficked pedestrian street that runs adjacent to the site. Before redevelopment, passers-by were always made aware of what it was that they were passing by, and often haunted by it. But with storefronts and rental units soon to be lining Queen Street, what is taking place within CAMH-use buildings will be less visible to the public eye, less accessible in the public imaginary, and thus hidden away from public concern. Thus the physical form of the redeveloping institution works in both overt and covert ways. It overtly separates and contains us from them but also conceals from the public imagination what continues to take place within this site, "that is, what they *don't* see, does not exist" (Razack 2010, 100).

Finally, what is to become of the non-CAMH lands? While in theory, anyone concerned with disability incarceration would be optimistic to hear that the land that is devoted to mad sites is shrinking, deinstitutionalization has taught us that often times what comes in place of carceral containment is not a big improvement. We must query just how this redevelopment coincides with the redistribution of biomedical investments, the shrinking of institutional beds being replaced with a greater investment in corporate interests (especially pharmacology) that have been redispersed through community care setting provisions. The question as to whether non-CAMH sites will be sold or long-term ground leased is a decision that is left up to the CAMH Board of Trustees to determine, on a case-by-case basis, decisions based on "if the sale is deemed to be in CAMH's best interests" (CAMH, New Neighbours in the Urban Village, 2011a).

Resistance: Remembering Our Histories

While the erasure of mad incarceration continues on at the Queen Street site (through renaming, retelling, and redevelopment), the consumer/survivor movement has been working hard to stake a claim on our own history, and ensure the circulation of discourses that exist outside of hegemonic meta-narratives produced by the psy disciplines. One example of this retelling is the annual Mad Pride event, which takes place in July of each year during what the City of Toronto has declared Mad Pride week. Organized by consumers/survivors, advocates, and allies, the parade, called "psychiatric survivor pride day" when it first took place in 1993, was originally held "in response to local community prejudices toward people with a psychiatric history living in boarding homes in the Parkdale area of the city" (Mad Pride Toronto, About Me, 2011). This currently annual pride parade starts on the grounds of the Queen Street site, and slowly makes its way from the institutional grounds, through the surrounding community, and ending in the community's Parkdale Activity Recreation Centre. In recent years, pride walks have included a bed push, which involves pushing a hospital bed along the journey from institutional to community setting—signifying our transition from incarcerated to community care. This event works to celebrate our community history, as well as acts as a reminder to the neighborhood of the legacy of mental health interventions within Parkdale, and that we are still here.

Another example of consumer/survivor activist history is the work of Dr. Geoffrey Reaume (2002), whose book, *Remembrance of Patients Past: Patient Lives at the Hospital for the Insane, 1870–1940*, documents the experience of living within the Queen Street site by drawing on, among other research methods, letters that patients themselves wrote chronicling their stay. Reaume and other consumer/survivors (Reaume 2002; Morrison 2005) have worked to document the consumer/survivor movement and its resistance to "negative stereotypes associated with madness" (Reaume 2002, 424). Most relevant, Reaume and allies have worked hard to preserve the remaining patient built walls that originally enclosed the Queen Street site long ago (many of the patient-built boundary walls have been torn down, so that all that remains "of the original wall are portions along the southeast and southwest parts of the ground" (Reaume 2011, 2). Recognizing that the walls materially mark a "labour and social history of the patients of the former Toronto Asylum" (Reaume 2011, 2), Reaume and allies worked hard to ensure that what remained as a testament to unpaid patient labor was preserved as a landmark. Indeed, in 1997, the remaining walls as well as two storage buildings were designated as heritage properties by the City of Toronto, and the current redevelopment will have to work around the heritage buildings. Since 2000, Reaume has been conducting popular "psychiatric patient built wall tours" offered to the public, and notes how

> The patient built wall represents a genuine physical link to the institutional experience of those who preceded us. The wall is thus made relevant to people today who appreciate it as a memorial to people who have been previously forgotten and unmarked in public monuments, unlike the doctors and architects who, if anyone is remembered, they are usually the most likely to be marked publically, either with busts, statues or parks. (Reaume 2011, 3)

In addition, nine memorial plaques were unveiled in September 2010, a collaboration between the Psychiatric Survivor Archives, Toronto, and CAMH, which as stand alone, or used in conjunction with the tour, narrate the unfolding history of the site. The plaques include "a general introduction to the grounds; women's work, including domestic labour, laundry and sewing toil; men's work building the walls, construction, carpentry, maintenance and agricultural labour; death and burial" (Reaume 2011, 3). This intervention works to retain a history of incarceration at the site that the redevelopment is working to erase. As Reaume notes,

> Given the tour's purpose, which is to engage patients' history to fight prejudice towards psychiatric patients past and present by stressing our collective contributions, the goals of the wall tour in this sense are congruent with CAMH's efforts to reduce stigma, though our approaches differ, particularly in regard to interpretations of the medical model. (Reaume 2011, 3)

Conclusion

These two spatial case studies have illustrated the importance of examining the context of the redevelopment processes as they pertain to sites of disability incarceration. These spaces have their roots in policies that sought to identify, remove, and manage those who were deemed degenerate, a practice that persists. While these two sites may pose different challenges as advocates move forward, as one is within a continuous process of "repurposing" while the other has been abandoned completely by the province of Ontario, there are common threads throughout the redevelopment of these sites that speak to a legacy of exclusion. Furthermore, the redevelopment process has actively worked to obscure disability histories in an effort to alter public perceptions and reframe these sites of incarceration as "public assets." These revisionings of built sites of carceral containment and related efforts to sanitize the history of disability policy in Ontario impact disabled individuals and their shared histories of exclusion and confinement.

Lost in current official and more palatable retellings of these spaces are the histories of those confined within these sites, as well as what took place within these walls. While the ongoing process of redevelopment may be fueled by the rhetoric of "inclusion," there is nothing "inclusive" about a process that actively seeks to conceal the histories of those who were, and continue to be subject to various forms of confinement and incarceration. These sites, despite the redevelopment process, continue to serve as a powerful reminder to those with disabilities that their place within the community is far from secure. Indeed, systems of de- and reinstitutionalization require one another; any experience of "community living" is conditioned by the threat of what happened to those deemed mentally disabled historically, as well as what new mechanisms of policy and power are currently being enacted. Through these two spatial cases we show how policy and practice across disabilities share similar histories of spatial exclusion and confinement, as well as current divergent goals. While there may not be consensus with respect to what we do with these sites and how we remember those who experienced or continue to experience confinement, we argue that the deliberate rewriting of these spaces serves as yet another example of the way in which disabled people are erased from mainstream discourses. We hope that this analysis contributes to work that is aimed at thinking through how confinement is obscured through strategic redevelopment processes that place Ontario's social policy prominent as benevolent, but renders those that it serves invisible.

Acknowledgments

Both authors are grateful for doctoral funding support from the Social Sciences and Humanities Research Council of Canada.

Notes

1. We use person-first terminology as it relates to intellectual disability to reflect the preferred language of many self-advocates. Although historically, problematic and demeaning terms have been used, here, we use intellectual disability to speak to the experience of individuals who have historically been labeled for what the medical community perceives as delayed or impaired development in activities of daily living.
2. We use here the language of madness to resist current biomedical determinisms and to locate ourselves within the longer history of madness, orienting madness as a sustained social oppression that the consumer/survivor/expatient and mad movements continue to resist through critique of sanist and mentalist practices, and in following with the field of Mad Studies.

References

Agamben, Giorgio. 2005. *State of Exception*. Translated by Kevin Attell. Chicago, IL: University of Chicago Press.

Boyle, Theresa. 2010. "CAMH Launches Phase Two Redevelopment." Last modified August 1, 2011. http://www.healthzone.ca/health/mindmood/mentalhealth /article/790157--camh-launches-phase-two-redevelopment

CBC News. 2011. "Rideau Regional Centre Site Sold in Smiths Falls," Last modified July 11. http://www.cbc.ca/news/canada/ottawa/story/2011/07/11/ott-rideau-regional-sale612.html

Centre for Addiction and Mental Health. 2011a. "New Neighbours in the Urban Village." Last modified July 20. http://www.camh.net/News_events/Redeveloping _the_Queen_Street_site/New%20Neighbours%20in%20the%20Urban%20 Village/EN_NewNeighbours.html

———. 2011b. "Redeveloping the Queen Street Site." Last Modified July 20. http:// www.camh.net/News_events/Redeveloping_the_Queens_Street_site/index.html

Crawford, Pleasance Kaufman. 2000. "Subject to Change: Asylum Landscape." In *The Provincial Lunatic Asylum in Toronto: Reflections on Social and Architectural History*, edited by Edna Hudson. Toronto, ON: Toronto Region Architectural Conservatory.

Cross, Simon. 2010 *Mediating Madness: Mental Distress and Cultural Representation*. Basingstoke, UK: Palgrave Macmillan.

Dowbiggin, Ian Robert. 2011. *The Quest for Mental Health: A Tale of Science, Medicine, Scandal, Sorrow, and Mass Society*. Cambridge: Cambridge University Press.

———. 1997. *Keeping America Sane: Psychiatry and Eugenics in the United States and Canada, 1880 – 1940*. Ithaca: Cornell University Press.

EMC News Smiths Falls. 2011. "Plans to Designate RRC Heritage Delays Land Sale." Last modified June 30. http://www.emcsmithsfalls.ca/20110630/news/Plans+to+de signate+RRC+heritage+delays+land+sale

———. 2001. "RRC Sale is Nearing Completion." Last modified May 26. http://www .emcsmithsfalls.ca/20110526/news/RRC+sale+is+nearing+completion

Everett, Barbara. 2000. *A Fragile Revolution: Consumers and Psychiatric Survivors Confront the Power of the Mental Health System*. Waterloo, ON: Wilfred Laurier Press.

Fabris, Erick. 2011. *Tranquil Prisons: Chemical Incarceration under Community Treatment Orders*. Toronto, ON: University of Toronto Press.

Gilman, Sander L. 1985. *Difference and Pathology: Stereotypes of Sexuality, Race, and Madness*. Ithaca, NY: Cornell University Press.

Goffman, Erving. 1961. *Asylums: Essays on the Social Situation of Mental Patients and Other Inmates*. New York: Anchor Books.

Hudson, Edna. 2000. "Asylum Layouts." In *The Provincial Lunatic Asylum in Toronto: Reflections on Social and Architectural History*, edited by Edna Hudson. Toronto, ON: Toronto Region Architectural Conservatory.

Ingram, Richard. 2007. "Reports from the Psych Wars." In *Unfitting Stories: Narrative Approaches to Disease, Disability and Trauma*, edited by Valerie Raoul, Connie Canam, Angela D. Henderson, and Carla Paterson, 237–245. Waterloo, ON: Wilfred Laurier Press.

Lake 88.1. 2011. "No Comment from Province on Regional Centre Sales Negotiations." Last modified June. http://lake88.ca/lake88/index.php?option=com_content&task= view&id=991&Itemid=1

McRuer, Robert. 2006. *Crip Theory: Cultural Signs of Queerness and Disability*. New York: New York University Press.

McDonagh, Patrick. 2009. "What are We Talking about When We Talk about the History of Intellectual Disability." *Canadian Disability Studies Newsletter – 'Making Connection'* 1(2), http://madpridetoronto.blogspot.com/

Mental Health 'Recovery' Study Working Group. 2009. *Mental Health "Recovery": Users and Refusers. What do Psychiatric Survivors in Toronto Think about Mental Health "Recovery"?* Toronto, ON: Wellseley Institute.

Metzal, Deborah S., and Pamela M. Walker 2001. "The Illusion of Inclusion: Geographies of the Lives of People with Developmental Disabilities in the United States."*Disability Studies Quarterly.* 21(4):114–128.

Michalko, Rod. 2009. "The Excessive Appearance of Disability." *International Journal of Qualitative Studies in Education* 22(1):65–74.

Miller, Peter, and Nikolas Rose. 2008. *Governing the Present.* Cambridge: Polity Press.

Morrison, Linda. 2005. *Talking Back to Psychiatry: The Psychiatric Consumer/Survivor/Ex-Patient Movement.* New York: Routledge.

Museum of Mental Health Services (Toronto). 1993. *The City and the Asylum: Celebrating the Bi-Centennial of the City of Toronto, 1793–1993.* Toronto, ON: The Museum of Mental Health Services.

Nease, Kristy. 2011. "Former Rideau Regional Centre to become seniors' complex." *Ottawa Citizen.* Last modified July 12. http://www.ottawacitizen.com/Former+Rideau+Regional+Centre+become+seniors+complex/5086775/story.html

Oliver, Michael. 1999. "Capitalism, Disability and Ideology: A Materialist Critique of the Normalization Principle." In *A Quarter-Century of Normalization and Social Role Valorization: Evolution and Impact,* edited by R. Flynn, and R. Lemay, 163–174. Ottawa, ON: University of Ottawa Press.

———.1990. *The Politics of Disablement.* New York: St. Martin's Press.

Ontario Ministry of Community and Social Services. Last modified April 12, 2011. "History of Development Policy," http://www.mcss.gov.on.ca/en/dshistory/first Institution/rideau.aspx

Ontario Realty Corporation. 2010. "Sales Brochure." http://www.ontariorealty.ca/Assets/Properties+for+Sale/Rideau+Regional+Centre+brochure.PDF

———. 2007a. "Expression of Interest." Last Modified December 4. http://www.ontariorealty.ca

———. 2007b. "Rideau Regional Centre Eastern Ontario, Canada.". http://www.ontariorealty.ca/Assets/Business+with+ORC/Rideau+Regional+Centre+-+brochure+2007+-FINAL.pdf

Ottawa Citizen, 2011. "Province Sells Former Home for Disabled for $100,000." Last Modified July 13. http://www.ottawacitizen.com/health/Province+sells+former+home+disabled/5093118/story.html

Park, Deborah, C., and Radford John. 1999. "Rhetoric and Place in the 'Mental Deficiency' Asylum." In *Mind and Body Spaces: Geographies of Illness, Impairment and Disability,* edited by Ruth Butler, and Hester Parr, 70–97. New York: Routledge.

Pick, Daniel. 1989. *Faces of Degeneration: A European Disorder, c.1848-c.1918.* Cambridge: Cambridge University Press.

Poole, Jennifer. 2011. *Behind the Rhetoric: Mental Health Recovery in Ontario.* Halifax: Fernwood Publishing.

Porter, Roy. 2002. *Madness: A Brief History.* Oxford: Oxford University Press.

Pos, Robert. 1975. "A Discussion." In *Howard Building Renovation Feasibility.* Toronto, ON: Ontario Heritage Foundation.

Razack, Sherene. 2010 "A Hole in the Wall; A Rose at a Checkpoint: The Spatiality of Colonial Encounters in Occupied Palestine." *Journal of Critical Race Inquiry* 1(1): 90–108.

Reaume, Geoffrey. 2011. "Psychiatric Patient Built Wall Tours at the Centre for Addiction and Mental Health (CAMH), Toronto, 2000–2010." Last modified July 10. http://activehistory.ca/papers/historypaper-10/

———. 2002. "Lunatic to Patient to Person: Nomenclature in Psychiatric History and the Influence of Patients' Activism in North America." *International Journal of Law and Psychiatry* 25(2002): 405–426.

———. 2000. *Remembrance of Patients Past: Patient Lives at the Toronto Hospital for the Insane, 1870–1940.* Don Mills, ON: Oxford University Press.

Simmons, Harvey G.1982. *From Asylum to Welfare.* Downsview: National Institute on Mental Retardation (NIMR).

Snyder, Sharon L., and David T. Mitchell. 2006. *Cultural Locations of Disability.* Chicago, IL: University of Chicago Press.

Thobani, Sunera. 2007. *Exalted Subjects: Studies in the Making of Race and Nation in Canada.* Toronto, ON: University of Toronto Press.

Titchkosky, Tanya. 2000. "Disability Studies: the Old and the New." *The Canadian Journal of Sociology* 25(2): 197–224.

Urban Strategies. 2002. *Master Plan: Executive Summary for the Centre for Addiction and Mental Health.* Toronto, ON: Centre for Addiction and Mental Health.

Voronka, Jijian. 2008. "Re/Moving Forward? Spacing Mad Degeneracy at the Queen Street Site," *Resources for Feminist Research* 33(1/2):45–61.

Whitaker, Robert. 2010. *Anatomy of an Epidemic: Magic Bullets, Psychiatric Drugs, and the Astonishing Rise of Mental Illness in America.* New York: Crown Publishers.

White, Kimberley. 2009. "Out of the Shadows and into the Spotlight: The politics of (In) visibility and the Implementation of the Mental Health Commission of Canada." In *Configuring Madness: Representation, Context and Meaning,* edited by Kimberley White. Oxford: Inter-Disciplinary Press.

Wolfsenberger, W. 1969. *The Origin and Nature of Our Institutional Models.* Washington, DC: President's Committee on Mental Retardation.

8

The New Asylums: Madness and Mass Incarceration in the Neoliberal Era

*Michael Rembis**

In a revealing article in the December 2010 issue of the *Journal of American History*, historian Heather Ann Thompson argues that "focusing new historical attention...on the advent of mass incarceration after the 1960s, helps us understand some of the most dramatic political, economic, and social transformations of the postwar period" (734). After reading Thompson's account, there is little doubt that this is indeed the case. Yet in an otherwise comprehensive and incisive analysis of the rise of mass incarceration and the prison industrial complex in the postwar United States, Thompson unsurprisingly fails to account for perhaps one of the most critical social transformations in this process; the so-called deinstitutionalization of well over 550,000 Americans who had been living incarcerated lives in mental hospitals (Palermo, Smith, and Liska 1991; Penrose 1939).[1] Recent researchers in various fields have referred to what they call the *criminalization of mental illness* (Slate and Johnson 2008). Yet those historians who engage in a critical assessment of mass incarceration in the late twentieth century do not consider the important relationships among the rise of the prison industrial complex and the increasing psychiatrization of both socially "deviant" behavior and incarcerated populations, as well as the psychic trauma associated with incarceration. In 2007, the Council of State Governments declared that, "The three largest inpatient psychiatric facilities in the country are jails, with the Los Angeles County Jail, Rikers Island Jail in New York City, and the Cook County Jail in Chicago each individually housing more persons with mental illnesses than any psychiatric institution in the United States." (Slate and Johnson 2008, 59) In this chapter, I engage in a critical assessment of the relevant literature in an effort to outline the growing connections among "deinstitutionalization" and the rise of mass incarceration from the 1960s to the early twenty-first century. In the process, I point toward the critical importance of including this analysis in the larger history of mass incarceration in the postwar United States and make an argument for the centrality of disability studies (or mad studies) in any examination of United States history.

The omission of madness and mad prisoners from the recent historical record is pervasive in the literature on incarceration. For decades, activists and academics like Angela Davis (2005) have done the vital work of helping us "think about the possibility that punishment may be a consequence of other forces and not an inevitable consequence of the commission of crime" (40–41). Yet many scholars and activists who engage in a critical assessment of the rise of the prison industrial complex do not interrogate (in any systematic way) the links between madness and incarceration (Alexander 2010; Thompson 2010). Instead, they focus on race and poverty. Davis, for example, argues that, "Regardless of who has or has not committed crimes, punishment, in brief, can be seen more as a consequence of racialized surveillance…Those communities that are subject to police surveillance are much more likely to produce more bodies for the punishment industry." According to Davis (2005), incarceration has become a powerful means of "disappearing…dispensable populations from society…in the false hope of disappearing the underlying social problems they represent." She contends that "imprisonment is the punitive solution to a whole range of social problems that are not being addressed by those social institutions that might help people lead better, more satisfying lives" (40–41). Davis is certainly (and rightly) not alone in her focus on the social, cultural, and economic forces that produce the surveillance and incarceration of racialized bodies, which is extremely important. The vast majority of incarcerated Americans are poor men, women, and children of color. While recognizing the essential work that has been done in this area, I would like to propose that race alone is inadequate to explain the rise of mass incarceration in the United States since the 1960s. We cannot begin to grasp the complex and powerful role that mass incarceration has taken on in the era of neoliberalism without making serious consideration of the extent to which our modern lives have become embedded within and dependent on a medicalized, psychiatrized, and ultimately punitive, discourse of madness (Foucault and Senellart 2008; Harvey 2005; Phillips-Fein 2009).

First, a Word on Madness, Foucault, and the "Carceral System"

Foucault (1995) first referred to the power-knowledge regime that undergirds mass incarceration as the carceral network or carceral system. According to Foucault, a vast carceral network that developed gradually from what he refers to as the "classical age" (ca. 1600–1700s) down through the end of the nineteenth century, linked, through "innumerable relations," the punitive and the abnormal, transforming the "social enemy" into the "deviant" or "delinquent" and making the power to punish both "natural" and "legitimate." Once embedded in this system, which is still with us today and extends well beyond the prison, one is capable of moving through a "slow, continuous, imperceptible gradation that [makes] it possible to pass naturally from disorder to offence and back from a transgression of the law to a slight departure from a rule, an average, a demand, a norm" (Foucault 1995, 298). "We are in the society," Foucault argues, "of the teacher–judge, the doctor–judge, the educator–judge, the 'social worker'–judge; it is on them that the universal reign of the normative is based; and each individual, wherever he may find himself, subjects to it his body, his gestures, his behavior, his aptitudes, his achievements." In the end, Foucault (1995) concludes that, "the carceral network, in its compact or disseminated forms, with its systems of insertion, distribution, surveillance, observation, has been the greatest support, in modern society, of the normalizing power" (304). The prison is merely an extension of the disciplinary power that governs us all.

Foucault's fundamental insight—that an insidious "normalizing power" exists in modern Western societies that ultimately affects us all—while constrained by his methodology, nevertheless remains eminently useful for analyzing the incarcerated mad subject in the late twentieth century. Though he understood power as a "multiplicity of force relations" that operated through "ceaseless struggles and confrontations," and encouraged discursive "insurrections" from subjugated sources, in much of his writing Foucault curiously—given his involvement during the early 1970s with the prison information group or GIP—leaves unexamined the utterances and actions of those individuals whose lives were touched most deeply by the carceral system (Foucault 1990, 92,93; 1995; Foucault et al. 2003, 7–19; Foucault and Khalfa 2009; Foucault and Lagrange 2006). Instead, he relies almost exclusively on prescriptive and descriptive literature; on philosophies of the mind (epistemologies), the body, law, economy, and society; on various laws, codes, and official orders; on reform tracts and psychiatric treatises written by the most well-known medical men; and finally on material culture produced largely by those individuals who assumed the most dominant positions within (mostly European) society. This can be seen in the oft-cited preface to the 1961 edition of *History of Madness*, in which Foucault declares that, "madness can only be heard from the heights of the fortress in which it is imprisoned...To write the history of madness will therefore mean making a structural study of the historical ensemble–notions, institutions, judicial and police measures, scientific concepts–which hold captive a madness whose wild state can never be reconstituted." In his mystification of madness and mad people, Foucault refers to madness as "that inaccessible primitive purity" (Foucault, Michel, and Jean Khalfa 2009, xxxii–xxxiii). Although Foucault's corpus leaves largely untouched any direct critical analysis of the lived experiences of subjugated bodies and complex forms of embodied knowledge, he recognizes (in the abstract) innumerable potential sites of resistance and revolution.

In this chapter, I use insights provided largely by Foucault to rethink the positionality (*vis-a-vis* doctors and the state, for example) of mad subjects in late twentieth century discourse on incarceration. Beginning our analysis from a complexly embodied mad standpoint forces us to reevaluate common notions of "the archive."[2] The voices and actions of the mad and the incarcerated can be found throughout the records and artifacts produced during the earlier periods in which Foucault situates his studies; they are even more prevalent in the modern era. As long as psychiatric power–knowledge has existed, there has been resistance to it. Since the 1960s, a diverse group of mad people the world over has coalesced to form an "anti-psychiatry" movement (of sorts). The mad people's movement, which in various times and locations has sought to dismantle psychiatric power–knowledge and end incarceration and other forms of forced treatment emerged out of (and remains rooted in) the individual embodied experiences of movement participants. Though many individuals who aligned themselves with the mad people's movement found intellectual sustenance in the work of Foucault (1965), R. D. Laing (1965), Thomas Szasz (1961), Erving Goffman (1961), Phyllis Chesler (1972), and other scholars and activists, their challenges to psychiatric power–knowledge were born out of individual and collective experiences of violence and oppression.

From the beginning, movement participants challenged what came to be called the medical model of madness; the idea that madness is something that is experienced individually and internally, and is fixed, natural, timeless, neutral or value-free, and rooted in our biology (neurochemistry). This critique of the medical model of madness became part of a grassroots movement—often referred to as the consumer/survivor/ex-patient or C/S/X movement—that began to take shape in North America during the early 1970s and included a broad range of people living with an equally expansive list of psychiatric labels (Crossley 2006; Morrison

2005). Increasingly, movement participants began to discard those medical labels and (re)claim a mad identity. For people living within the culture or participating in the movement this identity took on politicized, empowering connotations. It also served as a means of unifying (more or less) groups of individuals who, under the medical model of madness, came to be separated by a seemingly infinite list of conditions, disorders, syndromes, illnesses, and impairments. In the spirit of the mad people's movement, I use the term "madness" throughout this chapter to refer to a broad range of behaviors, identities, and ways of being in the world that have, in the waning decades of the twentieth century, taken on new medicalized meanings and may include everything from Attention Deficit Hyperactivity Disorder (ADHD) and Affective or Mood disorders, to acute psychosis, schizophrenia, or the increasingly popular schizo-affective disorder and borderline personality disorder. In doing so, I seek to decenter medicalized notions of madness and direct our attention toward the long silenced voices, the largely hidden culture, and the often obfuscated actions of the "mad among us" (quote from, Grob 1994). I call this taking a "mad" approach to the study of mass incarceration.

Taking a mad approach to analyzing the specific manifestations of the carceral network that have emerged since the 1960s opens up new ways of thinking about incarceration, as well as what we currently refer to as "mental illness" and the lived experiences of our mad citizens. One of the central tenets of the mad people's movement and mad studies has been to offer both practical and scholarly critiques of incarceration and involuntary "treatment" in all of their many guises, and to highlight the voices and experiences of the psychiatrized or otherwise "mad identified" (Fabris 2011). Most mad activists and mad scholars maneuver within a liminal space between a medicalized or biologized notion of madness and a more social or relational understanding of what it means to live a "mad" existence; others reject medical madness wholesale. While it is beyond the scope of this chapter to explore all of the fascinating points of convergence and divergence within the C/S/X movement and mad studies (Crossley 2006; Morrison 2005; Staub 2011), I contend that beginning an analysis of deinstitutionalization and the rise of mass incarceration from a complexly embodied mad standpoint provides us with a valuable means of (re)evaluating both social processes.

The (Hi)stories We Tell

As an historian, I am deeply concerned with the stories we tell about our past and about our present—the two are often related in significant ways. The narratives we construct determine our reality; they determine what we know and what we know to be true, and they have very real material consequences in our lives. The stories we tell affect policy formation, for example. They also define what constitutes criminal behavior, and what we think we know about mental illness.

To date, the few accounts we have of the complex process we generally refer to as deinstitutionalization consist largely of scathing polemics written by those individuals located within the various "caring professions." The authors of these narratives accept medical notions of madness wholly and uncritically. They also tend to characterize our current situation as the unintended outcome of left-leaning activists, pragmatic politicians, and ideologically driven "civil liberties" lawyers, who, beginning in the immediate post-World War II period, worked (sometimes together) to dismantle an aging, ineffective, and perhaps most important, expensive state hospital system, and to reform outdated commitment procedures, with little or no thought about what might replace either system of intervention. These stories tend to demonize social activists, especially those considered part of the "anti-psychiatry" movement, and to attack liberal lawyers who were intent on protecting the rights of so-called mental patients without considering the importance of maintaining their safety and well-being. The state, in most of these accounts, is comprised largely of inept politicians primarily concerned with reducing the bottom line (Erickson and Erickson 2008; Eghigian 2011; Grob 1991; Isaac and Armat 1990; Johnson 1990; Torrey 1988; 1997; 2008). Within this retelling, the criminalization of madness becomes an "unintended consequence" of the failed attempt to move America's mental patients out of the back wards and into the community (Etter, Birzer, and Fields 2008). A complex tale gets reduced to "untreated illness." Former mental patients' mental illnesses go untreated in the community, ultimately leading to their arrest and incarceration.

While this may be an accurate caricature of the social and cultural forces that produced both deinstitutionalization and the criminalization of mental illness, it only reveals part of the story. We cannot rely on the "untreated illness" narrative wholly, or even partially to explain this past. A mad studies approach would tell us first that we cannot accept mental illness at face value. The ways in which we define mental illness are deeply rooted in our social, cultural, and historical location. What modern-day psychiatry deems mental illness, may not have been considered pathological in other periods of US history, or within all of the many diverse socioeconomic and cultural groups that make up the United States. That is not to say that madness is merely a social construct; that it somehow does not exist in the "real" world. Quite the contrary, what we currently refer to as "mental illness" exists across the human spectrum. It is something we all experience in one way or another. It is the values and meanings that we attach to madness that change over time and vary across cultures and classes, and ultimately affect who gets defined as mad, why, and in what setting. Rather than deal in meaningful ways with the social and historical contingencies of madness, contemporary social critics (especially those associated with the medical and "helping" professions) attempt to avoid the difficulties inherent in defining both "treatment" and "mental illness" by referring to something they call "serious mental illness" as if it were discrete, scientifically knowable, and readily self-evident. The term "serious," in this case, performs important cultural work. It simultaneously reveals latent anxieties (among doctors) in the diagnosis of "mental illness," and (paradoxically) places the diagnosis seemingly beyond interrogation. The notion that a "mental illness" is "serious" discreetly, yet powerfully shifts it into the register of "obviously or objectively true" or a "scientific fact." This is something that eminent medical historian Charles Rosenberg (2007), writing in a different context, has referred to as part of the "tyranny of diagnosis." Any critical assessment of madness and mass incarceration must begin by thinking critically about madness itself.

We must also begin by taking an equally expansive and critical approach to analyzing various forms of "treatment," including incarceration. A mad studies approach allows us to engage in meaningful ways with the long history of violence and isolation experienced by mad people. Throughout the nineteenth and twentieth centuries, the increasing pathologization and psychiatrization of aberrant behavior, the utter (though often unspoken) disregard for disabled or mad bodies, and the stigma associated with madness led directly to the disappearing of a "dispensable" and "defective" population and the "social problems" it represented. By the mid-1950s, approximately 559,000 Americans lived incarcerated lives inside crumbling mental institutions. Current efforts to incarcerate mad citizens are only the most recent manifestation of a centuries' old process of segregating and isolating those individuals deemed unworthy and incapable of full participation in society. In the waning decades of the twentieth century, as state hospitals emptied and many closed their doors permanently, both former patients and the newly mad increasingly found themselves alone and on the street or holed up in homes with overburdened, frustrated, exhausted, or uncooperative and insensitive family members. At the same time, lawmakers, business owners, neighborhood residents, and some family members began fashioning local, state, and federal policies and programs designed primarily to segregate, isolate, and in many cases criminalize behaviors that in earlier decades or other settings may not have warranted legal or juridical intervention. This profoundly punitive system of intervention emerged within and through an expanding psychiatric and pharmaceutical industry, forming a carceral system that proved critical in a process that Foucault adeptly described four decades ago as the normalization of the power-knowledge of normalization. But the mass incarceration of America's mad citizens in the late twentieth century involved much more than a normalizing discourse ("mental illness" and "criminality") embedded within power-knowledge systems and enacted through various state apparatus. Until we begin to take the experiences and utterances of mad people seriously, we will only be telling part of this critically important story.

Counting Mad Prisoners

When we begin to investigate mass incarceration, the story that we commonly read is that race and class alone (or at least disproportionately) determine one's criminality. Yet upon further analysis we see that this is not always the case. In order to explore this point in more detail, we must take a turn through the stories told by social scientists who analyze the demographics of incarceration. By the first decade of the twenty-first century, the incarcerated and supervised population of the United States was, overwhelmingly, a population of color. By 2006, more than 7.3 million Americans had become entangled in the criminal justice system, up from about 500,000 during the 1970s. As of 2009, the United States held 25 percent of the world's prisoners, while it contained only 5 percent of the world's population (Human Rights Index: US Prisons 2009–2010). The American prison population had, by 2006, increased more rapidly than had the resident population as a whole, and one in every 31 US residents was under some form of correctional supervision (prison, jail, probation, or parole) (Thompson 2010, 703). African American men were 6.5 times more likely than white males and 2.5 times more likely than Hispanic males to find themselves imprisoned. By 2006, one in fifteen black men over the age of eighteen and one in nine black men age twenty to thirty-four were incarcerated. The overall incarceration rate for women increased 832 percent from 1997 to 2007 (Human Rights Index: US Prisons 2009–2010). The imprisonment rate for African American women was almost double that of Hispanic women and three times the rate of white women. By the early twenty-first century, more African Americans found themselves in penal institutions than in institutions of higher learning (Thompson 2010, 703).

Research in various fields indicates, however, that the number of mad prisoners has also risen steadily in recent decades. For a number of reasons and to meet their own needs, Federal (US) census takers steeped in medical discourse break madness down into those individuals who "have mental health problems" and those individuals who "are seriously mentally ill," with the former consisting largely of "mood disorders" or "affective disorders" and "chemical dependencies," and the latter consisting of more intractable manifestations of madness, namely "schizophrenia," "bipolar disorder," and "major depression." A 2006 Bureau of Justice Statistics study reported that more than half of all prison and jail inmates have a mental health problem, which includes 64 percent of jail inmates, 45 percent of federal inmates, and 56 percent of persons confined in state prisons (Erickson and Erickson 2008, 4–5; Slate and Johnson 2008, 62). A separate report by the US Department of Justice released in 1999 and based on a survey of inmates, indicated that 16 percent of all inmates in state and federal jails and prisons "had schizophrenia, bipolar illness, major depression," or some other "serious mental illness." This meant that on any given day there were approximately 283,000 persons with "serious mental illnesses" incarcerated in federal and state prisons, and an additional 70,000 mad persons in public psychiatric hospitals (Erickson and Erickson 2008, 4–5; Kupers 1999, xvi). The number of mad prisoners increases dramatically when we include individuals living with "mental health problems." Human Rights Watch (2006) estimates the number of mad prisoners to be close to 1.25 million, twice the number (in absolute terms) of mad citizens incarcerated in state hospitals during the peak years of institutionalization in the mid-1950s. Although a mad studies approach would tell us that we must remain wary of the medical labeling that takes place within the judicial and "correctional" systems—a point to which I return—it seems undeniable that many mad Americans continue to live incarcerated lives.

When we delve deeper into the stories told by social scientists, we find that the prevalence of "mental health problems" seems to vary by racial or ethnic group. White inmates appear to have higher rates of reported "mental health problems" than African Americans or Hispanics, while African Americans, and especially African American men, seem to be labeled "seriously mentally ill" more often than their white counterparts (Erickson and Erickson 2008, 4–5). Explanations for these apparent racial disparities abound in the social-scientific literature on incarceration. This, however, is not the place to engage in these debates. A mad studies approach would tell us that we must take this opportunity to start to question not only the widely disparate rates of diagnosis but also the creation, maintenance, and in some cases, expansion of the diagnostic categories themselves.

In The Protest Psychosis, historian-psychiatrist Jonathan Metzl (2009) documents not only the changing meanings of "schizophrenia" over the course of the twentieth century, but also the disproportionate number of black men attached to that label. As Metzl aptly elucidates, race, which had been important in defining madness since the mid-nineteenth century, got "written into" modern notions of madness during what he calls the "civil rights era" of the 1960s and 1970s. Beginning in the 1960s, schizophrenia went from being a label applied largely to middle-class white housewives (1920s–1950s) to being a "violent social disease" attributed primarily to black men. Studies conducted by the National Institute of Mental Health in the 1960s found that "blacks have a 65% higher rate of schizophrenia than whites" (Metzl 2009, ix–xxi). According to Metzl (2009), a series of studies published in the Archives of General Psychiatry in 1973 "discovered" that "African-American patients were 'significantly more likely' than white patients to receive schizophrenia diagnoses, and 'significantly less likely' than white patients to receive diagnoses for other mental illnesses such as depression or bipolar disorder"

(Metzl 2009, ix–xxi). Metzl (2009) goes on to argue that, "Throughout the 1980s and 1990s, articles from leading psychiatric and medical journals showed that doctors diagnosed the paranoid subtype of schizophrenia in African American men 5–7 times more often than white men, and also more frequently than other ethnic minority groups" (Metzl 2009, ix–xxi). Metzl attributes elevated rates of schizophrenia diagnosis among black men not to any individual bias or prejudice (though that certainly exists), but rather to what the civil rights and black power activist Stokely Carmichael once referred to as "institutional racism." "To a remarkable extent," Metzl (2009, ix–xxi) argues, "anxieties about racial difference shape diagnostic criteria, health care policies, medical and popular attitudes about mentally ill persons, the structures of treatment facilities, and, ultimately, the conversations that take place there within." Though Metzl may not call himself a "mad studies scholar" and he does not concern himself directly with deinstitutionalization, it is evident from his study that the onset of deinstitutionalization and the nearly simultaneous rise of "law and order" politics, which would dominate centrist or mainstream political discourse throughout the late twentieth century, not only affected the rise of mass incarceration but also, in many ways, determined who would be labeled "mad" and in what setting. Black men, who for complex reasons found themselves in clinical or "correctional" settings, were much more likely than white or Hispanic men to be labeled in contemporary (medicalized) terms, "seriously mentally ill."

Gender also becomes important when we consider madness and incarceration. Both the 1999 and 2006 DOJ reports found that women inmates had higher rates of "mental health problems" than men. The 1999 Bureau of Justice Statistics report, which was based on a survey of prisoners, found that "29% of white females, 20% of black females and 22% of Hispanic females in state prison were identified as mentally ill. Nearly four in ten white female inmates age twenty-four or younger were mentally ill" (Human Rights Watch 2003, 38). In a more recent survey of available data, Human Rights Watch (2006) reports that approximately 73 percent of all women in state prisons have a "mental health problem."

A growing number of juvenile offenders, especially young women, have also been pathologized and psychiatrized since the introduction of the significantly revised third edition of the *Diagnostic and Statistical Manual of Mental Disorders* (DSM) in 1980.[3] Following the controversy surrounding the removal of "homosexuality" from the DSM in 1973/4, and feeling pressure not only from drug companies and third-party insurance companies but also from their own patients to create discrete diagnostic categories and a standardized system of classification, the American Psychiatric Association (APA) formed a task force led by Robert Spitzer and charged it with the seemingly incomprehensible task of bringing order to madness. Over the course of six years, Spitzer and his task force, which was part of a larger movement of biologically based psychiatrists who sought to move psychiatry away from Freudian or "dynamic" approaches to madness, fundamentally and perhaps permanently altered modern notions of madness. The result was the DSM-III, published in 1980, which nearly completely abandoned dynamic psychiatry and greatly expanded the number of disorders and syndromes within the APA's purview.[4] Armed with the thoroughly revised DSM, juvenile courts and some parents have been using juvenile detention facilities as de facto asylums for "mad" youth since the 1980s (Erickson and Erickson 2008, xiii).

As I have noted elsewhere, researchers in a number of fields, as well as judges, prosecutors, politicians and many parents, maintained the assertion that an overwhelmingly high percentage of delinquent girls manifested "signs" of a broad array of mental "disorders" (Rembis 2011). *Psy* researchers and practitioners have also created a number of new disorders with which they label and through which they are able to medicate, incarcerate, and otherwise surveil delinquent girls. The list of disorders involved in girls' delinquency is long, but it is well worth citing. It includes but is not limited to: conduct disorder, disruptive behavior disorder, anti-social personality disorder, anxiety disorder, bipolar disorder, depression, ADHD, substance abuse disorder, oppositional defiant disorder, and borderline personality disorder. One recent study found that 71.2 percent of delinquent girls met the "diagnostic criteria for a psychiatric disorder." A separate study found that 57 percent met the "criteria for at least two disorders" (Feld 2009). Barry Feld (2009), one of America's leading scholars of juvenile justice, has argued that both rising incarceration rates and the high percentage of "disordered" delinquent girls can be attributed, at least partially, to both "psychiatric hospitals' quest for profits..." and "malleable diagnostic categories [that have] enabled entrepreneurs to 'medicalize' adolescent deviance and parents to incarcerate troublesome children without any meaningful judicial supervision" (261).

Madness and incarceration ultimately affect the mental and emotional well-being of the nation's communities as well. According to the Bureau of Justice Statistics, at the end of the twentieth century, "state and federal prisoners were parents to 1,498,800 children under age eighteen" (Thompson 2010, 713). By 2002, one in every 45 minor children had at least one parent in a state or federal prison, and by 2008 "52% of state inmates and 63% of federal inmates reported having an estimated 1,706,600 minor children"—the majority of whom were under the age of ten (Thompson 2010, 716). In major cities like Chicago, African American children were more than eight times more likely to have a parent in prison than were white children (Thompson 2010, 716). Most teachers and students in America's urban classrooms have had to contend not only with the social and economic fallout of mass incarceration, but with its psychological consequences as well. As one researcher has stated, "children of prisoners often suffer from anxiety and attention disorders, or from post-traumatic stress" (Thompson 2010, 715). Researchers are increasingly coming to the conclusion that the negative behavioral and learning consequences that many children experience may be at least partially explained by their sense that through the incarceration of a parent or other relative they have lost "their homes, their safety, their public status and private self-image, their primary source of comfort and affection" (Thompson 2010, 715).

If we believe these accounts, we must come to the conclusion that increasingly biological notions of madness have become deeply enmeshed in the institutional and discursive apparatus first identified by Foucault (1995) as the "carceral system" and that mass incarceration has had a significant effect on America's mad citizens, on a growing segment of the incarcerated population, and on communities outside the walls of the jail or prison. I will leave it up to future mad and disability studies scholars, as well as those individuals who study mass incarceration, to analyze all of the nuanced implications of the demographics of incarceration. For now, I would like to focus on the stories we use to explain the apparent rise in mad prisoners.

Why So Many Mad Prisoners?

In this section, I begin to answer this deceptively complex question by exploring the most readily available explanations, namely those provided by key players within the Federal government and the National Alliance on Mental Illness (NAMI) and its associates. Since its founding in September 1979, primarily by family members and other relatives of people living with "serious mental illness," NAMI has worked to align itself closely with what psychiatrist Peter Breggin (1994; 2009) calls the "psycho–pharmaceutical complex"—the APA, the National Institute of Mental Health, "big pharma," and lawmakers (at the state and federal level). By 1996, NAMI had 130,000 members and chapters in every state. In its 2010 annual report, NAMI claimed to provide "support, education and empowerment for more than 500,000 members and supporters" (NAMI 2010). Referred to as a mother's march for madness and often derided by their critics as "NAMI mommies," the National Alliance on Mental Illness has been very influential in advocating for a strict biologically deterministic definition of madness, and for the use of psychopharmacology and other controversial forms of "treatment," such as ECT or electroconvulsive therapy and psychosurgery, commonly known as lobotomy. For three decades, NAMI has worked with psychiatrists, drug companies, and state and federal governments not only to promote its own biopsychiatric ideas, values, and goals but also to silence or marginalize any opposing viewpoints. The result, at least in part, has been the acceptance by a majority of Americans living in the twenty-first century of what Breggin and others have referred to as the "unproven credo" and the "unfounded slogans" that "mental illnesses" are "brain related disorders" that "involve strong genetic influences" (Breggin 1994; 2009; Morrison 2009; Whitaker 2010). This is the oft-told tale of the "chemical imbalance" and its links with madness; a tale that one psychiatrist recently characterized as "a kind of urban legend—never a theory seriously propounded by well-informed psychiatrists" (Pies 2011).

When we examine the seemingly parallel histories of deinstitutionalization and mass incarceration through the lens provided by NAMI and government agencies, such as the National Institute of Mental Health and the Department of Justice, we see that they intersect at several critical points and that trends that have become evident in the early twenty-first century are no mere coincidence or "unintended consequence." As one NAMI father explained in a session at a 2006 NAMI convention, "We've made them [our children] criminals as well as mentally ill" (McManamy 2006). In the NAMI narrative, stricter commitment and treatment procedures, the advent of the so-called war on drugs in the late 1960s and early 1970s, the initiation of "get tough" policies in the 1980s and 1990s, and the slashing of social welfare and health care programs, especially those aimed specifically at mad citizens, came together to produce rising numbers of mad prisoners. In 1992, NAMI and Public Citizen's Health Research Group (PCHRG, founded 1971) released a report that described alarmingly high numbers of mad people incarcerated in jails across the country. The report documented that most of the arrested individuals had not committed major crimes but rather misdemeanors or minor felonies directly related to their "untreated illnesses" (Erickson and Erickson 2008, 4).

Both the 1999 and 2006 studies by the DOJ point to some important background characteristics of mad inmates. They found that homelessness in the year before incarceration was more common among inmates who had seemingly less serious and more preventable and ultimately treatable "mental health problems." Living in a foster home and experiencing sexual and physical abuse as a child was also a common experience among mad inmates (Erickson and Erickson 2008, 5). According to the dominant (NAMI) discourse, the advent of the so-called war on drugs and the increasing salience of "ordinance infractions" and "quality-of-life violations," have pushed the criminal justice system onto the front line in modern efforts to "treat" the "mentally ill" (Alexander 2010; Slate and Johnson 2008). The nation's failing health care system and its especially inadequate mental health care services have intensified the apparent shift in "treatment" to new sites, including the criminal justice system, in most cases solely for political and economic reasons. During the Reagan/Bush era, from 1980 to 1992, there was a 154 percent increase in the reported number of mad persons in the nation's jails (Slate and Johnson 2008, 45–46). Although the NAMI account is an insightful and potentially powerful critique of our current situation, it leaves untouched the notion that incarceration is anything other than the direct result of "untreated illness."

Though (or perhaps because) other groups—members of the C/S/X movement, some psychiatrists and most mad studies scholars—remain critical of the "untreated illness" narrative, NAMI continues to promote this deceptively straightforward explanation for our current condition. The plot line is a rather simple one: Since the introduction of Thorazine in the 1950s and the move to deinstitutionalize the country's mental patients in the 1960s, increasing numbers of mad citizens have been forced to survive on the streets and ultimately in the nation's burgeoning prisons and jails. The "seriously mentally ill," who suffer from a medically diagnosable and treatable chemical imbalance, and who must take drugs for the rest of their lives, are not receiving the care and treatment they require to live in the community. Punitive (carceral) solutions to medical problems show no signs of abating largely because politicians on both the left and right continue to support neoliberal fiscal policies that slash domestic spending on health, education, and welfare, while leaving fiscal support for law enforcement nearly untouched. State budgets for mental health care, which have been declining steadily (in the aggregate) since the 1970s, have fallen by an additional $2 billion since 2008. Yet as H. Clarke Romans of the National Alliance on Mental Illness of Southern Arizona points out, "the [mental health care] costs were not really eliminated; they were just pushed down to less visible areas in the community, and we're responding to the difficulties with the most expensive form of services that the community has to offer to people; that's emergency rooms, hospitalization, law enforcement intervention. So, the communities are spending the money, even though it appears that the lawmakers believe that they have actually cut the budget and saved money" (*Democracy Now!* 2011). According to NAMI, mental patients have not received the treatment they require, which has resulted in their being forced into the carceral system through various social and structural forces.

The trends outlined by Romans (and NAMI) have accelerated throughout the 1990s and into the new century. From 1992 to 2003, according to the Center for Disease Control (CDC), the number of mad persons visiting emergency rooms across the country increased by 56 percent, from 2,381,000 to 3,718,000. Often emergency rooms were overcrowded, under staffed, under funded, and lacked the proper connections for referral services, resulting at least in part in the inadequate treatment and early release of mad patients, which in most cases meant increased entanglement with the criminal justice system. One scholar (Coleman 1997) found that two-thirds of US hospitals "dump[ed]" mad patients who were unable to pay for their care (Slate and Johnson 2008, 45–46). Yet another researcher (Markowitz 2006) found that "public psychiatric hospital capacity ha[d] a statistically significant negative effect on crime and arrest rates, and that hospital capacity affect[ed] crime and arrest rates in part, through its impact on homelessness" (Markowitz 2006). Put simply, as public psychiatric hospitals closed, arrest and crime rates increased. The negative or inverse relationship between the availability of hospital beds and arrest rates becomes more evident when we look at a specific state, such as New York, which has been a national leader in institutionalization, deinstitutionalization, and mass incarceration since it first consolidated its state hospital system in 1890. In 1973, there were approximately 93,000 New York residents in state hospitals and approximately 12,500 New Yorkers in the Department of Corrections. By 2000, those numbers had flipped, with only 5,000 New Yorkers in state hospitals and approximately 72,000 individuals in the New York State Department of Corrections (Wagner 2000). Though there is most likely considerable overlap, in many cases these are not the same people. This, however, is not the most important point to be drawn from the demographic shift in resident populations over the past four decades. This "transinstitutionalization," as it is often called, the move from asylum to jail or prison, is the direct result of the increasing medicalization and biologization of madness in the late twentieth century and the concomitant devaluing of other forms of treatment, care, and support within the community. The criminalization of madness in recent decades should not only be a national health care concern, but also a human rights concern, especially as more states move to restrict expenditures for inpatient care (Slate and Johnson 2008, 45–46). Yet few Americans outside NAMI—and those individuals directly associated with the mad people's movement (who I discuss in the next section)—have raised any alarms regarding the apparent push to incarcerate (rather than treat or support in some other way) the nation's mad citizens.

According to NAMI and their associates, the type of community care envisioned in the 1960s, which never really included the "seriously mentally ill," has clearly eluded most Americans. Mid-twentieth century reformers and politicians had intended that America's mad citizens be released from state hospitals and returned to their communities, where they would receive the support they needed through local community mental health centers. Emerging out of the mental hygiene movement and the push for deinstitutionalization, both of which had gained momentum over the first four decades of the twentieth century, as well as the idealism and egalitarian politics of the early 1960s, and enacted by Congress in 1963, the community mental health care act was meant to provide an alternative to the state hospital and a relief to family members and other care providers (Grob 1991; Isaac and Armat 1990; Johnson 1990; Torrey 2008; 1997; 1988). Speaking before Congress in February 1963, President Kennedy described community mental health care provided through community mental health centers (CMHCs) as "a bold new approach." Kennedy assured Congress that when the new plan was "carried out, reliance on the cold mercy of custodial isolation will be supplanted by the open warmth of community concern and capability" (Quoted in Torrey 1988, 108). Yet, as E. Fuller Torrey—perhaps the most well-known psychiatrist associated with both NAMI (formerly), and more recently, his own Treatment Advocacy Center—has noted, the community mental health centers and many of the ideals upon which they had been founded were "dead" by the early 1970s, replaced by the law and order rhetoric and (domestic) fiscal conservativism of the newly realigned Republican right (Torrey 1988, 131). Though it is difficult to discern its validity, Torrey offers the following anecdote, which neatly highlights the emerging priorities in mental health care in the early 1970s: "President Nixon's former personal physician suggested that all 6-year-olds in the United States should be psychiatrically tested to determine their potential for future criminal behavior. Those found to be deviant would be sent to 'camps' so they could receive intensive 'treatment' of their problems" (Torrey 1988, 132).

By most accounts, neglect and an utter disregard for human life have plagued community mental health care since its inception. "Discharge planning" has been nearly nonexistent. Anecdotal evidence suggests that many patients/prisoners were/ are simply released from the hospital/prison with no plan at all. Heather Barr of New York's Urban Justice Center's Mental Health Project has noted recently that mad prisoners from Rikers Island (New York) continue to be dropped off early in the morning with none of the medicine they were taking while incarcerated, no prescriptions for any medication, no referral to a mental health clinic, and no referral to a shelter with mental health services. According to Barr, exprisoners are given only $1.50 in cash and a $3 dollar Metro card. Ex-prisoners' plight is further compounded by the fact that it takes three months, or sometimes longer, to become eligible for Medicaid (state health insurance), which could help pay some of the cost of their care (Wagner 2000). Once on the streets, ex-prisoners find themselves "in trouble" with business owners, neighborhood residents, and in most cases law-enforcement officials. All of this has led, at least in part, to much higher rates of recidivism among mad prisoners—the so-called revolving prison door (Baillargeon et al. 2009).

One of the few studies of mad citizens behind bars has found that a large proportion of prisoners, especially those labeled "seriously mentally ill," ran into trouble with the law because of drug and alcohol abuse, and that there is no evidence that incarceration makes them less prone to substance abuse after they are released, which has been a common fallacy deployed by those individuals seeking to prop up the carceral system (Kupers 1999, xxii; Rhodes 2004). The author of the study (Kupers 1999) concludes that placing prisoners who were not, in most cases, convicted of violent crimes in what he calls a "hellish" environment for several years only makes them "angrier, meaner, and less caring toward others upon release," which can only intensify their own madness and the emotional and psychological distress of those around them.[5]

Since the release of the initial Bureau of Justice Statistics report in 1999, various government agencies have been working to create what they call "diversion" programs in an effort to reduce the number of mad prisoners. In 2000, Congress passed "America's Law Enforcement and Mental Health Project" (Public Law 106–515), creating Mental Health Courts, which ideally would help relieve the overburdened criminal court system. By the end of the first decade of the twenty-first century, more than 150 Mental Health Courts existed throughout the United States. State and local governments have also increasingly implemented what they refer to as "pre-arrest" or "pre-booking" diversion strategies, which may include police training, the deployment of "mobile crisis response teams" and transportation to treatment facilities rather than the local jail. There have also been a number of "post-booking" procedures implemented in recent years, usually through the Mental Health Courts, which may include mandatory treatment and/or compliance with medication, "case management," or inpatient hospitalization (Mental Health America n.d.). Although many of the newer strategies of intervention continue to come under fire for their human rights violations, they remain popular with advocates and activist groups, like NAMI, who are determined to keep America's "mental patients" out of the nation's jails and prisons.

"...the 'aunt in the attic'"

There is at least one other way in which we can begin to think about the move toward mass incarceration since the 1960s. It will require acknowledging and listening to the voices of mad people themselves, something that most Americans, including some of those who have called themselves allies, have been reluctant to do for over 40 years. David Oaks, long-time mad activist and editor of the US-American magazine *Dendron* recognized this reluctance in 1996, when he wrote, "Since the very origins of psychiatry, psychiatric survivors have individually resisted human rights violations and sought humane alternatives. In the past 25 years [since 1971], however, a small wave of diverse organized groups, networks, publications, have sprung up and connected internationally...In the family of social change movements this past 25 years, the psychiatric survivors liberation movement has been the 'aunt in the attic' who is usually ignored" (Reaume Unpublished).

Scholars interested in studying mass incarceration must stop ignoring the aunt in the attic and begin exploring seriously and systematically the ways in which psychiatrized citizens have resisted psychiatric oppression and incarceration, and worked to form their own systems of support and legitimation, and ultimately their own diverse culture. Scholars also need to grapple in meaningful ways with those individuals and groups who have embraced psychiatry and the psychiatric labels bestowed upon them, while simultaneously shaping their own understanding of these concepts and forging their own experiences and organizations. In short, we must engage with all of the complexities of human subjectivity; with what Foucault referred to as the "points of the body," "moments in life," and "types of behavior," that become "mobile and transitory points of resistance, producing cleavages in a society that shift about, fracturing unities and effecting regroupings, furrowing across individuals themselves, cutting them up and remolding them, marking off irreducible regions in them, in their bodies and minds" (Foucault 1990, 96; Mollow 2006; Rembis 2009; Wilson and Beresford 2002). We cannot hope ever to understand the history of mass incarceration in the late twentieth century if we continue to ignore the aunt in the attic.

Since the early 1970s, mad activists, and mad and disability studies scholars, have been working to highlight and put an end to human rights violations, and provide a counter to incarceration and other forms of involuntary treatment (Beresford and Wilson 2002; Crossley 2006; Morrison 2009; Staub 2011). What began in the early 1970s as a movement of primarily well educated, primarily white "psychiatric survivors" has grown over the last four decades into an international movement that includes survivors of psychiatric intervention, consumers of psychiatric services (including psychotropic drugs), and exinmates (of various types of institutions). This loose organization of psychiatrized citizens and their nonpsychiatrized allies has, like any social movement, experienced its own internal divisions (Pelka 2012; Reaume unpublished). Yet it has remained consistent in its critique of modern medicalized forms of psychiatric intervention (Crossley 2006; Morrison 2009).

From the beginning, movement participants aligned themselves with larger struggles for civil and human rights. Early activists drafted a "Patients' Bill of Rights" and shortly thereafter, in 1973, convened their first conference, which they called "The Conference on Human Rights and Psychiatric Oppression." For the nascent mad people's movement, centered primarily in Boston, New York City, and Berkeley, California, all activist work came down to, in the words of long-time movement leader Judi Chamberlin, "very simple issues of human dignity"

(Pelka 2012, 284). A right to have control over one's own body and a voice in their own treatment became paramount; as Chamberlain later recalled, psychiatric survivors continually advocated for "patient controlled alternatives" to standard psychiatric care (Pelka 2012, 285). They also worked to end the discrimination and violence that pervaded modern US society.

Psychiatric users and survivors have, to varying degrees, always thought of their movement as broad-based and occurring on many levels simultaneously. Participants in the mad people's movement often identified with and felt part of other social movements, including what long-time activist David Oaks has called the "prison justice movement," as well as the feminist, African American, gay liberation, and disability rights movements (Pelka 2012, 285). Perhaps the most well-known (currently active) activist group is MindFreedom International (MFI). MFI is the product of years of organizing done primarily by Oaks and his associates, many of whom began their efforts in the 1970s. Following several years of internal conflict within the broader mad people's movement during the 1980s, primarily over issues of funding, Oaks formed Support Coalition International in the early 1990s to create an activist space free of government and corporate (big pharma) influences (Morrison 2009). In 2005, Support Coalition International changed its name to MindFreedom International. MFI, which has been called the "epicenter of the mad movement," has a board of directors, a scientific advisory board, and an academic alliance, all intent on fulfilling the basic mission of MFI, to lead "a nonviolent revolution of freedom, equality, truth and human rights that unites people affected by the mental health system with movements for justice everywhere" (MindFreedom International n.d.).

Activists have been critical in forging national and international human rights initiatives. In the 1970s, they prodded the United Nations Sub-commission on Prevention of Discrimination and Protection of Minorities to undertake "a study of the question of the protection of those detained on the grounds of mental ill-health" (UN 1991). The work of the Sub-commission led to the formation of a working group that drafted a "body of principles for the protection of persons with mental illness and for the improvement of mental health care," which ultimately became a formal UN resolution in December 1991 (UN 1991). Around the same time (1994), World Federation of Psychiatric Users Co-chair Paolo del Vecchio developed a Human Rights Position Paper, which was recently (2001) modified and reaffirmed by the World Network of Users and Survivors of Psychiatry (WNUSP) General Assembly in Vancouver, Canada (World Network...2001). Those individuals who have been part of the C/S/X movement have engaged in direct "street-level" action against human rights violations, in policy formation, and in a multitude of consciousness-raising activities that center on the task of relocating (both practically and discursively) "problems" that are usually viewed by the dominant culture as private and individual (medicalized and pathologized) in the public and social world. Through a growing number of published memoirs and other life writing, annual meetings, news publications, such as *Madness Network News*, and later *Dendron News*, and most recently, numerous internet websites, chat-rooms, and blog posts, C/S/X participants and their allies have been able to organize, mobilize, educate, and support one another (Morrison 2009).

For four decades, MFI and the organizations that preceded it have provided movement participants with a safe space to make their voices public. In one sense, MFI and other organizations have enabled what Foucault has called the "strategic codification" of multiple shifting points of resistance that make "a revolution possible" (Foucault 1990, 96). Stories like the one told by Jody A. Harmon represent a critical front line in the struggle to create an effective counter narrative; as such, they cannot be ignored. Harmon (n.d.) describes herself and her experiences in the following ways: "I'm a psychiatric survivor, and I don't use that term loosely. I have been stored in warehouses labeled hospitals. I have endured weekly lectures termed therapy. I have been zapped until my brain burns white. I have been held down, tied down, put down. I have had pills forced down my throat and needles plunged into my flesh. All this to make me 'normal,' a mold I will never fit." "I didn't win my human rights," Harmon concludes, "I stood up and demanded them." Historians, and humans more generally, can learn from mad people's experiences. Harmon says, for example, that she tries, "hard not to stereotype people—police officers, psychiatrists—and [she tries] to forgive people" (Harmon n.d.). We, in our roles as scholars, activists, and citizens should listen to movement participants, such as Leonard R Frank, who demands of his fellow activists: "We have to be witnesses for those millions who are not speaking up now for whatever reason...[We have to] tell the truth about what we have known, what we have experienced in our own lives" (Frank n.d.). Finally, scholars need to work to accomplish the transformative goal set forth by MFI member and leader of its oral history project, Oryx Cohen, who hopes that "eventually the general public will hear our stories and take them as their own" (Cohen n.d.). Only when we begin to listen to the stories of psychiatric survivors can we affect lasting change in a far ranging carceral system that for decades has become increasingly enmeshed with an equally expansive and ostensibly objective and scientific psychomedical establishment.

To return once again (briefly) to Foucault, it can easily be argued that psych-survivors, consumers, and ex-inmates have for 40 years placed themselves in the vanguard of the battle for psychiatric power–knowledge in an effort "to render problematic everything that is habitual" (Foucault and Lagrange 2006). Though they have at times relied upon what generally and traditionally has been considered intellectual or academic discourse, theirs is a critique born of their own individual and collective experiences. It is embodied knowledge, rooted in what the social philosopher Bill Hughes (2005), writing in a different context, has referred to as "practical sensuous activities" and "various forms of embodied praxis;" what Antonio Gramsci might have called "organic intelligence" (Gramsci, Hoare, and Nowell-Smith 1972). The C/S/X movement has emerged out of numerous encounters with a reluctant psychiatric system, an unforgiving carceral system, and a saneist and ableist public. Theirs is knowledge that has been mediated through bodies that have been shocked, drugged, confined, isolated, or otherwise violated; bodies that have known all too well the material and emotional effects of living a mad existence. The stories told by the participants of the mad people's movement, their history and their culture, cannot be ignored. Nor can their insistence on maintaining their own human dignity (cf. Mollow 2006; Wilson and Beresford 2002). Yet mad people remain devalued and dismissed, and their stories and acts of protest are held up as signs of nonconformity and a "lack of insight" into their own "condition" and into the world around them. For many movement participants, token efforts made by organizations, such as NAMI, to entertain "alternative forms of treatment" remain at best laughable and at worst deeply disconcerting; yet another attempt at co-optation by a more powerful organization. In the words of MindFreedom activists, we need a "creative revolution" in which we all "mobilize our healing resources."

Conclusion

Writing a history of incarceration in the postwar period from a complexly embodied mad standpoint enables us to gain a fresh perspective on the social, economic, and political forces that undergird the creation and maintenance of an ostensibly unbiased and corrective or rehabilitative legal and judicial system and begin to explore its deep connections with modern medical, health care, and social welfare policies and practices. It is clear from social scientific research that a significant percentage of inmates in the nation's jails and prisons have been labeled mad and indeed may be experiencing a mad existence. The reification of medicoscientific and legal labels such as "seriously mentally ill" and the disproportionate pathologization of bodies and experiences as "mad" by organizations such as NAMI, the National Institute of Mental Health, and the broader *psy* industries does the important cultural work of removing madness and mad people's experiences from any type of meaningful critique or analysis of this critically important past. Situating madness and mad people wholly or even partially within a starkly medicalized discourse of deviance effectively individualizes, marginalizes, and ultimately alienates mad people in some cases from their own embodiment, but perhaps more frequently from the types of human interaction and dialogue that most citizens value and respect. In many ways, mad people become a "case" in the Foucauldian sense; something to be defined, measured, managed, monitored, and punished. Yet, as Foucault acknowledges, the continually shifting terrain of power–knowledge systems and the human relations within which they are embedded expose fissures and fault lines, both practical and discursive, that have been exploited by mad people themselves and their allies in an effort to redefine the boundaries of debate and actively resist psychiatric and legal/juridical oppression. Taking a "mad" approach to the study of mass incarceration in particular and to US history in general can help us to question and ultimately challenge medical and legal labeling, forced treatment, and taken for granted social–power relations in transformative ways that engender new questions and provide new pathways toward social justice.

Notes

* I would like to thank Susan Burch, Susan Cahn, Dwight Codr, David Herzberg, Kim Nielsen, Marion Quirici, and all of the wonderful folks who attended the Disability Studies Workshop at the University of Connecticut (March 2012) and the meeting of the Foucault Circle at Canisius College, Buffalo (March 2012), as well as my editors Liat Ben-Moshe and Chris Chapman for their thoughtful comments on various drafts of this chapter.

1. By no means am I attempting to imply that we engage in a rudimentary rearticulation of the "balloon theory" that has been popular in the social sciences since the 1930s and draws a direct correlation (and causal role) between declining hospital populations and rising jail and prison populations and *vice versa*. I am not attempting to argue here that precisely the same individuals being discharged from mental hospitals *ipso facto* ended up in jail or prison. Rather, I am arguing that the social and structural changes wrought in the name of "deinstitutionalization" have, over the last 50 years, created a situation in which jails and prisons have become the primary site of "treatment" of many "mad" citizens. For more on the "balloon theory" and the ways in which disability studies scholars are reconceptualizing

"deinstitutionalization and "transinstitutionalization," see: Ben-Moshe, Liat. 2011. "Disabling Incarceration: Connecting Disability to Divergent Confinements in the USA," *Critical Sociology* (published online).

2. Throughout this chapter, I am building upon Tobin Siebers' notion of the "complexly embodied" disabled subject (Siebers 2008).

3. White girls with economic means, who comprise the majority (86 percent in 2000) of drug-related referrals to the juvenile court, tend to be medicalized and "hospitalized" more than racial/ethnic minorities, while girls of color tend more often (than whites) to experience incarceration (Feld 2009).

4. According to Allan Horwitz, the number of "discrete diagnoses" in the DSM-III (1980) increased to 265 diagnoses, up from 14 basic diagnoses two decades earlier. The number of categories expanded to 292 in the DSM-III-R (1987), and to nearly 400 in the DSM-IV (1994) (Horwitz 2002; Kutchins and Kirk 1997).

5. The average prisoner will be released in less than five years, 95 percent of all prisoners will be released eventually, despite harsher sentences (Kupers 1999).

References

Alexander, Michelle. 2010. *The New Jim Crow: Mass Incarceration in the Age of Colorblindness*. New York: New Press.

Baillargeon, Jacques, Ingrid A. Binswanger, Joseph V. Penn, Brie A. Williams, and Owen J. Murray. 2009. "Psychiatric Disorders and Repeat Incarcerations: The Revolving Prison Door." *American Journal of Psychiatry* 166:103–109.

Beresford, Peter, and Anne Wilson. 2002. "Genes Spell Danger: Mental Health Service Users/Survivors, Bioethics, and Control." *Disability & Society* 17(5):541–553.

Breggin, Peter Roger. 2009. *Medication Madness: The Role of Psychiatric Drugs in Cases of Violence, Suicide, and Crime*. New York: St. Martin's Griffin.

———. 1994. *Toxic Psychiatry*. New York: St. Martin's Press.

Chesler, Phyllis. 1972. *Women and Madness*. Garden City, NY: Doubleday.

Cohen, Oryx. n.d. "Personal Stories." Accessed June 3, 2012. http://www.mindfreedom.org/personal-stories/cohenoryx ()

Crossley, Nick. 2006. *Contesting Psychiatry: Social Movements in Mental Health*. London: Routledge.

Davis, Angela Y. 2005. *Abolition Democracy: Beyond Empire, Prisons, and Torture*. New York: Seven Stories Press.

Democracy Now! 2011. "Jared Loughner, Mental Illness and How Budget Cuts Have Slashed Behavioral Health Services in Arizona," *Democracy Now!* (democracynow.org) Originally aired: January 11. Accessed January 18 http://www.democracynow.org/2011/1/11/jared_loughner_mental_illness_and_how

Eghigian, Greg. 2011. "Deinstitutionalizing the History of Contemporary Psychiatry." *History of Psychiatry* 22(2): 201–214.

Erickson, Patricia E., and Steven K. Erickson. 2008. *Crime, Punishment, and Mental Illness: Law and the Behavioral Sciences in Conflict*. New Brunswick, NJ: Rutgers University Press.

Etter, Gregg, Michael Birzer, and Judy Fields. 2008. "The Jail as a Dumping Ground: The Incidental Incarceration of Mentally Ill Individuals." *Criminal Justice Studies* 21(1):79–89.

Fabris, Erick. 2011. *Tranquil Prisons: Chemical Incarceration Under Community Treatment Orders*. Toronto, ON: University of Toronto Press.

Feld, Barry C. 2009. "Girls in the Juvenile Justice System." In *The Delinquent Girl*, edited by Margaret A. Zahn, 225–264. Philadelphia, PA: Temple University Press.

Foucault, Michel. 1995. *Discipline and Punish: The Birth of the Prison*. New York: Vintage Books.

———. 1990. *The History of Sexuality. Volume 1, An Introduction*. New York: Vintage.

———. 1965. *Madness and Civilization: A History of Insanity in the Age of Reason*. New York: Pantheon Books.

Foucault, Michel, and Jacques Lagrange. 2006. *Psychiatric Power: Lectures at the Collège de France, 1973–74*. Basingstoke, UK: Palgrave Macmillan.

Foucault, Michel, and Jean Khalfa. 2009. *History of Madness*. New York: Routledge.

Foucault, Michel, and Michel Senellart. 2008. *The Birth of Biopolitics: Lectures at the Collège De France, 1978–79*. Basingstoke, UK: Palgrave Macmillan.

Foucault, Michel, Mauro Bertani, Alessandro Fontana, François Ewald, and David Macey. 2003. *Society Must be Defended: Lectures at the Collège de France, 1975–76*. New York: Picador.

Frank, Leonard R. n.d. "Personal Stories." Accessed June 3, 2012. http://www.mind-freedom.org/personal-stories/frankleonardr

Goffman, Erving. 1961. *Asylums; Essays on the Social Situation of Mental Patients and Other Inmates*. Garden City, NY: Anchor Books.

Gramsci, Antonio, Quintin Hoare, and Geoffrey Nowell-Smith. 1972. *Selections from the Prison Notebooks of Antonio Gramsci*. New York: International Publishers.

Grob, Gerald N. 1994. *The Mad Among Us: A History of the Care of America's Mentally Ill*. New York: Free Press.

———. 1991. *From Asylum to Community: Mental Health Policy in Modern America*. Princeton, NJ: Princeton University Press.

Harmon, Jody A. n.d. "Personal Stories." Accessed June 3, 2012. http://www.mind-freedom.org/personal-stories/harmonjodya

Harvey, David. 2005. *A Brief History of Neoliberalism*. Oxford: Oxford University Press.

Horwitz, Allan V. 2002. *Creating Mental Illness*. Chicago, IL: University of Chicago Press.

Hughes, Bill. 2005. "What Can a Foucauldian Analysis Contribute to Disability Theory?" In *Foucault and the Government of Disability*, edited by Shelley Tremain, 78–92. Ann Arbor, MI: The University of Michigan Press.

Human Rights Index. 2009–2010. "US Prisons" *International Accents* 26(Winter). The University of Iowa. Accessed January 12, 2012. http://accents.international.uiowa.edu/worldviews/human-rights-index-us-prisons-winter-2009–2010–26/

Human Rights Watch. 2006. "Number of Mentally Ill in Prisons Quadrupled: Prisons Ill Equipped to Cope." Accessed January 12, 2012. http://www.hrw.org/print/news/2006/09/05/us-number-mentally-ill-prisons-quadrupled

———. 2003. "Ill-Equipped: U.S. Prisoners and Offenders with Mental Illness." New York: Human Rights Watch.

Isaac, Rael Jean, and Virginia C. Armat. 1990. *Madness in the Streets: How Psychiatry and the Law Abandoned the Mentally Ill*. New York: Free Press.

Johnson, Ann Braden. 1990. *Out of Bedlam: The Truth About Deinstitutionalization*. New York: Basic Books.

Kupers, Terry Allen. 1999. *Prison Madness: The Mental Health Crisis Behind Bars and What We Must Do about It*. San Francisco: Jossey-Bass.

Kutchins, Herb, and Stuart A. Kirk. 1997. *Making Us Crazy: DSM: The Psychiatric Bible and the Creation of Mental Disorders*. New York: Free Press.

Laing, Ronald David. 1965. *The Divided Self: An Existential Study in Sanity and Madness*. Harmondsworth, Middlesex, UK: Penguin Books.

Markowitz, F. E. 2006. "Psychiatric Hospital Capacity, Homelessness, and Crime and Arrest Rates," *Criminology* 44: 45–72.

McManamy, John. 2006. "Forced Meds and Phantom Rights." Accessed February 2, 2012. http://www.mcmanweb.com/foced_meds.html

"Mental Health America, Position Statement 52: In Support of Maximum Diversion of Persons with Serious Mental Illness from the Criminal Justice System." Accessed January 12, 2012. http://www.mentalhealthamerica.net/go/position-statements/52

Metzl, Jonathan. 2009. *The Protest Psychosis: How Schizophrenia Became a Black Disease*. Boston: Beacon Press.

MindFreedom International. n.d. "About Us." Accessed June 3, 2012. http://www.mindfreedom.org/about-us

Mollow, Anna. 2006. "'When Black Women start going on Prozac': Race, Gender, and Mental Illness" in Meri Nana-Ama Danquah's 'Willow Weep for Me.'" *Multi-Ethnic Literature of the U.S.* 31(3): 67–99.

Morrison, Linda J. 2005. *Talking Back to Psychiatry: The Psychiatric Consumer/Survivor/Ex-Patient Movement*. New York, NY: Routledge.

"NAMI 2010 Annual Report." Accessed February 21, 2012. http://www.nami.org/Content/NavigationMenu/Inform_Yourself/About_NAMI/Annual_Reports/Annual_Reports.htm

Palermo, George B., M. B. Smith, and Frank J. Liska. 1991. "Jails versus Mental Hospitals: A Social Dilemma." *International Journal of Offender Therapy and Comparative Criminology* 35: 97–106.

Pelka, Fred. 2012. *What We Have Done: An Oral History of the Disability Rights Movement*. Amherst, MA: University of Massachusetts Press.

Penrose, Lionel. 1939. "Mental Disease and Crime: Outline of a Comparative Study of European Statistics." *British Journal of Medical Psychology* 18:1–15.

Phillips-Fein, Kim. 2009. *Invisible Hands: The Making of the Conservative Movement from the New Deal to Reagan*. New York: W. W. Norton & Company.

Pies, Ronald. 2011. "Psychiatry's New Brain-Mind and the Legend of the 'Chemical Imbalance,'" *Psychiatric Times*, July 11. Accessed January 27, 2012. http://www.psychiatrictimes.com/print/article/10168/1902106?printable=true

Reaume, Geoffrey. unpublished."MAD ACTIVISTS AND THE LEFT IN ONTARIO, 1970–2000."

Rembis, Michael A. 2011. *Defining Deviance: Sex, Science, and Delinquent Girls, 1890–1960*. Urbana, IL: University of Illinois Press.

———. 2009. "(Re)Defining Disability in the 'genetic age': Behavioral Genetics, 'new' Eugenics and the Future of Impairment." *Disability & Society* 24(5): 585–597.

Rhodes, Lorna A. 2004. *Total Confinement Madness and Reason in the Maximum Security Prison*. Berkeley, CA: University of California Press.

Rosenberg, Charles E. 2007. *Our Present Complaint: American Medicine, Then and Now*. Baltimore, MD: Johns Hopkins University Press.

Siebers, Tobin. 2008. *Disability Theory*. Ann Arbor, MI: University of Michigan Press.

Slate, Risdon N., and W. Wesley Johnson. 2008. *The Criminalization of Mental Illness: Crisis & Opportunity for the Justice System*. Durham, NC: Carolina Academic Press.

Staub, Michael E. 2011. *Madness Is Civilization When the Diagnosis Was Social, 1948–1980*. Chicago, IL: University of Chicago Press.

Szasz, Thomas Stephen. 1961. *The Myth of Mental Illness: Foundations of a Theory of Personal Conduct*. New York: Harper & Row.

Thompson, Heather Ann. 2010. "Why Mass Incarceration Matters: Rethinking Crisis, Decline, and Transformation in Postwar American History." *Journal of American History* 97(3): 734.

Torrey, E. Fuller. 2008. *The Insanity Offense: How America's Failure to Treat the Seriously Mentally Ill Endangers Its Citizens*. New York: W. W. Norton.

———. 1997. *Out of the Shadows: Confronting America's Mental Illness Crisis*. New York: John Wiley.

———. 1988. *Nowhere to Go: The Tragic Odyssey of the Homeless Mentally Ill*. New York: Harper & Row.

United Nations General Assembly. 1991. "The Protection of Persons with Mental Illness and the Improvement of Mental Health Care," A/RES/46/119, 75th plenary meeting,17 December.

Wagner, Peter 2000. "Incarceration is Not a Solution to Mental Illness." Originally published in the April 2000 issue of *Mass Dissent*. Reprinted on *Prison Policy Initiative*. Accessed January 12, 2012. http://www.prisonpolicy.org/articles/mass-dissent040100.html

Whitaker, Robert. 2010. *Anatomy of an Epidemic: Magic Bullets, Psychiatric Drugs, and the Astonishing Rise of Mental Illness in America*. New York: Crown Publishers.

Wilson, Anne, and Peter Beresford. 2002. "Madness, Distress and Postmodernity: Putting the Record Straight." In *Disability/Postmodernity: Embodying Disability Theory*, edited by Mairian Corker and Tom Shakespeare. London: Continuum

World Network of Users and Survivors of Psychiatry General Assembly. 2001. "Human Rights Position Paper." General Assembly, Vancouver, Canada.

II

Interlocking Oppressions, Contemporary Lockdown, and Contested Futures

9

It Can't Be Fixed Because It's Not Broken: Racism and Disability in the Prison Industrial Complex

Syrus Ware, Joan Ruzsa, and Giselle Dias

Introduction

Prisons[1] are dangerous places, especially if you are racialized and disabled. Because of the ways that prisons are constructed, imagined, and maintained, rampant ableism and racism affect the daily lives of many prisoners. In this chapter, we explore how disability and experiences of racialization are constructed throughout the Prison Industrial Complex (PIC)[2] within the Canadian context (Turtle Island). Further, we contend that colonization, racism, and ableism are inherent to the functioning of the penal system. The PIC is based on a set of interests created and maintained to support capitalism, patriarchy, imperialism, colonialism, racism, ableism, and white supremacy. It acts as a form of social control for the rich and powerful. As such, it benefits politicians, governments, big businesses, developers, law enforcement, and the nonprofit industrial complex. Angela Davis (2003) explains,

> To deliver up bodies destined for profitable punishment, the political economy of prisons relies on racialized assumptions of criminality—such as images of Black welfare mothers reproducing criminal children—and on racist practices in arrest, conviction, and sentencing patterns. Colored bodies constitute the main human raw material in this vast experiment to disappear the major social problems of our time. Once the aura of magic is stripped away from the imprisonment solution, what is revealed is racism, class bias, and the parasitic seduction of capitalist profit. The prison industrial system materially and morally impoverishes its inhabitants and devours the social wealth needed to address the very problems that have led to spiraling numbers of prisoners. (55)

Disabled people,[3] racialized people, and disabled People of Color experience prison in unique ways. In this chapter, we assert that the PIC reinforces colonialism, racism, and ableism, and this leads to targeted policing, criminalization, and higher incarceration rates of People of Color, people with disabilities, and People of Color with disabilities. The PIC criminalizes the experience of disability and creates new experiences of disability both within prison and after people get out. With the introduction of new crime legislation, Canada is moving toward mass incarceration, which will only exacerbate colonialism, racism, and disabilities within the PIC. In our view, these systems are not broken, they function as extensions of racist and genocidal policies and practices that seek to criminalize and imprison Indigenous and racialized people, and people with disabilities.

In order to understand how this happens, we rely on stories from our work in prisons and other stories collected by prisoners about their experiences of racialization, disability, and prison.[4] We use these stories as our data because it is so rare to actually hear about prisons from prisoners themselves. We also use anecdotal and personal stories because there has been little research conducted about the experiences of race and disability in carceral spaces. Lastly, because there is so little information about this topic, we have had to make many links that have previously not been made. We are committed to making this chapter accessible to a broader audience, including prisoners and ex-prisoners for whom academic language could be alienating or exclusionary.

To expand on our arguments about how the PIC criminalizes experiences of disabilities, we must look at the prison environment itself. We must examine the devastating effects that prison has on people's psyches. Prison is both detrimental for people with disabilities and responsible for creating new experiences of disabilities. For the purpose of this chapter, we are going to focus solely on the prison environment (although we recognize that the PIC is an ever-expanding interest that includes all carceral spaces). In Foucault's (1977) work *Discipline and Punish: The Birth of the Prison*, he speaks to the experience of power and disciplinary mechanisms in prison settings. Prior to the birth of prisons, people who committed an offense were physically punished through torture, hangings, or dismemberment—that is, through bodily punishments. It is argued that penitentiaries were conceived of by the Quakers, who were trying to find more humane ways of treating "offenders," and were built with the intention of prisoners spending time in solitude focused on penance as a form of rehabilitation (see McShane and Williams 2005). Foucault (1977) argues that the shift in the methods of punishment went from punishing people's bodies to punishing their souls.

In the final section of this chapter, we discuss the ways in which the Conservative Government[5] has created legislation that is a move toward mass incarceration in Canada. Currently, our prisons are bursting at the seams. Prisons are overcrowded, which creates tension and violence. With the introduction of Bill C-10, which includes mandatory minimum sentences for drug offenses, we are beginning to see a move toward sky rocketing incarceration rates for drug users (as witnessed in the United States). Although the legislation is geared toward "organized crime," evidence from the United States indicates that this new legislation will mostly affect poor and racialized bodies—especially Black women (Lapidus et al. 2004; Mauer, Potler, and Wolf 1999). Through prisoners' stories, we hear about targeted policing in low-income Black neighborhoods and the system's creation of fear around "gangs" and rising crime rates. In fact, crime rates and the severity of crime in Canada have been decreasing since 1992 (Brennan 2012).

Critical disability theory and critical race studies have done a poor job of making connections in a way that is meaningful for racialized disabled people (Bell

2006; Ejiogu and Ware 2008). Because disability and race are not often considered together in critical disability theorizing and research and because of the lack of research about the experiences of people in prison in general, it is hard to fully understand the ways that race and disability intertwine to create unique experiences for racialized disabled people in prison. We need more research/information into the experiences of these prisoners. In this chapter, we consider the stories of criminalized, racialized, and disabled prisoners, intentionally making a connection between the experience of ableism and racism/colonialism and the PIC. This chapter tells that story. We begin by considering how racism and ableism play out together in the prison system.

Colonialism, Racism, and Ableism within Prison

In Canada (Turtle Island), the PIC has been used as a tool for the ongoing colonization of Indigenous communities. Our goal here is not to create a detailed history of the colonization process in Canada, but to frame the context in which the overincarceration of Indigenous people has become an extension of the colonization process and an integral part of the PIC. We discuss the historical trauma of First Nations, Métis, and Inuit People to help illuminate the Canadian government's process of ethnocide—which can be defined as the deliberate eradication of a people's culture, usually through political power (Aboriginal Healing Foundation 2003).[6] The main form of eradication was through the assassination of Indigenous people. The Aboriginal Healing Foundation (2004) explains, "In 1492, an estimated ninety to one hundred and twelve million Indigenous people lived on the American continent" (12) and goes on to detail that,

> At least until 1918, various epidemics devastated the lives of Indigenous people across the continent, some reaching as far north as Alaska and west to British Columbia. Dobyns (1983) suggests that 90 to 95 per cent of the Indigenous population was wiped out by epidemic disease, warfare, slavery, starvation and complete and utter despair, with most dying within one hundred years of contact. (Cook 1973)

It is not just that there was this attempt to depopulate such a significant proportion of the Indigenous people on Turtle Island, Indigenous people also faced assimilation practices that impeded the possibility of retaining and rebuilding their cultures. The goal of this assimilation strategy was to create a world where there would be almost no means (oral or written) to pass along and explain traditional ceremonies, cultures, or belief systems. The sheer loss of life ensured that there were fewer elders, teachers, warriors, healers, and artists (Aboriginal Healing Foundation 2004). Despite fierce resistance and continued survival, it is important to note that only 5 to 10 percent of that original population of Indigenous people remain alive after five centuries of epidemics, slavery, war, and colonization (Aboriginal Healing Foundation 2004). In the last half century alone, Indigenous people have been sent to residential schools,[7] where they were punished for participation in their cultural practices and where ongoing (and often violent) attempts were made to force them to assimilate into European Christian culture. In the 1960s, Indigenous children were stolen from their homes and placed in non-Indigenous homes, where they were often beaten, verbally abused, and sexually assaulted (Aboriginal Healing Foundation 2009). John's[8] story lends insight into the reality of these atrocities:

> I am writing this story on behalf of an individual who has been in prison for over 20 years serving a life sentence. As a young Micmac he was often in trouble with the nuns that ran the [residential] school he was sent to. Eventually, because of his inability to conform to the nun's demand of "silence and subservience" they sent him to the psychiatric asylum (prison) at the age of 9. It was at this facility [that he] was raised to adulthood and when he was 21 years old the asylum released him from their custody…with a lack of social skills and [the] deep loneliness of a person raised in a psychiatric prison he soon began to use drugs.[9] It was not long after this that in a horrible turn of events…someone was found murdered [and he was arrested]. (Collins 2012)

The brutality of the attempted genocide of Indigenous people has had, and continues to have, a disabling affect. This experience of disability is exacerbated by the PIC. In John's story, resistance to being held in the carceral space of the residential school resulted in him being labeled with a psychiatric disability, which led to time in the carceral space of the "asylum," where he experienced social isolation and loneliness. Peter and John's analysis of the story explains the experience of isolation that led to the use of drugs, which contributed to "a horrible turn of events" in which a murder happens. Although it is unclear from John's story if he is responsible for the murder, the story reads as if this is the case. John's story illustrates both a link between colonization and incarceration as well as disability and incarceration. It also shows how acts of resistance to attempted assimilation and colonization force people into the PIC, in its various forms. When Indigenous people attempt to resist ongoing colonization through settling land claims or demands for self-determination (e.g., Mohawk resistance in Kanehsatake/Oka,[10] Tyendinaga,[11] and Caledonia, etc.), they are arrested and put in prison. Indigenous people make up 3 percent of the general population, but 23 percent of the federal prison population (Gebhard 2012; Trevethan and Rastin 2004). In some provinces, those numbers rise to almost 80 percent (Gebhard 2012; Trevethan and Rastin 2004). While these statistics are used by the state to support the fallacy that Indigenous people are more criminal, in reality they reflect the impact of the historical and ongoing colonization and oppression of Indigenous peoples.

In addition to the driving force of colonialism, the PIC is driven by racism. It is not an accident that there is a significant overincarceration of people from racialized communities; the PIC was designed as a form of social control within racialized communities (see Devon 2012). Mark T. Carleton (1971) suggests that the control of racialized bodies through their conversion into active labor units extended beyond the period of slave labor camps in the United States and into the development of the penal system. He states, "The survival of agricultural operations within the penal system into the 1960s suggest that the terms 'convict,' 'slave,' 'Negro,' and 'farm work' have remained unconsciously interchangeable in the mind of institutional Louisiana" (Carleton 1971, 7). As Matthew J. Mancini (1996) further explains, as prisons formed, the concept that prisoners had forfeited their liberty was tied into understandings of slavery; in 1871, the Virginia Supreme Court determined that a convicted offender "has, as a consequence of his crime, not only forfeited his liberty, but all his personal rights except those which the law in its humanity accords to him. He is for the time being the slave of the state" (as cited in Alexander 2010, 31). Black people are the second most overrepresented population within Canada's PIC, after Indigenous people (Trevethan and Rastin 2004). The Correctional Investigator of Canada recently launched a study to look into the 50 percent spike in the number of Black people in the prison system in the past decade. Despite making up only 2.5 percent of the general population, Black people account for 9 percent of the federal prison population, and in Ontario those numbers jump to 20 percent (Crawford 2011). Provincially, statistics are not kept on racialized communities, and the only race-based statistics that are kept in provincial prisons are for Indigenous people. This lack of statistical information is problematic in that it prevents us from getting a broader numeric-based picture of racism within the PIC. Unfortunately, there has been little systematic research connecting the history of racism and colonialism in Canada to the PIC. It would be important work to trace the relation between the history of slavery and immigration policy and the PIC.

Kevin, a Black prisoner from a marginalized and under-resourced community in Toronto serving time inside a federal prison, writes of his experience of targeted policing in his community. He states,

> We as a group would just be outside hanging out doing absolutely nothing...and the police would...harass or arrest us for things that we did not do. Sometimes this was as regular as...a daily basis for a period of time as if the police had or needed to fill some sort of arrest quota. I'm still dumbfounded as to...why the police would carry on this way, seeing how they are hired to protect and serve the law, not abuse their powers. I personally have been arrested for crimes such as "Assault Police" to "Resist Arrest," "Drug Trafficking," "Drug Possession"...crimes that I am one million percent not guilty of committing. (Dias 2012)

Targeted policing, as in Kevin's story, illustrates how racialized bodies get picked up and then kept in the prison system. Once inside, the intersectional experience of class, race, and gender can keep people from getting out and staying out. The police are the main enforcers of the law, and officers have a great deal of discretion in terms of how they deal with the public.[12] In our experience, this discretion, married with the systemic racism, colonialism, and ableism[13] leads to the targeting and overpolicing of disabled and racialized communities. In Toronto, the police have repeatedly murdered disabled people, in particular, disabled People of Color with mental health issues.[14]

Ableism in the PIC manifests itself in many ways, including the targeting of disabled communities through overpolicing;[15] the physical construction of carceral spaces for nondisabled bodies that do not work well for disabled bodies (something we explore in more detail in a moment); the maintaining of a hostile environment that is designed to affect the mental health of prisoners (Foucault 1977); and so on. This ableism is intrinsically linked to systemic racism and classism. As Eli Clare elaborates,

> Race, class, gender, sexuality, and disability are so integrally tied together. For instance, racism is strengthened and fueled by ableism, by the belief that any body/mind labelled as "stupid" is worthless and expendable. One of the ways racism functions is to define People of Color—particularly, in a

US context, poor African Americans and Latinos–as stupid, which in turn drives racist unemployment rates, lack of access to education, and incarceration rates. (Fritsch 2009)

Interconnected experiences of racism and ableism affect the lives of racialized disabled people in particular ways. As Clare explains, the ableist assertion that intelligence governs value and usefulness in society is intertwined with characterizations of racialized people as inherently without value because of perceived intelligence, making it all the more complicated for racialized disabled people to be considered valuable in an ableist racist society. This directly affects employability, and lack of employment and access to resources fuels incarceration rates (Reece 2010). The stigma associated with being an ex-prisoner also affects future employability (Reece 2010). It is from this intersectional perspective so clearly articulated by Clare that we come to understand the ways that prisons are intrinsically tied up in the business of race, class, and disability. We now consider the specific experiences of disabled people labeled with mental health diagnoses, living with HIV/AIDS, and experiencing mobility disabilities.

In 2010, a report was released by the Correctional Investigator's Office (an Ombudsman for the federal prison system) to talk about the growing needs of prison populations. Howard Sapers, a Correctional Investigator states,

> Canadian penitentiaries are becoming the largest psychiatric facilities in the country. The Correctional Service of Canada assumes a legal duty of care to provide required mental health services, including clinical treatment and intervention. In failing to meet this legal obligation, too many mentally disordered offenders [sic] are simply being warehoused in federal penitentiaries. This is not effective or safe corrections. (Office of the Correctional Investigator 2010)

Sapers' quote suggests that (1) prisons are being used in lieu of providing supportive services for psychiatric survivors/consumers in the community and that (2) once inside prison, folks labeled with psychiatric disabilities are not receiving health services available to them in the community. Thus, psychiatric survivors/consumers have a higher likelihood of incarceration and, as a result, are less likely to access supportive services.

There is anecdotal evidence of a trend in Canadian prisons of using long-term segregation to isolate people with mental health issues from the rest of the population. Isolating people with mental health issues is cruel and excessively punitive. One documented example of this is the case of Ashley Smith,[16] a young woman who asphyxiated herself in her segregation cell while several guards looked on. The Smith case is one example that demonstrates that people with mental health issues need access to community resources, not incarceration. Unfortunately, cruel and unusual punishment is commonplace in the PIC, part of the essence of its daily functioning. This has dramatic effects on all prisoners. For prisoners who have psychiatric disabilities or are psychiatric survivors, the prison environment exacerbates existing mental health issues.[17]

In addition, a study released by the Correctional Service of Canada[18] in 2010 reported that rates of HIV in prison are 15 times higher than in the community and rates of Hepatitis C (HCV) are up to 39 percent higher, with an infection rate of 31 percent (Zakaria et al. 2010). These are staggering rates of infection and are due in large part to the CSC's "zero-tolerance policy" on drug use and refusal to introduce a needle exchange program (see Chu 2010). Without proper distribution of harm reduction materials in prison, these numbers will continue to grow. When looking at intersections of disability and prisons, HIV/AIDS and HCV infection rates are essential to the discussion. Overcrowded prisons without proper harm reduction programs will ensure the further transmission of HIV/AIDS and HCV, leading to greater disability in prison and in the community.

In the next section, we examine how prisons further criminalize and punish people with disabilities and create further disability.

Criminalization and Creation of Disability in the PIC

In order to understand how people's health is affected by incarceration, it is important to look at people's relationship to the social determinants of health *before* incarceration. Juha Mikkonen and Dennis Raphael (2010) list 14 factors that shape the health of Canadians in *The Social Determinants of Health: The Canadian Facts*; reading through this list is like reading the story of who is in prison and why they are there. The factors include: poverty; lack of education; unemployment or low-paying employment/poor working conditions; childhood trauma; food insecurity; insecure housing/homelessness; social exclusion; lack of a social safety network; little or no access to health services; Aboriginal status; race; gender; and disability. The last four factors on the list highlight the fact that racism, sexism, and ableism determine people's living conditions and correlate to the communities and identities that are targeted by the police, criminalized, and imprisoned.

Mental and physical health is negatively impacted by one's relationship to the social determinants of health, or lack thereof. This is true in the community, and it is even more painfully apparent in the prison system. According to the Corrections and Conditional Release Act (the legislation that governs the federal prison system),

> The Service shall provide every inmate with (a) essential health care; and (b) reasonable access to non-essential mental health care that will contribute to the inmate's rehabilitation and successful reintegration into the community...The provision of health care under subsection (1) shall conform to professionally accepted standards...The Service shall take into consideration an offender's state of health and health care needs (a) in all decisions affecting the offender, including decisions relating to placement, transfer, administrative segregation and disciplinary matters; and (b) in the preparation of the offender for release and the supervision of the offender.[19]

As we have suggested, the service does *not* provide every prisoner with "essential heath care" that "conforms to professionally accepted standards." In order to clearly outline what is covered under the term "health services," the Commissioner's Directive 800[20] lays out what is meant by "essential health services" in more detail:

> Inmates shall have access to screening, referral and treatment services. Essential services shall include a) emergency health care (i.e., delay of the service will endanger the life of the inmate); b) urgent health care (i.e., the condition is likely to deteriorate to an emergency or affect the inmate's ability

to carry on the activities of daily living); c) mental health care provided in response to disturbances of thought, mood, perception, orientation or memory that significantly impair judgment, behaviour, the capacity to recognize reality or the ability to meet the ordinary demands of life (this includes the provision of both acute and long-term mental health care services);...Inmates shall have reasonable access to other health services (i.e., conditions not outlined above) which may be provided in keeping with community practice (e.g. prenatal care for women). The provision of these services will be subject to the length of time prior to release, operational requirements, etc....In support of essential health services, emphasis will be on health promotion and illness prevention. (Correctional Service of Canada 2011)

These guidelines suggest that the physical and mental health of prisoners are a high priority for the Correctional Service of Canada and that health services are easily accessible and on par with community standards. Yet, research suggests that the reality of access to care is different than what is outlined in these guidelines, particularly for people living with disabilities (Ford and Wobeser 2012; McLay and Silversides 2011; Sapers 2009). In addition, our stories from prisoners in federal prisons in Canada suggest that prisoners are not accessing health care at community standards and that, in fact, the prison environment both exacerbates existing disabilities and creates new ones. Many prisoners who are suffering from serious health issues put in repeated requests over the course of weeks or months before actually getting to see a doctor. We examine access to health care in relation to mental health diagnoses, HIV/AIDS seroconversion,[21] and mobility in prisons.

In terms of psychiatric disabilities, the World Health Organization (2007) states that, "prisons are bad for mental health" because of overcrowding; violence; solitary confinement; lack of privacy; separation from family and friends; lack of meaningful activity; and uncertain futures in terms of housing, work, and relationship. Prisons affect the ways our brains and bodies work, creating experiences that don't fit within social notions of mental "health."[22] Additionally, there is a lack of appropriate health care—especially care for emotional health—in prison, which leads to increased rates of depression and suicide (WHO 2007). When people are in prison, they are fully under the control of the state. This is true in a logistical sense: in that they have lost their physical freedom and are in a government-run facility. It is also true in the sense that their personal agency is taken away. They are told when to wake up, when to eat, when and for how long they can use the phone, when and in what conditions they can see their families, when they can go outside, what they can read, etc. This lack of autonomy extends to almost every aspect of life in prison, and it is done by design in order to erode people's sense of self-efficacy, so that they become compliant (Foucault 1977); this directly affects their mental health. Powerlessness is a result of this experience. The North American Nursing Diagnosis Association recognizes that,

The environment in which health care is provided can influence the recipient's perception of personal control. Institutional rules and regulations, autocratic caregivers, and social isolation can increase one's sense of powerlessness. (NANDA International 2009, 190)

The creation of the experience of powerlessness is essential to the functioning of the prison environment, and it is highly relevant to the experience of people with disabilities trying to access health care services in prison. Despite the claims of the Corrections and Conditional Release Act and Commissioner's Directive (Correctional Service of Canada 2011) listed earlier, prisoners experience difficulty accessing needed health care services, receiving adequate and appropriate ongoing treatment in a timely fashion, and being allowed to meaningfully participate in their own plan of care. The impact of this lack of access on mental health is illustrated in a study by Smith et al. (2008). In a series of experiments to determine the effect of powerlessness on cognitive functioning, these researchers found that,

> Assigning someone a certain position can alter their mental skills in a way that confirms their standing. The powerful retain power because of the improved mental processes that it brings about, while impairments in the same processes keep people without power on the bottom rung. These effects make hierarchies incredibly stable, and lead the powerless into what Smith calls "a destiny of dispossession." (Yong 2008)

It is difficult for people to get access to any counselling and mental health services in prison. When people do get access to these supports, they are rarely offered in an ongoing way or over the long term. Anecdotal evidence suggests that some people request counselling because they are struggling acutely, yet have to wait years before they can see someone trained to help. Because all psychiatrists/psychologists available to prisoners work for Correctional Services Canada and because there is no confidentiality or privacy during therapeutic sessions, these sessions may not provide the support needed. It is hard for people to open up about any challenges they are experiencing in prison, particularly because anything they say will end up in their prison file and could potentially be used against them.[23] Knowing that their responses within psychiatric assessments and during counselling sessions could affect their access to release is hugely stressful and affects willingness to disclose challenges and seek assistance.

When people get out of prison, many leave with what has been termed "Post-Incarceration Syndrome" (PICS) (Gorski 2002),[24] which are understandable responses to living in an oppressive, restrictive, violent, and dehumanizing environment.[25] Gorski (2002) defines PICS as a cluster of symptoms that are usually present in prisoners and ex-prisoners caused by long periods of incarceration. Prolonged incarceration where there is a lack of education and no job training or "rehabilitation," coupled with punishment, ensures that people coming out of prison are worse off than when they went into prison. Prisoners who have experienced long periods of time in solitary confinement and significant abuse while in prison are most severely affected. The severity of these symptoms is subject to the person's ability to cope prior to incarceration; the length of time they are in prison and the prison environment itself; the level of abuse a prisoner faces while in prison; the length of time in solitary confinement; and the degree of involvement in education, work, and other programs while inside (Gorski 2012). He outlines the five clusters of the Post-Incarceration Syndrome as:

> a) Institutionalized Personality Traits resulting from the common deprivations of incarceration, a chronic state of learned helplessness in the face of prison authorities, and antisocial defences in dealing with a predatory inmate milieu;
> b) Post Traumatic Stress Disorder (PTSD) from both pre-incarceration trauma

and trauma experienced within the institution; c) Antisocial Personality Traits (ASPT) developed as a coping response to institutional abuse and a predatory prisoner milieu; d) Social-Sensory Deprivation Syndrome caused by prolonged exposure to solitary confinement that radically restricts social contact and sensory stimulation; e) Substance Use Disorders caused by the use of alcohol and other drugs to manage or escape the Post-Incarceration Syndrome symptoms. Post-Incarceration Syndrome often coexists with substance use disorders and a variety of affective and personality disorders. Our goal is not to pathologize but to name a cluster of symptoms that deeply effects one's ability to navigate the world post incarceration. (Gorski 2012)

Another area of disability that needs to be examined within the prison context is HIV/AIDS, which is prevalent in Canadian prisons. As of 2010, the rates of HIV in federal prisons were 4.6 percent, according to Correctional Service Canada (CSC 2012); this rate is ten times the rate of HIV/AIDS in the community (McLay and Silversides 2011). Hepatitis C rates are also high in prisons. Current estimates suggest that 31 percent of prisoners have Hepatitis C, a rate which is 39 times higher than that of the general population. (Silversides 2010). Research suggests that many prisoners are seroconverting while inside prison (Canadian HIV/AIDS Legal Network 2013). It is impossible to know how many prisoners are seroconverting while in prison because people would need to be tested when they first arrived in prison, after three months of low/no risk activity, and again upon release. Recognizing the stigma and discrimination facing HIV positive prisoners, community advocates do not encourage this kind of testing. Unfortunately, this means that we have no record of the number of people seroconverting *while* in prison. What we do know is that people are engaged in a number of activities, including drug use, unprotected sex, and tattooing, without the necessary harm reduction tools needed for their own personal health. Because of the criminalization of drug users, there are a lot of people who use drugs in prisons without access to the tools they need to use safely.

Because of the presumption that all past drug users are "drug seeking" when they ask for pain medication (C-Change 2001), it is almost impossible for prisoners to access opiate-based medications, even if they had previously been prescribed these same medications by a doctor outside of prison. The lack of proper pain management forces prisoners into a position where they have to self-medicate, sometimes through the use of injection drugs. Much has been written about the prevalence of injection drugs in prison (e.g., Canadian AIDS Society 2012; Wood, Lim, and Kerr 2006), which is fuelled in part because injection drugs can pass through one's system more quickly, making them less detectable on urine-based drug tests. Because of the lack of access to new needles and harm reduction materials that could make injecting drugs safer, this self-medicating to treat pain often leads to the transmission of HIV or Hepatitis C or both (C-Change 2001).

The experiences of prisoners with HIV inside prison are marked by HIV-phobia and ableism. One of our colleagues inside further explains John's experience:

[As] he started showing signs of the HIV illnesses (sweats, vomiting etc.) the other prisoners and staff became aware of his HIV status. He was fired from his prison job because of it and the instructor was sanctioned for the wrongful dismissal and he was given his job back. However the supervisor was not happy with this and would make a big production of telling everyone very loudly that they were not to bother him because he was HIV+ and as such a special case whom no one was allowed to bother. He would say it in a sneering, trouble making way. Eventually that shop instructor found another way to fire him and the game continued. Eventually he was transferred to this prison and he faced the same systemic racism, HIV stigma, ridicule and aggression from guards and prisoners... The health care treatment was horrible and the food services were just as bad. His medications were often cut off for no reason and with HIV treatments this can not only make your body resistant to the treatment it also opens you up for additional problems. The food services workers would not provide him with more food even after he had vomited his breakfast, lunch or supper and the man simply had no extra weight to lose. (Collins 2012)

John's story illustrates that prisoners with HIV rarely "have reasonable access to... health services" that emphasize "health promotion and illness prevention," as outlined in the Corrections and Conditional Release Act (Government of Canada 1992). By limiting his access to medications, neglecting to provide a stable diet offered at times that worked for someone with nausea and vomiting related to HIV, and fostering an environment that promoted anti-HIV/AIDS sentiment and ableism, the prison did not provide health services in an environment that supported health promotion and illness prevention. In fact, these limitations created a dangerous and hostile environment for John and contributed to his experience of disability.

Further to our discussion on disability in prisons, it is essential that we discuss mobility issues. As an example, Peter Collins, a prisoner at Bath Penitentiary, suffers from a degenerative back condition that leaves him in constant pain. In 2010, CSC was found guilty by the Canadian Human Rights Tribunal (CHRT) of failing to accommodate his disability by forcing him to stand for "count" (a security measure in federal prisons in Canada involving counting prisoners in each range to ensure everyone is present that can take place multiple times a day and that can require standing for long periods of time). Despite the results of the tribunal and direction to provide Peter with an assistive device for walking, the prison failed to give the device to him for several months:

Discussions between the CHRT and the Warden had included providing me with a cane in order to assist me when forced to stand for protracted periods of time... I asked why I was not told about this (since I had been denied a walker when I requested one)... he did not answer, but did indicate that all I had to do was ask. So, in fact, I did ask repeatedly. I asked at the hearing verbally, I was advised to put it in a written request, which I did, which was not responded to so I followed up with a verbal request and more written requests, none of which resulted in the production of a cane. I had a lawyer write to the prison (twice), this did not result in the production of a cane. I asked my sister to pay for a cane in the community and have the medical supply store send it to the prison. This did not result in the production of the cane. It was not until members of Parliament wrote to the prison (at the request of members of the community) that the cane was given to me, more than 2 years after the CHC stated during the Tribunal that all I had to do was ask. (Collins 2012)

Peter's story illustrates again that prisoners who require tools to move rarely "have reasonable access to…health services." He needs a cane to be able to move around the prison or stand for prolonged periods of time, things he is expected to do as part of his work duty and participation in security counts. His inability to participate fully in work duty or the security counts affect him dramatically, both in terms of access to funds for the canteen and in more serious ways, such as being perceived as uncooperative and even anti-authority—things that are punishable in prison and also affect his release from prison. Peter's story is typical of the experience of disabled people in prison: there is little support or care to help with the experience of physical and mental difference in prison; as a result, the experience of physical or mental difference can be exacerbated and these experiences then become punishable offenses.

Because prison staff is generally untrained and unqualified to identify or understand physical and mental differences, prisoners whose physical bodies, mental states, and health status are labeled as different are often seen as troublemakers and end up being further punished through institutional charges and administrative segregation. Additional punishments often mean that disabled prisoners spend longer periods of time incarcerated.

Given that prison is an oppressive, violent, dehumanizing environment that worsens existing disabilities and creates new ones, what does this mean for prisoners when they are released into the community? Many come out to the same poor living conditions and systemic discrimination they faced before being incarcerated. In fact, the situation may be worse because of the loss of housing, employment, and social supports that can result from imprisonment. Some people will have had their disabilities aggravated by prison conditions. Others may have developed serious health issues while inside, such as HIV or Hepatitis C, or be suffering from psychological trauma as a result of the isolation, loss of agency/autonomy, deprivation, and oppressive nature of the prison environment.

New Legislation: It's Only Going to Get Worse

> My opinion is that many of the new laws in this bill will only affect the lower class individuals and these prison cells will be stocked disproportionately with individuals from intercity communities who have lack of finances with the door to the community openly revolving with other lower income families stuck in a helpless position of having to reside in these Low Income Neighbourhoods to begin with. Not everyone is rich who are born in this country or immigrate to Canada. (Kevin, federal prisoner, cited in Dias 2012)

In 2011, Conservative Prime Minister Steven Harper pushed through an omnibus crime bill called the "Safe Streets and Community Act," also known as Bill C-10. The bill comprised nine separate bills that the government had previously been unable to pass as a minority government. This crime bill was passed despite the fact that the national crime rate has been dropping since 1992 and is at its lowest rate since 1972 (Brennan 2012). Furthermore, the bill was passed without appropriate consultation, against serious recommendations from experts, and against all evidence-based research. Today, Canada is experiencing its highest incarceration rate with prisons bulging at the seams. The result is an increase in prison expansion for profit and further genocide and racism with particularly disproportionate effects on Indigenous and Black communities. Looking at the United States, mandatory minimums such as are being implemented with this legislation have had a particularly dangerous effect on Black women (Levy-Pounds 2006). We must contextualize Black and Indigenous women's experience within the PIC in Canada. Dr. Rai Reece (2010) points out,

> Critical analysis of feminist criminology and Black women's incarceration ought to explicitly involve discussions of colonialism and imperialism. In retrospect the legacy of colonial conquest connects with the legacy of socio-cultural exclusion, racism and citizenship rights for Black women in Canada. Evidence of this is seen in contemporary practices of over-policing, monitoring, and social exclusion in Canada where understandings of race, gender, class, dis/ability and sexuality flow out of colonial relations and structural ideologies. By exploring the divergent tenets of colonialism, specifically the making of Canada as a white settler society, it is evident that the experiences of incarcerated Black women are connected to the historical ways in which racism and racialization were and still are central organizing features. (6)

For the purposes of understanding how this new crime legislation is going to affect Indigenous and Black communities and how it will create disabilities for prisoners, we focus on just one aspect of the crime bill: the Penalties for Organized Drug Crimes Act.[26]

For the first time ever, changes to the Controlled Drugs and Substances Act included new mandatory minimum sentences for trafficking, import/export, and production. Although there has been a consistent war waged on people who use drugs in Canada (see VANDU 1998; Global Commission on Drugs 2012), mandatory minimums will exacerbate the effects of this war. Despite claims that the government is targeting serious drug offenses as part of organized crime, evidence shows that drug laws and enforcement of these laws predominantly target people most marginalized, including those who are poor, Indigenous, or racialized drug users (Mauer and King 2007; Moore and Elkavich 2008).

For the purposes of this chapter, we consider the disabling experience of drug use as disability with the lens of understanding that drug use is not in itself the "problem" but that the War on Drug Users, lack of harm reduction programming, and lack of access to social support for drug users creates disabling experiences for many users.[27] However, we are also aware that people with undiagnosed psychiatric disabilities often use drugs to try and find relief from the ways that society does not allow for differing mental states, such as anxiety and experiences that are labelled as mania, depression, etc. Evidence shows that 30 percent of people living with psychiatric disabilities also use substances, and 53 percent of people who use drugs have also been labelled with "mental health issues" (Mood Disorder Society of Canada 2009). From our collective experience working in prisons and with harm reduction both on the inside and outside in communities, the authors would estimate these statistics to be higher. What we see from research is that there is a correlation between drug use and psychiatric disabilities that needs to be explored when looking at disabilities and prisons. We look to forms of structural violence that both create and reinforce disability and affect drug users' social determinants of health. Intersectional experiences of marginalization affect both tendency to use drugs and access to supports once using drugs. Drug use by women is often heightened by experiences such as sexual harassment; emotional, physical, and sexual abuse; poverty; racism; and mental illness (see Martin and Macy 2011; Millay et al. 2009; Stevens-Watkins et al. 2012).

As mentioned in the first section, experiences of mental health issues and drug use by Indigenous people can be directly connected to ongoing realities of colonization. The continued relocations of entire communities and the removal of Indigenous children to residential schools and white foster families resulted in disrupted families and communities, which has created a generation of traumatized peoples, along with the perpetuation of both "mental health and substance use issues" through intergenerational effects (Mussell, Cardiff, and White 2004) and eventually lead to higher incarceration rates for Indigenous people. In an excerpt about Alan's life story, Peter Collins explains:

> Alan is an Aboriginal man who identifies as 2-Spirited…In his early childhood he turned to drugs and alcohol as a means to escape the lack of inclusion that is the natural result of entrenched racism and homophobia. Later on as a teenager he was involved in a violent incident in which a man was significantly injured and he was charged with attempted murder. The proceedings were stayed in the sense that he was found Not Criminally Responsible. Under a Governor General's warrant he was committed to a psychiatric prison.
>
> While incarcerated in the psychiatric prison he was, among other things, subjected to sensory deprivation chambers in combination with courses of psychotropic drugs (LSD) all part of the state's experiments on those people considered disposable and without rights. After some years under those conditions he was released to a community-based therapeutic centre. After being a patient there for some time he was given a job as a Peer working in that facility. However, substance use and a lack of meaningful support eventually led to more violence and a sexual encounter resulted in violence and left one man dead. This time he was found to be criminally responsible (which is a questionable state sleight of hand in which the administration of justice views mental health issues as a ploy to avoid the full force of the law). He was sentenced to life in prison with a minimum parole eligibility of 10 years. That was 34 years and three strokes ago. (Collins 2012)

Alan's story illustrates the ways that intersecting experiences of racialization, homophobia, colonization, drug use, and being labelled with psychiatric disabilities affect the way that one's time in carceral spaces is served and the choices available once inside. With the understanding that Indigenous communities and People of Color (especially individuals with intersecting identities) face increased police surveillance and incarceration, we can begin to see how the new Bill C-10 legislation will play out within our communities.

When analyzing the drug trade in particular, it has been suggested that there is a difference between involvement in the drug trade based on one's experience of gender, and that this differentiation is rooted in poverty (Reece 2010). Women, and particularly Black women and Indigenous women, face poverty at much greater levels than men, leading to increased incarceration rates for women as the "war on drugs" rages on (Reece 2010). Research shows that women do not play a central role in the drug trade but act primarily as "small scale carriers, sellers' couriers or drivers. In many cases, their roles are limited to answering telephones or living in a home used for drug related activities" (Lapidus et al. 2004). Furthermore, when caught, women are less likely than men to give information to the police (Lapidus et al. 2004). As a result, they do not get to take advantage of plea bargains offered by the police to give names of dealers in exchange for reduced prison sentences. The reality of mandatory minimum sentencing means that low-level drug "offenders" receive the mandatory minimum sentence, while many mid-level or higher level drug offenders (the main targets of legislation) avoid long sentences through plea bargains with the crown and get shorter sentences for naming other people in the drug trade (Lapidus et al. 2004).

We need more information about the experiences of racialized women in prison in order to fully understand how they will be affected by the new legislation. Rai Reece (2010) explains that the despite the overrepresentation of Black women in prison in Canada there is little research about their experiences:

> Analysis depicting the configuration of Black women's bodies as central factors in Canadian nation building is undeveloped. In regard to incarceration and detention, the stories of Black women often rest on the periphery of our environments, if not excluded entirely. Much of the written, visual or verbal experiences of incarcerated Black women remains elusive in feminist criminological and theoretical study. In Canada, Black women and women of color in prison are the silent forgotten population. (6)

Because of sexism, racism, and colonialism, women's stories are often silenced; yet, we know that the new mandatory minimum sentencing will have the greatest effect on women. We know this because the effects of the war on drugs on women in particular have been staggering in the United States. In 1980, there were 12,300 women in prison in the United States; in 2002, there were 182,271 (Lapidus et al. 2004; Mauer, Potler, and Wolf 1999). Lapidus et al. (2004) continue: "By 1999, drug offenses accounted for 72% of the female population in federal prisons" (16). Despite the relatively similar patterns of drug use by all women, racialized women (Black women in particular) in the United States are incarcerated at higher rates than their white counterparts. For example, Black women's incarceration for drug related offenses has increased by 800 percent, while white women's incarceration has increased by 400 percent (Lapidus et al. 2004). Chief Justice William Rehnquist of the US Supreme Court has stated,

> There is a respectable body of opinion which believes that these mandatory minimums impose unduly harsh punishment for first time offenders–particularly for "mules" who played only a minor role in a drug distribution scheme. Be that as it may, the mandatory minimums have also led to an inordinate increase in the federal prison population and will require huge expenditures to build new prison space. (as cited in Lapidus et al. 2004, 38)

Overall rates of incarceration have increased significantly since the war on drugs began in the United States. In 1980, there were approximately 40,000 people in prison for drug-related offenses, and by 2003 the number had increased tenfold to almost 450,000, which is equivalent to almost a quarter of all prisoners in the United States (Mauer 2003).

As evidenced in the United States, we have every reason to believe that the new legislation in Canada will lead to further increased rates of incarceration for Black and Indigenous communities, particularly women. Understanding the link between the disabling effects of the criminalization of drugs and drug use leads to a greater understanding of how disability is being criminalized and what that means for mass incarceration in Canada.

Conclusion

The PIC is based on a set of interests created and maintained to support capitalism, patriarchy, imperialism, colonialism, racism, ableism, and white supremacy.

When we begin to see the magnitude of the tentacles of the PIC and how it works to maintain power and control, we begin to understand that it is not a mistake that poor disabled racialized bodies fill these spaces. We need further research regarding the lived experiences of racialized disabled prisoners and how disability plays out inside the PIC in Canada. This research is essential to understanding how to dismantle the PIC in Canada. We need to correlate the ways that intersectional experiences of marginalization are intrinsically connected to the foundation of the PIC and, by doing so, consider how to work together across communities to try to alter this prison state in which we live. It is not a matter of educating politicians and policy makers. We have come to understand that the PIC is not broken, that it can't be fixed or reformed, and that it continues to keep the rich richer and the poor and racialized in prison. It is within this context that we come to see the intersections between all forms of oppression, but specifically the intersections between the PIC, race, and radical disability politics.

In order to change our society to be a place where we all can have access to the right to self-determination and to create communities that are truly safer and more secure built on foundations of social justice and critical politics, we must not work to change the PIC. Instead, we must work to abolish it. As we have illustrated, the tentacles of the PIC stretch out into so many systemic structures in society, including the police system, the education system, housing, health care systems, and more. Thus, what we are advocating for in our will to abolish the PIC is in fact an abolishment of all of these systems—a revolution to bring in a new way of working, loving, and living together that brings a complexity of analysis and an understanding of intersectional realities into its core.

Notes

1. We use the term prison in this context to refer to actual prison structures, as well as other carceral spaces including, but not limited to, immigration detention centers, jails, holding facilities, psychiatric holding spaces, and more. We include consideration of the broader experience of detention in our analysis.
2. The Prison Industrial Complex includes policing (and targeted policing of particular communities), the legal/(in)justice system, carceral spaces, probation periods, release conditions, and other ways that confinement and imprisonment extend into our daily lives before arrest and after release from detention.
3. We use the term disabled intentionally as part of our understanding of the social model of disability and the power in owning disability as a celebrated identity. As Fran Branfield (1999) suggests, "Thus, to claim 'I am disabled' is a political

statement. It is to align oneself with other disabled people in a struggle for equality, inclusion and full citizenship. As a political statement it does not claim that all disabled people's experience of oppression is the same. It certainly does not claim that there is anything natural or inevitable about the way in which people with impairments are disabled. On the contrary, to 'come out' as disabled is to acknowledge that the oppression we experience is a direct consequence of our society's construction and understanding of disability" (399).

4. To better understand how the prison environment affects prisoners, we asked Peter Collins to gather stories of disabled prisoners. Peter Collins has been working as a peer health educator in prison for the past 15 years of his incarceration. During that time, he became an outspoken advocate for the health of prisoners and, in 2008, won the Award for Action on HIV/AIDS and Human Rights given by the Canadian HIV/AIDS Legal Network and Human Rights Watch. Peter has been a tireless activist on many prisoners' rights issues and has been instrumental in the movement to end the PIC. Through Peter's work he has come across hundreds of prisoners with disabilities who have been criminalized, and then further punished within the penal system, because of their disabilities. It is through his work and personal experience fighting against the PIC that he helped gather stories of Indigenous prisoners whose voices would otherwise be lost because of colonization practices. It is unfortunate that some of these stories were not written in the first person or could not be told by the individuals in their oral tradition; however, without Peter's work with these individuals their stories may have been lost, as has been the case with so many others.

5. Canada has three dominant political parties: the Conservative Party, the Liberal Party, and the New Democratic Party. The current Conservative Government represents right-wing, pro-market, Christian values.

6. Although we recognize the many ways in which Indigenous people and Black communities have resisted colonization and racism, we will not be talking about this resistance in great detail in this chapter. We do want to note that this resistance has been a significant and important part of dismantling the PIC.

7. The Aboriginal Healing Foundation (2009) further explains, "The literature pertaining to the effects of residential schools on the health of Aboriginal peoples in Canada is, at best, limited...Kirmayer and colleagues note the implications of the residential school legacy...'The origins of the high rates of mental health [issues] in Aboriginal communities are not hard to discern. Aboriginal peoples in Canada have faced cultural oppression through policies of forced assimilation on the part of Euro-Canadian institutions since the earliest periods of contact' (2003, S16). Particularly notable was the establishment of the residential school system, a result of federal government policy and culmination of a formal partnership between the government and Roman Catholic, United, Anglican, and other churches to educate Aboriginal children. Both church and state had significant roles in the lives of Aboriginal people. Through education, it was thought that Aboriginal children could be integrated into the emerging British Canadian society and imbued with the principles and knowledge required to [assimilate]" (Kirmayer, Simpson, and Cargo 2003) (7).

8. We were asked to change the names in the stories to avoid further punishment of these individuals.

9. We do not conflate drug use with violence. We recognize that the prohibition of drugs is often the cause of violence.

10. See Obomsawin (2000).

11. See Schertow (2008).

12. See, for example, *Introduction to Policing* by Gene L. Scaramella, Steven M. Cox, and William P. McCamey (2011), which states, "For a variety of reasons, a police

officer may decide not to enforce the law. The exercise of discretion involving individual choice and judgment by police officers is a normal, necessary, and desirable part of policing" (100).

13. Elizabeth Cormack (2012) provides an explanation of the history of the role of policing and the powers given to police during the initial period of colonization in Canada. Similarly, the Committee to Stop Targeted Policing (2000) explains that "the police in Canada have a long history of functioning as a tool to control and limit Aboriginal populations" (11). Backhouse (1999) also documents the ways that systemic racism (including within policing) has been an instrumental part of Canadian history.

14. See police treatment of Edmund Yu (City of Toronto Council and Committees 2000) and Otto Vass ("Inquest Begins into Otto Vass Death," *City News Toronto*, October 16, 2006). For the overrepresentation of police shootings of people with mental health issues see Brink et al. (2011). For the differential treatment, and heightened murder rates, of people of color by the police see Jiwani (2002). See also Hils (2012) for an interview with Leroy Moore about his work against police brutality directed toward people of color with disabilities. Also, in the May 2012 edition of "Voices," the Newsletter for the Psychiatric Survivor Archives of Toronto, Don Weitz (2012) outlines a partial list of psychiatric survivors; young men who have been killed by the Toronto police—half of whom were of African descent.

15. Ibid.

16. See Zlomislic (2009).

17. Ibid.

18. Correctional Services Canada administers and maintains the federal prison system in Canada for prisoners serving a sentence of two years or longer.

19. Corrections and Conditional Release Act, S.C. 1992, c. 20. (Can.). http://laws-lois. justice.gc.ca/eng/acts/C-44.6/page-24.html

20. The Commissioner's Directive 800 is a policy concerning health care in federal prisons in Canada.

21. Seroconversion is the process in which a person's HIV status changes from HIV negative to HIV positive through the development of HIV antibodies.

22. We challenge the notion of "mental health" and "mental illness" and instead support the idea that humans have many different emotional experiences and mental states. Terminology that suggests that there is but one valid mental state (one deemed to be "healthy") and several invalid mental states (described as "illnesses") is inherently ableist and contrary to the tremendous work and advocacy against these categorizations by psychiatric survivors, consumers, and so on.

23. Regarding the release of inmate psychiatric information, the Forum on Corrections Research of Correctional Service Canada states, "the duty of confidentiality, which requires openness and honesty between patient and physician, must be balanced against the public interest in the administration of justice" (Correctional Services Canada 2012).

24. See Terrance Gorski, "Post Incarceration Syndrome and Relapse," http://www .tgorski.com/criminal_justice/cjs_pics_&_relapse.htm. Also refer to "Is There a Recognizable Post-Incarceration Syndrome among Released 'Lifers'?" *The International Journal of Law and Psychiatry.*

25. For a critique of the pathologizing of systemically induced responses to experiences of trauma and violence in the context of the "Residential School Syndrome," (but applicable to the "Post-Incarceration Syndrome"), see Chrisjohn and Young (1995).

26. However, it is important to acknowledge that all of these laws combined will have a very significant effect, particularly on racialized communities

27. The authors do not believe that drug use is a disability.

References

Aboriginal Healing Foundation. 2009. "Residential Schools, Prisons, and HIV/AIDS among Aboriginal People in Canada: Exploring the Connections." Accessed September 9, 2012. http://www.ahf.ca/publications/research-series

———. 2004. "Historic Trauma and Aboriginal *Healing*." Accessed September 9, 2012. www.ahf.ca/downloads/historic-trauma.pdf

———. 2003. "Aboriginal People, Resilience and the Residential School Legacy." Accessed September 9, 2012. www.ahf.ca/downloads/resilience.pdf

Alexander, Michelle. 2010. *The New Jim Crow: Mass Incarceration in the Age of Color Blindness*. New York: New Press.

Backhouse, Constance. 2000. *Colour-Coded: A Legal History of Racism in Canada, 1900–1950*. Toronto, ON: University of Toronto Press.

Bell, Chris. 2006. "Introducing White Disability Studies: A Modest Proposal." In *The Disability Studies Reader* (2nd ed.), edited by Lennard J. Davis. New York: Routledge.

Branfield, Fran. 1999. "The Disability Movement: A Movement of Disabled People – A Response to Paul S. Duckett." *Disability & Society* 14(3): 399–403.

Brennan, Shannon. 2012. "Police-Reported Crime Statistics in Canada, 2011." Statistics Canada Catalogue No. 85–002-XWE. Accessed September 14. http://www.statcan.gc.ca/pub/85–002-x/2012001/article/11692-eng.htm

Brink, Johann, James Livingston, Sarah Desmarais, C. Greaves, Victoria Maxwell, Eric Michalak, Rick Parent, Simon Verdun-Jones, and Carnia Weaver. 2011. A Study of How People with Mental Illness Perceive and Interact with the Police. Calgary, AB: Mental Health Commission of Canada. Accessed September 3, 2012. http://www.mentalhealthcommission.ca

Canadian AIDS Society. 2012. "HIV/AIDS and Men in Prison." Accessed September 4. http://www.cdnaids.ca/hivaidsandmeninprison

Canadian HIV/AIDS Legal Network. 2013. "Prisons." Accessed September 4, 2013. http://www.aidslaw.ca/EN/issues/prisons.htm

Chu, Sandra Ka Hon. 2010. "'Do the Right Thing': An Evidence-Based Response to Addiction and Mental Health in Federal Prisons – Brief to the House of Commons Standing Committee on Public Safety and National Security Regarding its Study Federal Corrections: Mental Health and Addiction Canadian HIV/AIDS Legal Network." Accessed September 7, 2012. www.aidslaw.ca/publications/interfaces/downloadFile.php?ref=1678

Carleton, Mark T. 1971. *Politics and Punishment: The History of the Louisiana State Penal System*. Baton Rouge, LA: Louisiana State University Press.

C-Change. 2001. "The Nature and Extent of Hepatitis C Related Discrimination." Accessed September 7, 2012. http://www.lawlink.nsw.gov.au/lawlink/adb/ll_adb.nsf/vwFiles/HepC_Chapter2.pdf/$file/HepC_Chapter2.pdf

Chrisjohn, Roland, and Sherri Young. 1995. *The Circle Game: Shadow and Substance in the Residential School Experience in Canada*. Penticton, BC: Theytus Books Ltd.

City of Toronto Council and Committees. 2000. "Toronto Police Service Response to the Recommendations of the Coroner's Inquest into the Death of Edmond Wai-Kong Yu," prepared by Norman Gardner (Chairman). Toronto, ON. http://www.toronto.ca/legdocs/2000/agendas/committees/adm/adm000208/it014.htm

City News Toronto. 2006. "Inquest Begins into Otto Vass Death," October 16. http://www.citytv.com/toronto/citynews/news/local/article/23905

Collins, Peter. 2012. "Stories from Prisoners: Joan, Alan, Peter." Unpublished letter to Giselle Dias and Joan Ruzsa. May.

Committee to Stop Targeted Policing. 2000. "Who's the Target? An Evaluation of Community Action Policing." Accessed September 15, 2012. tdrc.net/resources /public/Report-00–08.doc

Cormack, Elizabeth. 2012. *Racialized Policing: Aboriginal People's Encounters with the Police.* Black Point, NS: Fernwood Publishing.

Correctional Service of Canada (CSC). 2012. "Forum on Corrections Research: Release of Inmate Psychiatric Information." Accessed September 3. http://www.csc-scc .gc.ca/text/pblct/forum/e023/e023o-eng.shtml

———. 2011. "Commissioner's Directive 800: Health Services." Accessed September 5, 2012. http://www.csc-scc.gc.ca/text/plcy/cdshtm/800-cde-eng.shtml

Crawford, Alison. 2011. "Prison Watchdog Probes Spike in Number of Black Inmates," CBC News, December 15. http://www.cbc.ca/news/canada/story/2011/12/14 /crawford-black-prison.html

Davis, Angela. 2003. "Masked Racism." In *Sing, Whisper, Shout, Pray: Feminist Visions for a Just World,* edited by Jaqui Alexander, Mab Segrest, Lisa Albrecht, and Sharon Day, 50–57. Fort Bragg, CA: EdgeWork Books.

Devon, D. B. 2012. "Slavery By A Different Name: The Convict Lease System." Centre for Research on Globalization. Accessed September 3. http://www.globalresearch. ca/slavery-by-a-different-name-the-convict-lease-system/31176

Dias, Giselle. 2012. "Kevin." Unpublished letter to Giselle Dias. February.

Ejiogu, Nwadiogo, and Syrus Marcus Ware. 2008. "How Disability Studies Stays White, and What Kind of White it Stays." Paper presented to Society for Disability Studies, Baruch College, New York.

Ford, Peter, and Wendy L. Wobeser. 2000. "Health Care Problems in Prison." *CMAJ* 162(5): 664–665.

Foucault, Micheal. 1977. *Discipline and Punish: The Birth of the Prison.* New York: Random House.

Fritsch, Kelly. 2009. "Resisting Easy Answers: An Interview with Eli Clare." Upping the Anti-Journal 9. Accessed September 3, 2012. http://uppingtheanti.org/journal /article/09-resisting-easy-answers/

Gebhard, Amanda. 2012. "Pipeline to Prison: How Schools Shape a Future of Incarceration for Indigenous Youth." Briarpatch Magazine, September 1. Accessed September 9. http://briarpatchmagazine.com/articles/view/pipeline-to -prison

Global Commission on Drugs. 2012. "Six Former Presidents, Richard Branson and Other World Leaders: Criminalization of Drug Use Fuels the Global HIV/AIDS Pandemic." Accessed September 24. http://www.globalcommissionondrugs.org /hivaids-pandemic/

Gorski, Terrance. 2012. "Post Incarceration Syndrome and Relapse." Accessed September 7, 2012. http://www.tgorski.com/criminal_justice/cjs_pics_&_relapse .htm

Hils, A'ishah. 2012. "Interview with Leroy Moore." Accessed September 3. http://dis-abilityrightnow.wordpress.com/tag/ableism/

Jiwani, Yasmin. 2002. "The Criminalization of 'Race,' the Racialization of Crime." In *Crimes of Colour: Racialization and the Criminal Justice System in Canada,* edited by Wendy Chan and Kiran Mirchandani, 67–86. Peterborough, ON: Broadview Press.

Lapidus, Lenora, Namita Luthra, Anjuli Verma, Deborah Small, Patricia Allard, and Kirsten Levingston. 2004. "Caught in the Net: The Impact of Drug Policies on Women and Families." Accessed September 15, 2012. http://www.aclu.org/files /images/asset_upload_file431_23513.pdf

Levy-Pounds, Nekima. 2006. "Beaten by the System and Down for the Count: Why Poor Women of Color and Children Don't Stand a Chance Against U.S. Drug-Sentencing Policy." *University of St. Thomas Law Journal* 3(3):462–495.

Martin, Sandra L., and Rebecca J. Macy. 2011. "Sexual Violence Against Women: Impact on High-Risk Health Behaviors and Reproductive Health." Harrisburg, PA: National Resource Center on Domestic Violence. Accessed September 3, 2012. http://www.vawnet.org/applied-research-papers/print-document.php?doc_id=2034

Mancini, Matthew J. 1996. One Dies, Get Another Convict Leasing in the American South, 1866–1928. A Cruel Chapter in Southern Criminal Justice. Columbia, SC: University of South Carolina Press.

Mauer, Marc. 2003. "Comparative International Rates of Incarceration: An Examination of Causes and Trends." Washington, DC: The Sentencing Project. Accessed September 16, 2012. http://www.sentencingproject.org/doc/publications /inc_comparative_intl.pdf.

Mauer, Marc, Cathy Potler, and Richard Wolf. 1999. "Gender and Justice: Women, Drugs, and Sentencing Policy." Washington, DC: The Sentencing Project. Accessed August 28, 2012. www.sentencingproject.org/doc/publications/dp_genderandjustice.pdf

Mauer, Marc, and Ryan S. King. 2007. *Uneven Justice: State Rates of Incarceration by Race and Ethnicity*. Washington, DC: Sentencing Project.

McShane, Marilyn D., and Frank P. Williams III, eds. 2005. *Encyclopedia of American Prisons*. Taylor & Francis e-Library.

Mikkonen, Juha, and Dennis Raphael. 2010. "The Social Determinants of Health: The Canadian Facts." Accessed September 4, 2012. http://www.thecanadianfacts.org/

Millay, Tamara A., Veena A. Satyanarayana, Catina C. O'Leary, Robert Crecelius, and Linda B. Cotter. 2009. "Risky Business: Focus-Group Analysis of Sexual Behaviors, Drug Use and Victimization among Incarcerated Women in St. Louis." *Journal of Urban Health* 86(5): 810–817.

Mood Disorder Society of Canada. 2009. "Mental Illness and Addiction in Canada." Accessed September 5, 2012. http://www.mooddisorderscanada.ca/documents /Media%20Room/Quick%20Facts%203rd%20Edition%20Eng%20Nov%20 12%2009.pdf

Moore, Lisa D., and Amy Elkavich. 2008. "Who's Using and Who's Doing Time: Incarceration, The War on Drugs, and Public Health." *American Journal of Public Health* 98(5): 782–786.

Mussell, B., K. Cardiff, and J. White. 2004. "The Mental Health and Well Being of Aboriginal Children and Youth: Guidance for New Approaches and Services." Accessed September 16, 2012. http://www.mheccu.ubc.ca/

McLay, David, and Ann Silversides. 2011. "Behind the Walls: Living with HIV in Prison Comes with Its Own Set of Challenges, and Some Aren't the Ones You'd Expect." CATIE. Accessed August 28, 2012. http://www.catie.ca/en/positiveside /winter-2011/behind-walls

North American Nursing Diagnosis Association (NANDA International). 2009. *Nursing Diagnosis Definitions and Classification 2009–2011*. Oxford: Wiley-Blackwell Publishing.

Obomsawin, Alanis. 2000. Rocks at Whiskey Trench. [film]. National Film Board of Canada Collection. http://www.onf-nfb.gc.ca/eng/collection/film/?id=33895

Office of the Correctional Investigator. 2010. "Report Finds Serious Gaps in the Planning and Delivery of Mental Health Services for Federally Sentenced Offenders." Accessed September 12, 2012. http://www.oci-bec.gc.ca/comm/press/press20100923-eng .aspx

Reece, Raimunda. 2010. *Caged (No)Bodies: Exploring the Racialized and Gendered Politics of Incarceration of Black Women in the Canadian Prison System*. Toronto, ON: York University.

Sapers, Howard. 2009. "Annual Report of the Office of the Correctional Investigator 2008–2009." Accessed August 5, 2012. http://www.oci-bec.gc.ca/rpt/annrpt/annrpt20082009-eng.aspx#1

Scaramella, Gene L., Steven M. Cox, and William P. McCamey. 2011. *Introduction to Policing*. Thousand Oaks, CA: Sage Publications.

Schertow, John Ahni. 2008. "Urgent Help Needed: Mohawks Surrounded by OPP." *Intercontinental Cry*. Accessed August 5, 2012. http://intercontinentalcry.org/urgent-help-needed-mohawks-surrounded-by-opp

Silversides, Ann. 2010. "HIV and Hepatitis C: Diseases that Run Rampant in Canadian Prisons." *Rabble*. Accessed August 5, 2012. http://rabble.ca/news/2010/05/hiv-and-hepatitis-c-diseases-run-rampant-canadian-prisons

Stevens-Watkins, Danielle, Brea Perry, Kathi L. Harp, and Carrie B. Oser. 2012. "African-American Women: The Protective Effects of Ethnic Identity, Affirmation, and Behavior." *The Journal of Black Psychology* 38(4): 471–496.

Smith, P. K., N. B. Jostmann, A. D. Galinsky, and W. W. van Dijk. 2008. "Lacking Power Impairs Executive Functions." *Psychological Science* 19(5): 441–447. DOI: 10.1111/j.1467–9280.2008.02107.x

Trevethan, Shelley, and Christopher J. Rastin. 2004. "A Profile of Visible Minority Offenders in the Federal Canadian Correctional System." Research report delivered to Correctional Services Canada. Accessed September 9, 2012. www.csc-scc.gc.ca/text/rsrch/reports/r144/r144_e.pdf

VANDU. 1998. "About VANDU." Accessed September 4, 2012. www.vandu.org.

Weitz, Don. 2012. "Stop Killing Us! A Critique of Toronto Police Responses to Psychiatric Survivors." *Voices: Newsletter of the Psychiatric Survivor Archives of Toronto* 3(2): 4–5.

World Health Organization (WHO). 2007. "Mental Health and Prisons." Accessed September 14, 2012. http://www.who.int/mental_health/policy/mh_in_prison.pdf

Wood, Evan, Ronald Lim, and Thomas Kerr. 2006. "Initiation of Opiate Addiction in a Canadian Prison: A Case Report." *Harm Reduction Journal* 3: 11.

Yong, Ed. 2008. "Feeling Powerless Impairs Higher Mental Abilities." Scienceblogs.com. May 19. http://scienceblogs.com/notrocketscience/2008/05/19/feeling-powerless-impairs-higher-mental-abilities/

Zakaria, Diane, Jennie Mae Thompson, Ashley Jarvis, and Frederic Borgatta. 2010. "Summary of Emerging Findings from the 2007 National Inmate Infectious Diseases and Risk Behaviours Survey" Research Report. Correctional Service of Canada.

Zlomislic, D. 2009. "Ashley Smith Suicide Prompts Probe into Other Prison Deaths." *The Toronto Star*. Accessed September 9, 2012. http://www.thestar.com/news/canada/article/711798–ashley-smith-suicide-prompts-probe-into-other-prison-deaths

10

Chemical Constraint: Experiences of Psychiatric Coercion, Restraint, and Detention as Carceratory Techniques

Erick Fabris and Katie Aubrecht

Introduction

The body can be restrained for long periods using psychiatric drugs. Psychiatric patients in the 1970s started to fight against such practices, used primarily on people considered "mentally disordered." Some patients rejected the "mentally ill" label, calling themselves psychiatric survivors (Morrison 2005) in memory of eugenic practices like Nazi Germany's T4 program (Friedlander 2001). They considered what psychiatrists call chemical restraint, which has been in use for centuries (Fennell 1996), to be a chemical straitjacket and a "prison of drugs" (Chamberlin 1978; Janet Gotkin, from a US Senate Hearing in 1975, cited in Whitaker 2001, 176). The links between chemical restraint and incarceration are not only physical ones.

Chemical incarceration (Fabris 2011) is a term we use to describe mandatory drugging of people considered mad or mentally ill, but also anyone in an institution who is drugged without informed consent, with or without a diagnosis. In *Tranquil Prisons* (2011), Erick introduced this argument to show how drug treatment is often coercive, and tranquilizing drugs are regularly used to constrain. Psychiatric drugs may not be safe or effective, though they are a standard treatment response for distress or social conflict (Jackson 2005; Whitaker 2010). Major "neuroleptic" tranquilizers called antipsychotic medication do not usually stop hallucinations or delusions (in fact they can bring them on, especially during withdrawal). Furthermore they change the brain's chemical processes and structure, resulting in a loss of attention, feeling, and will, as well as other negative effects such as nervous tremors and rapid weight gain (Whitaker 2010). These are primary effects, once thought to constitute therapeutic response as Whitaker (2010) shows; however, the use of drugs to restrain people, supposedly for the purpose of therapy, has become commonplace in schools, prisons, hospitals, and residential facilities. This is an unconstitutional and unethical form of restraint, and over time a biological form of detention (Fabris 2011).

Erick's experience as a mental patient informs his research. As a result of his experience, he questions the given narrative that says those labeled mentally ill are generally confused, noncompliant, and dangerous, as well as the idea that drugging people is less coercive than "locking them up." While it could be argued that imposing drugs on people when they are violent is humane, the negative effects of drugs can last a lifetime. Drug withdrawal can make original distress treated with drugs much worse. Many people resign themselves to drugs to prevent withdrawal after they have been forced onto them. This preemptive coercion of drugs that starts the chain of dependency must be stopped. The dependency itself is a worse form of coercion than the actual restraint or "incarceration" of drugging, because it makes a person agreeable to being managed, despite what can be said of tranquilization as a form of help. Hence, it is not just the fact that drugs are ordered on patients that makes them coercive alone, but that they restrain the body and create dependency, using the body against the person, which results in an indefinite form of detention. *Tranquil Prisons* only shows the legal instruments of drug coercion, however, by looking at the legal orders used to keep people on "medications" after they leave a facility, such as the Community Treatment Order (CTO) in Canada and the Involuntary Outpatient Committal (IOC) in the United States. Coercion occurs in many ways.

Katie's experience of coercion in mental health treatment was just as frightening and restrictive as the more formal arrangements Erick discusses. She identifies as a disabled person and a psychiatric survivor, and relates to Mad identities and communities (Fabris 2011) as expressions of resistance to psychiatric oppression, and as such, political commitments. Her work seeks to understand the socially and historically transformative implications of resistances that erupt from *within* individuals, communities, institutions, and epistemologies (Aubrecht 2012; 2010; Titchkosky and Aubrecht 2009).

Using a letter exchange based on a method of narrative inquiry used by Carola Conle (1999), we show how chemical constraint informs prescription, restraint, and constraint in any institution, facility, or home. These letters, which act as the main body of this chapter (and the conclusion), inform issues of identity, experience, and political theory. Jijian Voronka's (2008; 2003) critical cultural analysis of the relations between the construction of mad carceral sites in Ontario and Canadian nation-building, and Geoffrey Reaume's (2009) archival research on life in a mental hospital from a patient's perspective, suggest a need to question how state-sanctioned responses to "madness" are situated historically and politically. Katie and Erick's dialogue through letters explores how biomedical understandings and practices perpetuate inequity and the prison industry by making the lived experience of marginalization appear as an individual's problem. We also explore how psychiatric medication offers an initiation into normalcy—a rite of passage that is represented as essential to survival within institutional settings. Implicit in the letter exchange is the understanding that psychiatric survival is so much more than an "overcoming story" (Price 2011). It is a collaborative work of *speaking with others*, and of "bearing witness" (Mcguire 2010) to the subversive possibilities of Disability and Mad movements and studies working in solidarity to disrupt taken-for-granted relations to "progressive" social institutions and disciplinary practices.

Bio-textual practices of distancing and division, like drugging, can be understood as what Mike Oliver and Jane Campbell refer to as "divide and rule" tactics (1996, 73). Such practices are "bio-textual" in the sense that the experience of the body comes to life through texts, whether legislative or medical, and ways of acting are enforced by texts. Bodily experiences are organized and ordered through diagnoses. Erick examines this in relation to the physical body and sensory and cognitive experiences, while Katie considers how formal and informal psychiatric prescriptions to be better selves alter how situations are understood and experienced. In both instances, the materiality of the body is made present by alienating the individual from experience, and the experience from the world. Such practices play an essential role in the individualization, dehistoricization, and depoliticization of marginalized people and communities. Psychiatric prescriptions make it possible to define social suffering and dissent as signs or symptoms of the existence of personal disorder and moral weakness, rather than embodied responses to inequitable social systems. Such practices also work to sanction and produce double and triple consciousnesses, which W. E. B. Du Bois (1903) and Frantz Fanon (1967) describe as the sense of having no single unified consciousness, but instead "of always looking at oneself through the eyes of others, of measuring one's soul by the tape of a world *that looks on with amused contempt and pity*" (Du Bois 1903, 8–9; emphasis added). Critical race and anticolonial theory (Chapman 2010; 2012; De La Torre-MacNeill 2011; Dei and Asgharzadeh 2001; Fanon 1965; Freire 2005; Kempf 2009; Wane 2008), as well as post-structural feminisms (Haug 1999; Scott 1999) and feminist disability studies (Garland-Thomson 2005; 2001; Wendell 1989), have all demonstrated a need to examine the complex relations between consciousness of self and the societal values and power relations of the day. An anticolonial analysis of psychiatry thus offers an occasion to question how dominant conceptions of madness and disability have been used to maintain oppressive systems of power. It provides a theoretical framework for understanding the abuse of power, the rationalization of the abuse of others, and the extraction of some valued commodity or power.

Implicit within this letter exchange is a commitment to resist the colonial imperative to pathologize resistance and interpret anguish, distress, and dissent as signs of personal deficiency, imbalance, and disorder. In *The Wretched of the Earth*, Frantz Fanon (1965) argues that it is often the case that the first buds of collective resistance emerge in what appear to be spontaneous defensive reactions to colonial domination and cultural repression—confusion, anger, aggression—what psychiatry refers to as *acting out*. Fanon also shows that such "reactions" do not simply demonstrate the truth of a naturally disturbed, culturally deficient, or chemically unbalanced individual. They are, rather, embodied performances of the violence of the colonial encounter (Aubrecht 2010; Fanon 1965). This encounter is lived not once, but repeatedly, many times over, met and re-met daily in ideas, images, and institutions that are structured by ableist ideals, and rationalities. In speaking of resistance we do not assume that all experiences and behaviors considered to be madness and labeled as "mental illness" represent self-conscious acts intended to challenge colonial violence; rather the implicit challenge to a normate world (Garland-Thomson 2005) in which "mad" embodiments are treated with carceratory techniques make this form of difference a critical challenge to the status quo.

Psychiatry's premise of reordering or curing identity (the disorderly "mad" body) leads to the apparent intent to immobilize it first, then to treat it. The corpus, chemically restrained for the purpose of "stabilization" (Fabris 2011), is made "ill" figuratively, and in everyday life. Drugging "side-effects" are the ledger of a two-sided truth: you don't naturally belong, but you can stay if you prove that you are committed to wanting to belong. Disability studies theorist Rod Michalko (2002; 1998) discusses a similar insight in *The Mystery of the Eye and the Shadow of Blindness* and *The Difference that Disability Makes*; that is, a sense of what

Michael Trask (2003) and David Theo Goldberg (2009) refer to as the "temporary temporality" of one's place in the world. Psychiatry offers a way of understanding and treating the violence of contemporary forms of colonial capitalism, and the resulting confusion, anguish, anger, and distress this violence produces, as a transitional phase or "momentary detour" (Trask 2009) on the path to progress. However, in this chapter we argue that ableist, mentalist (Chamberlin 1978), and sanist (Birnbaum 2010) imprisonment is torture (Minkowitz 2006/07), in part because of its indefinite confinement by use of the body (Fabris 2006), but also its potential for deadly side effects (Whitaker 2010).

First Letter from Erick to Katie

Hi Katie, how are you? I'm glad we have chosen to tell our stories. We have decided to link them to the expansion of the prison industrial complex under colonial practices of power. We want people to consider how some medical or psychiatric treatment can be used to restrain and, over time, detain bodies. Drugging people with "antipsychotics" or "neuroleptics" is becoming a part of the process of criminalization, detention, and control of bodies across institutions including corrections, education, social work, and general medicine. Some people might choose to try "meds" in distressing times, but neuroleptic tranquilizer effects can be quite damaging, leading to a repeated cycle of dependency, withdrawal, and often "re-hospitalizations," as well as loss of emotion, expression, cognitive depth, will power, and other iatrogenic (i.e., medically induced) impairments (Fabris 2012). Such drugs can also bring on what they are meant to stop: hallucinations, aggression, delusion, suicidality, and long-term iatrogenic impairments like Tardive Dyskinesia in which hand tremors and other parkinsonian symptoms appear (Breggin 2012; Whitaker 2010), among broader iatrogenic effects.

Katie, we've talked about the puzzle of "mental illness," or what used to be called madness, and how this ableist idea is often used to excuse or punish strangeness as if it were the single cause for evil or violence. This mentalism is part of the problem, and it grounds bioscience struggling to find and eradicate mental disability or disorder. However, as many have said, the real phenomenon of distress or social difference is not something we can simply ignore. We each have ways of understanding differences described as mental or emotional, and we do this across disabilities and disorder categories, but we do not reduce these "mad" or "ill" experiences to problems of the individual. We also see our experiences not as faulty or disordered, but as lived experiences that are connected to oppression, social disparity, and conflict.

As people with experience of psychiatric coercion, we welcome alliances with antiprison activists, as well as disabled, Deaf, antiracist, anticolonial, feminist, anti-heterosexist, antipoverty, and many other activists concerned with systems of control. These forms of resistance are considered together, to share our complaints about drugging across structural or societal arrangements, and to help us recognize oppressions across borders. I hope our letters relate not only the information we need to share but also the feelings and thoughts we remember in struggle, because these are as important for theorizing about oppression through psychiatric constraints.

The issue for me is how drugs work on bodies as a restraint. Tina Minkowitz (2006/07) argued that chemical restraints used only on the mentally disabled (or "psychiatrically" or "psychosocially" disabled) is a discriminatory practice. Disability, regardless of its supposed origin as mental or physical—which are not separable anyway—cannot be used as a premise for mistreating people, especially under the pretense of "treatment." People considered less than deserving of rights, like those considered "mad" or "ill," are not only arrested or detained, but are medically impaired and told to stay on "medication" for the purpose of control.

In my experience, I was hauled into an emergency ward of a general hospital for acting "strange" at work, which like most such experiences was not dangerous. When I asked to be put in another room at the hospital, I was swarmed by orderlies, forced onto a gurney, strapped down and given an intramuscular injection of the old drug Haldol (Haldoperidol). I fell unconscious and woke up many hours later. I was then expected to conform to the psych ward's routines and told I had a mental illness that would prevent me from working and having primary relationships. I was put on a newer form of neuroleptic drug for an indefinite time.

On the locked ward, I was put on a privilege system, which figured as a carrot for complying with routines on the ward. On the second step of this system I was allowed fresh air for ten minutes in my hospital gown, which seemed to me an attempt at modifying behavior through shaming and manipulation. I was released a month later. I saw a shrink who grudgingly allowed me to tweak my meds, which I successfully reduced by 1/5th of the total dose every two or three weeks. I managed this mostly because of the support I got from my friends in the psychiatric survivor movement. Only ten months after my forced "treatment," I started working for a tiny patient advocacy organization in the largest psychiatric institution in Canada, then called the Queen St. Mental Health Centre, in Toronto. I have since taken up academic work, researching coercions like CTOs. It is only now that, with you, I have a chance to relate coercive and forced treatment to broader or nuanced methods of institutional control.

Erving Goffman (1961) considered total institutions to restrict movement and association with others. Outpatient drugging performs the same function, and the way that laws have been bent to encourage it shows how the industries of control are expanding. It is well documented (see Dreezer and Dreezer 2007; Fabris 2011; Trueman 2003) that most people put under CTOs and IOCs are not dangerous, or even resisting drugs. What is most startling is that treatment is often foisted on people and the resulting negative effects are blamed on a "mental illness," yet they become the burden of the treated individual. Stories of indiscriminate drugging provide for theorization about institutional control in contemporary colonial practices, what some call transinstitutionalization (Guy 1985). Transinstitutionalization is how people are shuffled around from one institution to another, such as from education to prison or psychiatry. Such top-down practices erode the individual's sense of self, the narrative of one's life.

Recently a student of mine wrote about what happened to her while being drugged. It did not occur on the ward, but began in school. She remembered in detail how her right to decide was immediately denied, supposedly because of her inability or "incapacity" (the legal term) to make her own decisions. Yet she had only wanted a bit of help with her situation. There are so many options in dealing with each other's situational crises if we use open communication channels. However, the effects of drugs soon started to take hold, and she began to experience lethargy and somnolence. She was alarmed by this, but had no way to contest it because of how she was denied agency by medical determinations about her medical and legal status. Young people that do not fit in as students in the educational system are most vulnerable to surreptitious and coercive drugging. In many students' stories, information about medication is withheld (supposedly until the person has become more reasonable, or sedated I would say), and clinicians and others rarely discuss or concern themselves with "side effects," saying that the risks of madness outweigh the risks of toxic drugs. Even if drugs reduce pain in the short term, they restrain and destroy the body over the long term and do not cure "madness," resulting in a chemical incarceration.

First Letter from Katie to Erick

Hi Erick, thanks for your letter. I have really enjoyed our conversations and email exchanges, and value the opportunity we've been given to think and talk together about our positions, philosophies, life stories, and works. My attention to what you have described as chemical incarceration is animated by recognition of the prevalent, and increasingly normalized, reference to psychotropic drugs as a source of agency in North American societies. Often justified as a tool for taking control, "correcting" "problem behavior," "overcoming" adversity, increasing "resilience," and even "enhancing" performance, psychiatric medications are depicted in a way that makes them appear as though they are simply accommodations, comparable to other adaptive or augmentative devices. This version of meds, as an accommodation, is to some extent championed in the consumer movement. However, it seems to gloss over ways which medications and the normative prescriptions they enforce affect the lived experience of the body. Differences in thinking, feeling and acting (variously labeled as "mental illness," "mental disability," "psychosocial disability," and even "whatever you want to call it"), can provoke disability studies movements and analyses to question the relationship between accommodation and social justice. The term chemical incarceration makes it possible to consider psychiatric drugging as a form of legitimized violence intended to restrain movement, remove agency, and deny self-determination. It makes explicit the need to interrogate the sociopolitical dimensions of what Irving Kenneth Zola (1978) describes as "disabling medicalization."

You and I come to understand chemical incarceration from different lived experiences, backgrounds, and interests. I have never been institutionalized and cannot claim to know what it is like. We do, however, share a common goal of stopping coercion. We also both write from the cultural location of the academy. Although we write and speak from other locations, to discount the significance of formal education, particularly higher education, on the experience of what we are referring to as chemical coercion might be to miss an essential part of the story. The possibility of this exchange was conditioned by our activities in the University in the form of discussions in academic and activist conferences, classrooms, department corridors, and campus pubs. It was also in the university that I was first formally introduced to psychiatry, and to myself as a problem which psychiatry alone could answer.

Under the watchful gaze of a physician, I was taught to read experiences, red cheeks, heavy hearts, and knots, as symptoms of mental illness and as tests of my character. I was constantly quizzed about how well I knew the experiences I had were actually true experiences. I couldn't be sure what I felt, liked, or wanted anymore. I did, however, become ever more familiar with what doctors felt, liked, and wanted, and that those would be the right things to feel, like, and want. It was at this time that I was introduced to anxiety disorder and depression in the form of a prescription for an antidepressant. Under the pretense of care, I became increasingly dehydrated—spiritually, emotionally, as well as physically. The instructions that came with the medication were more moral than medical. I owed it to myself and others to learn how to dispense with confusion and draw clean boundaries between who I was, who I am, and who I could be. At the time, the doctor guaranteed that if I followed his directions and took the medication, I would become a better person—more "social," and, if not "back to normal," at the very least more comfortable with the task of needing to become someone else. Someone who could *do better* and therefore *deserved better*. The drugs, I was told, would help me be a better me.

As part of his sell, he claimed to have many patients on anti-anxiety and antidepressant medications, students and other "people of my age." The high prevalence of students taking medication for depression or anxiety was all really very normal, ordinary even. Really, they are just like vitamins. With the exception that these vitamins came with a prescription: take ritually, repetitively, resolutely, alone, and in secrecy. Suffer the headaches, nausea, cramps, agitation, and anxiety far worse than before, but don't talk about it, at least not in public. It's all very normal, he assured me, and no one ever has to know. If it was all so very normal, how come it felt so very strange? The restraints of this ritualistic chemical (dis)placement, and not "mental illness," altered the very way I moved. When I was on medication I thought, talked, and postured myself in ways that seemed unfamiliar, even to me. I stood and sat too stiff or loose, arms too straight against my sides, or pressed-down and spread flat along a table, head down; the spaces between me and others, when they were there at all, felt predetermined and over calculated. Psychiatric medication, at least the antidepressants and anti-anxietants I was on, produced a persistent and simultaneous sense of fatigue and disorientation, a restlessness, which made it difficult to focus, and nearly impossible to concentrate. They made it possible to *get up and get going*, make it to class, but seemingly impossible to *be where I was*. I stopped taking notes and stopped talking in class.

What you describe as chemical incarceration, for me, meant being restrained in what felt like someone else's body. Pharmaceutical reason confined me within a glass bubble that separated me from my body and my body from the world. Voices were muffled, and responses were delayed and over determined. Within a biomedicalized world of one, I was encouraged to imagine the medication as a guide that would lead me to adjust to the timelines of respectable "reality." As I write this, I am reminded of Jijian Voronka's (2008) pivotal work on respectability and asylum-building in colonial Canada. For me, this initiation into respectability, embodied in assumptions about the look and feel of successful academic performance, was like a hazing process involving harassment, abuse, and humiliation. Prescription adjustments were accompanied by interrogations which always began with, "How are you doing in school?" but inevitably ended in "Are you having sex?", "Do you ever feel worthless?", and "Do you ever think of committing suicide?" They usually also involved adjustments of other kinds, including birth control pills that were switched to higher or lower dosages of estrogen. I was informed that experimenting with different methods of birth control offered a way to test for the source of the emotional distress which I had come to know simply as depression and anxiety, but which I felt so fully in terms of the way I was positioned in relation to time—to where "I" was and wasn't, should and couldn't be. It was "naturally assumed" that too little or too much estrogen might very well be the "real" source of *my problem*.

Second Letter from Erick to Katie

Katie, thank you for your great letter. In legal terms, how choices are constrained in the operationalization of drugging is informative. Sometimes constraint is legitimized through rules of medical consent, and this makes it easy to wonder about "consent." To understand consent, there are examples we can draw upon from the Canadian legal system. Take, for instance, the case of Scott Starson, a forensic psychiatric inmate (held "not criminally responsible" in a criminal case) here in Ontario. The Supreme Court of Canada authorized drugging to remedy unwanted behaviors, despite the availability of less physically damaging treatments. This authorization, which the Court claimed would offer a way to balance autonomy rights held by all individuals, at least sound ones, is enacted when a psychiatrist deems a patient legally "incapable" to make treatment decisions (I think of it like the "insane" category in a civil case). To do so, the psychiatrist must inform the patient under assessment of the following: the diagnosis, the treatment, its associated risks and benefits, and whatever alternatives are available. Then, acting with the authority of the province of Ontario's Health Care Consent Act (1996), as an example, a psychiatrist tests for capacity by deciding if an inmate presents the ability to understand her own symptoms and the treatment suggested, as well as her ability to appreciate the consequences of deciding or not deciding to use such treatment. The test is not whether the person can repeat specific terms or agree with the psychiatrist's terminology or specific diagnosis, as the Starson decision now provides; the Court says a psychiatrist must decide whether the person recognizes that some condition affects her, and that a treatment decision will affect her, but the patient must not base her treatment decision on a delusion (*Starson v. Swayze* 2003 at para. 18). Remember that this is not the civil commitment itself but the treatment imposition, so the rules are a bit different, relating to choice.

Now that these legal rules have been described, I will use the term psychiatric "detainees" rather than patients, if only because a person under a 72-hour assessment is denied legal oversights or even substantive legal appellation (the term "patient" is insufficient for being detained for an illness, and inmate is too substantive as this legal designation provides rights denied to psychiatric detainees in both civil and forensic streams). The term detainee is used to precisely denote what is legally occurring under Ontario's Mental Health Act Form 1: a detention (isolation, sequestration, containment in a controlled space or posture), especially for an indeterminate period. For the purpose of treatment, the drugging comes with the detention. However, a Form 1 assessment is only one instantiation of legal procedures that confuses restraint with treatment, so that anyone under compulsory psychiatric arrangements is in danger of environmental detention (isolation, sequestration) or restraint (chemical or mechanical), and is conceivable as a detainee insofar as chemical restraint impairs, limits, and constrains the body in social and physical space. This is compounded by the problem of withdrawal symptoms that force a person to "choose" the treatment that was originally imposed.

In some circumstances of psychiatric coercion, such as when (trans)institutionalized people (e.g., in schools, prisons) are drugged into a stupor without diagnosis, I believe the term chemical incarceration or detention could be applied without official patient status being imposed. I will continue to use terms like patient and client when the context calls for it, such as when a situation applies to all patients of any medicinal practice, or when considering a client of advocacy services. In my prior work (2006) I have used the term "inmate" in keeping with Goffman's (1961) terminology to describe people under compulsory psychiatric arrangements as well as in institutions. I also meant to suggest that if patients were at least conceived as inmates they might be more ready to protect their legal rights, though in practice this might not be the case. However, "detainee" more exactly describes the social location of subjects of outpatient committals, involuntary statuses, and incapable statuses.

Second Letter from Katie to Erick

Thanks Erick. Reading what you say of a clinical emphasis on individuals' capacity to recognize their "conditions" and make treatment choices in the "Starson decision" has raised the importance of questioning how our "conditions" are defined.

Psychiatric drug regimes keep madness at a distance, and as Michel Foucault (1995) says in "Madness, The Absence of Work," always "within distance" (290). Within westernized narrative schemas, stories of madness have played a central role in the telling and retelling of histories of colonialism and conflict, enlightenment, eugenics, industrialization and urbanization, and control. Important critical analyses and critiques of how such stories are used to perpetuate inequitable social relations can be found within Disability Studies (Price 2011) and Mad Studies (Costa, et al. 2013). Geoffrey Reaume (2009) cautions that stories of madness, however prevalent, are rarely told from a mad perspective. When such stories are told, they tend to depict madness and mental illness as conditions that produce isolated individuals naturally at home in the shadows.

Speaking of shadows, I find myself thinking about the Mental Health Commission of Canada, announced by Prime Minister Stephen Harper in August 2007 in response to a key recommendation of the 2006 report of The Senate Standing Committee on Social Affairs, Science and Technology entitled *Out of the Shadows at Last: Transforming Mental Health, Mental Illness and Addiction Services in Canada* (The Senate Standing Committee on Social Affairs, Science and Technology 2006). The Commission, which was "created to focus national attention on mental health issues and to work to improve the health and social outcomes of people living with mental illness" (Mental Health Commission 2008), has helped bring mental health issues to the top of the agendas of Canadian institutions, not least of which includes Canadian educational institutions. *Out of the Shadows at Last* begins with what the report depicts as one woman's "story of mental illness" (Senate Standing Committee 2006, 1). She describes telling her employers that she was depressed, a claim which she was required to qualify in the form of notes from experts, questionnaires, and "pills" (Senate Standing Committee 2006, 27): "When I came to my employers and told them that I was depressed, they said, 'Well, you will have to prove that.' I said, 'I intend to. I have a note from a psychiatrist that says so. If you would like to see my purse, I have lots of pills that I have to take and I have to suffer through'" (Senate Standing Committee 2006, 1). Rather than relieve suffering, this story of "mental illness" offers a view of "pills" as way of making difference legible, and a cultural currency that also must be suffered.

Third Letter from Erick to Katie

Hi Katie, what you were saying with regard to the emotional experiences of drugging gets me thinking beyond the legal and administrative use of chemical restraint.

Is drugging not like being inducted into a cult? You are told things no thinking person would accept, and then you are disoriented by drugging, so that you have less capacity to act, and all this goes unnoticed in sterile and dehumanizing interactions. So when we speak of chemical incarceration we speak of experiences, not simply the legal elaboration of clinical arrangements. These experiences inform how psychiatric exploitation, torture, and capture bonding are carried out.

Incarceratory schemes to control certain expressions more readily are some of the colonial "gains" of drugging people *en masse*. Add to this the general acceptance of drugging: a perfect storm of indiscriminate treatment appears and gives way to thousands of mad people's protests all over the world, decrying forced treatment and overuse of drugs. So the experience of being drugged has resonances. But in my own experience, as I have said elsewhere, I felt like there was no future, no past, only a kind of shallow present in which I could make myself amenable, but not fully engaged in relating. I was agreeable, constantly jittery, and ever faithful to what I was being told. I was less prone to argument; people wondered what I wanted. And I went over the same ground a lot. There are a lot of experiential accounts, in Whitaker (2010), for example, that speak to the issue of being spellbound, or silenced, or slowed, or being split up, and so on.

Incarceration of bodies considered irrational and irresponsible ("incapable" and "insane") is disrespectful of the body. It also allows for a total reduction in central nervous system function for the sake of preventing any possible risk. Drugging has been used for centuries, at least since English mad house directors used ox horns to pour tranquilizing "physic" down the throats of their seventeenth century inmates. The trade in madness continues to draw millions of people into tranquility for profit. As we tell this story of the capture and constraint of so many bodies and brains, and recall our own experiences, I feel we have a better chance of demanding change from within and without prison systems, including the mental illness system.

Third Letter from Katie to Erick

Erick, you raise an important point about the disabling effects of psychiatric drugs, a fact that is often glossed-over in references to "madness" or "mental illness" as a kind of "invisible disability."

Although prescribed under the auspices of stabilizing "moods," psychiatric medications produce new sensitivities and effects such as changes in patterns and disruptions to waking and sleeping life, which often generate the need for additional treatments. Even when prescriptions are followed, there is always the possibility of an unexpected interaction that can lead to bad reactions and even worse conditions than before, which you have described as iatrogenic impairments. I was so troubled when you told me that iatrogenic impairments are often identified as mental disorders and drugged more, leading to what you call "the cycling of chemistry" (Fabris 2011). I once read an article by Carl Sherman (2002) about this. In it, he talks about how antidepressants such as selective serotonin reuptake inhibitors, or SSRIs, produced memory problems in elderly persons, which were interpreted as symptoms of dementia. This led to dementia diagnoses, and with these diagnoses, a greater likelihood of hospitalization and institutionalization. Sherman, however, does not address the fact that within hospitals and institutions, persons with dementia and other cognitive impairments are often subject to the use of physical and pharmacological restraints to prevent "wandering" and exit. However, the solution to the "problem" of institutionalization that Sherman proposes does not involve questioning the harmful effects of drugs that are prescribed in the name of increasing happiness and well-being, nor even the practices of institutionalization. Although his research shows that prescriptive practices increase rather than decrease the likelihood of institutionalization and medical dependencies, Sherman calls for policies that increase the monitoring and surveillance of people taking SSRI's, so that reactions can be identified in time to prevent further "damage!" Much like "the story of mental illness" within the government document *Out of the Shadows at Last*, Sherman's research is presented as proof of a need for "more of the same" kinds of ways of dealing with human suffering. This just confirms for me the importance of Mad understandings of iatrogenic impairment within critical analyses of the "revolving doors" of mental hospitals and prisons.

Concluding Letter from Katie to Erick

What our dialogue contributes to an understanding of disability and incarceration is the need to consider the social and institutional linkages that connect compulsory and voluntary admissions and treatment. This could also lead to new understandings of how we make distinctions between rights and privileges, which is a dialogue that this broader collection, *Disability Incarcerated*, takes up. In my letters I have tried to account for what Josephine Ross (2010) refers to as the "subtle coercions" that structure everyday interactions and disenfranchise individuals and groups on the basis of their failure to successfully demonstrate dominant social norms. According to Lori Janelle Dance (2009), "Within a colonial or administrative nation-state context, disenfranchisement is an active process by which the colonizing power, state or state-sanctioned institutions deny colonial subjects or citizens basic rights" (1). Legal arrangements such as CTOs blur the lines between consent and coercion under the guise of "progressive medicine" and the promise to advance social and individual well-being (Aubrecht 2009). Rather than an alternative to institutionalization, they could also be read as constitutive of less obvious forms of incarceration. In placing the onus on the individual (through self-management and customized individual "treatment plans"), new legal arrangements must be read in relation with the common policies and practice of other social institutions, such as the university, the hospital, and the long-term care residential facility.

What does thinking of compulsory community treatment legislation and the normalization of psychiatricizing practices in the university in conversation do? It provokes a need to question whether and how supports and services that are represented as accommodations may actually work to regulate experience, coerce uninformed consent to normative regimes, and constrain the possibilities of resistance against inequitable social orders and disciplinary institutions. Considering these two distinct sites together (the prison industrial complex and the higher education system) also draws attention to the need to distinguish what is happening in situations of mandatory treatment from situations that occur within such privileged spaces as the North American university. Thinking with our conversation, it has become clear to me that systems of education and incarceration are not analogous. They rather extend one another, and this is important insofar as it suggests that resistances in one realm could very possibly inform destabilizations in the other.

Concluding Letter from Erick to Katie

In terms of a conclusion, Katie, I was hoping to address some questions we left out of our letters. For me this runs the gamut from our social positions as white settlers doing academic work to our theoretical choices and terminologies, which I will try to touch on very briefly. *Disability Incarcerated* started from a panel on disability and imprisonment. Psychiatric survivors often feel caged for differences they do not consider illnesses or disabilities. But my work on chemical incarceration has tried to show how our feelings actually correspond to legal and physical impositions by the state, which informs how we qualify experiences as impairments. State mandated drugging physically disables us and prevents us from resisting. I seek political remedies for this violence, which calls for solidarity with activists from disability and prison justice movements, some of whom use antiracist and anticolonial critiques. My experience as a white settler who was labeled with a mental illness and chemically restrained may be different from a disabled person who is considered mad and institutionalized, or a person of color who is wrongly convicted of a drug offense and is imprisoned. I wanted to write with you because your experience shows that even without "orders," or legal means, being drugged can be disorienting, destructive, and restraining. So emotional distress and difference are not that far removed from criminality and disability where state coercion is concerned. With our privilege, we use critical scholarship to show how psychiatry, medicine, and prisons work together within a white supremacist, eugenic, patriarchal, colonial capitalism, constraining certain bodies in and out of schools, hospitals, and jails. Wherever disability, racialization, "madness," or any difference is unwanted, drugging can be used to impair the body, compound distress, and embed coercion in the "helping" professions. Contrary to the notion of safe and effective treatment, drugging is not "less restrictive" than a cage because our very thoughts and feelings are compromised, restraining people physically, and diverting our will to escape. Drugging reveals the ties between disability, imprisonment, and various industries that reinforce the modern legacy of colonialism.

Acknowledgments

We are grateful to the editors and reviewers for the invitation to contribute to this collection and for their insightful dialogue.

References

Aubrecht, Katie. 2012. "Disability Studies and the Language of Mental Illness." *The Review of Disability Studies: An International Journal* 8(2): 31–44.

———. 2010. "Re-Reading the Ontario Review of the Roots of Youth Violence Report: The Relevance of Fanon for a Critical Disability Studies Perspective." In *Fanon and Education: Thinking through Pedagogical Possibilities*, edited by George Dei and Marlon Simmons, 55–78. New York: Peter Lang.

———. 2009. "CTOs: A New Order of Terror?" In *Engaging Terror: A Critical and Interdisciplinary Approach*, edited by Marianne Vardalos, Guy Kirby Letts, Herminio Meireles Teixeira, Anas Karzai, and JaneHaig, 323–330. Boca Raton, FL: BrownWalker Press.

Birnbaum, Rebecca. 2010. "My Father's Advocacy for a Right to Treatment." *Journal of the American Academy of Psychiatry & the Law* 38(1): 115–123.

Breggin, Peter. 2012. "Tardive Dyskinesia Caused by Antipsychotic Drugs." Accessed July 22, 2012. http://www.breggin.com/index.php?option=com_content&task=view&id=45&Itemid=66

Chamberlin, Judi. 1978. *On Our Own: Patient-Controlled Alternatives to the Mental Health System*. New York: McGraw-Hill.

Chapman, Chris. 2012. "Colonialism, Disability, and Possible Lives: The Residential Treatment of Children Whose Parents Survived Indian Residential Schools." *The Journal of Progressive Human Services* 24(2): 127–158.

———. 2010. "Becoming Perpetrator: How I Came to Accept Restraining and Confining Disabled Aboriginal Children." Paper presented at *PsychOut: A Conference for Organizing Resistance Against Psychiatry*, Ontario Institute for Studies in Education, University of Toronto, Toronto, Ontario, Canada. Accessed December 1, 2011. http://aecp.oise.utoronto.ca/psychout/papers/Chapman_paper.pdf.

Conle, Carola. 1999. "Why Narrative? Which Narrative? Struggling with Time and Place in Life and Research." *Curriculum Inquiry* 29(1): 7–32.

Costa, Lucy, Jijian Voronka, Danielle Landry, Jenna Reid, Becky McFarlane, David Reville, and Katherine Church. 2013. "Recovering Our Stories: A Small Act of Resistance." *Studies in Social Justice* 6(1).

Dance, Lori Janelle. 2009. "Struggles of the Disenfranchised: Commonalities Among Native Americans, Black Americans, and Palestinians." Accessed October 1, 2012. http://www.alhewar.org/Lori_Dance-StrugglesOfDisenfranchised.pdf

De La Torre-MacNeill, Joaquin. 2011. "Consciousness Raising and Reality Construction within Oppressed Groups: Bridging the Gap between Feminist Theory and Critical Race Theory." *Res Cogitans* 2(1): 29–36.

Dei, George J. Sefa, and Alizera Asgharzadeh. 2001. "The Power of Social Theory: The Anti-Colonial Discursive Framework." *Journal of Educational Thought* 35(3): 297–323.

Dreezer and Dreezer, Inc. 2007. *Report on the Legislated Review of Community Treatment Orders, Required under Section 33.9 of the Mental Health Act for the Ontario Ministry of Health and Long-Term Care*. Toronto, ON: Queen's Printer for Ontario.

Du Bois, W. E. B. 1903. *The Souls of Black Folk: Essays and Sketches*. Chicago, IL: A. C. McClurg & Co.

Fabris, Erick. 2012. "Iatrogenic Impairment: Disability and Psychiatric Survivors." Paper presented at the Annual Meeting for the Society for Disability Studies, Denver, Colorado, June 20–23.

———. 2011. *Tranquil Prisons: Chemical Incarceration under Community Treatment Orders*. Toronto, IL: University of Toronto Press.

———. 2006. "Identity, Inmates, Insight, Capacity, Consent: Chemical Incarceration in Psychiatric Survivor Experiences of Community Treatment Orders." M.A. thesis, Ontario Institute of Studies in Education, University of Toronto.

Fanon, Frantz. 1967. *Black Skin, White Masks*. New York: Grove/Atlantic.

———. 1965. *The Wretched of the Earth*. New York: Grove Press.

Fennell, Phil. 1996. *Treatment without Consent: Law, Psychiatry, and the Treatment of Mentally Disordered People since 1845*. New York: Routledge.

Foucault, Michel. 1995. "Madness, The Absence of Work." Translated by Peter Stastny and Deniz Şengel. *Critical Inquiry* 21(2): 290–298.

Freire, Paulo. 2005. *Education for Critical Consciousness*. London: Continuum International Publishing Group.

Friedlander, H. 2001. "The Exclusion and Murder of the Disabled." In *Social Outsiders in Nazi Germany*, edited by Robert Gellately and Nathan Stoltzfus, 145–164. Princeton: Princeton University Press.

Garland-Thomson, Rosemarie. 2005. "Feminist Disability Studies." *Signs: Journal of Women in Culture & Society* 30(2):1557–87.

———. 2001. *Re-shaping, Re-thinking, Re-defining: Feminist Disability Studies*. Washington: Centre for Women Policy Studies. Accessed November 31, 2011. http://www.centerwomenpolicy.org/pdfs/DIS2.pdf

Goffman, Erving. 1961. *Asylums: Essays on the Social Situation of Mental Patients and Other Inmates*. New York: Doubleday Anchor.

Goldberg, David Theo. 2009. *The Threat of Race: Reflections on Racial Neoliberalism*. Oxford: Blackwell Publishing.

Guy, Glen. 1985. "Community-based Care: Deinstitutionalization or Transinstitutionalization?" *Exceptional Child* 32(3): 137–147.

Haug, Frigga. 1999. *Female Sexualization*. Translated by Erica Carter. London: Verso.

Jackson, G. E. 2005. *Rethinking Psychiatric Drugs: A Guide for Informed Consent*. Bloomington, IN: Authorhouse.

Kempf, Arlo, ed. 2009. *Breaching the Colonial Contract: Anti-Colonialism in the US and Canada*, New York: Springer.

Mcguire, Anne. 2010. "Disability, Non-Disability and the Politics of Mourning: Re-conceiving the 'We.'" *Disability Studies Quarterly* 30(3/4). Accessed December 29, 2011. http://dsq-sds.org/article/view/1282/1309

Mental Health Commission of Canada. 2008. "Out of the Shadows Forever." Accessed December 5, 2008. http://www.mentalhealthcommission.ca/english/pages/default.aspx

Michalko, Rod. 2002. *The Difference that Disability Makes*. Philadelphia, PA: Temple University Press.

———. 1998. *The Mystery of the Eye and the Shadow of Blindness*. Toronto, ON: University of Toronto Press.

Minkowitz, Tina. 2006/07. "The United Nations Convention on the Rights of Persons with Disabilities and the Right to be Free from Nonconsensual Psychiatric Interventions." *Syracuse Journal of International Law and Commerce* 34: 405–428.

Morrison, Linda. 2005. *Talking Back to Psychiatry: The Consumer/Survivor/Ex-patient Movement*. New York, NY: Routledge Press.

Oliver, Mike, and Jane Campbell. 1996. *Disability Politics: Understanding Our Past, Changing Our Future*. London: Routledge.

Ontario Health Care Consent Act. 1996. S.O. 1996, Chapter 2, Schedule A.

Price, Margaret. 2011. *Mad at School: Rhetorics of Mental Disability and Academic Life*. Michigan: University of Michigan Press.

Reaume, Geoffrey. 2009. *Remembrance of Patients Past: Patient Life at the Toronto Hospital for the Insane, 1870–1940*. Toronto, ON: University of Toronto Press.

Scott, Joan. 1999. *Gender and the Politics of History*. New York: Columbia University Press.

Sherman, Carl. 2002. "SSRIs Are Associated with Mild Cognitive Impairment." *Clinical Psychiatry News*. Accessed June 18, 2011. http://findarticles.com/p/articles/mi_hb4345/is_4_30/ai_n28912964/

Starson v. Swayze. 2003. 1 S.C.R. 722, 2003 SCC 32.

The Senate Standing Committee on Social Affairs, Science and Technology. 2006. "Out of the Shadows at Last: Transforming Mental Health, Mental Illness and Addiction

Services in Canada." Accessed June 27, 2011. http://www.parl.gc.ca/Content/SEN/Committee/391/SOCI/rep/rep02may06part1-e.htm

Titchkosky, Tanya, and Katie Aubrecht. 2009. "The Power of Anguish: Re-mapping Mental Diversity with an Anti-Colonial Compass." In *Breaching the Colonial Contract: Anti-Colonialism in the US and Canada*, edited by Arlo Kempf, 179–201. New York: Springer Press.

Trask, Michael. 2003. *Cruising Modernism: Class and Sexuality in American Literature and Social Thought*. New York: Cornell University Press.

Trueman, Shelly. 2003. "Community Treatment Orders and Nova Scotia – The Least Restrictive Alternative?" *Health Law Journal* 11: 1–33.

Voronka, Jijian. 2008. "Re/Moving Forward?: Spacing Mad Degeneracy at the Queen Street Site." *Resources for Feminist Research* 33(1/2). Accessed June 12, 2011. http://findarticles.com/p/articles/mi_hb6545/is_1–2_33/ai_n31524744/?tag=content;col1

———. 2003. "The Race to Space Madness: Making Respectability through Mad Sites in Ontario." MA thesis, Ontario Institute for Studies in Education, University of Toronto.

Wane, Njoki. 2008. "Mapping the Field of Indigenous Knowledges in Anti-Colonial Discourse: A Transformative Journey in Education." *Race, Ethnicity and Education* 11(2): 183–197.

Watters, Ethan. 2010. *Crazy Like Us: The Globalization of the American Psyche*. New York: Free Press.

Wendell, Susan. 1989. "Toward a Feminist Theory of Disability." *Hypatia* 4(2): 104–124.

Whitaker, Robert. 2010. *Anatomy of an Epidemic: Magic Bullets, Psychiatric Drugs, and an Astonishing Rise in Mental Illness in America*. New York: Crown.

———. 2001. *Mad in America: Bad Science, Bad Medicine, and the Enduring Mistreatment of the Mentally Ill*. New York: Basic Books.

Zola, Irving Kenneth. 1978. "Healthism and Disabling Medicalization." In *Disabling Professions*, edited by Ivan Illich, Irving K. Zola, John McKnight, Jonathan Caplan, and Harley Shaiken, 41–67. Boston, MA: Marion Boyars

11

Racing Madness: The Terrorizing Madness of the Post-9/11 Terrorist Body

Shaista Patel

Introduction

In this chapter, I explore several key questions: What does the circulation of the figure of the "mad Muslim terrorist" do for secular-liberal Western democracies and their subjects? What needs to be in place for this figure to emerge in particular ways post-9/11? What kind of political rationalities are mobilized to legitimize extra-juridical incarceration of these "mad Muslim terrorists"? How does racial logic intersect with popular psy discourse in the emergence and circulation of the figure of the "mad Muslim terrorist"? I explore these questions in relation to a newspaper article entitled *Insanity and Terrorism* by Stewart Bell (2004) in the *National Post*, a nationally distributed right-leaning newspaper in Canada with a daily readership of 1.3 million, including online posts (National Post Staff 2012). Bell is an award-winning, popular Canadian journalist and senior reporter for the *National Post* where he regularly contributes columns on terrorism. His last two books dealt with terrorism in Canada, and his articles on terrorism have appeared in several magazines across the country. He is hailed as one of Canada's "foremost reporters on terrorism." A quick examination of his major publications reveals the racist "Canada as a safe haven for terrorists" logic that has been mobilized to legitimize the draconian anti-terrorism (read anti-Muslim) legislation and security regime post-9/11 (Patel 2012). Therefore, while I am investigating just one of Bell's articles, I want to emphasize that the discourse of the "mad Muslim terrorist" is not unique to this article, but offers an opening for studying complex questions about how the resistance and political movement of bodies produced at the nexus of race/religion and madness become recognizable figures of danger in our current geopolitical context.[1]

In addition, I have chosen a newspaper article for investigating the social organization of terrorism and madness for two reasons: First, newspaper articles are insidiously powerful texts in that they are ordinary and can be found anywhere—the doorstep, the convenience store, the street, the subway station, the bus—and they are accessible to a significant segment of the population. We, ordinary people, actively participate in forming "news" as the "truth" of our society by discussing news stories as "facts," as the "reality" of our world and the state of our being. News media is about power, and that power is not restricted to its influence on audiences. As Teun van Dijk (1995) argues, the power of news media is consistent with the "broader framework of the social, cultural, political, or economic power structures of society" (9). Second, I believe that reading is an important political act of meaning making and (potentially) disrupting ordinary truths about others and ourselves. In her book *Reading and Writing Disability Differently*, Tanya Titchkosky (2007) encourages us to attend to our reading, to "read our reading" in order to understand our encounter with a text and to see what meanings emerge between the nexus of words and our act of reading.

Reading is an identity-forming meeting where both the text and we the readers are ascribed certain meanings and responsibilities. It is through encountering others that we begin to understand ourselves and the world we inhabit in specific ways. The meanings formed through these encounters are within the limits of the cultural and political imaginaries within which we live. However, reading is an act through which we may re/produce or disrupt the systems of order that have given us a sense of ourselves and of the others. Our reading of texts is mediated through various categories of culture that we tend to see as natural or universal, and it allows us to question these categories.

The words "mad," "crazy," and "insane"—not to mention the more specific terms such as "psychotic," "anxious," "neurotic, " and "depressed"—are common parts of our vocabulary today, both in reference to those who have been psychiatrized and in reference to those who have not. Erick Fabris (2011) discusses how discourses of madness have become a regular part of our everyday conversation, and how it "alludes to ideas well outside the psychiatric or psychological categories, a kind of arcane of strangeness" (28). We invoke madness in all sorts of social situations, such as madness-as-lack, absurdity, suffering of some sort, illness, death, disorientation, failure, risk, violence, excitement, to name just a few such occasions (Fabris 2011).

What is it about the ways in which madness has been invoked that makes it commonsense to us, the normalized subjects, and what image of the person occupying this category occupies "our" imagination? I do not exhaust all that could possibly be said about the category of mad as deployed in the newspaper article. Rather, I discuss the links between race/religion, madness, and terrorism discourses with the particular aim of investigating what the label "mad" is doing to readers' sensibilities regarding the political actions of racialized others, specifically those deemed as "mad Muslim terrorists." As I argue later, bodies are produced at the nexus of race/religion and madness through violence, and marked for the violence of incarceration and, eventually, death. The next section of this chapter presents the framework within which I later examine Bell's article. I discuss how Orientalist and racist narratives of Muslim bodies facilitate the transition of the raging Muslim into "mad Muslim terrorist" who threatens the white social order, and therefore must be incarcerated or eliminated. Having set the theoretical framework, I then examine Bell's article to argue that making resistance movements of Muslims into their madness and terrorism is necessary for refusing to engage with them on an ethical, political, and humane level.

Raging Mad Muslims

Race and disability have worked closely in the extermination of millions seen as bearing human otherness. According to Zygmunt Bauman, "racism proclaims that certain blemishes of a certain category of people cannot be removed or rectified—that they remain *beyond* the boundaries of reforming practices, and will do so forever" (quoted in Snyder and Mitchell 2006, 110, emphasis added). Such positioning beyond the boundaries of reforming practices places racialized Others beyond the category of the human, and into the realm of subhuman and animal-like creatures. Snyder and Mitchell (2006) suggest that race and disability are a mutual project of human exclusion legitimized through scientific rationales of what constitutes a perfect human body. The authors are careful to point out that their goal is not to set up a comparison between the extent and kind of violence done to racialized bodies versus disabled bodies. While these categories have never been mutually exclusive, Snyder and Mitchell (2006) want us to acknowledge the fact that "our current theories of racial eugenics exclusively reference 'race' as the social locus ascribed insufficiency, while leaving disability as the default category of 'real' human incapacity" (111). An analysis of how disability and race work together need to unsettle the seemingly ordinary and prevalent understanding of bodies marked by race and disability.[2] The figure of the so-called "mad Muslim terrorist" needs to be carefully placed at the intersection of race/religion and psy discourses in order to understand how it is constructed and mobilized.

The fascination of racist and Orientalist writing with explaining the "Muslim mind" has a long history. The quest for Orientalist knowledge about the psyche of the Muslim became a career for Orientalist scholars during the nineteenth century, and is part of legacy of the official and ordinary racist and Orientalist discourses of the West.[3] Orientalism, as Edward Said (1994) explains, "is a style of thought based upon an ontological and epistemological distinction made between 'the Orient' and (most of the time) 'the Occident'" (2).[4] This distinction is framed in Cartesian dualisms of the civilizational and racial superiority of the West versus the inferiority and barbarity of the East, from where Muslims are imagined to come (regardless of our hundreds of years of presence in the West and the Islamic influence on European Christendom, especially in the move from the middle ages to the modern period).[5]

Drawing upon nineteenth century discourses of racist scientific categorizations of the Self and Other, the West constructed Muslims into a distinct race, which allowed the Orientalists to make essentialist statements about the way Muslims necessarily "think and behave." The irrationality of Muslims remains as a persistent discourse in any and all discussions about them in mainstream Western media, and can be seen in racist talk of the notorious key figure in modern day Orientalist thought, such as Bernard Lewis. In the *Atlantic Monthly*, Lewis (1990) wrote an article entitled "The Roots of Muslim Rage," in which he states:

> There is something in the religious culture of Islam which inspired, in even the humblest peasant or peddler, a dignity and a courtesy toward others never exceeded and rarely equalled in other civilizations. And yet, in moments of upheaval and disruption, when the deeper passions are stirred, this dignity and courtesy toward others can give way to an explosive mixture of rage and hatred which impels even the government of an ancient and civilized country—even the spokesman of a great spiritual and ethical religion—to espouse kidnapping and assassination, and try to find, in the life of their Prophet, approval and indeed precedent for such actions. (5)

This strange (but familiar) caricaturing of Muslims is an example of everyday racist and Orientalist discourses about their barbarity. The wild, untamable Muslim, who is solely defined by his passion rather than his politics, and whose mindset is so evil and so irrational that people of the civilized white West cannot understand it, has been the focus of all Western discourses about Muslims since the nineteenth century. The psychologizing discourse of the Muslim mind turns political actions into their emotions, their instability (of character), and their "passion," which is constructed as apolitical and a sign of their antimodernity (as opposed to the rational, civilized, and modern white Westerner). Lewis(1990) easily dismisses political motives and actions of Muslims as being about their emotions only. He gives no context to how those "deeper passions are stirred" by draconian foreign policies and invasions of Muslim countries and resources. The childlike Muslim might burst into an "explosive mixture of rage and hatred" at apparently some "upheaval and disruption," presumably of their own doing. This leaves no room to consider the historical and political context of the violence of the neocolonial and imperial policies of Western governments. These have colonized Muslims and their lands for ages and continue in the neocolonial and imperial invasion on the sovereignty of Muslim nation-states, lands, and bodies. Muslims' "rage and hatred" are seemingly inspired from their Prophet's seventh century teachings as if they have no political analysis of the contemporary anti-Muslim world order. When it becomes about religion, continuing war against Muslims becomes about Western obligations of secularity and ongoing struggles for maintaining (bloodthirsty and racist) democracy.

Muslim groups and governments around the world have highly sophisticated and diverse means of resisting the continuing encroachment upon their territories, bodies and integrity, but they remain framed as angry, uncivilized crowds far from the edges of Western civilization. Emotions, substituted for sophisticated political motives, can never enter Western juridical and public realm. A Muslim is such an antimodern madman, so outside the realm of (Western notions of) rationality that we (the civilized Europeans) can never know him, but clearly recognize him as not being part of the West.[6] However, this discourse of the madness of the racialized Other is not unique to Muslims only. In his study of the construction of Blacks and Jews as mad bodies, Sander Gilman (1985) discusses how both Blackness and Jewishness became associated with innate madness. White plantation owners held the madness of the black slave's body, rather than the social institution of slavery in the antebellum South, as the source of their anxiety and fear (Gilman 1985). Black people, it was believed, had a list of diseases particular to them and these diseases simply predisposed them to madness. As Dorothy Roberts (2011) notes, "schizophrenia became a metaphor for any black dissatisfaction with racial inequality" (91). Similarly, in *The Protest Psychosis*, Jonathan Metzl (2009) discusses how schizophrenia became primarily a Black disease during the 1960s civil rights movement. In the late 1960s when the second edition of the *Diagnostic and Statistical Manual of Mental Disorders* (DSM-II) was released, mental illnesses, and the diagnosis criteria of schizophrenia in particular, reflected the cultural and race tensions of racially segregated America, where Blacks were rising against the state and white citizens (Metzl 2009). Schizophrenia, a disease that was until the 1950s associated primarily with the "neurosis" of middleclass white women, was now being described using male pronouns and came to stand in for Black (hyper) masculinity itself. Two New York psychiatrists Walter Bromberg and Franck Simon described schizophrenia as "protest psychosis, a condition in which the rhetoric of the Black Power movement drove 'Negro men' to insanity" (Metzl 2009, 100). They made it clear that this connection was not metaphorical or allegorical, but that participation in Black Power movement actually *caused* the list of symptoms associated with schizophrenia. As Metzl (2009) explains, the diagnosis of "masculinized black anger and unrest" was necessary not because it was harmful to the patient, but because it threatened the white racial order of the doctors, and by extension, the White civilization (102). The so-called hostility and anti-White delusions of Black men were the consequences of joining civil rights protests, rather than resulting from racial oppression of Blacks by white-dominated national and global reality. Similarly, Jews were seen as "especially prone to hysteria and neurasthenia" (Gilman 1985, 154). Their demand for political equality was seen as the very proof of their psychopathology. While the political conditions underpinning the construction of the slave body, the Black body during the civil rights era and the body of the Jew were different, and the conditions of violence were different and were mobilized for different end goals, in both cases it was their status outside of Western civilization and threat to the white racial social order that was held as a cause of their mental illnesses.

While white people are rational and have complex thinking process and sophisticated lives and aspirations, those who are not part of the white race are locked outside the aspirational possibility of humanity, a space where violence is carried out on their bodies with impunity. What is ironic is that it was the resistance of Jews and Blacks to the violence done to them that came to be seen as a symptom of disease. They could not be seen as modern political beings in a world order organized along the lines of white supremacy. While those seen as pitiable move into the category of premodern very fluidly, Muslims consistently figure in the category of the antimodern premodern. When politics are dismissed as culture, when reactions to racist and xenophobic state and foreign policies are rejected as the antimodern culture of the other and as their innate desire destruction of the "values" of the West, there is no space for engaging with politics of the other in an ethical way. The question then becomes about the "Islamic mindset" or "terrorist mindset" rather than about diverse Muslim politics. Echoing how white society explained the resistance of slaves and Jews as a symptom of disease, the politics of Muslims engaged in various resistance movements becomes about an antimodern and dangerous "Islamic mindset."

The work which racial difference does in the construction of "terrorist" Muslim men, versus the construction of the likes of Timothy McVeigh, Anders Breivik, and Wade Page, to name just a few white men charged with terrorism, is significant.[7] While the treatment meted out to Muslim and white terrorists under law might not be different, and while both white terrorists and Muslim terrorists are psychologized, the difference is that while the latter are seen as always mad and guilty as a people, the former do not stand in for all white people or Western civilization itself. While *all* Muslim men remain psychologized as mad, with the potential to burst into an "explosive mixture of rage and hatred" at any time, as Lewis (1990) argues, white terrorists remain as individual white men who committed heinous "senseless violence" because they were not "sound of mind." And while they are considered dangerous, they are still seen as part of the West, even if as its excess, or an aberration. In cases of white terrorists, the focus of the media coverage is on their alleged individualized mental illness, whereas in case of Muslim terrorists, their alleged mental illness is always connected to the religious ideology of Islam and some archaic seventh century teachings of Islam, which allows the Orientalist/

Western subject to make overgeneralized, sweeping assertions about "that population" of Muslims. Especially now, as Bell (2004) asserts, psychologists have the much-awaited "rare chance to collect psychological data on a large pool of subjects and to develop a profile of what makes them [Muslim terrorists] tick."

Psychologizing the perpetrator in both cases masks the asymmetrical historical and contemporary power differentials within which some lives are deemed more worthy than others. Making these men into irrational mad men makes their actions into an aberration, rather than allowing the public to engage with social inequalities marking the current geopolitical order. For instance, in the case of Anders Breivik, the trial and its media coverage focused almost exclusively on his in/sanity, rather than on the political context within which he wrote his 1,500 page hate manifesto against Muslims and killed innocent people, even while he continued to argue that he was perfectly sane and that his actions were necessary to stop the "Islamisation" of Norway and the rest of Europe. As Aslak Sira Myhre (2012), astutely points out in his article, *Anders Breivik Verdict: Now Norway Must Ask How It Created a Killer*, "The question is not who Breivik is, but why he became a rightwing extremist, an anti-feminist, anti-Marxist and a racist" (par. 4). Considering this question would compel an analysis of white supremacist and Islamophobic politics of ordinary Norwegians and of other Europeans, something which needs to be avoided at all costs for racist and imperialist foreign policies and invasions of Muslim countries by Western governments to continue. It was much easier to dismiss Breivik as a schizophrenic outcast even by the prosecutors of the case, rather than to critically engage with the social and political context within which Breivik was not alone in his ideologies, even if he was alone in his actions. In contrast, the so-called terrorism of Muslim men has a unique racial status where Islam itself comes to stand in for the "race" of all Muslims who need to be evicted from Western nation-states or killed in their own countries (something which "coincidentally" Breivik also argued in his hate manifesto).

It is within this Orientalist/colonial and racialized framework that Bell's (2004) article mentioned at the outset of this paper must be considered. The news article's narrative of the raging-without-reason-Muslim begins with the question, "Who becomes a terrorist and why?" Rather than beginning with an examination of political conditions in the so-called regions of "economic and political instability" (RB1), the prominent narrative is one of racializing the terrorist suspects through the trope of madness. Bell (2004) quotes Colonel Larry James, chief psychologist at the Walter Reed Army Medical Center in Washington, DC, who in a talk to Ontario psychologists in Toronto stated, "It is surprising the number of Axis I psychological disorders we have among *that population*" (par. 7, emphasis added). Whereas "that population" of terrorists is never named as Muslim, the article clearly states that the "research" was conducted "on the hundreds of terrorists captured since Sept. 11, 2001," leaving no doubt in the reader's mind about who constitutes that "terrorist" population. The next sentence in the article defines in brackets what those "Axis I psychological disorders" are according to the "psychologists' bible." "Depression, schizophrenia and phobias" all constitute mental illness and play a role in the making of terrorist, according to Col. James. Naming these mental illnesses enables readers to understand the both familiar and foreign mindset of the Muslim "terrorist," in part because the Orientalist history of their so-called maddening rage is already well in place by the likes of Bernard Lewis and hundreds of Orientalists before and after him, and the wide acceptance of these discourses in the West.

The fact that this so-called research is carried out on bodies of the incarcerated without any ethical overview is not challenged or even considered, once labels such as "mentally ill" and "terrorist" are attached to the already subhuman Muslim bodies of the incarcerated. In fact, what is labeled as "research" is simply a part of covering up illegal and inhumane experimentation on prisoners, in addition to the crimes of torture post-9/11, as the *Experiments in Torture* report released by the Physicians for Human Rights (2010) reveals. The report details how doctors, psychologists, and other professionals monitored the effects of sleep deprivation, "waterboarding" (more appropriately known as mock drowning), and other so-called enhanced interrogation techniques on prisoners under CIA interrogation in order to collect information on the "physical and psychological impact of the CIA's application of the 'enhanced' interrogation techniques, which previously had been limited mostly to data from experiments using US military volunteers under very limited, simulated conditions of torture" (Physicians for Human Rights 2010, 3). The history of unethical "experiments" conducted on bodies of those incarcerated is dark and long.

The racialized and the disabled, especially when incarcerated in mental asylums, hospitals, or prisons, constitute the excess of society, those nonhuman subjects whose lives are not worth grieving over in their pain and even in their deaths. In fact, their pain and death are sometimes seen as their redemption and as necessary for our lives. For instance, in his research on scientific experimentation on Canadian inmates from 1955–1975, Geraint B. Osborne (2006) states that researchers who were conducting these unethical studies on the inmates often argued that prisoners actually felt like a part of society through their participation in something useful for public service. In his 1963 memo, the director of medical services for the federal penitentiary services, Dr. Gendreau, noted that participating in these studies provided inmates,

> An opportunity to identify themselves with society, whose laws they have violated. It gives participating inmates a feeling of self-respect. It builds up the self-esteem of those who have a low opinion of themselves; they know they can become useful to millions of people. (Osborne 2006, 298)

This is just one of the examples of the long history of coercing the bodies of incarcerated for these dangerous medical and pharmaceutical experiments and, of course, is not unique to Canada. The Holocaust in Europe is full of examples where German physicians used those incarcerated and marked for death as guinea pigs for all sorts of experimentations. Robert Whitaker (2002) outlines some such examples in his book where he states that the Jews and other prisoners killed were considered inferior beings, and the knowledge gained from their deaths were used to save important lives, such as those of the German pilots and other superior Germans. And the Nuremberg Code was barely in place when American psychiatrists such as Paul Hoch began giving LSD and other untested medicines to those diagnosed with schizophrenia, without informing their patients of the effects of these drugs (Whitaker 2002). As Snyder and Mitchell (2006) aptly argue, "*the exhaustion of disabled research subjects comes by way of our historical investment in believing that disability makes a person available for excessive experimentation and bureaucratic oversight*" (28, emphasis in original). Race and disability work together in complex ways to make some lives disposable, allowing various medical experiments to be carried out on bodies of the incarcerated, and so that the West at large will accept this with little critical interrogation of the ethical underpinnings of such experiments.

The discourse of the uniqueness of the terrorist mind and body (of color) haunts Bell's article and the broader discourse about terrorism in the West. Col. James, the expert Bell (2004) continues to refer to, states: "We need a new way of conceptualizing these men and women, because the categories we have, they don't fit neatly into" (par. 15). This basically comes down to the Orientalist and racist belief that the "terrorist mindset" is so foreign that we (Westerners) cannot understand it with the categories of analysis we have available. The rationale guiding the statement is also that once we know this seemingly homogenous "terrorist mindset" [of Muslims], we will be in a better position to win against them. The so-called terrorism of these Muslim bodies is so foreign to us Western subjects that we need an entirely different way of looking at it.[8] This belief, in fact, has generated an entire field of academic and policy studies known as "terrorism studies." The psyche of the terrorist is the "privileged site of investigation" here, as Amit Rai (2004) astutely notes in his study of the field of terrorism studies. He explains:

> A very particular psyche undergirds such theories: a homogeneous, non-conscious, non-rational, non-intentional and uniformly violent field of forces. The lines that crisscross this field are themselves given through discourses of, for instance, normative heterosexual kinship – white mythologies such as 'inconsistent mothering' (and hence the bad family structure apparently common in the East) are presented as psychological compulsions that effectively determine and fix the mind of the terrorist. (545)

This "personality defect model" for understanding the terrorist mindset can be illustrated through statements in Bell's article about just who exactly these terrorists are. As Col. James states in the newspaper article, "The folks that are looking for a sense of belongingness, family outcasts...This person tends to be the black sheep of the family and really doesn't connect well with the rest of the family" (Bell 2004, par. 27). James goes on to describe how Osama Bin Laden was the "family outcast," which led him to do what he did. He then differentiates between upper class or privileged family outcasts versus poor terrorists, who are tired of the daily grind and are the more "sociopathic-type characters." Negative experiences of childhood facilitate the progression of one into a terrorist, and racism and Islamophobia do the work of translating this individualistic psychologizing into a cultural characteristic for these psychologists.

Another common aspect of terrorists according to studies on terrorism examined by Rai (2004) is the notion of failed heterosexuality. The terrorist is constructed as sexually frustrated so that the Orientalist myth of sexually frustrated Muslim men being promised the heavenly reward of virgins if they are martyred in *jihad* is given as an explanation of the motives of those who are constructed as terrorists in the West. Bell's expert on terrorism, Col. James, affirms this stereotype when he explains that often terrorists are abducted at a young age and sexually abused by their commanders at terrorist camps. This sexual abuse somehow leads to their sexual frustrations (such as having had [forced] homosexual encounters, not feeling manly enough, not having easy access to women), which, in turn, leads them to blow themselves and others up. All these explanations depoliticize complex social, political, economic, and historical struggles into "Western psychic models rooted in the bourgeois heterosexual family and its dynamics" (Rai 2004, 547).

For Muslim bodies, their religious affiliation is itself taken as a sign of mental disorder. A Muslim can never be rational unless half-rescued by the civility of the West. As Lewis (1990) explains, "there is something in the religious culture of Islam" itself that drives the Muslims to heights of illogic and passion, and extends it to a metaphysical level where the rational, secular Western subject refuses to go (and is not expected to go). A resonant historical example comes from David Edwards' (1989) examination of the construction of the "mad mullah" (the mad Islamic leader) in colonial encounters between the British and Indian Muslims in uprisings against the British rule in 1897. In the summer of 1897, there were anti-British uprisings led by a religious mendicant known as the "mad fakir" or "mad mullah" (Edwards 1989, 652). Winston Churchill, who was posted in that part of India at the time, played on all the common stereotypes of this anticolonial resister and his forces, to paint them as "savage tribesmen possessed by an extraordinary fervor" (Edwards 1989, 653). Stories that were common about the "mad mullah" and his force were given a twist by Churchill to make them sound completely barbaric and hostile to (Western) civilization, and thus a threat to the colonial order. Instead of understanding the mullah's actions as political, British rage and ridicule dismissed his actions as mere acts of savagery of a mad man and his uncivilized force. Hence, there could be no political engagement with them. The stories about the "mad mullah" performing miracles became the basis of Churchill's polemical repudiation of the anticolonial visionary as "evidence of the fanatical nature of the local people" who followed the mullah in resistance against the British power. Edwards (1989) argues that "Establishing the enemy as fanatical denies him moral status and affords those whose moral superiority is thus affirmed a free hand in defending their interests" (655). In Bell's article, the discourse of miracles as irrational is replaced by the discourse of their [Muslims] irrational hatred toward us [Western subjects] and our values. Bell (2004) mentions a debate that psychologists are apparently engaged in, about whether or not "mental illness" is a factor in terrorism, but he gives the impression that hatred and mental illness are two key factors in manufacturing Muslim terrorists. And while Col. James agrees that economic factors play a role in who becomes a terrorist, there is still no space to engage with political rationales of these so-called terrorists, for those economically marginalized are rendered "sociopathic-type characters." Bell ends with a short statement on how these terrorists are "divorced from reality," rather than fighting and resisting the long legacy of racial and colonial violence that generations of them have lived through as a result of colonialism and imperialism. He quotes a videotaped message, apparently coming from a bomber responsible for the Madrid attacks, as saying, "You love life and we love death" (Bell 2004, par. 39). He then ends with this question to his readers: "Are these the words of sane men?" The rhetorical answer is no, of course, so that we are never invited to consider any rational or strategic motives behind the violence. And what makes this even more shocking, in terms of its taken-for-grantedness is that the videotaped message begins with a statement of political rationalization for the attacks: "This is a response to the crimes that you have caused in the world and specifically in Iraq and in Afghanistan" (Bell 2004, par. 38). How is it that Bell can cite this without feeling the need to even address it? The question, "Are these the words of sane men?" seems to render any kind of direct engagement with the stated political objectives of the bombings absolutely unnecessary. The rhetoric of their maddening barbarism versus our sane civility has been the basis of colonialism and remains so for ongoing wars of the Empire.

The deviant bodies must be incarcerated and marked for death, for our freedom and security.

As I have noted earlier, Bell (2004) also mentions a study that argues that terrorists are not insane. This too is a common component of the field of terrorism studies. But all these studies that hinge upon the sanity or insanity of the "terrorist" foreclose possibilities of engaging with actions such as suicide bombing in a political manner or considering them acts of resistance. While the Empire maintains its innocence and civility while standing on the blood and bodies of millions of marginalized people at home and around the world, the terrorists or suicide bombers can never be afforded any integrity as political actors. The "mad man" in our culture has already been rejected as an irrational man whose actions are not worth taking seriously. These links between terrorism and madness not only make the unknown an extension of the known but also depoliticize the constructions of madness and terrorism by "removing a political phenomenon [such as terrorism] from comprehension of its historical emergence and from a recognition of the powers that produce and contour it" (Brown 2006, 15).

As another illustration of this pervasive depoliticization, Alison Howell (2007) analyzes how suicide attempts of those incarcerated at Guantanamo Bay are constructed as a proof of their being "mad." She argues that while the Bush Administration had taken these attempts at committing suicide as the story of uncivilized and barbaric men who are not only suicidal but also homicidal, the oppositional discourse of the human rights organizations, leftist press and public have also worked at pathologizing the psyches of the detainees by labeling them as victims of torture and in fact demanding better psychiatric care for them. Thus, while the arguments put forth by the humanitarian agencies are different from that of the Bush Government, both operate within the same "regime of truth" in which the category of mad is reified as natural and (better) psychiatric treatment is the only viable solution to the given "problem" (Foucault and Gordon 1980). These two psychiatric/psychological discourses (which may be oppositional relative to one another) both render the detainees as passive. An alternative discourse, rather than an oppositional discourse playing with same categories, would allow us to consider the sociopolitical conditions at play that make American foreign policies and dehumanizing prison conditions possible in the first place. An alternative discourse might allow us to consider those incarcerated as human beings and not just as either terrorists or victims. Howell (2007) explains that although most of the detainees have gone on hunger strikes or attempted suicide during the period of their incarceration, these acts of resistance have been constructed by human rights organizations such as Amnesty International as proof of their psychological deterioration and "mental illness." She speculates, "representing the detainees as agents raises questions about what such people would do with their agency" (Howell 2007, 39). "Granting" agency to these men allows for their inclusion into the ranks of human, something which must be denied to these bodies in order to continue their incarceration.

The Agency of the Incarcerated

Acts of resistance by the incarcerated, such as their participation in prolonged hunger strikes which Howell (2007) discusses, have received little attention by the public, "perhaps because they highlight the agency of the detainees and fail to conform with the image of the detainees as passive victims, or because they seem to corroborate the military's image of the detainees as 'uncooperative' and 'manipulative'" (40). Agency when defined within a secular liberal Western imaginary can be afforded to only the individual who is decontextualized from history. It is afforded to individuals who seem to have no community or other affiliations, are not limited by the structures of the society, and can just pull himself up by his bootstraps and achieve whatever it is that he set out to do. Agency in such a framework can only be performed within a binary opposition between subordination and resistance. Saba Mahmood (2005), in contrast, conceptualizes agency as "capacity for action that specific relations of *subordination* create and enable" (18). Agency is produced through operations of power, rather than being a natural capacity for action that subjects are born with, or something that lives within subjects. Therefore, in drawing attention to agency of the incarcerated, I am not celebrating agency in a liberal individualistic manner where we assume that all human beings can change their lives if they have the will to do so. An analysis of the restraining conditions and possibilities for action these conditions create is important. And so, as Howell (2007) mentions, sometimes detainees themselves frame their concerns in terms of psy discourses by talking about how they have been psychologically affected by the incarceration and by the treatment of their fellow inmates. This is not simply a case of internalization of their diagnosis by the army of psychologists and interrogators working on them. As Metzl (2009) argues, W. E. B. Du Bois described and embraced the "double consciousness" of African Americans, and the discourse of their schizophrenia was celebrated by other Black intellectuals of the civil rights era because "they believed that it helped African Americans reject the pathology that resided not in the black psyche, but in the materialistic white civilization in which it was forced to reside" (126). If Blacks were indeed schizophrenic, argued Black intellectuals, the cause of their mental illness was the racist white society that continued to deny them their humanity. While it is debatable whether resistance through cooptation of black schizophrenia was a successful resistance strategy, what is important to note is that our resistance is carved out from within the set of discourses and practices that are accessible to us.

The deployment of psy discourses by the incarcerated men in Howell's study might be a strategic move, a way to best explain their human condition to the public at large. And while it could be an indication of the pervasiveness and, to some degree, an internalization of Western discourses about our bodies, either way the deployment of psy discourses by the detainees is an act of agency, of negotiating their humanity within the relations of violence that have marked them as terrorist and mad. These practices of reclaiming a label or condition by the detainees, or the suicide attempts of some prisoners as mentioned by Howell (2007), are themselves political interventions, something with which liberal secular understandings of agency would not be able to engage. Thinking about suicide committed under certain conditions as having moral and political consequences, for example, is necessary if we are to seriously and ethically engage with historical and political relations of power and violence. Suicide is understood as laying bare one's psychological (and sometimes bodily) pain, which, in the dominant secular discourses of liberalism, is always taken as a failing, a weakness, passive, and illogical. As Talal Asad (2003) notes, "pain is...often regarded as inimical to reason...[and] thought of as a human condition that the secular must eliminate universally" (67). When pain becomes the antithesis of reason itself, something that must be "eliminate[d] universally," pain is associated with a body *gone wrong*. Pain is rendered the signature of an irrational body that is no longer in control of the rational mind and is thus unable to exercise agency. It is assumed that pain, as an emotion, diminishes one's capacity for reason (moral judgment), reducing one's self-ownership of his or her body and faculties of reason. Pain reminds us of the materiality and limitations of our bodies. Hence, in secular-liberal theorizing of the body, pain is something negative, something that needs to be eliminated and is seen as a sign of weakness, rather than as a condition that allows us to relate to the world around us in more humane ways. In representations of the suicide attempts of the detainees at Guantanamo Bay, or in the so-called insane terrorists in Bell's article, any understanding of how those labeled "fanatic," "mad," or "insane" exercise their agency as political actors, shaped by and actively navigating local and global power relations as they do so, are eclipsed by their psychological failure. Once the label "mentally ill" is attached to incarcerated Muslim bodies through "research," their pain, their agency, and their histories all become meaningless—or, perhaps, they take on a specified meaning that we already know to be ultimately meaningless. The word "insane" is sufficient to conjure up an image of a person who is a danger, and who is therefore in need of containment. It also is an image of a person with nothing useful to offer society and who therefore can be contained without any resultant social loss. The image that arises at the nexus of the categories of "terrorist" and "insane" is of an "abnormal" body and mind that has no future, and no possibility of going anywhere, and is bent upon destroying us out of pure hatred.[9] The "mad Muslim terrorist" is destined to be incarcerated, regulated, tortured, and kept away from the public for our security and order.

In the case of suicide bombers and others labeled as "terrorists," especially in the post-9/11 geopolitical context, race and psychopathology make the liberal-secular Western subject refuse an engagement with the action of these "madmen." But in his analysis of "suicide bombing," Asad (2007) notes that perhaps the "suicide bomber" is not so exceptional after all:

> The right of liberal democratic states to defend themselves with nuclear weapons – and this seems to be accepted by the international community – is in effect an affirmation that the suicidal war can be legitimate. This leads me to the thought that the suicide bomber belongs in an important sense to a modern Western tradition of armed conflict for the defense of a free political community: To save the nation (or to found its state) in confronting a dangerous enemy, it may be necessary to act without being bound by ordinary moral constraints. (63)

This argument invites Western subjects to rethink the common assumptions about the body of the suicide bomber, and of the "mad Muslim terrorist" by extension. Those who believe that nuclear war was and could again be justified surely imagine that this justification lies in the political benefits. Like the political calculations to make, keep, and use nuclear weapons, suicide bombing and other acts of terrorism by those construed as Muslim terrorists are, likewise, not engaged because those responsible are stuck in some archaic interpretation of Islam, or because they are threatened by modernity, or because they are psychopaths. These people have chosen the same means of violence to affirm their politics as Western nation-states have mobilized from their very conception. Violence is at the very heart of modern liberal polities. It is histories of Orientalism and racism, then, that renders those who resist, and who kill in the name of their liberation, as mad, as insane, as terrorists, and as apolitical.

Asad (2007) further argues that "in the suicide bomber's act, perhaps what horrifies is not just dying and killing (or killing by dying) but the violent appearance of something that is normally disregarded in secular modernity: the limitless pursuit of freedom, the illusion of an uncoereced interiority that can withstand the force of institutional disciplines" (91). In response to horror, it is only when we begin to distance ourselves from the moment of horror that we begin to translate the affective experience of horror into sense-making. But Western subjects constituted through the difference between the self and the Other often remain stuck in that moment of awe and horror in response to the actions of the Other, especially when those Others are deemed "insane," "mad," and "barbaric." The mad bomber's "horrific" actions are just mad, instead of actions that require us to evaluate *our* complicity as Americans or other Western nationals in *their* sociopolitical realities. The secular liberal sensibility has to render that which it cannot understand, or does not want to understand, as irrational and mad, and it then incarcerates the "mad" bodies to a lifetime of violence. The refusal to engage with the politics of marginalized bodies maintains our complicity in ongoing relations of domination and subordination.

Conclusion

Situating resistance movements of "mad Muslim terrorists" as legibly human responses to foreign and domestic policies of Western nation-states entertains the possibility of politically and ethically engaging with the actions of these Others. This is in contrast to normative readings in which any resistance, any act of war, and any form of violence that is not approved by Western nation-states is dismissed as the madness of dangerous antimodern and anti-White bodies. The figure of the "mad Muslim terrorist" produced at the intersections of race/religion and madness conjures up an enemy of Western nation-states and White civilization that needs constant incarceration and eventually death for maintaining the white social order. What Bromberg and Simon labelled as the "protest psychosis" of Black civil rights activists in 1968 (Metzl 2009, 100) has become the "jihad psychosis" of incarcerated Muslims and all Muslims, by racial and Orientalist logic post-9/11. This "jihad psychosis" is shaped by cultural, sociopolitical, and institutional factors that make the link between Muslimness and madness a mark of death for Muslims and those who look like Muslims and are incarcerated on allegations of terrorism, which acts as a constant threat against Muslims everywhere in the post-9/11 world order.

Notes

1. See appendix for full text of Bell's article.
2. By "bodies marked by race," I mean all visibly non-White bodies. I understand that whiteness is not definitive, and not all White bodies have access to privileges conferred by whiteness within the neoliberal global world order. However, seemingly non-White bodies occupy a space other than that offered to White people, a space constructed as outside that of full humanity.

3. Neither the West nor the Orient are distinct, clearly demarcated physical spaces, but are conceptualized in relation to each other through relations of power (including history, geography, anthropology, and other discourses), like all categories.
4. Although the term "Orient" has also been used to refer to East Asia or the "Far East," Said is primarily referring to Muslim countries in Africa and Asia.
5. Said (1994) notes that there is a difference between the Franco-British involvement in the Orient versus that of the American post World War II. By Orient, he explains that he means "India and the Bible lands" (4) at least until the nineteenth century, which for America also included the Far East. See pp. 1–4 for more details.
6. Sherene Razack (2008) argues, three stereotypical figures have come to represent the "war on terror": the "dangerous" Muslim man, the "imperilled" Muslim woman, and the "civilized" European who must confront the violence of the former and rescue the latter using any and all means possible. These contemporary figures around and through which the narrative of the ongoing war is structured have a long Orientalist history and has been mobilized as the rationale for interventions and encroachment of the West into Muslim lands. Although the Muslim man is always uncivilized, dangerous, and misogynistic, the stereotype of Muslim woman as imperilled is mobilized to legitimize violent attacks of the West on lands and bodies of Muslim men and women. However, both Muslim men and women remain outside the fold of Western civilization (Razack 2008, 5).
7. See Erevelles, this volume, for a similar argument about the racialized discourses and practices surrounding school shootings and zero tolerance school policies.
8. Even when some of the alleged Muslim terrorists are from Western nation-states, they continue to be seen as being from someplace else, and in popular media discourses of today, they are seen as hailing from Pakistan, Afghanistan, or Iraq, even if they have never been to those countries.
9. In saying so, however, I do not mean to assert that there are no alternative readings or counter-hegemonic discourses challenging the dominant production of knowledges. Processes of identification are ongoing, and thus never complete or totalizing. Fissures for challenging norms through readings and other modes of actions always exist as a possibility.

References

Asad, Talal. 2007. *On Suicide Bombing.* New York: Columbia University Press.
———. 2003. *Formations of the Secular: Christianity, Islam, Modernity.* Stanford, CA: Stanford University Press.
Bell, Stewart. 2004. "Insanity and Terrorism." *National Post,* March 27.
Brown, Wendy. 2006. *Regulating Aversion: Tolerance in the Age of Identity and Empire.* Princeton, NJ: Princeton University Press.
Edwards, David. 1989. "Mad Mullahs and Englishmen: Discourse in the Colonial Encounter." *Comparative Studies in Society and History* 31(4): 649–670.
Fabris, Erick. 2011. *Tranquil Prisons: Chemical Incarceration Under Community Treatment Orders.* Toronto, ON: University of Toronto Press.
Foucault, Michel, and Colin Gordon. 1980. *Power / Knowledge: Selected Interviews and Other Writings, 1972–1977.* New York: Pantheon Books.
Gilman, Sander. 1985. *Difference and Pathology: Stereotypes of Sexuality, Race, and Madness.* Ithaca and London: Cornell University Press.
Howell, Alison. 2007. "Victims or Madmen? The Diagnostic Competition Over 'Terrorist' Detainees at Guantánamo Bay." *International Political Sociology* 1: 29–47.

Lewis, Bernard. 1990. "The Roots of Muslim Rage." *Atlantic Monthly*, September, Accessed December 1, 2012. http://www.theatlantic.com/magazine/archive/1990/09/the-roots-of-muslim-rage/304643/

Metzl, Jonathan M. 2009. *The Protest Psychosis: How Schizophrenia Became a Black Disease*. Boston, MA: Beacon Press.

National Post Staff. 2012. "National Post Readership Rising Across Canada: NAD Bank." *National Post*, September 26. Accessed December 1, 2012. http://news.nationalpost.com/2012/09/26/national-post-readership-up-across-canada-nadbank/

Osborne, Geraint, B. 2006. "Scientific Experimentation on Canadian Inmates, 1955 to 1975." *The Howard Journal* 45(3): 284–306.

Patel, Shaista. 2012. "The Anti-Terrorism Act and National Security: Safeguarding the Nation Against Uncivilized Muslims." In *Islam in the Hinterlands: Muslim Cultural Politics in Canada*, edited by Jasmin Zine, 272–298. Vancouver: University of British Columbia Press.

Rai, Amit. 2004. "Of Monsters: Biopower, Terrorism and Excess in Genealogies of Monstrosity," *Cultural Studies* 18(4): 538–570.

Razack, Sherene. 2008. *Casting Out: The Eviction of Muslims from Western Law and Politics*. Toronto: University of Toronto Press.

Roberts, Dorothy. 2011. *Fatal Invention: How Science, Politics, and Big Business Re-Create Race in the Twenty-First Century*. New York and London: The New Press.

Said, Edward. 1994. *Orientalism*. Toronto, ON: Random House of Canada Limited.

Sira Myhre, Aslak. 2012. "Anders Breivik Verdict: Now Norway Must Ask How It Created a Killer." *The Guardian*, August 24. Accessed December 13, 2012. http://www.guardian.co.uk/commentisfree/2012/aug/24/anders-breivik-verdict-norway.

Snyder, Sharon L., and David T. Mitchell. 2006. "The Eugenic Atlantic." In *Cultural Locations of Disability*, 100–129. Chicago and London: University of Chicago Press,

Titchkosky, Tanya. 2007. *Reading and Writing Disability Differently: The Textured Life of Embodiment*. Toronto, ON: University of Toronto Press.

van Dijk, Teun. 1995. "Power and The News Media." In *Political Communication In Action: States, Institutions, Movements, Audiences*, edited by David LPaletz, 9–36. Cresskill: Hampton Press.

Whitaker, Robert. 2002. *Mad in America: Bad Science, Bad Medicine, and the Enduring Mistreatment of the Mentally Ill*. New York: Basic Books.

12

Refugee Camps, Asylum Detention, and the Geopolitics of Transnational Migration: Disability and Its Intersections with Humanitarian Confinement

Mansha Mirza

Introduction

As of 2011 there were 42.5 million people around the world who had been forcibly dislocated from their homes and communities due to persecution or armed conflict (UNHCR 2012). This number subsumes all categories of displaced persons including refugees, asylum seekers, and the internally displaced. (UNHCR 2012).

The phenomena of human displacement trigger sociopolitical responses largely reminiscent of responses to disability. For example, both disability and displacement represent a disruption of "the natural order of things," the social categories that modern societies tend to be grounded in (Douglas 1966). The condition of displacement subverts social categories based on "nation-states," thereby generating anomalies, that is, persons embodying a transitional state—neither belonging to their country of origin nor to the country of asylum (Malkki 1995). Likewise, disability subverts social constructions of "personhood" whereby disabled people are also seen as anomalies, that is, embodying a transitional state—neither "full person" nor "nonperson" (Nicolaisen 1995). Disabled and displaced persons are often construed as "aberrations in need of therapeutic intervention" and become recipients of institutionalized practices targeted at returning them to the natural order of things, either back into the fold of the nation-state or back into the state of normalcy. And until this return to the natural order is achieved, people falling under both conditions may be subjected to long-term confinement. For people with disabilities, these spaces of confinement include (at least historically) mental asylums, treatment centers, and care institutions. For displaced persons, these spaces take the form of refugee camps and asylum detention centers. Though created for the beneficence of the confined population, both types of spaces signify deviance and being out of place.

Despite the above parallels, intersections between disability and displacement have not been sufficiently explored in the academic literature. This chapter explores these intersections primarily through a deconstruction of refugee camps and asylum detention centers as landscapes of long-term exclusion and marginalization. This chapter also traces how disabled people fare in these spaces of humanitarian confinement, and how discourses of disability intersect with the geopolitics of mass human displacement and transnational migration.

Genealogy of Refugee Camps: From Temporary Safe Havens to Enduring Landscapes of Humanitarian Confinement

Refugee camps are circumscribed spaces where masses of displaced persons are offered basic protection and care by the international humanitarian community, the conglomerate of international humanitarian agencies, governmental and nongovernmental organizations, and donor states. Today, camps have become consonant with humanitarian assistance. Yet ironically, the 1951 United Nations Refugee Convention, a legal framework for responding to large-scale human displacement, contains no mention of camps. The Convention's European framers developed it with their equals in mind, Eastern European refugees displaced by World War II. These refugees were envisioned as agents of democracy rather than passive recipients of aid and were expected to imminently integrate into their asylum countries. To suggest that these individuals be housed in temporary circumscribed encampments would have invoked unacceptable comparisons with concentration camps and forced labor camps, which were widely condemned in postwar, *civilized* Europe (Smith 2004).

The idea of housing and assisting displaced persons in camps did not emerge until the postcolonial era when the humanitarian community turned its attention to large-scale human displacements in Asia and Africa (Davies 2007). Confronted with non-European displacement contexts, humanitarian actors such as the Office of the United Nations High Commissioner for Refugees[1] turned for inspiration to development institutes such as the World Bank, with more operational experience in these regions. Noted refugee studies scholar Barbara Harrell-Bond (2000) argues that dominant economic development models of the time were unquestioningly adopted by the UNHCR to guide delivery of humanitarian aid. These models favored placing displaced populations in camps or settlements to facilitate delivery of aid and stimulate income-generating activities, the latter envisioned as a pathway to ease integration into the host country (Harrell-Bond 2000).

Despite the failure of this strategy, the camp-approach took hold as a favored mechanism for providing humanitarian aid to large swaths of displaced persons in an organized manner and on a temporary basis. Early success with the 1971 East Pakistan crises, one of the first non-European interventions launched by the international humanitarian community, further cemented this idea of refugee camps as temporary safe havens (Van Damme 1995). The nearly ten million refugees displaced during the crisis were spread over a large number of small camps and most returned home after ten months to newly independent Bangladesh (Van Damme 1995). However, unlike the East Pakistan crisis, which was temporary, most major crises since then have lasted much longer. Today, more than ten million displaced persons are believed to be living in exile for five years or longer; at least a third of them are estimated to be living in refugee camps mostly dispersed across Africa and Asia (UNHCR 2008; 2011a). Refugee advocates condemn the long-term confinement of displaced persons in camps as "human warehousing" (Smith 2004). Despite widespread criticism, refugee camps continue to proliferate for several reasons.

Humanitarian organizations, donor and host states, and occasionally displaced persons themselves have vested interests in creating and maintaining refugee camps. Sometimes refugee leaders are themselves inclined to keep their compatriots geographically concentrated in camps. Refugees confined within camps in a state of dependence become easy recruits for oppositional militias. Refugee camps also serve as a propaganda tool to pressure the international community to resolve the crisis in favor of exiled political leaders (Smith 2004). Poor and under-resourced host countries where displaced persons first seek refuge also stand to gain from containment of refugees in camps. Existence of camps not only prevents refugees' local integration but also attracts international aid for their care and maintenance (Crisp and Jacobsen 1998; Kibreab 1989). Refugee camps also trigger economic and social development through creation of local jobs and previously nonexistent social and medical services (Hyndman 2000). Sometimes donor governments collude with host governments (who might be potential political allies) and pressure humanitarian organizations to host displaced persons in camps (Morris 2007). Donor governments are also known to urge humanitarian organizations to assist displaced persons closer to their country of origin (Hyndman 2000; Stevens 2006), thereby perpetuating refugee camps. This preference for assisting displaced persons in camps "out there" instead of "over here" is reflected in the fact that only 1 percent of the world refugees are ever resettled in developed donor countries (UNHCR 2011a).[2] The general populace of many developed countries, although willing to donate large sums of money to fund humanitarian aid in camps, often resent the recipients of this aid when they show up at their door-step as asylum seekers (Hyndman 2000; Zembylas 2010).

Funding arrangements of humanitarian organizations also favor provision of humanitarian assistance in camps rather than integrated environments. Assistance provided in camps is conceived as emergency aid as opposed to long-term development aid, much in the same way as institutionalization of people with disabilities is seen as a short-term recourse rather than a lifelong arrangement. Funds are more readily available for emergency aid than for development aid, since donor governments frequently earmark funds for emergencies (Harrell-Bond 2000). To be certain, emergency aid has continued to increase dramatically and consistently over the years both in absolute terms and as a percentage of official development aid (Fearon 2008). For example, in 1995, emergency aid across all donors amounted to 1.9 billion[3] dollars, representing 1.8 percent of total official development assistance. By 2010, emergency aid had risen to 11.2 billion dollars, representing 6.7 percent of total development assistance (Development Co-operation Directorate 2012). Additionally, the humanitarian sector has grown into a highly competitive market with several more nongovernmental organizations entering the fray (Fearon 2008). This growth in the humanitarian sector possibly promotes self-interest in the continuing existence of camps (Agier 2005) in much the same way as growth in the disability sector promotes the continuation of nursing homes and sheltered workshops (Albrecht 1992).

Thus, misguided funding mechanisms contribute to the ongoing sociospatial exclusion of displaced persons in camps, paralleling the exclusion of persons with disabilities in institutions. Care for disabled persons in institutions is also promoted by misguided social policy and public financing (Gleeson 1997; Shirk

2006). Just like displaced persons are preferred "out there" than "over here" so also are disabled people preferred in institutions than integrated in communities and neighborhoods (Gleeson 1997; Piat 2000). Both types of institutions are driven by similar goals of managing deviant "others" in segregated spaces, metaphorically and often geographically distant from the mainstream. This segregation serves the interest of capitalist economies in the case of disability institutions, and in the case of refugee camps, it serves the self-interests of donor countries, host states, and arguably of humanitarian organizations.

The next section further explores similarities between refugee camps and other total institutions like prisons and mental asylums.

Geography of Refugee Camps: Exception, Segregation, and Social Hierarchies

The most remarkable feature of refugee camps is their geographical and juridical liminality. Refugee camps are often located at the fringes of host countries, and are also peripheral to the host country's juridicopolitical systems. Italian philosopher Giorgio Agamben describes such liminal spaces as "states of exception" (cited in de la Durantaye 2009). States of exception emerge at times of crisis, when abrogation of individual rights is sanctioned in the interest of crisis management. The confinement of displaced persons in refugee camps is often justified as a necessary temporary measure to manage emerging refugee crises. As noncitizens in their host country, camp inhabitants are deprived of the legal and political rights afforded to citizens. Frequently, however, these putatively temporary camps become permanent. Holding refugees' political rights in abeyance, a supposed exception to the rule becomes a banal normality. Thus refugee camps exist in a permanent state of exception (Diken 2004), a state that closely resembles other spaces of enclosure like prisons and mental institutions.

However, refugee camps are also distinct from other states of exception. Prisons and institutions, whether publicly funded or not, operate under the purveyance of the state. Their inhabitants, though excluded from political life, are ultimately state subjects. On the other hand, refugees are, by definition, stateless. They simultaneously exist inside and outside the jurisdiction of the state. While they are included in the forced encampment policies of host countries, they are excluded from the protective canopy of citizenship and from the political structures of their host country, and become simply bodies to be managed and fed (Diken 2004).

In the juridicopolitical vacuum of refugee camps, it is humanitarian organizations that perform the role of camp governance. They do so outside normal rules of law, under conditions of political neutrality, and frequently without any external oversight (Smith 2004). The dual role of controlling camp resources while enforcing order within camps creates intense power differentials between humanitarian workers and camp inhabitants. These power differentials between "managers" and those "managed" are symptomatic of most spaces of long-term confinement such as prisons and institutions (Goffman 1961). In refugee camps, these differentials have sometimes played out in disturbing incidents where camp administrators have withheld food distributions and forcibly relocated refugees to other camps in retaliation for *disrupting* camp law and order (Smith 2004). This power hierarchy does not only manifest as extreme incidents of the kind described earlier, it is also inscribed in the everyday reality and spatial ordering of camps.

Manuel Herz, an architect, points out that the spatial organization of refugee camps is remarkably consistent across time and geography. The typical camp design derives from modernist urban planning principles of the 1920s, based on trust in order, hierarchy, and hygiene. Important as these concepts might be in terms of efficient aid delivery and maintaining sanitation and public health, they also signify a social hierarchy (Herz 2007). In most refugee camps, humanitarian personnel and the people they serve are spatially segregated. In some settings, humanitarian personnel live in nearby towns and travel daily to and from camps, sometimes under police escort (Herz 2007). When housed within camp premises, humanitarian personnel reside in separate compounds, which are frequently located close to the perimeter of the camp, bound by security fences and occasionally guarded by armed security (Herz 2007; Hyndman 2000). These security measures are intended to protect humanitarian personnel from local bandits, border militias, and the displaced persons themselves, lest the latter start an agitation. Thus the spatial organization of camps casts inhabitants as volatile, dangerous, and liable to criminal activity.

The locations of key points of service, such as food distribution centers, medical clinics, and offices of various humanitarian organizations, are also based on ensuring security of the organizations' personnel rather than convenient access for camp residents (Herz 2007; Hyndman 2000). While this spatial layout is inconvenient for all camp inhabitants, it especially disadvantages women, the elderly, and persons with disabilities. A further disadvantage to persons with disabilities is that in addition to being distant, health centers, schools, and offices of humanitarian organizations are also inaccessible, especially for people with communication and mobility impairments (Shivji 2010).

Living conditions in camps are also starkly different for different groups. Humanitarian workers enjoy a higher standard of living with more space, better toilets, running water, electricity, and permanent weather-proof structures (Hyndman 2000). Conversely, other camp residents live in temporary tentlike structures, use makeshift latrines, and face long distances and wait times to collect their daily water supply. While some camps do offer more robust living accommodations, these give the impression of permanence. The semblance of permanence is disagreeable to host governments and possibly threatens the relevance of aid organizations whose mandate is often limited to emergency aid.

In addition to residential separation and distinct living conditions, food security is another marker of social hierarchy in camps. As camps proliferate and donor contributions decline, meeting the nutritional needs of camp residents becomes an ongoing challenge.[4] However, the resulting food insecurity only affects one segment of the humanity sharing the same spatiality—the displaced camp residents and not their humanitarian care providers. Nutritional deficiencies that result from food insecurity pose a greater threat to the well-being of persons with disabilities and also create conditions that make more people disabled.

Food insecurity in camps is probably worsened by the fact that camp residents are often prohibited by host governments from working outside the camps. At the same time, work experience and self-reliance are considered useful assets for displaced persons. These assets might prove advantageous in the event of opportunities to restart their lives after returning to their country of origin or after overseas resettlement (Smith 2004). To boost self-reliance among camp residents, aid organizations support various types of income-generating activities. However, these initiatives often reinforce existing social hierarchies, tending to favor powerful male members among camp communities. On the other hand, parallel activities like handicrafts are encouraged among other camp residents such as single women and people with disabilities. Although well-intended, these activities merely give a semblance of occupational activity, any economic profitability being incidental (Agier 2005). Occasionally, camp residents are permitted to leave camps and relocate temporarily to nearby urban areas to pursue advanced education, employment training, or to work as translators at headquarters of aid organizations. Once again, such opportunities, and the relative freedom of mobility that results, favor young, educated, able-bodied males while disadvantaging women, elderly people, and people with disabilities (Hyndman 2000). Those without educational and financial resources seek surreptitious alternatives such as sneaking past camp security to live and work illegally in surrounding towns and cities. The associated risks and uncertainty again preclude women and people with disabilities from taking advantage of these alternatives to camp habitation.

In summary, the spatial and programmatic organization of camps shapes the social routines and opportunities of camp residents, disadvantaging some more than others. Ironically, the humanitarian actors, who are quick to point out these disadvantages, are complicit in reinforcing them. Similar disadvantages are experienced by people living in many parts of the Global North. Yet these disadvantages are framed in ways that contrast "our" egalitarian ways with "their" cultural backwardness while ignoring how programs sourced from and funded by the Global North exacerbate existing inequities. There is now considerable discussion on how camp conditions exacerbate the disenfranchisement of women (Hyndman 2000; Rao 1997), and a similar concern regarding people with disabilities is also emerging (Shivji 2010; Women's Commission for Refugee Women and Children 2008).[5] The growing discourse on this topic acknowledges that gender- and disability-related disadvantages in refugee camps are not merely the manifestations of cultural peculiarities, but are intensified by sexist and ableist humanitarian policies and practices.

Thus far this chapter has discussed refugee camps as sites of humanitarian confinement. These camps serve the function of managing the refugee problem far from the shores of the Global North, at a safe distance from the rich, developed countries, which fund their day-to-day operations. Refugee camps are thus simultaneously within and outside the moral, economic, and political systems of the Global North. The next section addresses another site of humanitarian confinement, located within the boundaries of the Global North—the asylum detention center.

Asylum Detention Centers: More Proximate Refugee Camps?

Asylum detention centers, such as refugee camps, also represent a state of exception (Diken 2004). The only difference is that they are located "here" in developed countries, instead of "there" in the hinterlands of Asia and Africa. Like refugee camps, detention centers are also spaces of confinement that serve to manage and regulate the mobility of displaced persons. People confined in asylum detention, labeled asylum seekers, are also "refugees," who exist outside the protective fold of a nation state. In addition, they are also people who have subverted acceptable pathways of mobility across international borders.

The only acceptable pathway for a refugee to enter a developed country in the Global North is through official resettlement. Resettlement begins in refugee camps where refugees deemed in need of additional safety and protection are referred by humanitarian organizations for immigration to developed countries that participate in the UNHCR's overseas resettlement program. Refugees referred for resettlement are vetted by immigration authorities of the target resettlement country. Educational level, professional training, and language skills are duly noted before refugees are cleared for resettlement. Some countries like Australia and the Netherlands also screen refugees for their "suitability for social integration" (Agier 2005; UNHCR 2011c). Refugees are also screened for communicable diseases, and occasionally physical and mental disorders, that may threaten the public health or tax the service systems of destination countries. Having such a condition can lead to denials of refugee resettlement claims (UNHCR 2011c).[6] Health screenings to ascertain whether refugees are "fit" for resettlement can have significant ramifications for persons with disabilities. This issue is taken up in more detail in subsequent sections. The main point being made here is that refugees must undergo numerous vetting procedures and follow a regularized pathway toward resettlement in a developed country, and many barriers exist in this path (disability status being one of them).

Only a tiny fraction of refugees get accepted for resettlement. Those who do are entitled to the same social services available to citizens of the resettlement country, an entitlement that symbolizes their standing as deserving refugees who were compliant with orderly pathways of mobility. Thus, in order to enter the shores of the Global North, refugees must first live in confinement in camps in the Global South. Before seeking mobility, they must subject themselves to immobility. Thus resettlement is the preferred pathway to mobility and this is reflected in the fact that many countries such as Canada, Australia, and the European Union are expanding their resettlement programs while clamping down heavily on asylum seekers (Charter 2009; Gilbert 2011; Joint Standing Committee on Migration, Australia 2010). Asylum seekers are refugees who subvert this tolerated pathway of mobility. These are displaced people who arrive unannounced at ports of entry in the Global North and claim asylum on grounds of persecution and civil unrest. For this transgression, they are "held" in detention centers along with other "unwanted aliens" such as travelers without appropriate documents and noncitizens who have committed crimes and are in removal proceedings. Therefore, while the refugee is constructed as a potential threat by the spatial organization of the camp, the asylum seeker is constructed as a presumed threat by the political organization of detention, the act of seeking asylum itself being construed as a crime (Wilson 2006).

Across the developed world, detention centers have become an institutionalized mechanism for containing asylum seekers until they are considered worthy of entry or until they can be turned back. Australia, for example, has a long-standing policy of mandatory detention for all asylum seekers upon arrival (Carrington 2006, Lawson 2011). Detention centers have been established in extra-territorial zones through bilateral agreements with island nations like Nauru and Papua New Guinea in exchange for development aid. While the Australian state is absolved of any responsibility for conditions in these centers, it controls who is detained and for how long (Pickering 2005; Lawson 2011). While Australia certainly stands out as an extreme example, other countries are not too far behind. For example, Canada is creating a new detention regime loosely modeled after Australia's (Harrold and Lucier 2010). In the United Kingdom, capacity to hold people in immigration detention has increased tenfold between the 1990s and 2009. As of 2008, asylum seekers accounted for 75 percent of the immigrant detainee population in the United Kingdom (Global Detention Project 2011). Similarly in France, a centralized and permanent detention center has been established at the country's main international airport. The center replaces previous makeshift and fragmented sites such as police offices, hotel rooms, and waiting rooms at airport terminals. The new holding center boasts of greater managerial efficiency and better living conditions for detainees. Daily management of the center is under the purview of humanitarian actors like the French Red Cross, an arrangement made in response to sustained pressure from rights advocates (Makaremi 2009).

The progression from shabby detention facilities to "humane" centers for housing asylum seekers is similar to the evolution of crowded almshouses into mental institutions and convalescent homes for housing disabled people. Both represent paradoxical efforts to humanize the essentially inhumane practice of mass confinement. However questionable detention practices continue unabated because detention centers are justified by the same state of exception and a similar logic of "inclusive exclusions" that characterize refugee camps (Diken 2004). Frequently, detention centers are located sufficiently outside the borders of nation states, both politically and physically, so as to justify their existence. At the same time these centers are still subsumed under the juridical order of the very states from which they are excluded. Asylum seekers are kept out of the state at the same time as they are subject to the state's legal systems. Take, for example, the case of asylum detention in France, intricately analyzed by Makaremi (2010). In France, detention centers are characterized as "waiting zones." Asylum seekers can be detained in "waiting zones" because they are considered "not admitted" inside France. Thus detention of asylum seekers is justified by the French state by first declaring a portion of its own territory as an extra-territorial zone, and then claiming administrative and legal authority over this zone. Thus France's borders are rendered more malleable at the same time as they become more impermeable for asylum seekers (Makaremi 2010).

This "exceptional state" of being simultaneously inside and outside the law creates significant accountability deficits. For instance, locating detention centers in remote islands impedes oversight by human rights advocates (McCulloch and Pickering 2009). Furthermore, practices that would be illegal under ordinary circumstances become allowable under "exceptional conditions." As an example, management of detention centers is often subcontracted to private companies, some of which are also international providers of private prisons and prominent lobbyists in the arena of detention policy (Carrington 2006; Global Detention Project 2011; Pickering 2005). In the United Kingdom, seven of the country's eleven long-term detention centers are believed to be managed by one of four private companies. These companies receive a daily reimbursement fee for each inmate held in detention, thus rendering immigrant detention tantamount to any other for-profit business (Global Detention Project 2011). In a compelling example of the nexus between diminished accountability and business profitability, Diken (2004) cites the case of a multinational company charged with running a detention center in the United Kingdom, where detained asylum seekers were made to labor for one-tenth the British minimum wage.

This logic of exception also legitimizes confinement of asylum seekers for extended lengths of time. Unlike prisoners, who know the length of their sentence, immigration detainees have no knowledge of how long they will be detained.

Detention times vary across countries and range from a few months to two or three years (Amnesty International 2008). In the absence of fixed terms of stay, the only way out for detainees is to prove their case for asylum. If unable to do so, they are not merely returned to confinement; rather they incur further penalty in the form of removal proceedings back to their places of origin. In some cases, removal proceedings can be initiated even before asylum claims have been fully examined (Human Rights Watch 2010).

Additionally, the burden of proof falls upon the individual subjects and their ability to remember, synthesize, and articulate their displacement trajectories. This encumbrance confers a systemic risk especially for asylum seekers with cognitive and mental disabilities who might be unable to independently articulate their asylum claim, or satisfactorily respond to interrogation procedures. Cases of cognitively and mentally disabled persons in immigration detention have recently surfaced in some countries (Al-Mohamed 2008; McCulloch and Pickering 2006). One prominent case involved a mentally ill German citizen holding Australian permanent residency who was held in Australian detention for several months as an unauthorized immigrant. Her detention prompted a government inquiry into more than two hundred other cases of suspected unlawful detention (Palmer 2005). Such cases highlight disabled detainees' difficulty with communicating and processing information during their interrogation, and failure on part of officials to recognize their disability or provide them with needed supports during interrogation procedures. What is remarkable about these cases is that they only came to light because many of the detainees in question were found to be "wrongfully" detained. These individuals turned out to be citizens or legal permanent residents who were detained because they could not provide coherent details about their background when confronted by law enforcement or immigration officials. In most cases, these individuals were either relocated to hospitals or mental health facilities when their legal status was discovered, or returned to their country of citizenship/legal residence after being erroneously deported.

Thus while their disability exposed them to detention risks, their legal status helped counter this risk. What, then, becomes of those who have a disability *and* no legal status, such as refugees and asylum seekers with disabilities? The following section examines these intersections in detail.

Disability and the Geopolitics of Mobility

The containment of people in refugee camps and detention centers cannot be adequately understood without also considering its opposite condition, that of freedom of mobility across national borders. Hyndman (2000), for example, contrasts the transnational mobility of refugees who live in refugee camps and the expatriate humanitarian professionals who work in the same camps. The relative immobility of the former becomes accentuated when juxtaposed against the hypermobility of the latter. Where refugees need exceptional permits to travel even a few miles outside the camp, humanitarian personnel own special United Nations passports that afford them unrestricted travel over thousands of miles and across multiple borders. The same processes of migratory regulation that restrict the mobility of refugees facilitate the mobility of humanitarian professionals. Sociologist Zygmunt Bauman (1998) describes such disparities as a "global hierarchy of mobility," a system of social stratification marked by the extraterritoriality of a few elite and the forced territoriality of many others. The stratifications produced by this hierarchy represent important intersections, both discursive and concrete, with the construct of disability.

Let us consider first the discursive intersections between disability and the geopolitics of transnational mobility. In his manifesto for a "sociology of mobilities," Urry (2000, 50) alludes to "the various kinds of *disabling processes* (emphasis added) which limit or constrain the mobilities of many." The phrase "disabling processes" can be understood to subsume the gamut of ableist, racist, sexist, elitist, and nationalist policies that have created a whole underclass of people deprived of equal access to global mobility (Pickering and Weber 2006). Members of this underclass, people with and without disabilities, are not inherently disadvantaged, but rather disadvantaged by virtue of being denied their freedom of mobility. What Urry (2000) refers to as "disabling processes" are not new phenomena; rather they have a strong historical precedence. Immigration policies of many developed countries share a blatantly ableist history of not only excluding people with disabilities (Richards 2004) but also deploying the notion of disability to craft the image of undesirable immigrants (Baynton 2001).

Nation states continue to deploy "disabling processes" in order to control the membership of their polity. These processes are enacted both at state borders and as far from official borders as possible (Pickering and Weber 2006). Some countries, for example, have entered into migration partnerships with third countries whereby processing of asylum seekers has been outsourced to countries (some of them with dubious human rights records) like Morocco, Tunisia, Algeria, and Libya (Green 2006). Naval blockades and interdiction at sea are other examples of preemptive measures used to regulate migration before potential immigrants and asylum seekers arrive at state borders. Additionally, in the case of Australia at least, these measures have been accompanied by legislative amendments retroactively excising swaths of Australian territory so that boatloads of asylum seekers, landing on (formerly) Australian islands, can be claimed to have never arrived *in* Australia (McCulloch and Pickering 2009; Weber 2006).

Together, these measures comprise a new asylum paradigm where asylum seekers are intercepted before they reach their destination and are herded to distant camps and detention centers (Pécoud and Guchteneire 2006). Thus their subsequent confinement is not a distinct condition but a corollary of the geopolitics of mobility. For the most part this geopolitics of mobility has been successful in curbing asylum flows. The UNHCR reports that asylum applications have fallen internationally (UNHCR 2011b). Asylum seekers who manage to dodge interception and arrive at state borders are subjected to further "disabling" processes, including their systematic vilification as dangerous, fraudulent, manipulative, and most of all, welfare-seeking. Some heads of state and elected officials have publicly described asylum seekers and refugees as "swamping" welfare systems and from whom welfare systems "need to be protected" (Diken 2004). To achieve the dual goals of protecting welfare and controlling immigration, many countries are adopting a new type of "disabling" process—biometric technologies.

Technologies such as finger-printing, iris scanning, travel documents embedded with smart chips, and radio frequency identification are being increasingly used to monitor the entry and exit of people across countries (Shachar 2009). Outwardly, these new technologies are justified for security reasons. However, their real value lies in mechanizing the social stratification of travelers whereby the mobility of some is expedited while that of others is impeded (Wilson 2006). These technologies also enable digital monitoring of migrants' use of public services. For example, an electronic tagging system has been tested in the United Kingdom where all asylum claimants are issued a smart card. The smart card is intended to monitor their whereabouts, and also to discourage their fraudulent use of the British welfare system. Thus biometric technologies represent a new frontier in the "disabling" geopolitics of mobility. Unlike other "disabling" processes, which rely on amorphous policies and legal wrangling to socially construct people as less worthy of transnational mobility, biometric technologies are corporeal in that deviance and inadmissibility are permanently inscribed on people's bodies and identities (Maddern and Stewart 2010).

Moving on from discursive to more concrete intersections between disability and the geopolitics of mobility, what is the place of disabled refugees and asylum seekers in the global hierarchy of mobility? Historical evidence suggests that during one of the first formalized refugee resettlement efforts, involving people displaced by World War II, certain groups of refugees, including those who were sick, elderly, or disabled, were considered undesirable by resettlement countries and continued to live in a stateless limbo, scattered throughout Europe for many years (Loescher 2001). Contemporary immigration practices are also discriminatory against disabled people and pander to neoliberal, nationalist agendas whereby those allowed entry into the body politic of the state are those most likely to contribute to labor markets and economic growth. In some immigrant-receiving countries, even those granted labor visas are at risk of deportation if they or a family member acquires a disability that restricts their ability to work or renders them a potential "burden" for the country's social and healthcare systems (see e.g., Fragomeni 2012; Kirby 2009). Under such discriminatory immigration policies, disabled refugees and asylum seekers are likely to be deemed too unfit to contribute to the economy of the host society and too expensive to be given refuge (Meekosha and Dowse 1997).

This has indeed been the case as exemplified by the UNHCR's "Ten or More" plan launched in 1973. The plan was intended to encourage countries participating in the refugee resettlement program to accept, as part of their annual resettlement quotas, ten or more (later, 20 or more) persons with disabilities, plus their families, who might otherwise not meet admissibility criteria (Women's Commission for Refugee Women and Children 2008). Resettlement countries have responded variably to the UNHCR's efforts. A few countries (e.g. USA, Ireland) are generally open to resettling persons with disabilities and a few others (e.g. Denmark and New Zealand) follow the policy of reserving a percentage of their resettlement quotas for persons with disabilities and medical needs (UNHCR 2011c). However, other countries restrict resettlement opportunities for disabled refugees. Sweden, for example, allows resettlement for people with disabilities and medical needs "only in exceptional cases and provided the proper form of treatment is available [in Sweden]" (UNHCR 2004, Sweden chapter, 2). Likewise, Norway categorically states that their "capacity for resettling refugees with reduced mobility such as people confined to wheelchairs... is also limited" (UNHCR 2004, Norway chapter, 3).[7]Similarly, Canada, until recently, effectively barred the resettlement of those refugees seen as lacking the "ability to successfully establish [in Canada]" or who might present "excessive medical demand or cost for Canada" (Casasola 2001, 78). On the more extreme end of this spectrum is Australia, which has a long-standing and ongoing policy of denying resettlement and asylum to people with disabilities *and their families* on grounds of undue burden on the public health system (Meekosha 2005; Young and Finlay 2001). According to the Multicultural

Development Association, a prominent organization that assists refugees resettled in Australia, these restrictive immigration policies appear to be fulfilling their intent. Out of the thousands of newly arrived refugees assisted by the organization, only a small handful have evident disabilities, although several families report having disabled family members who they could not bring with them to Australia. There are numerous cases of refugee families in Australia having left behind a disabled family member to facilitate the separate migration of others in the family (Joint Standing Committee on Migration, Australia 2010).

Based on the above discussion, one could well argue that the "place" of disabled refugees and asylum seekers within the global hierarchy of mobility lies in camps in the Global South and possibly detention centers in the Global North. Their spatiality is more bounded, and their mobility more restricted than that of their nondisabled counterparts. While this is true overall, there also exist moments of rupture. These moments represent an inversion of the regular choreography of transnational mobility, where being characterized with a disability enhances rather than restricts mobility across national borders. The next section discusses these moments of rupture and how disability is produced, reproduced, and contested within these moments.

Disability and Ruptures in the Global Hierarchy of Mobility

The previous sections analyze refugee camps and detention centers as sites where displaced persons are segregated and managed in the interests of a global hierarchy of mobility. While these sites mark the creation of new social hierarchies, they also trigger situations that can unsettle existing hierarchies. Agier (2005), for instance, describes how former ethnic and gender-based hierarchies among refugees are contested and transformed as refugees encounter international aid organizations and their Western liberal ideal of universal equality. Aid organizations are expected to offer equal access to camp services and activities for all social groups. Often devalued social groups such as single women and ethnic minorities are given special attention. Favorable international attention confers a positive valence and improved social standing to these groups.

Recent evidence suggests a similar trend for people with disabilities living in camps. Over the past few years the international humanitarian community has been making efforts to improve conditions for disabled people living in camps (Mirza 2011b).[8] These efforts entail mainstreaming disabled people into regular programs as well as launching special programs for people with disabilities, including special considerations and opportunities for mobility outside camps. For example, in most refugee camps people with disabilities can obtain special permission (albeit with some difficulty) to leave the camps and live in nearby towns for availing medical treatment such as advanced surgeries and specialized rehabilitation care, which are often unavailable in camps (Mirza 2011b). In the 1980s, the UNHCR even sponsored a "medical evacuation" program that allowed refugees to temporarily relocate to a different, often more developed country if the medical intervention sought was not locally or regionally available (Women's Commission for Refugee Women and Children 2008).

Thus, in a reversal of routine hierarchies of mobility, having a disability and needing specialized medical services can also be a ticket to relocate outside camps, albeit temporarily. In some cases, and as a result of recent developments in the UNHCR's resettlement program, having a disability can also get refugees permanent resettlement in a developed country. The UNHCR encourages priority resettlement of those refugees deemed most "vulnerable." Among the categories of individuals identified as being "vulnerable," people with disabilities are included under the broader category of refugees with medical needs (Mirza 2010b). A few resettlement countries have responded favorably to the UNHCR's initiative. For example, New Zealand now accepts disabled refugees who "cannot be treated in their country of refuge" and whose resettlement in New Zealand "will significantly improve their medical condition and well-being" (Saker 2010, 25). The United States has also adopted a similar approach. In 2005, the United States partnered with the UNHCR in a group resettlement project where approximately two thousand disabled Somali refugees were resettled *en masse*, in the first (and perhaps only) endeavor of its kind to date (Mirza 2011a).

The above examples represent ruptures in the normal choreography of global mobility where disability becomes a facilitator rather than a barrier for mobility across borders. But this "revaluing" of disability is less straightforward than it seems and entails moments where the condition of disability is produced, reproduced, and contested. There are reports, for example, of nondisabled refugees "performing" disability and requesting specialized medical services for mental illness to procure permission to live outside camps. Such performances are often contested by medical professionals and declared as not legitimate (Hyndman 2000). On one hand, contestation of such disability claims reflects the general difficulty in diagnosing and confirming mental illness. On the other hand, such "productions" of disability reflect a strategy for survival and a desperate attempt to escape unlivable camp conditions. Regardless, the ultimate falsification of such claims likely reinforces the image of refugees as fraudulent and manipulative. Not to mention the likelihood of greater scrutiny over genuine mental health symptoms and future disability claims.

Even for people with "genuine" disabilities, the window of opportunity for off-camp or off-shore medical treatment can be quite constricted. First, their treatment requests need to be verified by medical professionals. The same professionals also need to confirm that the claimant's condition is treatable and that the treatment is not locally available. Evidence indicates that expert professionals who can make such endorsements are few and far between and, when available, are difficult to access (Mirza 2011b). Second, opportunities for overseas resettlement, which are based on medical need, necessitate the role of medical professionals as gatekeepers rather than recognizing disabled people's right to resettlement like all other refugees. Third, the medical treatment clause might preclude resettlement opportunities for people with disabilities whose condition might not be treatable. There are a large number of physical and cognitive impairments for which no known cure or treatment exists even in the most developed countries. Many resettlement countries, while outwardly open to accepting disabled refugees on grounds of medical need, require that the person's condition be treatable or likely to worsen without treatment. This represents a backhanded way of limiting the resettlement of persons with untreatable, and therefore more severe disabilities, while giving the appearance of being equitable. This also creates a hierarchy of mobility *among* people with disabilities, where those with less severe disabilities are considered more deserving of resettlement.

Finally, the language of "vulnerability" and "medical need" used to justify resettlement for disabled refugees does little to combat the general perception of disabled people as needy and dependent on welfare. For example, growing concerns about foreigners seeking asylum solely for the purpose of getting medical care have prompted changes in French immigration laws. These changes could result in revocation of medical visas and possible deportation of immigrants and asylum seekers seeking any medical treatment in France (Elzas 2011). In another example, the Netherlands' refugee resettlement policy seeks to balance "vulnerable" cases, that is, people with disabilities with "high profile" cases, that is, prominent human rights activists who can contribute to civil society while also being a support for their "vulnerable" compatriots (UNHCR 2004; 2011c). Thus "vulnerable" and "high profile" refugees are seen as mutually exclusive, implying that disabled refugees needing care and support have few benefits to offer to society. At the same time "high profile" refugees are seen as never requiring care and support. The main message underlying such policies is that not needing supportive resources is the hallmark of successful refugee resettlement and immigration.

Despite its negative connotations, the language of "vulnerability" continues to be deployed not only in pursuing resettlement opportunities for disabled refugees living in camps but also in seeking reprieve for disabled asylum seekers confined in detention centers. Multiple directives and guidelines have been developed that specify minimum standards for asylum detention. These guidelines identify categories of asylum seekers deemed "unfit" for detention. People with disabilities are included among those considered "unfit" for detention and therefore deserving of better alternatives (e.g., Amaral 2010; Cutler 2005; Sampson, Mitchell and Bowring 2011).

The idea and image of disability is also being increasingly deployed by human rights advocates to question asylum detention practices. Numerous investigations have revealed how disabled asylum seekers are detained for long periods of time without adequate access to healthcare (Refugee Council 2005; Shah and Trude 2009) and how conditions in detention are likely to worsen the physical and mental health of persons with disabilities (Cutler 2005; Shah and Trude 2009). Additionally, there is a growing body of evidence that highlights the negative impact of detention on the mental and physical health of asylum seekers, thus suggesting that detention practices can produce disability among those otherwise healthy and nondisabled (Amaral 2010; Laban et al. 2008; Sweet 2011). Expectedly, states have contested these allegations through discursive strategies suggesting that asylum seekers are only feigning disability to seek attention and receive visas (McCulloch and Pickering 2009). Therefore to legitimize such claims, human rights organizations often bring in medical professionals and use diagnostic criteria to establish the presence of physical or mental disabilities (Cutler 2005; McCulloch and Pickering 2009). Legal advocates follow a similar practice when challenging detention of individual detainees on grounds of disability (e.g., Burnham 2003).

The above trends are problematic for multiple reasons. First, they signify disability as a strictly medical issue by heightening the role of medical professionals in asylum procedures. Evidence suggests that a medical doctor's endorsement might favorably influence the outcome of asylum applications (Lustig et al. 2008). While a favorable outcome might benefit the detained asylum seeker, it might also result in unnecessary labeling of people as "vulnerable." For example, a multicountry investigation into asylum conditions for detainees with physical and mental impairments revealed that the detainees did not necessarily see themselves as "vulnerable" on account of their physical or mental health. Rather, they associated their "vulnerability" with the reality of being detained indefinitely in poor conditions without any supportive resources (Amaral 2010).

Additionally, using the "vulnerability" argument to challenge detention causes an individual's predefined characteristics to be seen as sole determinants of that individual's vulnerability. People with mental and physical disabilities are not vulnerable in any essentialist way and consistently categorizing them as such reinforces the image of disabled individuals as weak and needy. This image then feeds into cost-burden arguments against resettlement of disabled refugees and asylum seekers (Straimer 2010). Finally, when disability becomes a stand-in for everything that is wrong with asylum detention, it obscures the bigger issue. The overall message for society morphs from "detention is a violation of human rights" to "detention is unjustified because it produces or worsens disability."

Therefore, using disabled people and images of disability to spotlight injustices of confinement does little to challenge the widespread societal devaluation of people with disabilities and their inferior placement in the global hierarchy of mobility. Furthermore, it fails to dismantle the geopolitics of global mobility and the practice of holding refugees and asylum seekers in confinement. On the other hand, it might prompt states to respond with so-called "humane" detention procedures, thus further legitimizing practices that are inherently unjust.

Conclusion

This chapter traces the genealogy and geography of refugee camps and asylum detention centers in a bid to explore connections, both literal and figurative, between the conditions of disability and human displacement. Camps and detention centers serve similar purposes of holding displaced persons in humanitarian confinement while managing their transnational mobility. Where refugee camps are exclusive to the Global South, asylum detention centers represent their counterpart in the Global North. Much like prisons and institutions, camps and detention centers are characterized by a state of inclusive exclusions. Their inhabitants, stateless by definition, are simultaneously within the power of host states and outside the state's juridicolegal protection.

Camps and detention centers are also characterized by distinct power hierarchies, both between authorities and inhabitants, and among inhabitants themselves. These hierarchies create differences in material conditions within camps, and also in opportunities for outside mobility.

All inhabitants of refugee camps and asylum centers represent an underclass of people whose mobility across national borders is closely regulated and circumscribed. This chapter argues that refugees and asylum seekers with and without disabilities are similarly "disabled" by the arsenal of legal, political, and biometric strategies, which construct them as less worthy migrants. In this pecking order of global mobility, those with disabilities likely occupy one of the lowest positions. Faced with discriminatory immigration policies advanced by resettlement and asylum countries, the spatiality of disabled refugees and asylum seekers is more bounded, and their mobility across borders is more restricted. However, this chapter also highlights initiatives and opportunities, where being labeled with a disability can facilitate rather than limit cross-border mobility.

In recent times, members of the humanitarian community have advocated for disabled refugees and asylum seekers to be spared long-term confinement in camps and detention centers, and for their resettlement and asylum claims to be expedited. Images of disability have also been used to advocate for more humane asylum conditions. These advocacy efforts are justified on grounds that people with disabilities are vulnerable and in need of greater protection. While the vulnerability argument opens up closed migration channels for disabled refugees and asylum seekers, it is also a double-edged sword. The case that needs to be made is not that people with disabilities must be exceptional to confinement because they are inherently vulnerable in some way. The act of confinement itself must be an exception, used only in the rarest of circumstances when no better alternatives are available, such as when the immediate safety of refugees and asylum seekers is under threat. And even in these truly exceptional circumstances, preserving or restoring people's freedom of mobility must be the ultimate imperative.

Notes

1. Henceforth abbreviated as UNHCR.
2. Resettlement refers to the transfer of refugees from the country in which they have sought refuge to another state, usually a developed country in the Global North. This option is available only to refugees who have crossed international borders and not to internally displaced persons. Resettled refugees are usually granted some form of long-term residency rights and, in many cases, have the opportunity to become naturalized citizens (International Organization of Migration, http://www.iom.int /jahia/Jahia/about-migration/managing-migration/refugee-protection).
3. All figures based on constant 2010 US dollars.
4. Warnings about food shortages are frequently reported on UNHCR's website. See, for example, "UNHCR Concerned about Malnutrition Levels among New Somali Refugees," published July 5, 2011.
5. Note also that the latest edition of the influential *Sphere Project, Humanitarian Charter and Minimum Standards in Humanitarian Response* includes accessibility considerations for disabled people.
6. Notably, HIV/AIDS is no longer an inadmissible condition following strong advocacy by the UNHCR (Mirza 2010a).
7. This language is no longer retained in the latest 2011 edition of the UNHCR's *Resettlement Handbook*. However, the discriminatory tone of the previous edition provides recent historical context to this argument.
8. See also the Special Edition on Disability and Displacement (Volume 35) of the *Forced Migration Review*, a prominent periodical in the humanitarian field.

References

Agier, Michel. 2005. *On the Margins of the World: The Refugee Experience Today.* Cambridge: Polity Press.
Albrecht, Gary. 1992. *The Disability Business: Rehabilitation in America* [Sage Library of Social Research Vol. 190]. Newbury Park, CA: Sage Publications.
Al-Mohamed, Day. 2008. "Day in Washington Podcast #24 – Immigration and Customs Enforcement (Ice) and Disability." *In Day in Washington. Home of the Disability Policy Podcast.* http://dayinwashington.com/?p=90

Amaral, Philip. 2010. "Becoming Vulnerable in Detention. Civil Society Report on the Detention of Vulnerable Asylum Seekers and Irregular Migrants in the European Union (the Devas Project)." Belgium: Jesuit Refugee Service – European Regional Office.

Amnesty International. 2008. "French Detention Centre Highlights Mistreatment of Migrants." London: Amnesty International.

Bauman, Zygmunt. 1998. *Globalization: The Human Consequences.* New York: Columbia University Press.

Baynton, Douglas. 2001. "Disability and the Justification of Inequality in American History." In *The New Disability History: American Perspectives*, edited by Paul K. Longmore and Lauri Umansky, 33–57. New York: New York University Press.

Black, Richard. 1998. "Putting Refugees in Camps." *Forced Migration Review* 2: 4–7.

Burnham, Emily. 2003. "Challenging Immigrant Detention. A Best Practice Guide." London: Immigration Law Practioners' Association and Bail for Immigration Detainees.

Casasola, Michael. 2001. "Current Trends and New Challenges for Canada's Resettlement Program." *Refuge: Canada's Periodical on Refugees* 19(4): 76–83.

Carrington, Kerry. 2006. "Law and Order on the Border in the Neo-Colonial Antipodes." In *Borders, Mobility and Technologies of Control*, edited by Sharon Pickering and Leanne Weber, 179–206. Dordrecht: Springer.

Charter, David. 2009. "More Homes for Refugees as Europe Aims to End People-Trafficking." *The Times*, September 3.

Crisp, Jeff, and Karen Jacobsen. 1998. "Refugee Camps Reconsidered." *Forced Migration Review* 3: 27–30.

Cutler, Sarah. 2005. "Fit to Be Detained? Challenging the Detention of Asylum Seekers and Migrants with Health Needs." London: Bail for Immigration Detainees.

Davies, Sara E. 2007. "Redundant or Essential? How Politics Shaped the Outcome of the 1967 Protocol." *International Journal of Refugee Law* 19(4): 703–728.

de la Durantaye, Leland. 2009. *Giorgio Agamben: A Critical Introduction.* Stanford, CA: Stanford University Press.

Development Co-operation Directorate. 2012. "International Development Statistics (Ids) Online Databases on Aid and Other Resource Flows." Organisation for Economic Co-operation and Development.

Diken, Bulent. 2004. "From Refugee Camps to Gated Communities: From Biopolitics to the End of the City." *Citizenship Studies* 8(1): 83–106.

Douglas, Mary. 1966. *Parity and Danger: An Analysis of Concepts of Pollution and Taboo.* London: Routledge and Kegan Paul.

Elzas, Sarah. 2011. "French Medical Visas Threatened." Radio France Internationale.

Fearon, James D. 2008. "The Rise of Emergency Relief Aid." *In Humanitarianism in Question: Politics, Power, Ethics*, edited by Thomas G. Weiss and Michael Barnett, 49–72. Ithaca, NY: Cornell University Press.

Fragomeni, Carmela. 2012. "Canada Doesn't Want This Autistic Boy." *The Hamilton Spectator*, March 15.

Gilbert, Liette. 2011 "Politics of Immigration and the Controversial Refugee Reforms." *Canada Watch Spring*: 39–40.

Gleeson, Brendan. 1997. "Community Care and Disability: The Limits to Justice." *Progress in Human Geography* 21(2): 199–224.

Global Detention Project. 2011. "United Kingdom Detention Profile." Geneva: Global Detention Project.

Goffman, Erving. 1961. *Asylums: Essays on the Social Situation of Mental Patients and Other Inmates.* New York: Anchor Books.

Green, Penny. 2006. "State Crime Beyond Borders." In *Borders, Mobility and Technologies of Control*, edited by Sharon Pickering and Leanne Weber, 149–166. Dordrecht: Springer.

Harrell-Bond, Barbara. 2000. "Are Refugee Camps Good for Children?" In *New Issues in Refugee Research*, 1–11. Geneva: Policy Development and Evaluation Services, United Nations High Commissioner for Refugees.

Harrold, Daphne Keevil, and Danielle Lucier. 2010. "Bill C-49: An Act to Amend the Immigration and Refugee Protection Act, the Balanced Refugee Reform Act and the Marine Transportation Security Act." Ottawa, ON: Library of the Parliament.

Herz, Manuel. 2007. "Refugee Camps in Chad: Planning Strategies and the Architect's Involvement in the Humanitarian Dilemma." In *Research Paper No. 147*, 1–14. Geneva: Policy Development and Evaluation Services, United Nations High Commissioner for Refugees.

Human Rights Watch. 2010. "France: Amend Immigration Bill to Protect Asylum Seekers." New York: Human Rights Watch.

Hyndman, Jennifer. 2000. *Managing Displacement: Refugees and the Politics of Humanitarianism*. Minneapolis, MN: University of Minnesota Press.

Joint Standing Committee on Migration. 2010. "Family, Humanitarian and Refugee Migration." In *Enabling Australia. Inquiry into the Migration Treatment of Disability*, 103–38. Canberra: The Parliament of the Commonwealth of Australia.

Kibreab, Gaim. 1989. "Local Settlements in Africa: A Misconceived Option?" *Journal of Refugee Studies* 2(4): 473–474.

Kirby, Dean. 2009. "Kicked Out for Being Disabled." *Manchester Evening News*, January 19.

Laban Cornelis, Ivan Komproe, Hajo Gernaat, and Joop de Jong. 2008. "The Impact of a Long Asylum Procedure on Quality of Life, Disability and Physical Health in Iraqi Asylum Seekers in the Netherlands." *Social Psychiatry and Psychiatric Epidemiology* 43(7): 507–515.

Lawson, Timothy. 2011. "Thousands Rally Against Malaysia Deal, Mandatory Detention." *Green Left Weekly*.

Loescher, Gil. 2001. *The UNHCR and World Politics: A Perilous Path*. New York: Oxford University Press.

Lustig, Stuart, Sarah Kureshi, Kevin Delucchi, Vincent Iacopino, and Samantha Morse. 2008. "Asylum Grant Rates Following Medical Evaluations of Maltreatment among Political Asylum Applicants in the United States." *Journal of Immigrant and Minority Health* 10: 7–15.

Makaremi, Chowra. 2009. "Governing Borders in France: From Extraterritorial to Humanitarian Confinement." *Canadian Journal of Law and Society* 24(3): 411–432.

Malkki, Liisa. 1995. "Refugees and Exile: From 'Refugee Studies' to the National Order of Things." *Annual Review of Anthropology* 24: 495–523.

McCulloch, Jude, and Sharon Pickering. 2006. "The Violence of Refugee Incarceration." In *The Violence of Incarceration*, edited by Phil Scraton and Jude McCulloch, 225–243. New York: Routledge.

Maddern, Joanne, and Emma Stewart. 2010. "Biometric Geographies, Mobility and Disability: Biologies of Culpability and the Biologised Spaces of (Post)modernity." In *Towards Enabling Geographies: 'Disabled' Bodies and Minds in Society and Space*, edited by Vera Chouinard, Edward Hall, and Robert Wilton, 237–252. Surrey: Ashgate.

Meekosha, Helen. 2005. "A Feminist/Gendered Critique of the Intersections of Race and Disability: The Australian Experience." Invited distinguished lecture presented at the Department of Educational Studies, University of British Columbia, Vancouver, British Columbia, June 23.

Meekosha, Helen, and Dowse Leanne. 1997. "Enabling Citizenship: Gender, Disability, and Citizenship in Australia." *Feminist Review* 57: 39–72.

Mirza, Mansha. 2010a. "Global Ethnography with Disabled Refugees: Combining Individual Narratives with Systems and Policy Analysis." PhD diss., University of Illinois.

———. 2010b. "Resettlement for Disabled Refugees." *Forced Migration Review* 35: 30–31.

———. 2011a. "Disability and Cross-Border Mobility. Comparing Resettlement Experiences of Cambodian and Somali Refugees with Disabilities." *Disability & Society* 26(5): 521–535.

———. 2011b. "Unmet Needs and Diminished Opportunities: Disability, Displacement and Humanitarian Healthcare." *Research Paper No. 212*. Geneva: Policy Development and Evaluation Services, United Nations High Commissioner for Refugees.

Morris, Nicholas. 2007. "'Prisons of the Stateless': A Response to New Left Review." In *Research Paper No. 141*. Geneva: Policy Development and Evaluation Services, United Nations High Commissioner for Refugees.

Nicolaisen, Ida. 1995. "Persons and Nonpersons: Disability and Personhood Among the Punan Bah of Central Borneo." In *Disability and Culture*, edited by Benedicte Ingstad and Susan Whyte, 38–55. Berkeley, CA: University of California Press.

Palmer, Mick. 2005. "Inquiry into the Circumstances of the Immigration Detention of Cornelia Rau." Canberra: Department of Immigration and Multicultural and Indigenous Affairs.

Pécoud, Antoine, and Paul de Guchteneire. 2006. "International Migration, Border Controls and Human Rights: Assessing the Relevance of a Right to Mobility." *Journal of Borderland Studies* 21(1): 69–86.

Piat, Myra. 2000. "The NIMBY Phenomenon: Community Residents' Concerns about Housing for Deinstitutionalized People." *Health & Social Work*, 25(2): 127–138.

Pickering, Sharon. 2005. "Crimes of the State: The Persecution and Protection of Refugees." *Critical Criminology* 13: 141–163.

Pickering, Sharon, and Leanne Weber. 2006. "Borders, Mobility and Technologies of Control." In *Borders, Mobility and Technologies of Control*, edited by Sharon Pickering and Leanne Weber, 1–19. Dordrecht: Springer.

Rao, Tara. 1997. "An Unsettling Settlement: The Physical Planning of Refugee Settlements: A Gender Perspective." MA thesis, University of East Anglia.

Refugee Council. 2005. "A Study of Asylum Seekers with Special Needs." London: Refugee Council.

Richards, Penny L. 2004. "Points of Entry: Disability and the Historical Geography of Migration." *Disability Studies Quarterly*, 24(3). http://dsq-sds.org/article/view /505/682.

Saker, Rowan. 2010. "New Zealand: Beyond the Quota." *Forced Migration Review* 35: 25–26.

Sampson, Robyn, Grant Mitchell, and Lucy Bowring. 2011. "There Are Alternatives. A Handbook for Preventing Unnecessary Immigration Detention." Melbourne: The International Detention Coalition.

Shachar, Ayelet. 2009. "The Shifting Border of Immigration Regulation." *Michigan Journal of International Law* 30: 809–838.

Shah, Amanda, and Adeline Trude. 2009. "Out of Sight, Out of Mind: Experiences of Immigration Detention in the UK." London: Bail for Immigration Detainees.

Sharma, Nandita. 2000. "The Making of the Citizen Self and Citizen Other: Canada's Non-Immigrant Employment Authorization Programme." In *Globalization and Its Discontents*, edited by Stephen McBride and John Wiseman, 129–142. New York: St. Martin's Press Ltd.

Shirk, Cynthia. 2006. "Rebalancing Long-Term Care: The Role of the Medicaid HCBS Waiver Program." Washington, DC: The George Washington University.

Shivji, Aleema. 2010. "Disability in Displacement." *Forced Migration Review* 35: 4–7.

Smith, Merrill. 2004. "Warehousing Refugees: A Denial of Rights, a Waste of Humanity." *World Refugee Survey*, 38–56.

Stevens, Jacob. 2006. "Prisons of the Stateless: The Derelections of UNHCR." *New Left Review* 42: 53–67.

Straimer, Clara. 2010. "Vulnerable or Invisible? Asylum Seekers with Disabilities in Europe." *Research Paper No. 194*. Geneva: Policy Development and Evaluation Services, United Nations High Commissioner for Refugees.

Sweet, Melissa. 2011. "Mandatory Detention of Asylum Seekers Is Harming People and 'Demeans Us All': Leading Psychiatrist." In Croakey. The Crikey Health Blog. http://blogs.crikey.com.au/croakey/2011/03/29/mandatory-detention-of-asylum-seekers-is-harming-people-and-demeans-us-all-leading-psychiatrist/

United Nations High Commissioner for Refugees. 2012. "UNHCR Global Trends 2011." Geneva: United Nations High Commissioner for Refugees.

———. 2011a. "60 Years and Still Counting. UNHCR Global Trends 2010." Geneva: United Nations High Commissioner for Refugees.

———. 2011b. "Asylum Levels and Trends in Industrialized Countries 2010." Geneva: United Nations High Commissioner for Refugees.

———. 2011c. "UNHCR Resettlement Handbook." Geneva: United Nations High Commissioner for Refugees.

———. 2008. "Protracted Refugee Situations. High Commissioner's Initiative." Geneva: United Nations High Commissioner for Refugees.

———. 2004. "UNHCR Resettlement Handbook." Geneva: United Nations High Commissioner for Refugees.

Urry, John. 2000. *Sociology Beyond Societies: Mobilities for the Twenty-First Century*. London: Routledge.

Van Damme, Wim. 1995. "Do Refugees Belong in Camps? Experiences from Goma and Guinea." *The Lancet* 346: 360–362.

Weber, Leanne. 2006. "The Shifting Frontiers of Migration Control." In *Borders, Mobility and Technologies of Control*, edited by Sharon Pickering and Leanne Weber, 21–44. Dordrecht: Springer.

Wilson, Dean. 2006. "Biometrics, Borders, and the Ideal Suspect." In *Borders, Mobility and Technologies of Control*, edited by Sharon Pickering and Leanne Weber, 87–110. Dordrecht: Springer.

Women's Commission for Refugee Women and Children. 2008. "Disabilities among Refugees and Conflict-Affected Populations." New York: Women's Commission for Refugee Women and Children.

Young, Kylie, and Eloise Finlay. 2001. "Disabled? Sorry We Can't Afford It. Australia's Position on Refugees and Migrants with Disabilities." *Women in Action /Women and disabilities/* 4(2). http://www.isiswomen.org/index.php?option=com_content&task=view&id=660&Itemid=200

Zembylas, Michalinos. 2010. "Agamben's Theory of Biopower and Immigrants/Refugees/Asylum Seekers. Discourses of Citizenship and the Implications for Curriculum Theorizing." *Journal of Curriculum Theorizing* 26(2): 31–45.

13

Self-Advocacy: The Emancipation Movement Led by People with Intellectual and Developmental Disabilities

Mark Friedman and Ruthie-Marie Beckwith

Introduction

In October 1982, two disparate groups of individuals with disabilities[1] were taking steps to organize what ultimately became two of the most powerful self-advocacy organizations in the country—Speaking For Ourselves of Pennsylvania, Inc. and People First of Tennessee, Inc. Their multi-issue mission statements were in keeping with those of the more mainstream disability advocacy organizations at the time. However, the "self-help approach" the founders used to establish and attract their constituencies was considered by professional and parent advocacy organizations to be useful only to the extent it prepared people for membership within the established disability advocacy community—a "boot-camp" so to speak. As such, for the most part, their early efforts were largely ignored or at best met with a form of paternalistic acceptance.

The establishment's lack of attention served to provide the fledgling groups with the time to transform themselves from individuals who were considered by most to be incompetent, unable to benefit from education, and completely dependent on families and professional guidance into well-informed, tenacious leaders in the long haul fight to emancipate their counterparts from large, state-run institutions. Their respective campaigns for freedom resulted in seismic shifts in how people with developmental disabilities were perceived and the manner in which they receive services and supports.

The purpose of this chapter is to provide an explanatory critique of the challenges and resistance they encountered, the praxis[2] that informed their efforts, the evolution of their social change approaches, and the impact of their liberation movement on disability service networks in their respective states. Their collaboration with other emerging self-advocacy groups in Oregon, Washington, Illinois, Oklahoma, Alabama, New Hampshire, Minnesota, and New York, among others, would ultimately lead to the formation of Self-Advocates Becoming

Empowered (SABE), the national self-advocacy group, including its initial "Close the Doors" campaign in 1994. This was the first national effort by self-advocates to emancipate people with intellectual and developmental disabilities from institutions (Nelis and Ward 1995).[3]

This chapter conceptualizes emancipation as put forth by Lacey (2002, 9):

> Emancipation is, first, becoming rid of the state of oppression and second gaining the conditions for effective agency...Furthermore, to get rid of oppression requires getting rid of the causes of the absence of the conditions of effective agency.

In addition, throughout this chapter, the term "self-advocacy" is used in the context of self-determination, and as defined by SABE:

> It is about independent groups of people with disabilities working together for justice by helping each other take charge of our lives and *fight discrimination*. It teaches us how to make decisions and choices that affect our lives so we can be more independent. It also teaches us about our rights, but along with learning our rights, we learn responsibilities. The way we learn about advocating for ourselves is by supporting each other so we can speak out for what we believe in (Self-Advocates Becoming Empowered, cited in Hayden 2004).

Finally, for the most part, the data for this analysis are presented in the form of personal stories and insights from those on the front line of the struggles, including the nondisabled authors: Mark Friedman as the founding state coordinator for Speaking For Ourselves, Inc. and Ruthie-Marie Beckwith, as the founding staff advisor for People First of Tennessee, Inc.

The Challenges and Resistance They Overcame

The grassroots organizing activities used during the initial years focused on functions that maximized the participation of all members, regardless of the severity of their disability, thus assuring that no one would be left out. All involved in these efforts knew they had wandered into uncharted territory and the founders invested a great amount of time in assuring that their groups promoted authenticity as well as autonomy.

Debbie Robinson of Speaking For Ourselves described their efforts as "Advocacy in the Danger Zone."

> Interviewer: When you are working with people in a Danger Zone, what do self-advocates have to remember?
>
> Debbie: Self-advocacy people have to remember that you are going to come across a situation where you have to be really careful how you handle it, not be so hasty, and be patient. You have to be careful. You have to think about the people you are trying to help. The person is the first priority. They are living in that situation and you have to be really careful. You are dealing with people's lives (Hayden 1990/1991, 12–13).

In the early stages of organizing their self-advocacy groups, the members seldom mentioned their traumatic experiences of abuse. Insightful reflections shared by leaders like Debbie were dismissed as the product of manipulation and subversive mind control techniques employed by the nondisabled organizers and advisors (O'Connor, Fisher, and Robinson 2000). It would take several years before their collective voices were strong enough to silence the overt skepticism of many professionals and family members.[4]

As their organizations gathered strength and slowly evolved into a movement, the members began to talk about their experiences living in institutions. They overcame their fears and lack of experience and began reaching out to their incarcerated counterparts living in institutions. The members' efforts to expose the nature and insidiousness of their oppression were relentless.

As their voices grew in number and volume, so did the resistance they encountered from family members, professionals, family advocates, state officials, unions, and other individuals and entities with extensive conflicts of interest. Repression emerged at each juncture and had to be dealt with both on a personal and an organizational level. And, to add to the complexity of the resistance, the subordination of people with intellectual and developmental disabilities was commonly perceived as valid given the predominantly negative beliefs about disability in general and intellectual disabilities in particular. The following examples of specific barriers encountered by the organizations' members and their institutionalized counterparts, illustrate how the nature and scope of the resistance shifted in response to their growing collective power.

Barriers Faced by the Members

In order to organize, members had to overcome their lack of money, limited access to telephones, illiteracy, inability to drive and lack of other resources that most people take for granted in the twentieth century. Only a handful had attended public schools for any amount of time and, as such, members rarely demonstrated the ability to read, to write more than their first name, or to do basic arithmetic. At the time, most members were given access to no more than a dollar a day to purchase sodas at the sheltered workshops they were required to attend during the day. Despite the fact that they were adults, they had to seek "permission" to attend self-advocacy chapter meetings from parents or social workers (Beckwith 1996a, 241).

For most of their lives the members had been conditioned to be passive and patient—perpetually waiting for other people to make decisions about their lives. This "learned helplessness" (Seligman 1975)—and it was clearly learned rather than innate—was countered by 'speak-out' sessions and moral support from their local self-advocacy chapter's leadership and fellow members. The members' lack of life experiences, routinely taken for granted by middle class Americans, would at times cloud decision-making and necessitate more personal excavation by the organizers. For example, at a planning meeting for their first statewide conference, one member balked at participating because she had never experienced staying in a hotel room. Again, many of such difficulties that arose were a product of ableism and the effects of incarceration and paternalism, rather than inherent in members' intellectual disabilities.

Ultimately, the growth of membership in number and geography afforded access to new members to be recruited to the cause. In 1995, Speaking For Ourselves (1995) wrote its own manifesto with regard to membership recruitment as follows:

> "Ways to Attract New Members"
> Food for Thought
>
> When a new member enters
> our organization, we have to
> treat them like they're part
> of **our family**, where they can
> come for refuge from
> <u>the chains of bondage</u> of institutions.
> Also they can be cured from the
> <u>disease of dependency</u>
> to transform to a strong-willed
> being of independency—that is the
> **ONE TRUE TIE THAT BONDS**
> **US ALL TOGETHER**
> <u>Speaking For Ourselves</u>.

As participation in meetings and functions on local and state levels continued to grow, so did the resistance on the part of the professional and family advocacy organizations. People First of Tennessee, Inc. amassed a litany of examples of how its members (both inside and outside of the institutions) routinely encountered violations of their First Amendment Rights (People First of Tennessee, 1996).[5]

1. A member was not permitted to go to church because she had "mouthed off" to the house manager. Members of People First frequently change churches (even denominations) when the house managers change. Other members who are Jewish are not supported to go to synagogue and are even encouraged to go to Christian Churches.
2. People have their "privilege" to come to People First meetings revoked by staff when they "act up". (We are told that we have a "disruptive" influence on these people.) One member was told he could "choose" not to come to our board meeting as punishment for hitting someone at the workshop.
3. People are not permitted to come to the phone when a People First member or staff person calls. The person calling and or being called is grilled about what the call is about.
4. People routinely have to get "permission" to go to community events with people other than agency staff.

In Tennessee, institutional opposition to membership became full blown when People First turned to litigation as a liberation tool. Chapters no longer were afforded meeting space, and individual membership cards were returned to the People First office with hate mail attached. Filings for individual conservatorship over members who lived in the state-run institutions grew by over 50 percent in two years. Attempts to visit members who lived in institutions were rejected or the escort to a living unit shifted from a harried social worker to an armed guard. Death threats left on the People First answering machine reinforced the understanding that their advocacy work had ventured into ever deepening layers of Debbie Robinson's Danger Zone.

Barriers Faced by the Incarcerated

In addition to the problems of illiteracy and lack of resources, chapter members who were incarcerated had their lives completely controlled by staff and institutional rules. The rules were rigid and usually for the convenience of the staff or the institution. For example, in many institutions, people were awakened at 6 am due to the shift staff change over and then left to lie in their beds for an hour or two until the day shift was ready. In order to make a phone call to family or an advocate, people had to use the phone in the nursing station or their social worker's office, and access to the phone had to be earned with "good behavior."

The greatest challenge in the institution was abuse, both physical and sexual. Abuse came from everywhere, from the staff as well as other 'patients.' Rarely was staff held accountable for the damage they inflicted. Criminal charges filed by aggrieved family members were dropped when district attorneys and prosecutors believed their victims were too disabled to be credible witnesses. In a Pennsylvania case, institutional staff accused of abuse were brought to trial. The judge found the residents' testimony unreliable and dismissed the case.

Residents who spoke up too much or were considered "uppity" were punished and sent to 'behavior wards' where the use of locked seclusion rooms and straitjackets were still common practices. A team of four staff members, named "The Behavior Busters" was responsible for the beating death of one of the People First members who lived at the Arlington Developmental Center. Assaults secured their victims' silence and kept everyone else 'in line'—this is what will happen to you if you don't behave.

Self-advocacy chapter members fortunate enough to move out of the institutions were routinely threated with "being sent back" for not complying with minor rules or failing to "fit in" to smaller, but still segregated community homes. Nonetheless, some of these formerly incarcerated members would come to provide the most unassailable testimony to what they and others had endured. Betty Potts and Carol Talley were early spokespersons about their experiences, and their stories motivated their fellow members to take action on behalf of those who had not yet been released.

Betty Potts was 22 in 1978 when she left Pennhurst, after having lived there for 13 years. She had lived in North Philadelphia with her parents before entering Pennhurst. When Betty was a young child, her parents could no longer take care of her and she was sent to Pennhurst State School and Hospital. In Betty's own words she described her life at Pennhurst:

> I went to Pennhurst when I was nine. I got sent there because my Mom was getting sick and she couldn't take care of me. I remember being at Pennhurst and seeing people tied down to their beds and getting smacked and hit. Nobody hit me 'cause I could talk. I once spoke up about their hitting someone and handled rough but they said I lied about it but I didn't.
>
> It was hard living at Pennhurst. I guess it was also hard on the staff cause some of them were overworked. My Mom and Dad didn't put me there because they didn't love me. They put me there 'cause they couldn't take care

of me. I always went home to visit with my Dad and Mom even though I was living at Pennhurst (Potts 2011).

Life in the institution was hard. Women were particularly susceptible to sexual abuse. Carole Talley lived at many institutions including Pennhurst. At one of the pro-institution public hearings sponsored by Pennsylvania state legislators, she described her experience this way:

> You people don't know what it's like to be in an institution. When I was three years old, I was taken from my family. My family didn't have a choice. They didn't have the money. I grew up in Elwyn for 23 years and in plain words, they ain't no damn good.
> I feel everybody on earth has a right to live where they want to live, not in an institution. I feel every time people mention the work retarded; I get very angry because I hate that word. They should use the word disabled.
> I feel all institutions should be closed for good. I wish that families and government officials could be in an institution to see how it is for themselves. I lived in three of them and I can tell you how it was...
> They put me in an institution. My grandfather wanted me but my Mom said no. When I went to the institution they told my parents they would teach me reading, writing and arithmetic but they did not teach me anything. They left me alone in a classroom and a couple of boys got a hold of me and raped me. When my Mom left, the other kids beat me up. When you have an accident they would make you kneel on the floor and put your hands out and put the dirty panties over your face. Every time my Mom would come to see me she could see marks. When she would say something, I would get beat up and put in the locked side room. Every five minutes I was in the side room. My parents couldn't visit me (Speaking For Ourselves, 14).

The Praxis That Informed the Efforts of Self-Advocates

In *Political Consciousness and Collective Action*, Morris (1992, 351), outlined the need for a researcher's investigation of political consciousness to identify, describe, and analyze existing systems of domination that affect the oppressed opposition. As in the case of other incarcerated populations, the domination experienced by individuals with developmental disabilities in state-run as well as private institutions is absolute. Prejudice, indifference, and lack of purpose pervade the day-to-day existence of the incarcerated, ultimately robbing them of their humanity and rendering them invisible.

Although their first local chapters were organized in the same month of the same year, October 1981, the leaders of Speaking For Ourselves and People First of Tennessee did not meet one another until the Spring of 1990 at the annual conference of the American Association on Mental Retardation (currently referred to as the American Association on Intellectual and Developmental Disabilities) in Atlanta, GA.[6] The development of both organizations' structure and operations was evolutionary and organic. It wasn't add water and stir—there was no off the shelf leadership.

As with any other group of oppressed people, the members required the same investment in time and effort to grow their leadership. As their experience grew, so did their vision of how life could be different. Their understanding of the complexity of problems inherent in trying to fundamentally change social structures deepened. Ultimately, their unfaltering demand for universal emancipation for *all* of their incarcerated counterparts, and not just those perceived to be "ready" or "more capable" would represent such a shift in paradigms that many policymakers could not overcome the cognitive dissonance it created.

Consciousness Raising

In the early years, people had to overcome their fear of speaking up. Many members got into 'trouble' with their group home staff for sharing problems they had with the staff or agencies. Many self-advocacy chapters instituted stringent rules of privacy such as, "what's said here, stays here." As stated earlier, it took several years for people to be able to talk about their own institutional experiences. Many members had lived in institutions and had personally experienced physical and/ or sexual assault. It was very hard to talk about and many never did (Williams 1993).

People's feelings about their own experiences in institutions were complicated. In general, these feelings included: (1) feeling abandoned by their families and not wanting to talk poorly of them; (2) living in fear; (3) coping with the actual experience of abuse; and (4) dealing with the lingering feelings of shame and fear. These feelings were compounded by a sense that 'it must have been my fault,' and, 'I must have done something bad to have been put there.'

In 1989, Speaking For Ourselves visited the members who had been "placed" at Pine Hill, a facility that held 100 residents. It had originally been an Annex of the infamous Pennhurst (Haldeman 1977) but in 1980, the state had mysteriously converted it to a privately run facility operated by a nursing home company. At the institution, they met several small children who spent their whole day confined to their beds. Roland Johnson (1999), a former resident of Pennhurst who later became a national self-advocacy leader, came out in the hallway and said, "I saw the little babies crying, little infant babies, they was not being cared for right... It smelled like Pennhurst: it 'mind me of Pennhurst—the graffiti and the beds, just looked like Pennhurst. It was just a awful sight to see...I had tears when I came out of there" (Johnson 1999, 77). During the visit, he also heard a staff member slap a resident. Debbie Robinson (2012) described her experience, "I was stunned, I was dumbfounded and I've never seen anything like it in my life. There were no words you could say besides the smell in there. It made me sick. I've never seen anything like it."

Speaking For Ourselves reacted to the abuse they had seen by calling everyone they knew, including the Executive Director of the Association for Retarded Citizens, the state Director of Mental Retardation, local officials and advocacy lawyers. They met with the important state officials about the horrible conditions at the facility. An investigation was done and the state sent in monitors at the facility 24/7. Members visited this facility many times and had many meetings with officials about the conditions, but in the end little was done.

Culture: The Roots of Community Spirit and Power

Storytelling and songs have often been used to give people strength to face overwhelming forces of violence and oppression. Highlander Folk School, a famous civil rights training center, describes the significance of culture building in the following way:

> So now, just as in the past, people in struggling communities are turning to the strength and wisdom of their heritages to sustain them in their current struggles. Their songs, sermons, satires, dramatic direct actions, foods, extended families, and seasonal celebrations keep them going, keep them fighting. People in these communities know that they're fighting for nothing less than a quality life and the opportunity to define how they will live their lives. (Highlander Research and Education Center 1988)

Songs about resistance and getting out of institutions inspired the membership to continue their liberation efforts. The incorporation of storytelling and song into the self-advocacy movement served functions similar to other civil rights struggles against oppressive institutional structures. These functions helped members overcome fear, enhanced members' sense of identity, built solidarity at local and statewide meetings, and provided structure for the oral history members relied on as a way to overcome illiteracy. The Speaking For Ourselves song was one of the first, written in 1987 by Karl Williams (Perske 1996, 1). The song became very popular and was sung by self-advocacy groups across the United States and the world. It became the unofficial anthem of the self-advocacy movement (Perske 1996, 30). Later, several songs were written specifically to support the institution work. People First of Tennessee created its own song to support its institutional work entitled, *Clover Bottom Freedom Train.*

> Many years have come and gone since I've been in this place
>   Waiting for an opening to join the human race,
>   Three square meals are not enough to feed my lonely soul—
>   Won't you give me one more chance to be made whole? (Beckwith 1996b).

Similarly, storytelling in both organizations led to the publication of "Success Stories" (People First of Tennessee 2000; Speaking For Ourselves 1996) —compilations of the stories and photos of formerly incarcerated members that they would use as a tool to promote institutional closure.

Developing Position Statements and Taking a Stand

In the 1990s, it was still dangerous to speak out against institutions. In Pennsylvania, chapter meetings were open only to members and organization volunteers. Over time, meeting agendas included discussions about the problems members who were still incarcerated were experiencing. The issue was usually addressed as a question similar to, "How can we help all the people still living in institutions?" "What can we do to help them get out?"

In Tennessee, many chapters held their meetings at the agencies where they received supports, and outsiders were seldom excluded from participating. While this helped build internal support for those groups, discussions about experiences in the institutions, as well as efforts to close them, were relegated to events that brought the leadership together on a regional or statewide basis on nonagency turf.

Annual "Speak Up" contests held in each region became the forums for members to share their thoughts about any topic they felt strongly about while honing their own their public speaking skills. Experiences with incarceration and advocating for the closure of the state-run institutions became a common theme of these talks.

> The reason I pick institutions as my topic because I feel like we can do better for our people who live in institutions…Any person with a disability should have the same rights in receive support and services as anybody else. I think all services should be out in the communities…I also think the GOVERNMENT should take the money they spend on the up keep of the institutions and they should spend it to build homes for the people who live in the institutions…(Scott 1995)

Speaking For Ourselves began taking a stand against institutions as the leaders gained strength and allies and began to feel safe in speaking and standing up for others. In 1985, Jerome Iannuzzi, one of the early leaders of Speaking For Ourselves, was appointed by Governor Dick Thornburgh to serve on the Pennsylvania Developmental Disabilities Council. This gave him a platform to speak out against the institutions and promote their closure. He was one of the first self-advocates in the country to be appointed in his own right to serve on a Developmental Disabilities Council.

As people's knowledge of best practices for supporting individuals in the community with more complex medical and psychiatric disabilities grew, coupled with the interminable reports of abuse, neglect and deaths, so did the memberships' demands for full emancipation for all of their incarcerated counterparts. In Tennessee, incarcerated counterparts also included children. Frances Hamblen, People First State Vice-President, had worked for 20 years as a childcare aide. She was particularly disturbed about the neglect many of the children had experienced,

> The one child looked at me and said, 'Help me. Get me out of here.' He was about six or seven years old. His eyes penetrated me. It scared me, and I thought if I could just get that child outside…but they are still in that institution. I want all those places to be closed. (Byzek and Gwin 1997)

Fellowship Farm in Limerick, Pennsylvania and the Highlander Research and Education Center in New Market, Tennessee became familiar refuges from the tension and toll organizing exacted on leadership and served as the locations where the leadership formulated and adopted their first position statements opposing institutions and demanding their closure.

> We believe institutions are harmful and limit life choices. Institutions stop people from exercising their rights and leading a normal life. People with disabilities should have a choice to live where ever and with whomever they want. Any person regardless of disability should have the same opportunity to receive support and services as anyone else. All services and supports should be in the community. Therefore, we believe all institutions should be closed and the people set free. (People First of Tennessee Board of Directors 1994)

We believe that all institutions should be closed and abolished. Everybody with all types of disabilities should live in the community. People in institutions are getting abused and hurt real bad. People are dying and getting mistreated. People in institutions want to be part of the community, be free, have control of their lives, make decisions, vote, have jobs, have a better life. People's voices need to be heard and listened to and supported by technology.

People should have a quality place to live. Quality means:
- Where they want to live
- Friends and relationships
- Jobs
- Freedom to come and go
- Who you want to live with

No one should have the right to put people in institutions at all!! (Speaking For Ourselves Board of Directors, 1995).

People First of Tennessee was the first disability organization in Tennessee to take a position that all institutions should be closed. This caused a stir in the disability community and branded People First as a radical organization with unrealistic viewpoints about deinstitutionalization.

Evolution of Their Social Change Approaches

Visiting and Visibility

As in Tennessee, Speaking For Ourselves began their initial work to get people out of institutions with efforts to visit their members still living in institutions. They had taken the position to not to have local chapters in state institutions and instead worked to get the people living in the institutions to attend local chapters.

About a dozen people living at Embreeville State Center attended the local Chester County Chapter meetings. Jerome Iannuzzi and the Speaking For Ourselves State Coordinator made the first visits to state institutions in 1985. Jerome was a fearless advocate for people living in institutions. Jerome had lived at the notorious Pennhurst State School and Hospital for more than fifteen years as a child and young adult. He explained his reason for being sent to Pennhurst this way,

"When I was 13, my parents decided their lives would be better if I was cared for in an institution. Although an aunt and uncle wanted to adopt me, the Judge said no, and I was committed to Pennhurst. Today, I wish families and the government could be institutionalized and see how it feels for themselves." (Speaking For Ourselves 2000, 16–18)

Visiting these state institutions was very emotional and difficult. It was heart rending when at the end of the visit we were able to leave and the residents had to stay. On the way home in the car after one visit, while discussing the next steps they would take Jerome said, "I can't do this anymore." He said he couldn't visit the institutions anymore. It was just too difficult. It brought up all his own past painful experiences.

Debbie Robinson (2012) was the Philadelphia Chapter President and remembers:

They came to us telling us things and told us to come to see them, and to get them out. One of the members just stood out and said come visit me. That's when we went to this institution. State officials didn't want us visiting the institutions but they could not stop us from visiting our members who lived there.

Legislative Actions

Speaking For Ourselves, Inc. conducted its statewide Campaign for Freedom in 1997 and visited all of the seven state institutions in Pennsylvania. They traveled across the state because many of the institutions were in the remote corners of the state. In 1997, the Pennsylvania State Legislature proposed a law restricting the ability of the Governor to close an institution without legislative approval. State Representative Fairchild chaired Committee hearings on the proposed law at the State Capital building and at each of the state institutions. Because of the tremendous backlash against the efforts to close the state institutions, the hearings were certain to be packed with parents and employees of the institution opposed to closing institutions and in support of the proposed law.

Members attended all of the legislative hearings. The first hearing was held in a large hearing room at the State Capitol in Harrisburg. The room was packed and people overflowed into the hallway. Speaking For Ourselves' most experienced leaders who had been residents of institutions signed up to testify but were not allowed to speak. However, Ray Gagne was the only person with disabilities who was allowed to testify and Representative Fairchild attacked him verbally.

Prior to the hearings, Speaking For Ourselves had formed an alliance with the independent living centers and ADAPT disability activists. For a long time there had been a separation between people with physical disabilities and cognitive disabilities but the institutional issue represented an area of common interest.

The ADAPT activists had extensive experience in power politics and Speaking For Ourselves members had none. The Speaking For Ourselves leadership admired them. ADAPT activists attended the hearing in significant numbers and lined the walls of the room as a demonstration of solidarity. They did not testify or speak but were there to give the Speaking For Ourselves leadership support and strength and to bear witness to the proceedings.

This was the first time ADAPT members had fit into one of Speaking For Ourselves' organizing events. To their credit, ADAPT leaders were able to overcome the common societal prejudices held by many toward people with intellectual disabilities. They were able to see them as fellow activists rather than incompetent clients in need of services. The ADAPT leaders made a very significant contribution to Speaking For Ourselves' organizing efforts through their presence.

The hearings were tumultuous and painful. Before each hearing, Speaking For Ourselves members would tour the institution and meet as many people as they could. They would be mobbed with people wanting to hug them or touch them physically whenever they entered a living area. It was hard to see so many people living in such isolation and segregation. People had little to do all day long. It was difficult for all of them to stand up against such opposition and animosity, but they knew they were speaking for the people still living there who yearned for the chance to live in the community.

At their office Speaking For Ourselves received hundreds of letters support-ing institutions and chastising them for their actions. Many of the letters con-tained very hateful words. They were hard to read. They read them all, usually out loud to one another so those members who were illiterate could understand what was being said about them. They put the letters into large three ring binders to remember how strong the opposition was. Eventually there were three binders filled with these letters. Carolyn Morgan, Board President, used to tell everyone, "We just have to tap into our resources within ourselves. We can and we will make a difference."

The hearing at Polk State Center was the worst. Polk has long been considered one of the worst institutions in the State. It contained 700 residents. The year before the hearing, in 1996, the Health Department had issued a scathing report citing the death of four residents due to poor medical care. The report said a woman with a history of gastrointestinal bleeding went untreated for two days. A man developed gangrene from a cut on his leg (Associated Press 1997).

Polk was located in the far northeastern region of Pennsylvania hours from any major city. It employed 1,200 people and was the major employer in the area. The Committee Hearing was held in the institution's auditorium. There were about 300 parents and staff people present. The Committee members sat up on a big stage. Ron Brown was one of two members who testified at the hearing. He described his experience:

I was thirteen when I moved to Polk. They told me I would not make it on the outside. I have been out of Polk for 20 years now. I testified at the hear-ings to close Polk. It was very hard for me to go back there to testify. Now I can do whatever I want to see all institutions close (Speaking For Ourselves 2000, 7).

There was complete silence in the audience as the members gave their testimony about what happened to them when they lived at Polk; no one could dispute the actual voices of the people who had lived there. Members had placed copies of their book of success stories of people who had moved out of institutions on each of the 300 seats in the auditorium (Speaking For Ourselves 1996). Not one copy was left behind after everyone had left the auditorium.

What would turn out to be the last hearing was held at Woodhaven Center in Philadelphia on October 15, 1997. Woodhaven was an unusual institution of 200 residents that was a State institution operated by the Temple University Institute for Disabilities. It was initially designed to be a model program for people with behav-ioral problems but by the time it was built and operationalized its time had passed. Community programs were sprouting up and the benefits of community living were becoming abundantly clear. However, Woodhaven persisted in attempting to be a model program.

For the Woodhaven hearing, Representative Fairchild had decreed that no per-son with disabilities would be allowed to testify. He called them 'rabble rousers' and said they didn't represent the people living in institutions or their families. Speaking For Ourselves planned a rally outside the hearing room to protest not being allowed to testify. They arranged for the leaders of the national self-advocacy organization, Self-Advocates Becoming Empowered, to attend. Tia Nelis, chair-person of the group and a strong leader from People First of Illinois, participated, along with ADAPT and other advocates.

The issue of being excluded from testifying galvanized the disability community. Speaking For Ourselves was able to obtain twelve cross disability organizations to cosponsor the Rally. Debbie Robinson served as the organizer of the Rally. In the press release before the Rally, leaders of Speaking For Ourselves (1997) stated:

- "We are trying to get all the people out of the State institutions"—Steve Dorsey, Vice President of Speaking For Ourselves.
- "It's a violation of the constitution to not let us speak"—Octavia Green, Board President of Speaking For Ourselves.
- "These hearings have treated people with disabilities in a barbaric way. The Legislators think we are not human as if we don't have any brains"—Debbie Robinson, Board member and organizer of the Campaign for Freedom Rally.

More than 150 people attended the rally at the hearing. Toward the end of the hearing, people's anger boiled over at not being allowed to testify and they shut down the hearing. While the bill to prohibit the closure of any state institution without the specific approval of the state legislature did pass, the Governor later vetoed it.

Litigation

People First began escalating its concerns over the treatment of its incarcerated members following the release of a 21 page, single spaced, scathing Letter of Findings issued by the U.S. Justice Department in 1991 over the conditions at Arlington (US Department of Justice 1991). The director of the state Protection and Advocacy organization hadn't obtained a copy of the report but, nonetheless, was dismissive about its contents. Few among the community providers had any dealings with those who were incarcerated. Many providers as well as family members viewed possible deinstitutionalization efforts as competition for scare community based support resources.

While Speaking For Ourselves was able to galvanize allies in the disability community, People First of Tennessee had to go it alone—no other disability organizations were willing to ally themselves with People First. People First of Tennessee members watched with disbelief when the media reported that the Governor had conducted an unannounced tour of the Arlington facility and pronounced it "well-run." In June 1991, after much wrangling, state president Beth Sievers and other officers of the board of directors met with the Commissioner of the Department of Mental Health armed with a list of questions the board and local chapter members wanted addressed. The meeting did not go well.

The board had made it a priority to obtain a tour of the facility to make sure that People First members were safe and not being abused. The degree of paternalism in response to their questions raised even more questions in the leadership's minds. The Commissioner responded during the meeting to the three different requests for a tour of the facility made by Beth by assuring her that, "Your members and everyone else who lives at Arlington are fine. And, we'll be happy to give you a tour *after things settle down.*"

The Commissioner's denial of what the leadership believed to be a very reasonable request convinced the Tennessee self-advocacy membership that unlike their counterparts in Pennsylvania, working within the system would not secure the reforms they believed would need to be made. As such, after a six-hour debate at the next meeting of their Board of Directors, they voted to file the first federal lawsuit brought by formerly incarcerated individuals with developmental disabilities in the United States against a state-run institution. With representation from experienced public interest lawyers, Judy Gran of the Public Interest Law Center of Philadelphia (PILCOP) (Byzak 1998) and Jack Derryberry of Nashville they filed their first lawsuit on December 12, 1991. Three years later in 1994, they filed a second lawsuit that included the three remaining state-run facilities.

The organization's early work of visiting and recruiting members at Tennessee's four state-run developmental centers in the early 1980's turned out to be a significant factor in Tennessee People First's litigation efforts. Resistance to the litigation by state officials was to be expected. However, family members of those incarcerated strongly objected to the litigation and sought to use their status as legal conservators to remove their relative from inclusion in the definition of the "class." The families' attorney argued that the leadership of People First was incapable of representing the class due to their diagnosis of mental retardation.

The Judge dismissed the claims of the families' attorney and ordered the full class certified, citing case law related to Pennhurst with regard to issues of conservatorship. People First was given legal standing and named as the "class representative" based on the long-standing, active relationships with their incarcerated members.

> As discussed more fully above, the parents and guardians lack the authority to waive the fundamental rights of their children and wards; moreover, any authority by the parents or guardians to bring civil litigation on behalf of their ward is not exclusive. (US Department of Justice 1995)

Being named class representative provided assurance that the voices of the incarcerated themselves would not only be included but would also influence the long-term remedies that were ultimately included in multiple court orders.

People First's emancipation efforts intensified drastically following the court's ruling. Noncourt-related activities shifted to educating the membership about best practices in community services, continuing to visit incarcerated members to assure their safety,[7] mounting a wide ranging public relations campaign, and fundraising to support their involvement.

Court-related activities included maintaining a presence when court was in session (a challenge in that the case was in the United States District court based in Memphis, a four hour drive from Nashville and an even longer ride on the Greyhound Bus). As the organization prevailed in court, members became involved in court ordered planning sessions for deinstitutionalization as well as monitoring the State's compliance with the courts orders.

To carry out this wide array of initiatives on a statewide basis, People First formed "institution teams" that carried out their mandate with renewed passion and persistence. Members of these teams found themselves traveling outside of Tennessee to promote their cause. Ed Sewell, past president of People First of Tennessee, shared his perspective in Mouth Magazine (Byzek and Gwin 1997, 24–27).

> The Justice Department was against us. They didn't believe in what we were doing. I had a bunch of questions they wouldn't answer. They didn't want to work with us. They are now coming to see our side of the story, since they saw so many people die. We had more than 50 people die in there. They

get beatings. They get sexual abuse. They get neglect. They die. But now the word is getting around about what we did. I've been traveling to other states—Alabama, Wisconsin, Illinois. They want to learn from what we've done.

Collaborative efforts between Speaking For Ourselves, People First of Tennessee and a number of other self-advocacy organizations began to coalesce as more members shared their stories and strategies.

The addition of other strong voices coalesced on Valentines Day in 1996, when both organizations participated in a joint meeting of self-advocates from around the country with the U.S. Justice Department in Washington, D.C. The Justice Department had filed numerous lawsuits against state institutions under the Civil Rights of Institutionalized Persons Act (CRIPA). However, as Ed Sewell had indicated, they frequently settled the lawsuits by agreeing to court orders to fix up the institution rather than having people move out into community programs. They met with Deval Patrick, the Assistant Attorney General for the Civil Rights Division of the Department of Justice to demand more aggressive enforcement of civil rights laws on behalf of persons living in state-run institutions.

Pam Bard, the Chester County, PA Chapter President, summarized the purpose of the meeting quite succinctly when she told Mr. Patrick, "We are here today because we want to close institutions and you want to fix them up and make them look pretty" (Byzek and Gwin 1997, 27).

The Impact of Their Liberation Movement

Thousands of people with intellectual and developmental disabilities have left state-run and private institutions over the last 20 years. While the largest factor in this has been law suits, people's voices expressed through self-advocacy organizations have played a major role in freeing people from institutions. Ten states have now phased out all their institutions. These include: Arkansas, DC, Hawaii, Maine, Michigan, New Hampshire, New Mexico, Rhode Island, Vermont and West Virginia. Five other states are expected to close their last institutions in the next five years.

Much has changed due to self-advocacy. People's voices are now accepted as legitimate expression and are commonly heard in policy-making bodies and even solicited. People with intellectual disabilities are full members of most disability decision-making bodies. Self-advocacy organizations are perceived to be legitimate representatives of their members. People are more able to participate in collective action and organizing.

The majority of people with intellectual disabilities no longer live in institutions. Yet, exclusion and segregation remain the norm. Group homes and supervised apartments keep people separate and segregated in the community. While there are many efforts to increase employment, the majority of people with developmental disabilities remain unemployed at home or in sheltered workshops. Sheltered workshops continue to increase in size and numbers of people. Few people have competitive or integrated jobs in the community.

Conclusions

Ultimately, the self-advocacy movement is about helping people with intellectual and developmental disabilities gain power and influence. This is particularly difficult as the people are situated in and often dependent on a human service system. They are usually surrounded by paid professionals and caregivers who deny the power they exert over the people in their care. Human service workers are extremely uncomfortable with the idea of power. They often refuse to see how being powerless makes people vulnerable and defenseless. This denial of the 'elephant in the room' is a major barrier to overcoming it.

Gaining power is one of the core purposes of self-advocacy. Empowerment of the individual is at the heart of the movement. Individual power can keep people safe and be liberating. Collective power gives people influence to shape the future. People can accrue power when they gain the support of influential allies.

Self-advocacy is frequently misperceived as being an individual effort toward empowerment rather than a social movement by people with disabilities engaged in collective action to overcome oppression. Self-advocacy is often criticized as being segregated. The importance of organizing and the role of organizers is generally devalued and often outright rejected. Rosa Parks is often thought of as a hero because, as the story is told, one day she got tired of going to the back of the bus and refused and was arrested. It is widely misunderstood that Rosa was the Secretary of the local NAACP. She had attended civil rights retreats at the famous Highlander Folk School,[8] a Tennessee training center for worker's rights and racial equality. She was part of a group that mobilized and organized collectively to create a movement that would change the world (Powledge 1991, 74).

Self-advocacy has not yet achieved the level of acceptance, power and influence of the civil rights movement. Many leaders of the self-advocacy movement have made the shift from representing themselves to representing the group members. This is a major step in leadership and the development of successful movements (Toch 1965, 84). It is a continuing struggle to shift people's thinking from service models to civil and human rights because, in the end, self-advocacy is a movement for freedom and justice.

Notes

1. The founding members had, for the most part, developmental disabilities within the definition of the Developmental Disabilities Act of 1981.
2. Paulo Freire (1986, 36) defines praxis in *Pedagogy of the Oppressed* as "reflection and action upon the world in order to transform it." Through praxis, oppressed people can acquire a critical awareness of their own condition, and, with their allies, struggle for liberation.
3. Initial support for Self-Advocates Becoming Empowered was provided by the Institute on Community Integration, University of Minnesota and the Center for Human Policy, Syracuse University.
4. Indeed, when People First of Tennessee filed its first federal lawsuit in 1991, *People First of Tennessee v. the Arlington Developmental Center*, Tennessee state officials routinely referred to it by the name of the law firm in Philadelphia that was representing People First thus promoting the notion that the organization's leadership had been duped by those Philadelphia lawyers. Use of the true name of the case didn't begin until after People First of Tennessee filed its second-class action lawsuit against the three remaining state-run institutions.
5. First Amendment claims were included in the People First of Tennessee, Inc. v. Arlington Developmental Center and appealed by the Parent Guardian Association to the Supreme Court where they were denied certiorari, the right to a hearing.

6. American Association on Mental Retardation Annual Convention, Atlanta, Georgia, May 31, 1990.
7. Denials of access to incarcerated members served as at the basis for the First Amendment claims included in the original complaint. Following the Court's Order, access to all of the People First members living in institutions was guaranteed.
8. One famous photo shows Rosa Parks sitting in the front row along with Martin Luther King at the Highlander Folk Center, referred to as a communist training school. Retrieved from: http://www.martinlutherking.org/images/commie-school.jpg

References

Associated Press. 1997. "State Joins Probe into Deaths at Mental Facility." *Philadelphia Inquirer*. January 29.

Beckwith, Ruthie-Marie. 1996a. The Bruises Are on the Inside: An Advisor's perspective. In *New Voices: Self-advocacy by people with disabilities*, edited by, Gunnar Dybwad and Hank Bersani Cambridge, MA: Brookline Books.

———. 1996b. "Clover Bottom Freedom Song," In *I Get Respect: Stories of New Lives in the Community*. Nashville, TN: People First of Tennessee.

Byzak, Josie. 1998. What Drives You to Do What You Do? *Mouth Magazine*. May. http://www.mouthmag.com/says/judysays.htm

Byzek, Josie, and Lucy Gwin. 1997. Escape from Tenneesee's DD Centers. *Mouth Magazine* 8(2). http://www.mouthmag.com/peoplefirst.htm

Freire, Paulo. 1986. *Pedagogy of the Oppressed*. New York: Continuum, 36.

Haldeman v. Pennhurst State School & Hospital. 446 F. Supp. 1295 (F.D. Pa. 1977).

Hayden, Mary. 2004. *The Self-Advocacy Movement: The Unacknowledged Civil Rights Movement*. Washington, DC: National Institute on Disability and Rehabilitation Research.

———. 1990/1991. "Advocacy in the Danger Zone: Interview with Debbie Robinson" *IMPACT* 3(4): 12–13.

Highlander Research and Education Center. 1988. *Culture: The Roots of Community Spirit and Power: The Highlander Culture Program*.

Johnson, Roland. 1999. *Lost in a Desert World: An Autobiography (as told to Karl Williams)*. Massey-Reyner.

———. 1987. *WHYY Radio Interview by Marty Moss-Coan*. April 26.

Lacey, Hugh. 2002. "Emancipatory Critique and Emancipatory Movements." *Journal of Critical Realism*, (November).

Morris, Aldon. 1992. "Political Consciousness and Collective Action." In *Frontiers in Social Movement Theory*, edited by Aldon Morris and Carol McClurg Mueller. New Haven, CT: Yale University Press.

Nelis, Tia, and Nancy Ward. 1995/1996. "Operation Close the Doors: Working for Freedom." *Impact* 9(1): 15–17.

O'Connor, Susan, Ellen Fisher, and Debra Robinson. 2000. "Intersecting Cultures: Women of Color with Intellectual Disabilities." In *Women with intellectual disabilities: Finding a place in the world*, edited by Rannveig Taustadottir and Kelley Johnson, 229–239. Philadelphia, PA: Jessica Kingsley Publishers.

People First of Tennessee. 2000. *I Get Respect: Stories of New Lives in the Community*.

———. 1996. *Memorandum regarding First Amendment Rights Violations to Jack Derryberry, Attorney by Ruthie-Marie Beckwith, Staff Advisor*, Original document in author's personal files. (July 16, 1996).

———. 1994. Board of Directors, Nashville, Tennessee. http://www.clearinghouse.net /chDocs/public/MR-TN-0001–0005.pdf

Perske, Robert. 1996. "Self-Advocates on the Move." In *New Voices: Self-advocacy by people with disabilities*, edited by Gunnar Dybwad and Hank Bersani. Cambridge, MA: Brookline Books.

Potts, Betty. 2011. Interview by author. Philadelphia, PA. June 4.

Powledge, Fred. 1991. *Free at Last? The Civil Rights Movement and the People Who Made It*. New York: Harper Collins.

Robinson, Debra. 2012 "Visionary Voices Oral history, Temple University, Institute on Disabilities." Accessed December 12, 2012. http://disabilities.temple.edu/voices/detailVideo.asp?mediaCode=010–01

Scott, Bonita. 1995. *Institutions Speech*. People First of Tennessee Annual Conference. Nashville, Tennessee.

Seligman, Marvin. 1975. *Helplessness: On Depression, Development, and Death*. San Francisco: W. H. Freeman.

Speaking For Ourselves. 2000. *Out of Institution and You're Home: Success Stories 1969–1999*. Plymouth Meeting, PA. In personal files of author.

———. 1997. *Woodhaven Rally Flyer*. In personal files of author.

———. 1995. *Ways to Attract New Members*, Plymouth Meeting, PA. In personal files of author.

Speaking For Ourselves Board of Directors. 1995. Plymouth Meeting, PA. In personal files of author.

Toch, Hans. 1965. *The Social Psychology of Social Movements*. New York: Bobbs-Merrill.

US Department of Justice. 1995. "Order Granting Class Certification, People First of TN v. Arlington Developmental Center." http://www.clearinghouse.net/chDocs/public/MR-TN-0001–0001.pdf

———. 1991. Letter of Findings, Arlington Developmental Center. U.S. v. STATE OF TENN. 925 F.Supp. 1292 United States District Court, W. D. Tennessee.

Williams, Karl. 1993. "Held in Each Other's Hearts: Members of Speaking for Ourselves as told to Karl Williams." In *Friendships and Community Connections between People with and without Developmental Disabilities*, edited by Angela Amado, 241–276. Baltimore, MD: Paul H. Brooks Publishing.

14

Alternatives to (Disability) Incarceration

Liat Ben-Moshe

When thinking of disability and incarceration from an intersectional perspective (as suggested in the introduction to this volume), it is important to think about incarceration in a variety of locales that disabled and/or non normative bodies and minds are being swept into, such as psychiatric hospitals, residential institutions for those with intellectual and developmental disabilities, and prisons. I therefore focus, in this chapter, on discussions of alternatives to incarceration (broadly defined) that take place in three movements with an abolitionary framework: anti-psychiatry, prison or penal abolition, and the movement to close down institutions for those labeled intellectually and developmentally disabled. These movements seek not to reform prisons, psychiatric hospitals, and residential institutions for those labeled as developmentally disabled, but to do away with them altogether.

When incarceration is discussed from a critical (not to mention abolitionary) framework, the question posed most frequently is, "but what is to be done" (Gilmore 2011)? What could replace these systems of incarceration? Those who critique prison abolition, anti-psychiatry, and anti-institutionalization often do so because they feel that although the critique of prisons and institutions sometimes has merit, these perspectives do not provide any solutions, only condemnations of the current system. I want to suggest that this is not the case. Although varied, prison abolitionists, anti-psychiatry, and deinstitutionalization activists sketch alternative living arrangements, alternative responses to harm and ways of dealing with pain and altered states of mind, without resorting to hospitalization and imprisonment. Put together, such suggestions amount to a vision of abolitionist alternatives in praxis. Building on the work of activists and scholars in these movements, I provide below a rough sketch of some alternatives to incarceration from an abolitionary/noninstitutional framework.

Abolition as the Power of "what is not yet fully existing"

There are various organizations that could be characterized as penal or prison abolitionist in North America, such as Critical Resistance, Families Against Mandatory

Minimums, All of Us or None, Black and Pink, Project NIA, Justice Now, the Prison Moratorium project, American Friends Service Committee, Anarchist Black Cross, and the Prison Activist Resource Center, to name a few. Although they do not necessarily share the same ideas regarding alternatives to imprisonment, they all share the dream and struggle for a world with no prisons, or no penalty as a response to harm. Ruth Morris (1995) suggests that the goal of prison abolition is to envision a time where a prison could be built but no one would be put in it, because society will "say no" to caging human beings and to mechanisms advocating revenge instead of justice.

Similarly, I characterize deinstitutionalization in the fields of developmental disability and psychiatric disability not only as an exodus of oppressed people outside the walls of institutions. In the eyes of those who pushed for institutional closure and community living for people with a variety of disabilities/impairments/altered states, deinstitutionalization is perceived as a philosophy, not just a historical process or policy agenda. The resistance to institutionalization and psychiatric hospitalization arose from a broader social critique of medicalization and medical authority (Conrad 2007; Conrad and Schneider 1992; Zola 1991), which brought with it a new understanding of human value, especially in regards to people with disabilities, as seen in the anti-psychiatry and ex-patients movements (Szasz 1961; Chamberlin 1978) and the People First movement (Williams and Shoultz 1982). Taken together, these frameworks suggest that reforming the prison/institutional-industrial-complex (by creating more opportunities for employment for people while institutionalized, opening psychiatric wards in prisons, etc.) will only prolong systems that need to be eliminated altogether.

I suggest that abolition can become a useful strategy for resistance to all forms of incarceration, as it does not seek to reform the structure as is but envisions and creates a new worldview in which oppressive structures do not exist. It thus goes beyond protesting the current circumstances, to creating new conditions of possibility by collectively contesting the status quo. Thomas Mathiesen conceptualizes abolition as an alternative in the making: "The alternative lies in the 'unfinished,' in the sketch, in what is not yet fully existing" (1974, 1). According to Mathiesen, abolition takes place when one breaks with the established order and simultaneously breaks new ground. Abolition is triggered by making people aware of the necessary dilemma they are faced with—continuing with the existing order with some changes (i.e., reform) or transitioning to something unknown. The question becomes not "what is the best alternative" in its final formulation, but how this new order shall begin from current conditions. The second question, which emerges from the unfinished as alternative, is how to maintain it as such, a sketch, not a final result but a continual process of change (Mathiesen 1974).

Longtime anti-psychiatry activist Bonnie Burstow (2010) suggests that anti-psychiatry as a movement could benefit from the insights of prison abolitionists, especially as formulated by Quakers in the 1970s. Following the recommendations of Honey Knopp et al. (1976), Burstow suggests that the short term goals of anti-psychiatry activists, such as reform efforts, should be kept as such, as steps on the road that is not yet fully formulated—the unfinished road of abolition. Knopp et al. (1976) suggest that it is useful to imagine the long term goal of abolition as a chain that links together shorter campaigns on specific issues—such as jail diversion, restitution programs, or the move of those released to community placements.

In a recent conversation with Noam Chomsky, Angela Y. Davis (2012) encourages us to imagine radical futures, different than the ones we have now, as different as we can imagine in fact. But she also reminds us that the future is always connected to the present and past. Therefore, the examples that follow are meant as heuristic devices that might aid us in this work of reimagining a carceral-free society. They are not meant as "solutions" per se, as that is not the end goal of these struggles/movements for abolition. The aim is to create responsive and just communities, free from coercion, repression, oppression, and forced disappearance and segregation.

Alternatives to Imprisonment

When discussing the goals of abolitionary work in regards to prisons, the question that people ask most often is what could replace prisons or punitive responses to harm. This question could be charted as trying to understand what to do with those incarcerated at the present time, what to do with those deemed as dangerous in the absence of imprisonment as a viable strategy, or what to do when an offense takes place (like assault or mugging) if one is committed to nonpunitive responses to crime. It's important to stress that there is no one uniform abolition movement, and therefore the answers that activists provide to these questions are multiple and complicated. In this section, however, I sketch some of the ways abolitionist groups have responded to such questions (for more nuanced discussion see Ben-Moshe 2011b; Davis 2003; Saleh Hanna 2000).

One of the difficulties of conceptualizing a world without prisons is that many think about a monolithic system that will replace the punitive one we have now (Davis 2003). But abolishing the present system should instead lead to socially responding to specific behaviors and their outcomes in a myriad of ways, so that murder is not handled in the same ways as sex work, for example. Moreover, not every case of "murder," or killing another person, would be handled in the same way either. The response to one could be complete decriminalization and the response to the other could be counseling or access to peer support, for instance.

Some of the most scathing critiques of the abolition model are based on the fact that people view it as impractical, and as not offering any real-life solutions to the problems it names. But as early as 1976, when one of the first manuals on prison abolition was put into print, abolitionist alternatives were suggested and explored alongside the critiques they offered (Knopp 1976). These included the use of restitution as a means of making amends for harms done, especially if there are financial implications to those who were harmed by the act. Some alternatives that were already in place at the time, but were not yet widely used, included the increased reliance on such programs as community probation, supervision, and parole (Knopp 1976). A related suggestion involves widening the scope of jail and prison diversion and treatment programs for a wider variety of people, especially in relation to sex work and drug offenses. As we will see below however, although these are indeed alternatives to incarceration, they also have the potential of extending the scope of the carceral regime to more individuals and to acts that were not previously under its reach.

Other alternatives to incarceration could include community supervision programs, which can also have drawbacks such as the potential abuse of the power to supervise. But over the years, the efficacy of such programs seems to have proved itself over other measures, especially since they connect people to the community and to available services (Morris 1989). This is something segregationist approaches, such as jails or boot camps, cannot do. A more hybrid community based program can be gleaned in Ontario with the use of community resource centers. These are used for people serving the last portion of their sentence while getting access to jobs in the community (Morris 1989).

In regards to harms that are seen as violating and extreme (including sexual violence), abolitionists challenge the assumption that harsh sentences and retributive attitudes lessen victims' pain or deter the "offender" from repeating the same kind of harm. Some programs in the abolitionist spirit are peer support groups for those harmed and those who committed harm, reeducation, and noncoercive and holistic treatment programs.[1] Current strategies that follow an abolitionist framework can be found in the anthology by members of *Incite! Women of Color Against Violence* (2006), which articulates ways of thinking and reacting to violence and sexual assault that do not involve the State or its agents. For instance, neighborhood watches in areas that are known as problematic to the safety of women and LGBTQ folks reduce the reliance on the police and its agents when something suspicious or objectionable is taking place. The Audre Lorde Project (n.d.), for example, launched the Safe Neighborhood Campaign, which calls for prevention and response to violence against gender variant and nonconforming people of color in Brooklyn, NY.

In regards to street crime, there are some programs operational today that decrease the reliance on police and State intervention in crime control. These are perceived as alternatives because traditional law enforcement (like police and other State apparatuses) treat marginalized communities, especially communities of color, with oppressive and suppressive measures. In order to create nonstatist self-defense mechanisms of deterrence, community action groups (like CLASP in West Philadelphia described by Knopp et al. in 1976) are organizing using various self-help and self-reliance measures. Such techniques include hanging jingle bells on doors to signal the entrance of intruders, and neighborhood watches comprised several adults armed only with flashlights and horns. These techniques work not only as preventive measures to deter crime but also to create cohesive communities who feel responsibility for their own neighborhood and learn to trust one another in vouching for their own safety. This is part of the abolitionist measure of empowering communities, especially those marginalized and most affected by the reach of the carceral regime, to define and deal with issues that arise within them.

Some penal and prison abolitionists draw inspiration from precolonial societies and eras, in which prisons were never widely used. Such practices include the use of sentencing circles, which were created by indigenous communities in North America, and conferencing, traditionally practiced mostly in New Zealand and based on Maori traditions. Drawing on such practices, advocates of abolition point to the efficacy of victim-offender reconciliation programs. They suggest that in many cases, the reconciliation between the offender and the victim is much more powerful than the exile of the offender (Davis 2003). Some victim-offender reconciliation programs are also based on Christian faith principles, which originated with Quakers, Mennonites, and others (Leung 1999). Drawing on such traditions, criminologist Nils Christie (1977) called for the establishment of community based courts in which no professionals are involved and the offender faces directly those who were harmed by the act.

Alternatives to incarceration should be based on a new justice paradigm, according to abolitionists and social justice activists. For example, peace building justice is suggested by Magnani and Wray (2006) of the American Friends Service Committee. This framework is not based on punishment but on repentance, reparation, and reintegration. Repentance involves public acknowledgment of what has been done, issuing an apology for the harms done and the desire to atone for the action. For example, public acknowledgment of harms done was the centerpiece of the Truth and Reconciliation Committees in South Africa. Another example is the Navajo justice system, which is based on the practice of peacemaking and restoration (Nalyeeh)—demanding to discuss harms done and the pain it caused so that something positive will result from these actions. Navajo justice, in contrast to western concepts, confronts the action and its consequences, not the individual (Magnani and Wray 2006; Nielsen 2009).

Such practices are often referred to as representing restorative justice, as opposed to penal or criminal justice frameworks. Leung (1999) suggests that the restorative justice movement in North America arose out of four traditions: aboriginal justice, faith communities (especially Mennonites), the prison abolition movement, and alternative dispute resolution programs. Restoration refers to the process of righting wrongs or healing wounds caused by harm. This is a very broad definition, which will entail different outcomes for different parties. It does not necessarily mean returning to the relationships or conditions exisiting prior to the conflict, as that might be dangerous, for example in the case abusive relationships. Restitution programs offer a similar approach, but on narrower grounds, as they assign material value for the offense and do not address nonmaterial disputes (Leung 1999).

Despite the appeal of such suggestions, there are numerous abolitionist critiques raised against the restorative justice framework. First, as with other alternatives to incarceration, these ideas are increasingly being co-opted by the (criminal justice) system. The system uses the language of healing, restoring and justice but without implementing the necessary changes within the prison system and in society at large (addressing racism, sexism, capitalism etc.). The only change is often in the rhetoric used, not the value base of the programs and the system as a whole. For example, restitution and probation are now added on to long sentences, rather than as real alternatives to incarceration. In addition, the restorative framework is mainly advocated by white middle class activists, although its roots are mainly within indigenous communities worldwide. As a result, poor communities and communities of color could perceive this framework as a form of colonialism, as these activists go to indigenous communities and harvest their knowledge to bring it back to their own nonindigenous communities.

Ruth Morris was a particularly vocal critic of some alternatives to incarceration, which she describes as a continuation of the current state of affairs. Morris (1989) distinguishes between "true community alternatives" and prisons in the community. Prison-like institutions tend to: widen the net and regulate lives that would not be surveilled without such "alternatives"; create social isolation and segregation in the community; categorize people into staff vs. inmates; and promote control and violence as the basic tool for human interaction. In contrast, some characteristics of true alternatives to imprisonment include treating people in a humane fashion, creating meaningful integration into the totality of the community as much as possible, rejecting stigma and labels, and incorporating nonviolent ways of resolving problems. Morris (1995) critically reflects on her own activism, from 1975 to the 1990s, of attempting to bring underserved populations from prisons back into the community. She founded bail programs and the organization *My Brother's Place* (for chronically institutionalized men), as well as befriending many people who were incarcearated and bringing them into her home. According to Morris (1995), almost everything she worked toward has been co-opted by the State or the criminal justice system for its own use. The programs turned punitive and retributive, and she was essentially fired from participating in the programs she founded.

In addition, restorative justice, as opposed to punitive approaches, is very labor intensive for all involved. It is an ongoing process, and often there are no magical solutions that fit all parties. Each time one takes steps toward restoration, the terms need to be negotiated to fit the specific case and those involved. The strength of such approaches is that they are non coercive, but that can also be construed as their disadvantage. Since it is a voluntary operation, you cannot force someone who has done harm to take the route of repenting and atonement for wrong-doing (Magnani and Wray 2006). Other critiques of current formulations of restorative justice are that they assume communities that are very different conceptually from the ones we have now, as they draw from indigenous teachings.

The most significant critique of the restorative justice framework is that it does not address the structural inequalities that lead to injustice in the first place. It does not question the basic assumptions of the system, such as who gets to be defined as a criminal, and what gets defined as the community. Therefore, restorative justice can never restore the offender to the community without critiquing the embedded assumptions and definitions behind such a goal (Saleh-Hanna 2000). Due to these critiques, Morris (1995) and others, like Generation-Five (n.d.), suggest a shift from restorative justice toward *transformative* justice. The end goal is not only to restore relationships but to transform society in the process. The focus is not (only) on the specific harm done but on structures that create oppression and inequality in the first place. A deeper understanding of radical alternatives to imprisonment thus entails a multiplicity of actions starting with a redistribution of resources, demilitarization of schools, noncoercive physical and mental health care for all, a justice system based on reconciliation rather than vengeance, decriminalization of drug and sex work, and the defense of immigrant rights, to name just a few starting points (Davis 2003; Morris 1995; Saleh-Hanna 2000).

Alternatives to Psychiatry and Hospitalization

The same critiques that have been laid against the prison abolition framework have also targeted those who critique psychiatric commitments, especially with the perceived absence of alternatives to psychiatric or biomedical practices in relation to mental health. But although normatively sanctioned alternatives to psychiatry are not widespread in North America, they have always existed, and some of them predate the emergence of psychiatry as a field. But since medicalization and the pharmaceutical industry have their strongest hold in the United States, many of these alternatives are currently practiced elsewhere. It is also important to remember that the United States is the only Western country without some form of socialized health care system, which means that any investment in psychiatric alternatives or more holistic approaches is scarce and rarely funded by federal and state agencies.

In their groundbreaking collection, *Alternatives beyond Psychiatry*, Peter Stastny and Peter Lehmann (2007) collected ideas and lived experiences of those who have been psychiatrized and chose to live without psychiatric interventions. Some of the suggestions for practices that reduce the need for medication and hospitalization are quite straightforward and include the increased use of psychotherapy, as opposed to psychiatry and medication, in its different varieties such as group therapy, counseling, peer support and peer-counseling. Other alternatives suggested by users are various techniques of relaxation and contemplation such as yoga and meditation techniques, which many found to be useful to relieve stress and anxiety. Several authors also suggest that jogging, swimming, and other physical activities have helped them both in their recovery and in everyday life coping with stress (Stastny and Lehmann 2007). Although some of these suggestions may seem quite mundane, for people who have spent time within the psychiatric system, these proposals differ significantly from traditional medical approaches.

Other alternatives to hospitalization were actually developed by people with psychiatric training. Soteria is an often-cited pioneering model initiated in the early 1970s by American psychiatrist Loren Mosher. It is an alternative treatment model to traditional psychiatry and some of its characteristics are often taken up by psychiatric survivors. The original Soteria was a house in San Jose, California that offered a homelike environment for about seven patients at a time. It offered an array of activities such as yoga, art, music, dance, sport, outings, and gardening, and in which everyone shared the day-to-day running of the house to the extent they could. There were three phases identified for people in Soteria: the acute phase in which a phenomenological approach was used (interpreting the episode from each persons' own narratives and history[2]); then the person was expected to start sharing in daily activities and the staff shifted from a parent-supporter role to more of a peer relationship; and the third stage included diversification of roles and competencies inside and outside the house (Aderhold, Stastny, and Lehmann 2007).

Although the model is often cited by psychiatric survivors and those advocating for alternative models of treatments to this day, it has been marginalized in psychiatric discourse, even though empirical studies have proved its effectiveness in treating "psychotic breaks" and so-called disorders (Aderhold 2007, Calton et. al. 2008, and a discussion in Jones and Brown 2013). This neglect is probably due to the insistence that psychiatric drugs should be used only if no other options were working after a six-week period, a proclamation unheard of in biomedical psychiatry. There is also critique of the fact that there was no universal treatment plan developed in Soteria that could assist in management of "psychotic" patients. Mosher and others have argued that since the model is not about treating psychosis but about treating human beings, it cannot and should not have a plan that will fit everyone and every situation (Aderhold 2007).

Other networks to decrease dependence on hospitalization and provide alternative spaces for people in crisis have been attempted in Europe. In Sweden, a unique hotel setting was in operation from 1995–2004, and allowed people to stay for as long as they wanted, with no pressure to move to their own apartments because this may have been stressful for some. Some people moved there from prisons and institutions, and others were elderly and wanted to share their lives with others. There were no professionals involved except for maintenance workers. Other examples include the Runaway House in Berlin and the Crisis Hotel Project in New York State, where people who are at risk for psychiatric hospitalization can retreat to (Stanstny and Lehmann 2007). Bucalo (2007) also discusses La Cura, a network in Sicily, which operates a hotline that aids in legal strategies of avoiding psychiatric hospitalization and coercion. It also operates a network, Association Penelope, which provides housing, meals, and assistance with job applications, and is open to all people who need it without a requirement to get diagnosed or serviced by psychiatrists to attain these services.

In North America, Second Opinion Society in the Yukon, Canada, was founded by psychiatric survivors in the early 1990s and provides a drop-in center and resources for advocacy and support for local people of the region. It emphasizes community and holistic healing approaches instead of biopsychiatry and is run by survivors. They hold a weekly soup lunch, which is open to all and is attended by politicians, social workers, artists, tourists, holistic health practitioners and more.

They also established a community garden, which provides the food for the lunch and creates a concrete connection to the community (Sartori 2007).

Other alternatives to psychiatry lie not in the use of places and strategies of coping but in ways of warding off unwanted psychiatric interventions. For example, the use of advance directives, which are similar in terms of legality to a living will, allows a person to declare their wishes in case they have a psychotic break or other psychiatric episode (Krucke 2007). Unfortunately, these are not always upheld by psychiatrists, who feel that the person is not competent enough to refuse treatment. Advocates note ironically that people's competency is rarely questioned when giving consent to treatment. This practice received attention in the early 1980s when Thomas Szasz (1982) suggested the use of "psychiatric wills" which is still practiced today.

Probably the most pervasive way in which alternatives to psychiatry are conceptualized, imagined and practiced are through national and international networks and organizations created by psychiatric survivors, ex-patients, and consumers, as well as people within the anti-psychiatry movement more generally (and those who don't fit neatly into any of these categories). The importance of such organizations is that they build an alternative community to psychiatry, one that is supportive, caring, and often defiant. As in the critique of restorative justice, the point of these networks is not to restore the person to some sort of normative mental health but to discuss the social conditions that led to distress and, in many instances, to increased distress and oppression caused by attempts to biomedically "treat" a perceived behavior or outcome. People who self identify as Mad, for example, claim the category as a form of difference, one in which they find community and home, culture and pride. In a similar fashion to other disability rights and disability justice advocates, madness is seen as an identity, and not a disease. As such, it is a source for frustration, pride, and an entry point into a political stance.

For instance, *The Icarus Project* (n.d.) is a user-led organization/network, with an active online community. Its members refer to altered states of mind (focusing on bipolar and similar diagnoses) as "dangerous gifts" that need to be taken care of rather than diseases to be eliminated. They have an active website with resources, art work and discussion forums. In order to keep the group's initial activist fervor, many Icarus groups use a meeting format in which they allow for one hour of inward support followed by an hour of outward action. This allows members to connect and collaborate with each other, and also with the larger community. *Hearing Voices Network* (n.d.) is another dispersed organization that targets coping mechanisms used by those with "visions, voices and unusual perceptions" as opposed to advocating the annihilation of these experiences as prescribed by traditional psychiatry. According to the group's principles, the way people respond to their own beliefs and perceptions is the key to improving their quality of life, not developing the ability to think "normally" or rationally. A related network is InterVoice (n.d.) "Working across the world to spread positive and hopeful messages about the experience of hearing voices." Probably the largest user-led antipsychiatry organization today is *MindFreedom International (n.d.)*, which calls for a nonviolent revolution in the mental health system. *MindFreedom* began in 1986 as a newsletter and held its first counter-conference/protest against the American Psychological Association in 1990. Today it has consultive status with the United Nations, and operates as a nongovernmental organization with a human rights approach, but gets no funding from governments, mental health organizations, religious groups, etc. It organizes Mad Pride cultural events in six nation states, including in Africa.

Psychiatric survivors also emphasize that alternatives are often not about specific practices, but about who "calls the shots." Much like Ruth Morris and other penal abolitionists, famed anti-psychiatry activist Judie Chamberlin (1978) felt it is of utmost importance to distinguish between "real" alternatives to psychiatry and those that are alternatives in name only. A true alternative, according to Chamberlin, is one in which the power to make decisions lies with those the service is supposed to serve. Chamberlin (1978) distinguished between three ideal types of alternatives. The first is the partnership model in which professionals and nonprofessionals, including service users, work together and are all involved in decision-making. The second is the supportive model in which membership is open to all, and nonpatients and expatients are treated as equals. The last model is the separatist one in which ex-patients are both the users and the ones running the service. Chamberlin felt strongly that partnership type models are not real alternatives because they separate those who receive from those who provide help in a hierarchical manner. Currently though, most alternatives to psychiatry follow this seemingly collaborative model especially in relation to funding, which determines who runs the programs and who gets to be included/admitted to them. Such services, according to Chamberlin, are not alternatives because they mirror psychiatric practice, which is the core problem. When mental patients run the programs themselves they get more than help or services, according to Chamberlin (1978). They have opportunities to prove their competence and learn new skills regarding leadership and planning. Most alternative organizations operated by ex-mental patients operate in some collective way, which encourages the sharing of responsibility. When they work collectively, without professional control, hierarchies are broken and people are viewed as equal, not as inferior or lacking expertise. This is what makes them "real" alternatives.

The prevalent discourse in mental health care right now centers on notions of recovery, which is heralded as an "alternative" to traditional psychiatric models. But Howell and Voronka (2012) aptly point to the convenience of centering discussions on resilience and recovery of people under neoliberal frameworks, which signifies a retrenchment of the State from providing meaningful services. Under this framework, resilience is nothing more than a co-opted concept that falls right into the individualistic medicalized model of mental health and is not an alternative to it in any meaningful way. Although the concept of recovery emerged within the ex-patient movement, Howell and Voronka (2012) explain that the point was to recover in relation to oppression and psychiatrization, within a framework of rights, social justice, and peer support so the emphasis was on "recovery in" and not "recovery from." In other words, the framework (in Mad pride or in organizations like Icarus or Hearing Voices, discussed above) is based on social justice and healing within communities, with an emphasis on transforming social relations, systems of inequality and the ways madness is perceived. The emphasis is not on changing oneself in order to be more "normal," which seems to be the prevailing rhetoric in much of the recovery discourse currently.

Community Living as an Alternative to Institutionalization

While alternatives to psychiatry and hospitalizations are varied, it seems that the major alternative to institutional life for people with significant disabilities (especially intellectual and developmental disabilities) proposed by progressive professionals and self-advocates alike has been the idea of non-institutional living, especially in one's own home with supports as needed. This suggestion and the immense advocacy around it may seem trivial, especially coming from rigorous scholars and professionals. But even this seemingly benevolent idea is still fiercely debated, especially in many states and provinces that maintain large state institutions and nursing homes for people with developmental disabilities. If one subscribes to an ideology that views people with cognitive, psychiatric, and other diagnoses as mostly incompetent, "child-like" and unable to care for themselves or make meaningful decisions about their lives, then an idea such as independent living or living in a non-institutional setting is quite radical, which is why it was, and still is, so ferociously resisted.

It may be useful to understand what one means by a "dependent population" that cannot live "independently," which is what many proponents of institutional and group home living say of people with significant disabilities. Two dimensions could be affiliated with the term dependency: first, dependency on the state for financial support, health care, and other provisions; second, perceived inability of people to engage in their own self care without assistance from others (Oliver 1990). Some disabled people seem to fit both definitions. In everyday usage, dependence implies an inability to care for oneself and thus having to rely on other people's assistance. Conversely, independence implies not relying on anybody and requiring no assistance, a concept tied to an individualistic ethos (Oliver 1990). Disabled people often embody a different definition of independence, as exemplified in the principles of the Independent Living Movement. Under this framework, independence is perceived as the ability to control one's life, such as hiring one's own aides, and deciding on daily routines. It is not understood to mean doing things without any help from others.

When analyzing daily living in modern societies, it is hard to find situations in which any people are independent from one another. Thus, projecting dependence as a characteristic only of "fragile" members of our societies (i.e., elderly, disabled, and children) may seem natural, but it relies on a specific North American framework of rugged individualism (Ben-Moshe, Nocella, and Withers 2013). If anything, in many cases it is societal attitudes that create dependence amongst elderly and disabled people. Inaccessibility of the built environment, patronizing attitudes, historical exclusion from schooling and the increasingly fast pace of life in modern societies are all contributing factors to the social construction of disability (Wendell 1996) and dependence (Oliver 1990). Dependence is not inevitable or inherent within these populations. Dependence was prescribed to people with disabilities, and the elderly, so it seems detached from "normal people's" existence (Finkelstein 1993). An additional problem of the creation of forced dependence and infantilization is that it is often "masked by loving care" (Hockey and James 1993) of family members or professionals.

Living independently or in the community can also have multiple meanings, especially when used euphemistically by states/provinces and for-profit agencies. As Taylor, Bogdan, and Racino (1991) demonstrate, many "homes" in which people with developmental and psychiatric disabilities reside are agency owned, licensed or certified, which means they must follow codes and regulations, which often limit the residents' actions and choices. The staff is accountable to the agency, not to the residents, which often creates conflict in the "home," and funding is based on the facility, not the individual who resides in it. These homes are more like small institutions that do not have gates; they are not true to the spirit of independent living and community inclusion.

Often, what is an institution and what is community living is defined by public policy. Some define institutions in relation to the number of people housed therein. Some look at group homes as institutions on a smaller scale while others claim that they are not institutions at all but homes for people with shared characteristics who act as roommates (Center on Human Policy 2004). In such instances it might be most useful listening to people who reside in them to define whether they think of them as institutional in mindset, practice, and procedure. *Self Advocates Becoming Empowered*, a national advocacy group of people with intellectual/developmental disabilities, state that: "An institution is any facility or program where people do not have control over their lives. A facility or program can mean a private or public institution, nursing home, group home, foster care home, day treatment program, or sheltered workshop" (Center on Human Policy 2004). SABE's definition emphasizes agency and control over decision making as the decisive factor of whether one lives in an institutional setting. For instance, many group homes have features that remind one of an institution or hospital, such as set of rules that hang on the wall, emergency exits with lighted signs, regimented activities and schedules designed by staff and not residents, etc. In that sense, a single home could be equally institutional as a large facility housing dozens of people.

Over the years, some of the figures given for deinstitutionalization of public institutions for people with disabilities have been misleading, as significant proportions of people were transferred to other types of institutions such as nursing homes. By 2009, an estimated 86.4 percent of people with developmental disability labels who were receiving residential services in the US lived in community settings of 15 or fewer people, and 73.1 percent lived in residential settings with 6 or fewer people (Lakin et al. 2010). Although these smaller settings (of 4–6 or 6–15 residents per "home") are not typically counted as institutional placements, due to their size as well as daily routines and other aspects of life, many people with disabilities, family members, and advocates consider them to be mini-institutions within the community (Center on Human Policy 2004). In this sense the effectiveness of deinstitutionalization as a movement should be in ensuring noninstitutional community living. The closure of such institution is only a first step in such a process (Taylor 1995/6). Too often institutional closure is still embedded within the same circuits of power that created these massive institutions. As a result, the transition to smaller institutions appears to be the best-case scenario, unless closure is accompanied by a radical epistemic shift in the way community, dis/ability, and segregation are conceptualized (Ben-Moshe 2013).

Biklen (1991) offers a few guidelines to ensure that people who are living outside of institutions, with supports from staff, are not just living in smaller scale institutions but in something qualitatively different. These principles include: making the place as homelike as possible, one that you or everyone else would want to live in; involving residents in community activities, work and life in general; presuming that everyone is competent and has the ability to make decisions about their own lives; and refraining from letting bureaucracy and regulation take over and make people's homes into programs or treatment options.

In addition to supported living and group homes or small residential settings, there have been other forms of community living developed for and by people with developmental and significant disabilities. Often, these involved a reconceptual-ization of what "community living" entails (Ben-Moshe 2011a). Some of these arrangements draw on anarchist, socialist, and communist traditions, creating nonhierarchical and at times nonstatist communities in which everyone contributes to the shared production and consumption of goods. Norwegian sociologist and criminologist Nils Christie (1989) describes life and social arrangements in "com-munes for extraordinary people," as he refers to them. These are villages in various (usually rural) parts of Norway, which are also a part of a larger network of about 55 such villages all over Europe, and people move between them. I share their description (from Christie 1989; 2007) in some length to demonstrate the potential of such living arrangements as they exist outside of North America for the benefit of our analysis and activism around alternatives to (disability) incarceration.

The villages operate as alternative social arrangements in which people share households, work, and cultural life. There are no salaries given for residents for the shared work they do (although some residents get a disability stipend that goes toward their stay in the village), and no classifications such as staff or clients (which are prominent in group homes for example). The residents of the village come there for various reasons. Some are sent there by the State (as diversion from prison or institutional life) but most get there by choice. Some are not literate in the traditional sense and most likely would not get a job outside of the village that would sustain them within current economic structures, without government aid. Some have labels of cognitive or psychiatric disabilities, while some have pre-vious encounters with the legal system. Others come there in order to live in a more peaceful environment after encountering some personal tragedy or in order to "find themselves." There are a lot of foreigners who come to live in the villages, often from other villages in Europe. When outsiders enter the village they are often left to wonder who is "disabled," "mad," or "delinquent," but such labels are not formally used within the village. The only distinction that seems to be made is between those who have a bank account (and get a disability stipend), also known as a villager, and those who do not, often referred to as coworker, although this categorization would not necessarily be known to outsiders (Christie 1989). Going beyond such labels is of course a constant struggle.

The villages are run by: an executive board which meets twice a year and is comprised people who know the village but do not live there (similar to many boards for not-for-profit organizations); local boards which meet four times a year and mostly deal with financial matters; and the village assembly where real deci-sions are made regarding the everyday operations of the village. Assembly meetings resemble a town hall meeting. Their structure is nonhierarchical and encourages discussion by all, including those who are less verbal. This does not mean that all have equal power to influence decisions, but by having a democratic, noncen-tralized governing structure, these villages nevertheless offer an alternative to the hegemony of State power. Although some are paid with governmental stipends that support the village, others have no formal contact with the State. People come, stay as long as they like, work in the village and then leave without formal pay, just as they came. If this seems utopian or impossible, Christie (1989) reminds us that this is the way people used to live for most of history, and some still do, especially in nonindustrialized nations. When an individual becomes troublesome or does not seem to fit in with the village way of life, they are asked to leave. This does not seem to happen often, although there are probably more times when villagers feel unwelcome and choose to leave on their own.

Another example of shared communal living arrangements specifically for and with people with developmental disabilities are L'Arche communities. The L'Arche model was founded in France in 1964 by Jean Vanier, and it is now an international organization working in 40 countries, including the United States and Canada. L'Arche homes and programs operate according to a not-for-profit community model, which is distinct from client-centered, medical, or social service models of care. At L'Arche, people with disabilities, and those who assist them, live together in homes and apartments, sharing life with one another and "building community as responsible adults; everyone is believed to have the capacity to grow and to mature into adulthood, and to make a contribution to society, regardless of the physical or intellectual limitations with which they may be living" (L'Arche n.d.). L'Arche communities strive to "create small faith-based communities of friendship and mutuality between people who have disabilities and others; to develop life-long support systems with people who have disabilities, especially with those who are extremely vulnerable due to old age and/or multiple disabilities; and to highlight the unique capacity of persons with disabilities to enrich relationships and to build communities where the values of compassion, inclusion and diversity are upheld and lived by each person" (L'Arche n.d.).

As Christie (1989; 2007) suggests, perhaps the "extraordinary people" living in such "extraordinary" arrangements can direct the rest of us into converting parts of our communities into decentralized zones or independent villages. Perhaps their way of life is more ordinary or desirable than our own. But from the viewpoint of the disability rights movement, this view can be seen as idealistic and paternalistic. If such living arrangements are so great, why are they disability/difference focused? Another way to analyze the usefulness of these villages lays not so much in their contribution to so called outcast members of society, but as alternative governance structures that we can all benefit from (in the spirit of autonomous communities). Perhaps what such experimental villages teach us is that if they work for people requiring more support, then they might work for all of us, as prime examples of communities of interdependence. Of course, the drawback of this line of thinking is that if everyone lived in these seemingly ideal villages, they would essentially lose their main characteristics and their meaning as *alternative* ways of living.

It's important to emphasize that L'Arche communities and other alternate living arrangements for people labeled as intellectually disabled (such as those described by Christie) differ greatly from one another in the ways they implement the principles of equality and inclusion. More often than not, although the principles are certainly there, there are clear lines of demarcations between those who have disabilities (or disability labels) and those who do not, even if such distinctions are more informal than the professional/consumer divide produced in more traditional living arrangements.

Proponents of community-based services envision a world of both natural supports and paid services and push toward a system that is ultimately directed by the needs and guidance of service users themselves. Self Advocates Becoming Empowered (SABE) argue that any service provision that is not controlled by users is institutional, whether it is given in an enclosed segregated setting or not. Ultimately, they argue, decision-making and resources should come from the disabled person (hence their advocacy for legislation such as Money Follows the Person as well as person-directed services). This shift in perspective, from institutional to community based models, should not be made by disabled people or policy makers solely, but by all members of any given community that will value and include other members, including those who have been historically marginalized and segregated (Carey 2011).

The Possibility of a Noncarceral Future

If we take deinstitutionalization in the fields of developmental disability and mental health as historical case studies, we can learn from them about pitfalls to avoid when thinking about prison abolition and, more broadly, about alternatives to incarceration at present. Some view the shift from institutional life to community living as a victory, a move away from anachronistic approaches that segregate people with disabilities, into humanistic discourses that advocate for equality, inclusion, and integration. For those advocating the abolition of the institutional mindset, however, the concept of community-based services was supposed to be more than a change in the location of the provision of services, more than reforming or even closing institutions. It was meant as an epistemic shift in regards to the hierarchical system of care and the lack of meaningful relationships offered to people with disabilities. In theory, community based services were supposed to help in breaking down the barriers that prevent full participation of people with disabilities from all aspects of life. In reality, "community" often became a negation, a physical space outside the walls of the institution or mental hospital (Carey 2011). From an abolitionist perspective, it was a negative abolition (i.e., a removal of an oppressive institution), but the attempt to create something new out of the ashes of the old institutions (i.e., achieving meaningful relationships for people with disabilities) was not always successful (Ben-Moshe 2011a). Community services are certainly smaller and more dispersed, but the relations of power/knowledge at their core remain intact. Professionals created the programs and run them, with little change or input from service users. Under these conditions, it is not very surprising that many of these services foster further segregation and marginalization of people with disabilities.

This tension between self-directed "real alternatives" and a continuation of segregation outside the walls of carceral spaces, as suggested by Morris and Chamberlin earlier, reflects the nature of the relation between reform and abolition more broadly. The most serious potential problem with many incarceration alternatives, such as parole and probation, is that they create a net widening effect of the system and its control, and therefore do not fall within an abolitionist goal in relation to incarceration and penalty. As a result, people who would not have been sent to prisons are now under the control of new systems, originally meant to keep those en route to prison out of it. They are then surveilled (by computerized systems, reports sent to their work and home, and by police officers) for such "offenses" as traffic violations.

Our current moment is also one of intense neoliberal policies resulting in fiscal constraints, austerity measures and privatization of social services, which simultaneously constrains and holds possibilities for the closure of prisons and large state institutions. Because of the rising cost of construction and maintenance of these carceral edifices, the corporate world, criminal justice and health care systems are now turning to various "alternatives" to incarceration and institutionalization. But this turn mostly signifies the increased privatization of penalty and health care; not the decline of segregation, but its intensification through other means. Some corporations which privatized services once performed by the criminal justice system (like bail, fines, etc.) now lobby for alternatives to incarceration and use both the rhetoric of increased efficiency and that of restorative justice. But advocates point out that no restoration can occur when private companies take over meanings of what is just and do it for profit[3] (Selman 2010).

It is not only the neoliberal policies that activists, who fight and resist incarceration, should be wary of, it is the "progressive and dispersed installation of a new system of domination" (Deleuze 1992, 7). Disciplinary societies, according to Deleuze (1992), whose main characteristic is the organization of vast spaces of enclosure, are being replaced today by the societies of control, whose key feature is social control, and less focus is given to the location in which it is prescribed. It is the alternatives that are given to vast spaces of incarceration at present that brings to light Deleuze's proclamation. Advocacy efforts to create psychiatric care clinics in the community, for example, are seen by anti-psychiatry activists as measures to increase surveillance on those psychiatrized. This is especially the case in relation to compliance with the psychopharmaceutical regimen that has become an order and not a choice, contributing to what Erick Fabris (2011 and in this volume) describes as "chemical incarceration." In addition, prison abolition activists do not view measures such as electronic monitoring bracelets as adding to the freedom of those who had been criminalized, but as an increase to the net of incarceration and punitiveness at large. So resisting incarceration is not as much about abolishing carceral spaces, as it is about demolishing the ideology that necessitates the processes of incarceration and segregation.

Those who advocate for anti-institutionalization and prison abolition see community as in need of change, and do not see integration per se as the goal, but the formation of new caring, socially just communities. This could be characterized as one of the main differences between (newer) formulations of activism around the concept of "disability justice," as opposed to work geared toward disability rights. Disability justice represents a conceptual shift from notions of advocating for rights or equality in a system that is oppressive and unjust to begin with (such as increasing employment for people with disabilities in an unjust capitalist marketplace and discussing "community services" only through the discourse of for-profit health care system) to advocating for social change more broadly. Disability justice activists confront the ways various oppressions, such as racism, sexism, capitalism and ableism, intersect to influence the lives of disabled people in the arenas of education, self care, empowerment, housing, work, health, sexuality, and recreation. The goal is not to replace one form of control, such as a hospital, institution, and prison, with another, such as psychopharmaceuticals, nursing homes, and group homes. The aspiration is to fundamentally change the way we respond to difference or harm, the way normalcy is defined, the ways resources are distributed and accessed, and the ways we respond to each other.

Notes

1. In relation to abolitionary strategies regarding child sexual abuse through a transformative justice model, see the work of Generation Five (n.d.).
2. In the tradition of R. D. Laing (1960).
3. Another related problem that comes up in relation to implementing such "alternatives" is the already wide gap in terms of socioeconomic class inherent in the system as it stands now. Alternatives, such as fines, bail, or paying for home care out of

pocket, are discriminatory and so the rates of poor populations in prisons and institutions will only increase.

References

Aderhold, Volkmar, Peter Stastny, and Peter Lehmann. 2007. "Soteria: A Treatment Model and a Reform Movement in Psychiatry." In *Alternatives Beyond Psychiatry*, edited by Peter Stastny and Peter Lehmann, 146–160. Berlin: Peter Lehmann Publishing.

The Audre Lorde Project. n.d. Accessed on May 15, 2013. http://alp.org/safe -neighborhood-campaign

Ben-Moshe, Liat. 2013. The tension between abolition and reform. In *The End of Prisons: Reflections from the Decarceration Movement*, edited by Mechthild Nagel and Anthony J. Nocella II. Amsterdam: Rodopi Press, Value Inquiry Book Series

Ben-Moshe, Liat. 2011a. "The Contested Meaning of 'Community.' Discourses of Deinstitutionalization and Community Living in the Field of Developmental Disability." *Research in Social Science and Disability* 6(Special issue on disability and community): 241–264.

———. 2011b. *Genealogies of Resistance to Incarceration: Abolition Politics within Deinstitutionalization and Anti-Prison Activism in the U.S.* PhD Diss., Syracuse University.

Ben-Moshe, Liat, Anthony J. Nocella II, and A. J. Withers. 2013. Queer-Cripping Anarchism: Intersections and Reflections on Anarchism, Queer-ness, and Dis-Ability. In *Queering Anarchism*, edited C. Daring, J. Rogue, Deric Shannon, and Abbey Volcano. Oakland: AK Press.

Biklen, Douglas. 1991. "Small homes." In *Life in the Community: Case Studies of Organizations Supporting People with Disabilities*, edited by Steven J. Taylor, Robert Bogdan, and J. A. Racino, Baltimore, MD: Paul H. Brookes Publishing Co.

Bucalo, Giuseppe. 2007. "A Sicilian Way to Antipsychiatry: La Cura." In *Alternatives Beyond Psychiatry*, edited by Stastny, Peter and Lehmann, Peter, 217–222. Berlin: Peter Lehmann Publishing.

Burstow, Bonnie. (2010) The Withering Away Of Psychiatry: An Attrition Model For Antipsychiatry. Keynote lecture, Given at PsychOut : A Conference for Organizing Resistance Against Psychiatry. Toronto: University of Toronto. Accessed July 8, 2012. http://individual.utoronto.ca/psychout/papers/burstow_keynote_paper.pdf

Calton, Tim, Michael Ferriter, Nick Huband, and Helen Spandler. 2008. "A Systematic Review of the Soteria Paradigm for the Treatment of People Diagnosed with Schizophrenia." *Schizophrenia Bulletin* 34(1):181–192.

Carey, Allison C. 2011. "The Quest for Community: Intellectual Disability and the Shifting Meaning of Community in Activism." *Research in Social Science and Disability* 6(Special issue on disability and community): 189–214.

Center on Human Policy. 2004. "Community for All" Tool Kit: Resources for Supporting Community Living." Accessed October 20, 2009. http://thechp.syr.edu/toolkit/

Chamberlin, Judie. 1978. *On Our Own: Patient Controlled Alternatives to the Mental Health System*. New York: McGraw-Hill.

Christie, Nils. 2007. *Beyond Loneliness and Institutions: Communes for Extraordinary People*. Oslo: Wipf & Stock Publishers.

———. 1989. *Beyond Loneliness and Institutions: Communes for Extraordinary People*. Oslo: Norwegian University Press.

———. 1977. "Conflicts as Property." *British Journal of Criminology* 17(1): 1–26.

Conrad, Peter. (2007). *The Medicalization of Society: On the Transformation of Human Conditions into Treatable Disorders*. Baltimore, MD: Johns Hopkins University Press.

Conrad, Peter, and Joseph W. Schneider. 1992. *Deviance and Medicalization: From Badness to Sickness*. Philadelphia, PA: Temple University Press.

Davis, Angela Y. 2003. *Are Prisons Obsolete?* New York: Seven Stories Press.

Davis, Angela Y., and Noam Chomsky. 2012. "Radical Futures and Prospects for Freedom." Lecture given at the Berklee Performance Center, Boston, MA.

Deleuze, Gilles. (1992) Postscript on the Societies of Control. *October* 59 (Winter): 3–.7

Fabris, Erick. (2011). *Tranquil Prisons: Chemical Incarceration Under Community Treatment Orders*. Toronto: University of Toronto Press.

Finkelstein, Victor 1993. "Disability: A Social Challenge or an Administrative Responsibility." In *Disabling Barriers- Enabling Environments*, edited by J. Swain, V. Finkelstein, S. French, and M. Oliver. London: Sage and Open University Press.

Generation Five. n.d. "Generation Five's Mission is to End Child Sexual Abuse within Five Generations." http://www.generationfive.org/

Gilmore, Ruth Wilson. 2011. "What Is to Be Done?" *American Quarterly* 36(2): 245–265.

Hearing Voices Network. n.d. Accessed on June 1, 2013. http://www.hearing-voices.org/

Hockey, Jennifer Lorna, and Allison James. 1993. *Growing Up and Growing Older: Ageing and Dependency in the Life Course*. Sage: London.

Howell, Alison, and Jijian Voronka. 2012. "Introduction: The Politics of Resilience and Recovery in Mental Health Care." *Studies in Social Justice* 6(1).

Icarus Project. n.d. Accessed on May 25, 2013. http://theicarusproject.net/

Incite! Women of Color Against Violence. 2006. *Color of Violence: The Incite! Anthology*. Cambridge, MA: South End Press.

InterVoice. n.d. Accessed June 1 2013. http://www.intervoiceonline.org/

Jones, Nev, and Robyn Brown. 2013. "Absence of Psychiatric C/S/X Perspectives in Academic Discourse: Consequences and Implications." *Disability Studies Quarterly* 33(1).

Knopp, Fay Honey, and Prison Research Education Action Project. 1976. *Instead of Prisons: A Handbook for Abolitionists*. Syracuse, NY: Prison Research Education Action Project.

Krucke, Miriam. 2007. "Advance Directives: A Step towards Self Help." In *Alternatives Beyond Psychiatry*, edited by Peter Stastny and Peter Lehmann, 97–104. Berlin: Peter Lehmann Publishing.

L'Arche. n.d. Accessed May 7, 2011. http://www.larcheusa.org/

Laing, R. D. 1960. *The Divided Self; A Study of Sanity and Madness*. Chicago, IL: Quadrangle Books.

Lakin, K. Charlie Sheryl Larson, Patricia Salmi, and Amanda Webster. 2010. *Residential Services for Persons with Developmental Disabilities: Statues and trends through 2009*. Minneapolis, MN: University of Minnesota, Research and Training Center on Community Living, Institute on Community Integration.

Leung, May 1999. "The Origins of Restorative Justice. Paper from the Canadian Forum on Civil Justice." Accessed on April 7, 2008. http://cfcj-fcjc.org

Magnani, Laura, and Harmon L. Wray. 2006. *Beyond Prisons: A NewInterfaith Paradigm for Our FailedPrison System*. Minneapolis, MN: Fortress Press.

Mathiesen, Thomas 1974. *The Politics of Abolition*. New York: Halsted Press.

MindFreedom International. n.d. Accessed on May 25, 2013. http://www.mindfreedom
.org/

Morris, R.1995. *Penal Abolition, the Practical Choice: A Practical Manual on Penal
Abolition*. Toronto, ON: Canadian Scholars' Press.

———. 1989. *Crumbling Walls: Why Prisons Fail*. Oakville, ON: Mosaic Press.

Nielsen, Marianne O. 1999. Navajo Nation Courts, Peacemaking and Restorative
Justice Issues. *Journal of Legal Pluralism and Unofficial Law* 44: 105–126.

Oliver, Mike 1990. *The Politics of Disablement: A Sociological Approach*. New York:
St. Martin's Press.

Saleh-Hanna, Vivienne 2000. "Penal Abolition: An Ideological and Practical Venture
Against Criminal (In)Justice and Victimization." MA thesis, School of Criminology,
Simon Fraser University, Canada.

Sartori, Gisela. 2007. "Second Opinion Society: Without Psychiatry in the Yukon."
In *Alternatives Beyond Psychiatry*, edited by Peter Stastny, and Peter Lehmann,
199–209. Berlin: Peter Lehmann Publishing.

Selman, Donna. 2010. Remarks given at the 20th anniversary panel for "The rich get
richer and the poor gets prison." American Society of Criminology annual conference, Philadelphia.

Stanstny, Peter, and Peter Lehmann., eds. 2007. *Alternatives Beyond Psychiatry*. Berlin:
Peter Lehmann Publishing.

Szasz, Thomas S. 1982. "The Psychiatric Will: A New Mechanism for Protecting
Persons Against 'Psychosis' and Psychiatry." *American Psychologist* 37: 762–770.

———. 1961. *The Myth of Mental Illness; Foundations of a Theory of Personal
Conduct*. New York: Hoeber-Harper.

Taylor, Steven J. 1995/96. Thoughts and impressions on institutional closure. In M.
F. Hayden, K. C. Lakin, & S. Taylor (Eds.), *IMPACT: Feature Issue on Institution
Closures*, 9(1), 8–9.

Taylor, Steven J., Robert Bogdan, and J.A. Racino, eds. 1991. *Life in the Community:
Case Studies of Organizations Supporting People with Disabilities*. Baltimore, MD:
Paul H. Brookes Publishing Co..

Wendell, Susan. 1996. *The Rejected Body: Feminist Philosophical Reflections on
Disability*. New York: Routledge.

Williams, Pual, and Bonnie Shoultz. 1982. *We Can Speak for Ourselves*. London,
England: Souvenir Press.

Zola, Irving K. 1991. "The Medicalization of Aging and Disability." *Advances in
Medical Sociology* 2: 299–315.

Epilogue: Disability, Inc.

Robert McRuer

While this anthology was being completed, one of the most famous disabled people in the world, for a very short time, went to jail. Charged with the February 14, 2013 murder of his girlfriend Reeva Steenkamp, Oscar Pistorius—who is a double amputee also known as "The Blade Runner" due to the carbon fiber prosthetic blades he uses as a sprinter—spent eight days in the Brooklyn Police Station holding cell in Pretoria, South Africa, before being released on bond. He was indicted for the murder on August 19, 2013, and will face trial on March 3, 2014. Although Oscar Pistorius's story is not on the surface about what the subtitle to this volume terms "Imprisonment and Disability in the United States and Canada," the editors make clear in their introduction that "incarceration is not just normative in North America, but...worldwide, due to ongoing legacies of colonialism and neocolonialism." The Pistorius story, moreover (although in perhaps unexpected ways that I detail), also allows for a consideration of what the editors identify as "the neoliberal policies" (or, more broadly, the cultural politics of neoliberalism) that sustain "the growth of the [globalized] prison system, the reduction of affordable housing, and the lack of financial support for disabled people to live viably in the community." (Chapman, Ben-Moshe, and Carey, this volume). As essays such as those by Geoffrey Reaume, Shaista Patel, and Mansha Mirza make clear, the modes of identification, surveillance, securitization, and incarceration explored in *Disability Incarcerated* are certainly not contained to the North American continent.

Of course, the editors are not referring to someone like Pistorius when they invoke disabled people in the prison system, or disabled people without financial support or affordable housing. Prior to the murder charges, Oscar Pistorius actually exemplified a globalized disability that could not be contained. In fact, the trademarked slogan for the multinational Össur corporation that designs the Flex-Foot Cheetah blade that catapulted Pistorius to fame as a sprinter and ultimately enabled him to break the glass ceiling keeping disabled athletes from competing in the Olympic Games is "Life Without Limitations." "Though it seems unimaginable now," Rosemarie Garland-Thomson (2013) wrote one month after the death of Steenkamp, "to many disability rights advocates and activists, [Pistorius] had the potential to become a symbol as important as Rosa Parks." Indeed, six months earlier, during the London 2012 games (where he ran both in the Paralympic and Olympic Games), Pistorius' image circulated globally—in footage from the games, interviews, advertisements, and even sappy inspirational memes widely shared through social media—as a symbol of what "disability" might be beyond barriers and constraints.

I argue in this epilogue that the Pistorius story brings into purview the multi-layered and noninnocent ways in which disability is caught up in contemporary biopower. I return to the 2013 events—and to the ways in which both securitization and incarceration are central to them—momentarily, but I want to start (as it were) before the fall, with the (neoliberal) ways in which Pistorius was identified in advance of the killing. As I briefly examine the transformation of Pistorius from global representative of an uncontained disability to incarcerated prisoner, I want to mark what Jasbir Puar calls "the convivial relations between distinct yet entangled forms of power, part and parcel of what can be named the 'environmentality,' rather than governmentality, of mutually reinforcing, rather than teleological or serial, habitations of discipline and control" (2007, 117). The crip environmentality that we now inhabit has generated forms of discipline and control that at times look and feel like freedom and that we might well term "Disability, Incorporated": disability corporealized, destigmatized, identified, and integrated *as such* (out and proud) into the circuits of global capital. "Disability, Incorporated," however, is entirely convivial with the ongoing global hypostatization of "Disability, Incarcerated"—so convivial that "Disability, Inc." serves well to capture both their paradoxical entanglement and the indeterminacy perpetually in circulation around the sign "disability" in this particular moment in the history of capitalism. Neoliberal forms of "disability" have emerged that obscure the myriad ways in which other bodies and minds (also understood or materialized as impaired or disabled) are now caught up in what Michel Foucault famously called the global "carceral archipelago" (1975, 298)[1].

In August 2012, the London 2012 Games broadcast this paradoxical crip environmentality to the world. Disability, Incorporated was marketed globally via what Pistorius himself called "the most successful Paralympic Games ever" (Brown 2012). Ticket sales for the Paralympics reached £45 million, while sponsorship of both the Olympics and Paralympics (sold as a package for the first time and, across the country and the world, generating advertising that included Paralympians) reached £80 million (Topping 2013). "Great Britain," Pistorius insisted in an interview, "is at the forefront in terms of education on disability…I believe that's the only way to remove a lot of the stigmas, and to get over this being a taboo subject…My experience is that disability here is regarded in a really progressive way." With sentiments that would ironically not be unusual on the first day of an Introduction to Disability Studies class, he concluded, "People have not looked at it as a problem, but more as a challenge to change wider perceptions" (Brown 2012).

Meanwhile, Disability, Incarcerated was arguably visible just outside the stadium (and received a certain degree of attention even in the mainstream press), as activists protested the sponsorship of the Olympics and Paralympics by the private French IT company ATOS. Since 2010, the Tory-led coalition government in the United Kingdom has provided ATOS with a lucrative contract to carry out "work capability assessments." These assessments declare a wide range of disabled people in Britain "fit to work" and thus ineligible for benefits that would allow them to live independently, access attendant services, or utilize assisted transport. Thanks to ATOS and other players in the coalition's severe austerity plan, £18 billion were cut from the welfare budget in 2010, while £11 billion per year were scheduled to be cut through 2014 (Vale 2012). ATOS's contract costs British taxpayers £110 million and has left more than half of those subject to its assessments "destitute"—that is, without benefits *and* unemployed (Ferguson 2012). The sister of one disabled man jailed after making threatening comments to the assessors who found him fit to work suggested that ATOS's tests should be approached "with the wariness of a parole hearing" (Williams 2013), capturing well the ways in which a carceral logic subtends the situation in Britain, even as it seems to send disabled people out, "free" and "fit," into extra-carceral spaces. In the media, disabled people caught in this web of surveillance, assessment, and control have been portrayed as malingerers, "shirkers," and "benefit scroungers," and rates of abuse and suicide of people with disabilities have increased. Whatever Prime Minister David Cameron might have said about disabled athletes and the success of the London Paralympic Games, Owen Jones writes, "he leads a government that is systematically attacking the rights of the sick and disabled. Their financial support is being confiscated; their ability to lead independent lives attacked; they are subject to humiliating tests; they are demonised as 'scroungers' and drains on the public purse; and abuse towards them is soaring." (Jones 2012). For these reasons, at what they called the "ATOS Closing Ceremonies" on August 31, 2012 (timed to coincide with the Paralympics), beneath slogans such as "ATOS don't give a toss," a broad coalition of activists gathered at the corporate headquarters in Triton Square London (as they did across the country) to demand that the multinational be shut down and, more immediately, that their contracts with the government be terminated.

Chris Chapman, in this volume, overviews the various and local forms of what he calls "normalized everyday oppression" against marginalized groups; my point in contrasting the spectacularized disabled event that was London 2012 and disabled experiences on the ground in the United Kingdom is that whatever quotidian forms Disability, Incarcerated takes in our moment (from the racialized school-to-prison pipeline Nirmala Erevelles overviews in this volume, to the persistent back wards of custodial institutions examined by Phil Ferguson, to the life-or-death examination or testing by ATOS that leaves so many disabled people in the UK destitute), those forms are now shaped in the same environmentality that brings us Disability, Incorporated.

Disability, Inc. depends on what David Harvey calls "accumulation by dispossession" (2005, 137), given how centrally enmeshed it is with the neoliberal processes that centralize wealth through privatization and through redistribution of resources away from the public (a global austerity politics that protects the banks while slashing services to the poor—a politics particularly evident and punishing in the United Kingdom—is a clear example of such accumulation by dispossession). Both valences of Disability, Inc. can be read through dispossession: *incarceration*, of course, literally dispossesses individuals and groups of the freedom to shape their own lives (and this dispossession through incarceration is increasingly managed, as Mirza's chapter and others make clear in this volume, by private prison companies); *incorporation*, however, also involves dispossession through the spectacularization and individualization of experiences that can, in the end, only belong to a few. What Kevin Floyd terms "identity's glossy normalization" (2009, 203) appears to value and integrate difference, including disabled difference, but only by privatizing it, attempting to neutralize in the process the more radical forms of collective disabled or crip sociality that produced "disability identity" as resistance to isolation and pathologization in the first place. This neutralization of disabled difference, sociality, and solidarity, however, is only part of neoliberalism's quotidian violence; insidiously, Disability, Incorporated obscures, *yet enables through that obscuring*, Disability, Incarcerated.

In this volume, the chapter by Jihan Abbas and Jijian Voronka perhaps best exemplifies these processes, as the authors detail how the Canadian state's booster narrative in relation to its own development, inclusion, and "tolerance" explicitly facilitates the erasure of disabled histories of oppression, incarceration, and violence. In 2013, in South Africa, Oscar Pistorius' story exemplifies these processes when it is read as a melodrama of identity (disabled role model turned evil disabled killer) rather than as a story taking place in a system that is inherently violent and that actually thrives on melodramas of identity (thriving on such melodramas, with their stock characters removed from a more politicized analysis, is itself a form of neoliberal violence). Pistorius—out and proud, openly disabled—had in this context already been incorporated and securitized. He was living in one of South Africa's most secure, and almost entirely white, gated communities—the Silver Lakes Golf estate, which was voted in 2009 "the most secure estate in South Africa," due to 24-hour security guards, electrified fences, and gates with controlled and perpetually staffed access ("Pistorius's home" 2013). Even though (or precisely because) the majority of crime occurs in nongated (and non-white) spaces elsewhere, South Africa has one of the largest security industries in the world for white, monied, property owners (Durington 2013). Contemporary South Africa is in fact founded upon systems of privatization, securitization, dispossession, and identification (identification of the many who are supposed "threats" on the outside of the gates and identification of the few who can be incorporated inside). "Disability" (inc.) does not materialize in our moment in an environment apart from those systems.

The literal cover story in court at the time of this writing for Pistorius is one about a threat to his own safety that he felt that evening. Despite reports from neighbors who believe they heard a heated domestic argument, Pistorius claims he shot Steenkamp four times through the bathroom door because he believed she was a burglar. The cover story thus is currently about a threat to private space, property, and security (all in the masculinist space where the possession and use of firearms is entirely naturalized). That melodramatic story about private fears in private space, however, obscures the *systemic* violence acted out daily on South Africa's dispossessed. Such systemic violence (in South Africa, violence acted out *differentially* upon the bodies of women—particularly women of color and queer women) was actually something that Reeva Steenkamp herself had spoken out against.

For eight days, then, in February 2013, Pistorius went to prison—or rather, to a temporary holding cell at the police station. His tragic celebrity story and temporary incarceration, however, reveals virtually nothing about conditions for disabled prisoners in the South African prison system. Other groups or collectivities are necessary for the dissemination of that story. A few days before Pistorius was released on bail, the *Guardian* published an article on Pretoria Central Prison written by a member of the Wits Justice Project in Witwatersrand. The Wits Justice Project investigates and reports on conditions in South Africa's prisons. Pretoria Central Prison is where Pistorius likely would have been incarcerated had he not been granted bail. The article asks questions about disabled prisoners in South Africa using the words of a paraplegic man identified simply as "Prisoner A" (Raphaely 2013). Prisoner A's story resonates with many of the essays in this volume, particularly with the direct voices of interred subjects in the chapters by Syrus Ware, Joan Ruzsa, and Giselle Dias and by Mark Friedman and Ruthie-Marie Beckwith. Prisoner A has been held since late 2011 but—like one third of all those in South

Africa's prison system—has not been found guilty of any crime. Prisoner A, whom (in the spirit of this volume) I quote at length, reports:

> If I use my [crutches] I have to pull my legs and throw them out to the front. That's how I walk. I was shot in my spinal cord, which was cut in the middle during a hijacking in the driveway of my house three years before my arrest. Before I was transferred here I was in Johannesburg prison, where the doctor prescribed a wheelchair for me. The doctor here says I must get a wheelchair from an outside hospital but hasn't referred me.
>
> Living here is very hard. We are 88 men in this cell which is meant for 32. Sometimes there are more. Twelve people sleep in two bunks pushed together, that's six on top and six on the bottom. I have my own bed on the bottom, which is a privilege. Luckily, I don't have to share because of my medical status.
>
> There are eight or 10 people with TB in this cell and four or five we know are HIV-positive. A guy with multi-drug resistant TB sleeps on top of me. I feel vulnerable all the time. Not because I'm threatened physically but because I'm always called names and treated like an alien. I'd rather die than be here...It's so crowded people even sleep on 'sponges' on the toilet floor. Sometimes there's no water in the toilet and it doesn't work. The smell and the flies are horrible. The food in the kitchen is also covered in flies. (Raphaely 2013)

Chapman, in this volume, with a citation that arguably echoes across the chapter, notes Angela Davis' cautions about successful abolitions. In, through, and across successful abolitions, we need, Chapman writes, "to learn from how these abolitions led to new institutions of control and violence, such as today's Prison Industrial Complex." My play with the indeterminacy of "Disability, Inc." in this epilogue is offered in the spirit of Davis' and Chapman's caution: even if disability is no longer always and everywhere a spoiled identity (Goffman 1963), even if it is now at times incorporated into the global spectacle of difference, such incorporation—and the abolition of stigma that accompanies it—should not obscure the ways in which neoliberal dispossession continues to generate new forms of control, containment, and complicity.

Pointing out such complicities and contradictions around what Michael A. Rembis here calls "mass incarceration in the neoliberal era" is only one of the important contributions of *Disability Incarcerated*. The volume also makes clear linkages between imprisonment and other forms of incarceration that have frequently been made by disability activists but rarely by scholars in disability studies and prison studies; exposes the continuation (and even augmentation) of longstanding practices of oppression (such as the "chemical constraint," or forced drugging, that Erick Fabris and Katie Aubrecht write about); spotlights disability struggles around incarceration, with all their complexities, impurities, and contradictions (such as the historical tension Allison C. Carey and Lucy Gu trace between parents' groups seeking "choice" and "inclusion" in relation to institutions and those seeking a more radical abolition of systems of disability incarceration); works effectively—given that so many of these essays focus on madness, mental disability, or psychiatric conditions—at and with what we might see as the "mad turn" in disability studies, a turn that is reinvigorating the field of disability studies and changing or radicalizing the questions we might ask in it; and, perhaps most importantly, dares not only to imagine alternatives to "Disability, Incarcerated," but also to point to sites where those alternatives are already in operation, as Liat Ben-Moshe's concluding and aspirational contribution does so beautifully.

Building on Angela Davis' encouragement to "imagine radical futures," Ben-Moshe writes of a world beyond incarceration, a world (moreover) emerging from the world we currently inhabit. What Ben-Moshe terms "transformative justice" entails, as she modestly suggests, "to name a few starting points," "a redistribution of resources, demilitarization of schools, noncoercive physical and mental health care for all, a justice system based on reconciliation rather than vengeance, decriminalization of drug and sex work, and the defense of immigrant rights." These crip starting points are not located elsewhere; they are already called forth, Ben-Moshe insists, in innumerable places. But these starting points have no traffic with Disability, Inc.; Disability, Inc. cannot and will not comprehend them. *Disability Incarcerated* (the volume), however, comprehends, even as it is exceeded by, the multiple and creative ways in which we might refuse the impoverished alternatives and unhappy union of incorporation and incarceration.

Notes

1. Disability Inc. (Incarcerated), a phrase first coined by Liat Ben-Moshe (2009), was the original title for this anthology. This title was later changed to *Disability Incarcerated* to be more accountable to the myriad ways in which dis/ability/madness and incarceration writ large intersect, beyond the level of profit making. For a discussion of Disability Inc. as incarcerated/incorporated in the institution-prison-industrial-complex, see Ben-Moshe (2013).

References

Ben-Moshe, Liat. 2013. "Disabling Incarceration: Connecting Disability to Divergent Confinements in the USA." *Critical Sociology* 37(7).

———. 2009. "Disability inc. (Incarcerated) in the Prison-Industrial-Complex." Rethinking Marxism conference. Amherst, MA.

Brown, Oliver. 2012. "Oscar Pistorius Says the World Will Be Amazed by the London Paralympic Games." *The Telegraph*, August 29. Accessed May 28, 2013. http://www.telegraph.co.uk/sport/olympics/paralympic-sport/9504854/Oscar-Pistorius-says-the-world-will-be-amazed-by-the-London-Paralympic-Games.html

Durington, Matthew. 2013. "Pistorius and South Africa's Culture of Fear." *Baltimore Sun*, February 22. Accessed May 30, 2013. http://articles.baltimoresun.com/2013–02–22/news/bs-ed-pistorius-20130222_1_oscar-pistorius-south-africa-crime-levels

Ferguson, John. 2012. "ATOS Scandal: Benefits Bosses Admit Over Half of People Ruled Fit to Work Ended Up Destitute." *Daily Record and Sunday Mail*, September 26. Accessed May 28, 2013. http://www.dailyrecord.co.uk/news/scottish-news/atos-scandal-benefits-bosses-admit-1344278

Floyd, Kevin. 2009. *The Reification of Desire: Toward a Queer Marxism*. Minneapolis and London: University of Minnesota Press.

Foucault, Michel. 1975. *Discipline and Punish: The Birth of the Prison*. Translated by Alan Sheridan. New York: Vintage-Random House.

Garland-Thomson, Rosemarie. 2013. "Elegy for Oscar Pistorius." *Aljazeera Online*, March 14. Accessed May 26, 2013. http://www.aljazeera.com/indepth/opinion/201 3/03/20133148645751304.html

Goffman, Erving. 1963. *Stigma: Notes on the Management of Spoiled Identity.* New York: Touchstone-Simon & Schuster.

Harvey, David. 2005. *The New Imperialism.* Oxford: Oxford University Press.

Jones, Owen. 2012. "David Cameron Praises Paralympians, But His Policies Will Crush Them." *The Independent*, August 26. Accessed May 28, 2013. http://www .independent.co.uk/voices/commentators/owen-jones-david-cameron-praises -paralympians-but-his-policies-will-crush-them-8082036.html

"Pistorius's Home on Estate Voted Most Secure in South Africa." 2013. *The Guardian*, February 14. Accessed May 30, 2013. http://www.guardian.co.uk/sport/2013 /feb/14/pistorius-home-estate-most-secure-south-africa

Puar, Jasbir K. 2007. *Terrorist Assemblages: Homonationalism in Queer Times.* Durham and London: Duke University Press.

Raphaely, Caroly. 2013. "Oscar Pistorius Case Highlights Plight of South Africa's Disabled Prisoners." *The Guardian*, February 22. Accessed May 30, 2013. http:// www.guardian.co.uk/world/2013/feb/22/paraplegic-remand-south-africa

Topping, Alexandra. 2013. "Locog Hails Biggest and Best Paralympics in History." *The Guardian*, September 6. Accessed May 28, 2013. http://www.guardian.co.uk /sport/2012/sep/06/paralympics-ticket-sales

Vale, Paul. 2012. "Austerity in the United Kingdom Leaves Disabled in Fear for Their Lives." *Huffington Post*, July 17. Accessed May 28, 2013. http://www.huffingtonpost .com/2012/07/15/austerity-measures-uk-a-thousand-cuts_n_1670711.html

Williams, Zoe. 2013. "Visit to ATOS Adviser Leaves Man with Criminal Record." *The Guardian*. April 26. Accessed May 28, 2013. http://www.guardian.co.uk /theguardian/2013/apr/26/atos-zoe-williams

Appendix

Insanity and Terrorism*

Stewart Bell

New insights show terrorists are young, with little education or money. And many suffer from mental illness

The terrorists who blew up four packed commuter trains in Madrid on the morning of March 11 must have marvelled at their success. With 10 bombs, triggered with cellphones, they killed about 190 people and injured another 1,750.

But how could they do it?

What kind of person can coldly plan a terrorist attack, knowing it will result in the murder of hundreds of fellow human beings? What kind of person can condemn so many innocent civilians to horrible sudden death? Who becomes a terrorist and why?

Answers to that question have been debated for many years now but new insights into the terrorist mindset – some of them controversial – are now emerging from research on the hundreds of terrorists captured since Sept. 11, 2001.

The conclusion: The average terrorist is young, a family outcast with little formal education or money who was raised in a region of economic and political instability. And, says a U.S. Army expert familiar with the research, many are mentally ill.

"It is surprising the number of Axis I psychological disorders we have among that population," Colonel Larry James, chief psychologist at the Walter Reed Army Medical Center in Washington, D.C., said in a recent talk to Ontario psychologists in Toronto.

(The disorders classified as Axis I in the psychologists' bible, the Diagnostic and Statistical Manual, include most of the major mental disorders: anxiety, depression, schizophrenia and phobias.)

Last week, Jack Straw, the British Foreign Secretary, took a similar view when he described the men behind the current wave of terrorism as adherents of a "maniac" fundamentalism who suffer from a "cholera of the mind."

---

* This piece serves as the starting point for Patel's analysis of the conflation of terrorism and madness.

Such statements are controversial among both mental health and counter-terrorism experts. Previous studies have generally concluded mental illness was not a factor in determining who becomes a terrorist. Blind commitment to the cause, not a mental defect, drives terrorists, the argument goes; only Hollywood terrorists are crazy.

"Contrary to the stereotype that the terrorist is a psychopath or otherwise mentally disturbed, the terrorist is actually quite sane, although deluded by an ideological or religious way of viewing the world," said a landmark 1999 Library of Congress study, The Sociology and Psychology of Terrorism.

But that was before the war on terrorism. In particular, it was before hundreds of terrorists were captured and taken to places such as Guantanamo Bay, giving experts a rare chance to collect psychological data on a large pool of subjects and to develop a profile of what makes them tick.

"Mental illness is a factor," Col. James said in an interview. But the ones who are mentally ill are not the likes of Osama bin Laden, the late Sheikh Ahmed Yassin of Hamas or Shoko Asahara of Aum Shinrikyo, the Japanese cult that attacked the Tokyo subway with nerve gas. It is the low-level flunkies attracted to them.

"The leaders or the mastermind figures may or may not have mental illness, but again among the foot soldiers, that's where you'll see more of the psychiatric types of problems."

Col. James believes the reason why psychological disorders have not before been widely detected in terrorists is that the people testing them have not asked the right questions. "We need a new way of conceptualizing these men and women, because the categories we have, they don't fit neatly into."

The thinking that drives al-Qaeda – that Westerners are devils and that killing them is serving God – in itself should raise questions about the sanity of its adherents, he says. "That begs the question: Is that a normal healthy thought process?"

Radical Islamic terrorists might breeze through a standard psych test, he says, but they would surely fail what he called the New York City Taxi Driver Test: Even a cabbie with no formal training could tell that an al-Qaeda member was just "not right."

Psychologists have long argued that some high-ranking terrorists may be psychopaths or have personality disorders, while those in lower-level positions such as suicide bombers are more likely to have mental deficiencies or depression, making them easier to manipulate.

But are most terrorists mentally ill?

"Yes and no," says Steven Stein, CEO of Multi-Health Systems and a Toronto psychologist who specializes in the field. "While some terrorists may have mental health problems, I don't think it is a basic cause of terrorism."

"There are millions of people worldwide with mental health problems and only a small percentage of them are violent. Much more pervasive among terrorists is being indoctrinated in a culture of hatred. There are much stronger links between hatred and terrorism than any particular mental illness."

The Library of Congress study concluded potential recruits who showed signs of mental illness tended to be weeded out by terrorist groups because they were considered a liability: "Terrorist groups need members whose behaviour appears to be normal and who would not arouse suspicion."

But Col. James maintains mental health does seem to determine who becomes a terrorist, although it is not the only factor, just one of many. In an interview, he said he was not permitted to talk about specific cases (he was asked about the only Canadian at Guantanamo Bay, Omar Khadr) or about Guantanamo Bay but he gave his general profile of who becomes a terrorist and why.

Aside from mental illness, terrorists tend to have a low level of education, which makes it easier to indoctrinate and manipulate them, he says. "A large number of them are functionally illiterate," he says.

"The average foot-soldier terrorist is not a rocket scientist. That's a factual statement. I'm not talking about the Osama bin Ladens and the guys who are chemical engineers and have masters degrees and come from tremendously well-educated families.

"That may be one of the mastermind-type people behind it, but the person who gets on the train or the bus...with a bomb strapped to their back typically doesn't have a PhD."

Family dynamics also play a role, he says. "The folks that are looking for a sense of belongingness, family outcasts....This person tends to be the black sheep of the family and really doesn't connect well with the rest of the family."

"If you look at Osama bin Laden, same thing. If you look at his mother and father, he was born to an intact family, very wealthy, very well-educated but for whatever reason...he's the one family outcast, long before he got involved in al-Qaeda. So these folks will go out and seek out other organizations, and they are ripe psychologically."

Then there is economic status.

"The average terrorist really is fairly poor and doesn't have a stable job or goes from job to job...and so here comes an organization that's willing to take them in, feed them, clothe them, educate them and, in their interpretation of the Koran, make them a soldier for the cause and pay them some nominal wages."

Indeed, some terrorists are "soldier-of-fortune-mercenary" types, he says. "These are the more sociopathic-type characters."

"'Hey man, there's a fight and you're willing to pay for it. Sign me up, brother, I'm with you.'"

Perhaps least surprising is the finding that terrorists tend to come from regions that are in economic and political upheaval, partly because governments lack the will or the resources to challenge terrorist groups that set up shop in such environments, he says.

These parts of the world have a plentiful supply of idle youths, who are the cannon fodder of terror. "It's more likely to see younger adults and children involved in this. Why? Because they're more vulnerable."

Up to a third of the combatants in Afghanistan were under 13 years of age, he says, and many were in the 9–15 range. "This was truly a different kind of war." Many of those boys were abducted and forced to fight, and a large number were sexually abused by the commanders at terrorist camps.

"When we look at a lot of these terrorist organizations, these boys meet the criteria of all the things I just laid out. Things are not going well in their family, they're typically not doing well in school, they're kind of social outcasts, they're looking for a place to belong, they're 13, 14, 15, so they don't have a way of supporting themselves."

Some researchers have documented how terrorists gradually become divorced from reality as they live underground to evade capture, making it possible for them to kill masses of people in the name of the cause of their leader or organization.

"This is a response to the crimes that you have caused in the world and specifically in Iraq and in Afghanistan. And there will be more, God willing," according to a videotaped statement released in the aftermath of the Madrid bombings.

"You love life and we love death."

Are these the words of sane men?

National Post [Don Mills, Ont] March 27, 2004: RB1 Front.

Contributors

Jihan Abbas is a Vanier Canada Graduate scholar and PhD candidate in sociology at Carleton University. Her research interests include disability and the labor market, social and developmental policy, and inclusion and exclusion. Abbas has been involved in the disability movement for several years in both a personal and professional capacity. She is the former Director of Research and Policy for Independent Living Canada and has extensive volunteer experience related to access and inclusion in the public and nonprofit sector. Abbas's work aims to build a more inclusive and equitable society.

Katie Aubrecht, is a Canadian Institutes of Health Research Postdoctoral Fellow and instructor with the Graduate Department of Family Studies & Gerontology at Mount Saint Vincent University, Nova Scotia, Canada and incoming President of the Canadian Disability Studies Association. Her research questions how embodied responses to the violence of prevailing discourses of power are assimilated under colonial knowledge regimes and in mental illness and aging discourses in health regimes. In 2013 she edited the special issue of the journal *Health, Culture and Society*, "Translating Happiness: Medicine, Culture and Social Progress."

Ruthie-Marie Beckwith, PhD, is a national consultant who helps people with disabilities develop and implement strategies for greater autonomy in their daily lives. As the founder and principal partner of Blue Fire Consulting, she provides consulting services across the United States in areas of self-determination, community organizing, leadership development, and self-employment. Committed to grassroots approaches to empowerment and resource mobilization, she has served as the founder and Executive Director of the two statewide nonprofit organizations dedicated to helping people with disabilities: The Tennessee Association of Microboards and Cooperatives, Inc. and People First of Tennessee, Inc. She has served as Adjunct Faculty at Vanderbilt University and Middle Tennessee State University. She received her PhD and MS degrees in Special Education from George Peabody College and her BS degree from the State University of New York at Geneseo.

Liat Ben-Moshe is Assistant Professor of Disability Studies at the University of Toledo. She holds a PhD in Sociology with concentrations in Gender Studies and Disability Studies from Syracuse University. Her recent work examines the connections between prison abolition and deinstitutionalization in the fields of intellectual disabilities and mental health in the United States. She has interests in (and published work on) such topics as disability, anticapitalism, and anarchism; queerness and disability; deinstitutionalization and incarceration; the politics of abolition; inclusive pedagogy; academic repression; representations of disability and critiques of the occupation of Palestine. She enjoys working collaboratively and has presented at dozens of conferences, workshops, and activist venues.

Allison C. Carey is Associate Professor of Sociology and Director of the Interdisciplinary Minor in Disability Studies at Shippensburg University. She is author of *On the Margins of Citizenship: Intellectual Disability and Civil Rights in 20th Century America* (Temple University Press, 2009) and coeditor with Richard Scotch of *Community and Disability*, Volume 6 of the book series Research in Social Science and Disability (Emerald Press, 2011). She has published on a variety of issues related to disability, including sterilization, civil rights and citizenship, and disability in the family. She has served the Board of the Society for Disability Studies and as chair of the American Sociological Association's section on Disability and Society.

Chris Chapman is Assistant Professor of Social Work at York University and holds a PhD in Sociology and Equity Studies from OISE/UT. His research explores diverse ways that ethical self-governance and systems of oppression interact with one another. Chris' publications include: "Colonialism, Disability, and Possible Lives: The Residential Treatment of Children Whose Parents Survived Indian Residential Schools" (2012) and "Becoming Perpetrator: How I Came to Accept Restraining and Confining Disabled Aboriginal Children" (2010). He currently concentrates his energies on working against professional, disablist, colonial, and racist violence, and at other times has focused on heteropatriarchal, military, geopolitical, and economic oppression. He is currently cowriting a book that situates the history of social work within legacies of interlocking oppression.

Angela Y. Davis has been central to radical political struggles since the 1960s, particularly in relation to anticapitalist, feminist, Black power, and prison abolitionist movements. She is a philosopher, the founder of Critical Resistance and the National Alliance Against Racist and Political Repression, and a retired professor in the History of Consciousness Department at the University of California, Santa Cruz. She has lectured in Canada and in all 50 US states, as well as throughout Europe, Africa, the Caribbean, Russia, and the Pacific. She is author of *If They Come in the Morning: Voices of Resistance* (1971), *Angela Davis – An Autobiography* (1974), *Women, Race and Class* (1981), *Women, Race and Politics* (1989), *Blues Legacies & Black Feminism* (1999), *The Angela Y. Davis Reader* (1999), *Are Prisons Obsolete?* (2003), and *Abolition Democracy: Beyond Prisons, Torture and Empire* (2005).

Giselle Dias is a prisoners' rights activist and abolitionist. For the past 18 years she has engaged in public education on issues such as: transformative justice, drug policy reform, harm reduction, and HIV/AIDS/HCV in prisons. Giselle has written several policy papers on HIV/AIDS and Harm Reduction in prisons and coauthored an Intersectoral Strategy for HIV/AIDS, HCV and Harm Reduction in Canadian Prisons. Giselle recently began working as a psychotherapist in private practice and specializes in working with victims of violence, people coming out of prison, drug users, and people with mental health issues.

Nirmala Erevelles is Professor of Social and Cultural Studies in Education in the Department of Educational Leadership, Policy, and Technology Studies at the

University of Alabama. She has published widely in the areas of disability studies, critical race theory, transnational feminism, sociology of education, curriculum studies, and multicultural education. Her recent book, *Disability and Difference in Global Contexts: Towards a Transformative Body Politic* was published by Palgrave in 2011.

Erick Fabris is a psychiatric survivor who lectures in disability studies at Ryerson University. He has collaborated on projects like: Psychiatric Survivor Archives of Toronto, Mad Pride, No Force Coalition, and Repeal Mental Health Laws. His book, *Tranquil Prisons*, is a narrative study against forced treatment.

Philip M. Ferguson, PhD, is a professor in the College of Educational Studies at Chapman University in Orange, California. Before coming to Chapman University in 2007, he taught at the University of Oregon and the University of Missouri St. Louis. His research has primarily focused on family/professional interactions and support policy, social policy and the history of disability, as well as qualitative research methods in disability studies and education. He is a past President of the Society for Disability Studies and was the Chair of the Board of Directors for Missouri Protection and Advocacy Services. In addition to numerous articles, book chapters, and monographs, Dr. Ferguson's publications include *Abandoned to Their Fate: Social Policy and Practice toward Severely Disabled Persons, 1820–1920*—a book and accompanying video on the history of individuals with intellectual disabilities and their families.

Mark Friedman received his PhD in Organizational Leadership from the Union Institute and University and has worked for three decades to free people with developmental disabilities from institutions, to run their own organizations, and have power over their own lives. He is currently CEO of Blue Fire Consulting and Adjunct Professor at the City University of New York. Previously, he worked for the Pennhurst Special Master implementing one of the first Federal court orders requiring deinstitutionalization. He served as the statewide coordinator of the self-advocacy organization Speaking For Ourselves and served as the Vice Chairperson of the Pennsylvania Developmental Disabilities Council. He has been the recipient of ten public service awards, including awards from the Philadelphia Foundation, the Public Interest Law Center of Philadelphia, and the City of Philadelphia.

Lucy Ling Gu graduated with her Bachelor's Degree from Shippensburg University in 2012. She is currently a PhD student in Clinical Psychology at the University of Rhode Island. Her research interests include psychology across the lifespan, health psychology, cross-cultural coping mechanisms, and medical sociology.

Robert McRuer, PhD, is Professor of English and Chair of the Department of English at George Washington University, where he teaches queer studies, disability studies, and critical theory. He is the author of *Crip Theory: Cultural Signs of Queerness and Disability* (NYU, 2006) and *The Queer Renaissance: Contemporary American Literature and the Reinvention of Lesbian and Gay Identities* (NYU, 1997). With Abby L. Wilkerson, he coedited *Desiring Disability: Queer Theory Meets Disability Studies*, a special issue of *GLQ: A Journal of Lesbian and Gay Studies* (Duke, 2003). His most recent coedited volume is *Sex and Disability* (Duke, 2012). He is now working on a project tentatively titled *Cripping Austerity*.

Mansha Mirza, PhD, is Assistant Professor in the Department of Occupational Therapy at the University of Illinois, Chicago. She has an interdisciplinary background in occupational therapy, health services research, and disability studies. Dr. Mirza's research and academic interests focus on delivery of disability and health related services in resource-limited situations of humanitarian relief, experiences of refugees with disabilities in resettlement and in refugee camps, and health disparities among refugees and immigrants settled in the United States. Dr. Mirza has been awarded multiple grants to fund her research in this area. She has presented at several national conferences and has numerous publications to her credit including eleven peer-reviewed journal articles and two book chapters.

Shaista Patel is a PhD candidate at the Ontario Institute for Studies in Education (OISE) at the University of Toronto. She identifies as a Muslim antiracist feminist and her political and academic work is on analyzing and forming solidarities between people of color and Indigenous peoples of Canada.

Geoffrey Reaume is Associate Professor in the Critical Disability Studies graduate program at York University and is a cofounder of the Psychiatric Survivor Archives, Toronto. He is the author of *Remembrance of Patients Past: Patient Life at the Toronto Hospital for the Insane, 1870–1940* (Oxford University Press Canada, 2000; re-issued, University of Toronto Press, 2009, 2010) and *Lyndhurst: Canada's First Rehabilitation Centre for People with Spinal Cord Injuries, 1945– 1998* (Montreal & Kingston: McGill-Queen's University Press, 2007), as well as a coeditor with Brenda LeFrancois and Robert Menzies of *Mad Matters: A Critical Reader in Canadian Mad Studies* (Toronto: Canadian Scholars Press, 2013).

Michael Rembis, PhD, is Director of the Center for Disability Studies and Assistant Professor in the Department of History at the University at Buffalo (SUNY). His work, which has appeared in many journals and edited collections, has won several awards, including the 2008 Irving K. Zola Award, awarded annually by the Society for Disability Studies to emerging scholars. His first book, *Defining Deviance: Sex, Science, and Delinquent Girls, 1890–1960*, was published by University of Illinois Press in 2011. He has coedited *Disability Histories* with Susan Burch, forthcoming from University of Illinois Press, and is working on an Oxford University Press Handbook on Disability History, which he is coediting with Kim Nielsen and Cathy Kudlick. In 2012, Rembis and coeditor Kim Nielsen launched the *Disability Histories* book series also with University of Illinois Press.

Joan Ruzsa is the coordinator of Rittenhouse: A New Vision, an abolitionist organization that promotes community alternatives to imprisonment, as well as providing support and advocacy to prisoners, exprisoners, and their families.

Jijian Voronka is a PhD candidate at the Department of Sociology and Equity Studies at the Ontario Institute for Studies in Education of the University of Toronto. Her research explores the limits, conditions, and possibilities of service user participation and inclusion within mental health research and service provisions. She works as a consumer research consultant for the Mental Health Commission of Canada on a national research demonstration project that is studying how to best provide housing for those without homes.

Syrus Marcus Ware is a black, disabled, and queer visual artist, activist, researcher, and educator. Syrus holds a Masters in Sociology and Equity Studies from OISE/

UT. He is a prison abolitionist who, while working at PASAN, helped to write *Responding to the Epidemic: Recommendations for a Canadian Hepatitis C Strategy*. He is a former member of Friends of MOVE Toronto, and is one of the organizers of Toronto's Prisoners' Justice Day events. He is one of the creators of "Primed: A Back Pocket Guide for Trans Guys and the Guys Who Dig 'Em," the first sexual health resource for trans MSMs in North America. Syrus is the author of several publications including "Going Boldly Where Few Men Have Gone Before: One Trans Man's Experience of Fertility Clinics" (in *Who's Your Daddy?: And Other Writings on Queer Parenting*, Sumach Press, 2008), and the coauthored, "How Disability Studies Stays White and What Kind of White it Stays". He is currently co-editing a book chapter with Zack Marshall about disability, Deaf culture, and trans identities in the forthcoming *Trans Bodies, Trans Selves* (2014).

Index

CPSIA information can be obtained
at www.ICGtesting.com
Printed in the USA
FFOW05n0011140815

9 781137 404053